D0105153

Modern Critical Views

Chinua Achebe
Henry Adams
Aeschylus
S. Y. Agnon
Edward Albee
Raphael Alberti
Louisa May Alcott
A. R. Ammons
Sherwood Anderson
Aristophanes
Matthew Arnold
Antonin Artaud
John Ashbery
Margaret Atwood
W. H. Auden
Jane Austen
Isaac Babel
Sir Francis Bacon
James Baldwin
Honoré de Balzac
John Barth
Donald Barthelme
Charles Baudelaire
Simone de Beauvoir
Samuel Beckett
Saul Bellow
Thomas Berger
John Berryman
The Bible
Elizabeth Bishop
William Blake
Giovanni Boccaccio
Heinrich Böll
Jorge Luis Borges
Elizabeth Bowen
Bertolt Brecht
The Brontës
Charles Brockden Brown
Sterling Brown
Robert Browning
Martin Buber
John Bunyan
Anthony Burgess
Kenneth Burke
Robert Burns
William Burroughs
George Gordon, Lord Byron
Pedro Calderón de la Barca
Italo Calvino
Albert Camus
Canadian Poetry: Modern and Contemporary
Canadian Poetry through E. J. Pratt
Thomas Carlyle
Alejo Carpentier
Lewis Carroll
Willa Cather
Louis-Ferdinand Céline
Miguel de Cervantes
Geoffrey Chaucer
John Cheever
Anton Chekhov
Kate Chopin
Chrétien de Troyes
Agatha Christie
Samuel Taylor Coleridge
Colette
William Congreve & the Restoration Dramatists
Joseph Conrad
Contemporary Poets
James Fenimore Cooper
Pierre Corneille
Julio Cortázar
Hart Crane
Stephen Crane
e. e. cummings
Dante
Robertson Davies
Daniel Defoe
Philip K. Dick
Charles Dickens
James Dickey
Emily Dickinson
Denis Diderot
Isak Dinesen
E. L. Doctorow
John Donne & the Seventeenth-Century Metaphysical Poets
John Dos Passos
Fyodor Dostoevsky
Frederick Douglass
Theodore Dreiser
John Dryden
W. E. B. Du Bois
Lawrence Durrell
George Eliot
T. S. Eliot
Elizabethan Dramatists
Ralph Ellison
Ralph Waldo Emerson
Euripides
William Faulkner
Henry Fielding
F. Scott Fitzgerald
Gustave Flaubert
E. M. Forster
John Fowles
Sigmund Freud
Robert Frost
Northrop Frye
Carlos Fuentes
William Gaddis
Federico García Lorca
Gabriel García Márquez
André Gide
W. S. Gilbert
Allen Ginsberg
J. W. von Goethe
Nikolai Gogol
William Golding
Oliver Goldsmith
Mary Gordon
Günther Grass
Robert Graves
Graham Greene
Thomas Hardy
Nathaniel Hawthorne
William Hazlitt
H. D.
Seamus Heaney
Lillian Hellman
Ernest Hemingway
Hermann Hesse
Geoffrey Hill
Friedrich Hölderlin
Homer
A. D. Hope
Gerard Manley Hopkins
Horace
A. E. Housman
William Dean Howells
Langston Hughes
Ted Hughes
Victor Hugo
Zora Neale Hurston
Aldous Huxley
Henrik Ibsen
Eugène Ionesco
Washington Irving
Henry James
Dr. Samuel Johnson and James Boswell
Ben Jonson
James Joyce
Carl Gustav Jung
Franz Kafka
Yasonari Kawabata
John Keats
Søren Kierkegaard
Rudyard Kipling
Melanie Klein
Heinrich von Kleist
Philip Larkin
D. H. Lawrence
John le Carré
Ursula K. Le Guin
Giacomo Leopardi
Doris Lessing
Sinclair Lewis
Jack London
Robert Lowell
Malcolm Lowry
Carson McCullers
Norman Mailer
Bernard Malamud
Stéphane Mallarmé
Sir Thomas Malory
André Malraux
Thomas Mann

Modern Critical Views

Katherine Mansfield
Christopher Marlowe
Andrew Marvell
Herman Melville
George Meredith
James Merrill
John Stuart Mill
Arthur Miller
Henry Miller
John Milton
Yukio Mishima
Molière
Michel de Montaigne
Eugenio Montale
Marianne Moore
Alberto Moravia
Toni Morrison
Alice Munro
Iris Murdoch
Robert Musil
Vladimir Nabokov
V. S. Naipaul
R. K. Narayan
Pablo Neruda
John Henry Newman
Friedrich Nietzsche
Frank Norris
Joyce Carol Oates
Sean O'Casey
Flannery O'Connor
Christopher Okigbo
Charles Olson
Eugene O'Neill
José Ortega y Gasset
Joe Orton
George Orwell
Ovid
Wilfred Owen
Amos Oz
Cynthia Ozick
Grace Paley
Blaise Pascal
Walter Pater
Octavio Paz
Walker Percy
Petrarch
Pindar
Harold Pinter
Luigi Pirandello
Sylvia Plath
Plato
Plautus
Edgar Allan Poe
Poets of Sensibility & the Sublime
Poets of the Nineties
Alexander Pope
Katherine Anne Porter
Ezra Pound
Anthony Powell
Pre-Raphaelite Poets
Marcel Proust
Manuel Puig
Alexander Pushkin
Thomas Pynchon
Francisco de Quevedo
François Rabelais
Jean Racine
Ishmael Reed
Adrienne Rich
Samuel Richardson
Mordecai Richler
Rainer Maria Rilke
Arthur Rimbaud
Edwin Arlington Robinson
Theodore Roethke
Philip Roth
Jean-Jacques Rousseau
John Ruskin
J. D. Salinger
Jean-Paul Sartre
Gershom Scholem
Sir Walter Scott
William Shakespeare
  Histories & Poems
  Comedies & Romances
  Tragedies
George Bernard Shaw
Mary Wollstonecraft Shelley
Percy Bysshe Shelley
Sam Shepard
Richard Brinsley Sheridan
Sir Philip Sidney
Isaac Bashevis Singer
Tobias Smollett
Alexander Solzhenitsyn
Sophocles
Wole Soyinka
Edmund Spenser
Gertrude Stein
John Steinbeck
Stendhal
Laurence Sterne
Wallace Stevens
Robert Louis Stevenson
Tom Stoppard
August Strindberg
Jonathan Swift
John Millington Synge
Alfred, Lord Tennyson
William Makepeace Thackeray
Dylan Thomas
Henry David Thoreau
James Thurber and S. J. Perelman
J. R. R. Tolkien
Leo Tolstoy
Jean Toomer
Lionel Trilling
Anthony Trollope
Ivan Turgenev
Mark Twain
Miguel de Unamuno
John Updike
Paul Valéry
Cesar Vallejo
Lope de Vega
Gore Vidal
Virgil
Voltaire
Kurt Vonnegut
Derek Walcott
Alice Walker
Robert Penn Warren
Evelyn Waugh
H. G. Wells
Eudora Welty
Nathanael West
Edith Wharton
Patrick White
Walt Whitman
Oscar Wilde
Tennessee Williams
William Carlos Williams
Thomas Wolfe
Virginia Woolf
William Wordsworth
Jay Wright
Richard Wright
William Butler Yeats
A. B. Yehoshua
Emile Zola

Modern Critical Views

NATHANIEL HAWTHORNE

Edited and with an introduction by

Harold Bloom
Sterling Professor of the Humanities
Yale University

CHELSEA HOUSE PUBLISHERS
New York ◊ Philadelphia

Printed and bound in the United States of America

10 9 8

∞ The paper used in this publication meets the minimum requirements of the American National Standard for Permanence of Paper for Printed Library Materials, Z39.48–1984.

Library of Congress Cataloging-in-Publication Data
Nathaniel Hawthorne.
(Modern critical views)
Bibliography: p.
Includes index.
1. Hawthorne, Nathaniel, 1804–1864—Criticism and interpretation. I. Bloom, Harold. II. Series.
PS1888.N29 1986 813′.3 86–6877
ISBN 0–87754–695–9

Contents

Editor's Note

This book brings together what its editor considers to be the best criticism yet published upon Hawthorne, arranged here in the chronological order of its original publication. I am grateful to Marijke Rijsberman and Susan Laity for their erudition and judgment in helping to edit this volume.

The editor's introduction considers Hawthorne in the context both of Emerson's influence upon *The Scarlet Letter,* and of Henry James's ambivalent responses to the influences upon *him* of both Emerson and Hawthorne. A reading of the Emersonian strain in *The Scarlet Letter* is followed by an exegesis of Hawthorne's remarkable final tale, the more-than-ironic "Feathertop."

Clark Griffith's essay contrasting "substance words" and "shadow words" in *The House of the Seven Gables* introduces the chronological sequence, which continues with R. W. B. Lewis's influential account of "returns into time" in *The Marble Faun.* With Larzer Ziff's meditation on the ethics of Hawthorne's theory of romance in "The Custom House," we return to *The Scarlet Letter* by way of its celebrated Introduction. Complementing Ziff's study of morality and myth, the emphasis of Daniel G. Hoffman in his analysis of the "folklore of love" is on Hawthorne's personal nostalgia or dream of love in "The Maypole of Merry Mount."

We return to the novels with A. N. Kaul's deeply informed reading of *The Blithedale Romance* and the book's subtle tracing of the continuities between Puritan tradition and New England Transcendentalist utopianism. A very different emphasis, psychological rather than mythological or moral, is manifested by Frederick C. Crews in his discussion of compulsion in "Roger Malvin's Burial." Another welcome change in perspective is provided by John Caldwell Stubbs, who sees the overt comic artifice of *The House of the Seven Gables* as Hawthorne's deliberate attempt to reverse himself after the darkness of *The Scarlet Letter.* Yet another mode, the elegiac, is evoked in Nina Baym's presentation of *The Marble Faun,* which she regards as disfigured but not destroyed by Hawthorne's prudential moralism and augmenting nihilism.

Three crucial tales—"Young Goodman Brown," "The Artist of the Beautiful," and "Rappaccini's Daughter"—are adroitly analyzed by Leo B. Levy, Sheldon W. Liebman, and Richard Brenzo, respectively, as instances of Hawthorne's astonishing artistry at fusing belief, aesthetic perception, and eros into a composite image of the American morality of romance.

Richard H. Brodhead returns us to *The Scarlet Letter* in what seems to me the most distinguished reading Hawthorne has received, a reading that teaches us to see the revisionary elements in the novel's relation to literary tradition. A similar centering upon Hawthorne's ambivalences towards narrative art is the basis for Keith Carabine's way of presenting Miles Coverdale's stance as narrator in *The Blithedale Romance*. Finally, this book comes full circle with Michael J. Colacurcio's revisionist reading of "My Kinsman, Major Molineux" as national myth, or "the matter of America." Little as the editor's introduction and Colacurcio's historically learned investigation otherwise have in common, each sees Hawthorne as deflating all American typological historiography, though presumably Colacurcio would not ascribe this strategy to an Emersonian strain in Hawthorne, as I would.

Introduction

I

Henry James's *Hawthorne* was published in December 1879, in London, in the English Men of Letters series. Unique among the thirty-nine volumes of that group, this was a critical study of an American by an American. Only Hawthorne seemed worthy of being an English man of letters, and only James seemed capable of being an American critic. Perhaps this context inhibited James, whose *Hawthorne* tends to be absurdly overpraised, or perhaps Hawthorne caused James to feel an anxiety that even George Eliot could not bring the self-exiled American to experience. Whatever the reason, James wrote a study that requires to be read between the lines, as here in its final paragraph:

> He was a beautiful, natural, original genius, and his life had been singularly exempt from worldly preoccupations and vulgar efforts. It had been as pure, as simple, as unsophisticated, as his work. He had lived primarily in his domestic affections, which were of the tenderest kind; and then—without eagerness, without pretension, but with a great deal of quiet devotion—in his charming art. His work will remain; it is too original and exquisite to pass away; among the men of imagination he will always have his niche. No one has had just that vision of life, and no one has had a literary form that more successfully expressed his vision. He was not a moralist, and he was not simply a poet. The moralists are weightier, denser, richer, in a sense; the poets are more purely inconclusive and irresponsible. He combined in a singular degree the spontaneity of the imagination with a haunting care for moral problems. Man's conscience was his theme, but he saw it in the light of a creative fancy which added, out of its own substance, an interest, and, I may almost say, an importance.

Is *The Scarlet Letter* pure, simple, and unsophisticated? Is *The Marble Faun* a work neither moral nor poetic? Can we accurately assert that man's conscience, however lit by creative fancy, is Hawthorne's characteristic concern? James's vision of his American precursor is manifestly distorted by a need to misread creatively what may hover too close, indeed may shadow the narrative space that James requires for his own enterprise. In that space, something beyond shadowing troubles James. Isabel Archer has her clear affinities with Dorothea Brooke, yet her relation to Hester Prynne is even more familial, just as Millie Theale will have the lineage of *The Marble Faun*'s Hilda ineluctably marked upon her. James's representations of women are Hawthornian in ways subtly evasive yet finally unmistakable. Yet even this influence and its consequent ambivalences do not seem to be the prime unease that weakens James's *Hawthorne*. Rather, the critical monograph is more embarrassed than it can know by James's guilt at having abandoned the American destiny. Elsewhere, James wrote to some purpose about Emerson (though not so well as his brother William did), but in *Hawthorne* the figure of Emerson is unrecognizable and the dialectics of New England Transcendentalism are weakly abused:

> A biographer of Hawthorne might well regret that his hero had not been more mixed up with the reforming and free-thinking class, so that he might find a pretext for writing a chapter upon the state of Boston society forty years ago. A needful warrant for such regret should be, properly, that the biographer's own personal reminiscences should stretch back to that period and to the persons who animated it. This would be a guarantee of fulness of knowledge and, presumably, of kindness of tone. It is difficult to see, indeed, how the generation of which Hawthorne has given us, in *Blithedale,* a few portraits, should not, at this time of day, be spoken of very tenderly and sympathetically. If irony enter into the allusion, it should be of the lightest and gentlest. Certainly, for a brief and imperfect chronicler of these things, a writer just touching them as he passes, and who has not the advantage of having been a contemporary, there is only one possible tone. The compiler of these pages, though his recollections date only from a later period, has a memory of a certain number of persons who had been intimately connected, as Hawthorne was not, with the agitations of that interesting time. Something of its interest adhered to them still—something of its aroma clung to their garments; there was something about them which seemed to say that

when they were young and enthusiastic, they had been initiated into moral mysteries, they had played at a wonderful game. Their usual mark (it is true I can think of exceptions) was that they seemed excellently good. They appeared unstained by the world, unfamiliar with worldly desires and standards, and with those various forms of human depravity which flourish in some high phases of civilisation; inclined to simple and democratic ways, destitute of pretensions and affectations, of jealousies, of cynicisms, of snobbishness. This little epoch of fermentation has three or four drawbacks for the critics—drawbacks, however, that may be overlooked by a person for whom it has an interest of association. It bore, intellectually, the stamp of provincialism; it was a beginning without a fruition, a dawn without a noon; and it produced, with a single exception, no great talents. It produced a great deal of writing, but (always putting Hawthorne aside, as a contemporary but not a sharer) only one writer in whom the world at large has interested itself. The situation was summed up and transfigured in the admirable and exquisite Emerson. He expressed all that it contained, and a good deal more, doubtless, besides; he was the man of genius of the moment; he was the Transcendentalist *par excellence.* Emerson expressed, before all things, as was extremely natural at the hour and in the place, the value and importance of the individual, the duty of making the most of one's self, of living by one's own personal light, and carrying out one's own disposition. He reflected with beautiful irony upon the exquisite impudence of those institutions which claim to have appropriated the truth and to dole it out, in proportionate morsels, in exchange for a subscription. He talked about the beauty and dignity of life, and about every one who is born into the world being born to the whole, having an interest and a stake in the whole. He said "all that is clearly due to-day is not to lie," and a great many other things which it would be still easier to present in a ridiculous light. He insisted upon sincerity and independence and spontaneity, upon acting in harmony with one's nature, and not conforming and compromising for the sake of being more comfortable. He urged that a man should await his call, his finding the thing to do which he should really believe in doing, and not be urged by the world's opinion to do simply the world's work. "If no call should come for years, for centuries, then I know that the want of the Universe is the attes-

> tation of faith by my abstinence. . . . If I cannot work, at least I need not lie." The doctrine of the supremacy of the individual to himself, of his originality, and, as regards his own character, *unique* quality, must have had a great charm for people living in a society in which introspection—thanks to the want of other entertainment—played almost the part of a social resource.

The "admirable and exquisite Emerson" was "as sweet as barbed wire," to quote President Giamatti of Yale. Any reader of that great, grim, and most American of books, *The Conduct of Life,* ought to have known this. James's Emerson, dismissed here by the novelist as a provincial of real charm, had provoked the senior Henry James to an outburst of more authentic critical value: "O you man without a handle!" Hawthorne too, in a very different way, was a man without a handle, not less conscious and subtle an artist than the younger Henry James himself. *The Scarlet Letter,* in James's *Hawthorne,* is rightly called the novelist's masterpiece, but then is accused of "a want of reality and an abuse of the fanciful element—of a certain superficial symbolism." James was too good a reader to have indicted Hawthorne for "a want of reality," were it not that Hawthornian representation had begun too well the process of causing a Jamesian aspect of reality to appear.

II

Of the four principal figures in *The Scarlet Letter,* Pearl is at once the most surprising, and the largest intimation of Hawthorne's farthest imaginings. There is no indication that Hawthorne shared his friend Melville's deep interest in ancient Gnosticism, though esoteric heresies were clearly part of Hawthorne's abiding concern with witchcraft. The Gnostic *Gospel of Thomas* contains a remarkable mythic narrative, "The Hymn of the Pearl," that juxtaposes illuminatingly with the uncanny daughter of Hester Prynne and the Reverend Mr. Dimmesdale. In Gnostic symbolism, the pearl is identical with the spark or *pneuma* that is the ontological self of the adept who shares in the Gnosis, in the true knowing that surmounts mere faith. The pearl particularly represents what is best and oldest in the adept, because creation is the work of a mere demiurge, while the best part of us, that which is capable of knowing, was never made, but is one with the original Abyss, the Foremother and Forefather who is the true or alien God. When Hawthorne's Pearl passionately insists she was not made by God, we hear again the most ancient and challenging of all Western heresies:

> The old minister seated himself in an arm-chair, and made an

> effort to draw Pearl betwixt his knees. But the child, unaccustomed to the touch or familiarity of any but her mother, escaped through the open window and stood on the upper step, looking like a wild, tropical bird, of rich plumage, ready to take flight into the upper air. Mr. Wilson, not a little astonished at this outbreak,—for he was a grandfatherly sort of personage, and usually a vast favorite with children,—essayed, however, to proceed with the examination.
>
> "Pearl," said he, with great solemnity, "thou must take heed to instruction, that so, in due season, thou mayest wear in thy bosom the pearl of great price. Canst thou tell me, my child, who made thee?"
>
> Now Pearl knew well enough who made her; for Hester Prynne, the daughter of a pious home, very soon after her talk with the child about her Heavenly Father, had begun to inform her of those truths which the human spirit, at whatever stage of immaturity, imbibes with such eager interest. Pearl, therefore, so large were the attainments of her three years' lifetime, could have borne a fair examination in the New England Primer, or the first column of the Westminster Catechism, although unacquainted with the outward form of either of those celebrated works. But that perversity, which all children have more or less of, and of which little Pearl had a tenfold portion, now, at the most inopportune moment, took thorough possession of her, and closed her lips, or impelled her to speak words amiss. After putting her finger in her mouth, with many ungracious refusals to answer good Mr. Wilson's question, the child finally announced that she had not been made at all, but had been plucked by her mother off the bush of wild roses, that grew by the prison-door.

That Pearl, elf-child, is the romance's prime knower no reader would doubt. The subtlest relation in Hawthorne's sinuously ambiguous romance is not that between Chillingworth and Dimmesdale, let alone the inadequate ghost of the love between Hester and Dimmesdale. It is the ambivalent and persuasive mother-daughter complex in which Hester is saved both from suicidal despair and from the potential of becoming the prophetess of a feminist religion only by the extraordinary return in her daughter of everything she herself has repressed. I will venture the speculation that both Hester and Pearl are intense representations of two very different aspects of Emersonianism, Hester being a prime instance of Emerson's American religion of self-reliance, while Pearl emerges from a deeper stratum of Emerson, from the Orphism and Gnosticism that mark the sage's first anarchic influx of power and knowledge, when he celebrated his own version of what he called, following the Swedenborgians, the terrible freedom or newness. Emerson, Hawthorne's Concord walking companion, is generally judged by scholars and critics to be antithetical to Hawthorne. I doubt that judgment, since manifestly Hawthorne does not prefer the pathetic Dimmesdale and the mock-satanic Chillingworth to the self-reliant Hester and the daemonic Pearl. Henry James, like T. S. Eliot, considered Emerson to be deficient in a sense of sin, a sense obsessive in Dimmesdale and Chillingworth, alien to Pearl, and highly dialectical in Hester.

In the Gnostic mode of Pearl, the young Emerson indeed affirmed: "My heart did never counsel me to sin. . . . / I never taught it what it teaches me." This is the adept of Orphic mysteries who also wrote: "It is God in you that responds to God without, or affirms his own words trembling on the lips of another," words that "sound to you as old as yourself." The direct precursor to *The Scarlet Letter*'s Pearl is a famous moment in Emerson's "Self-Reliance," an essay surely known to Hawthorne:

> I remember an answer which when quite young I was prompted to make to a valued adviser who was wont to importune me with the dear old doctrines of the church. On my saying, "What have I to do with the sacredness of traditions, if I live wholly from within?" my friend suggested,—"But these impulses may be from below, not from above." I replied, "They do not seem to me to be such; but if I am the Devil's child, I will live then from the Devil."

Call this Pearl's implicit credo, since her positive declaration is: "I have no Heavenly Father!" Even as Pearl embodies Emerson's most anarchic, antinomian strain, Hester incarnates the central impulse of "Self-Reliance." This is the emphasis of chapter 13 of the romance, "Another View of Hester," which eloquently tells us: "The scarlet letter had not done its office." In effect, Hawthorne presents her as Emerson's American precursor, and as the forerunner also of movements still working themselves through among us:

> Much of the marble coldness of Hester's impression was to be attributed to the circumstance that her life had turned, in a great measure, from passion and feeling, to thought. Standing alone in the world,—alone, as to any dependence on society, and with

little Pearl to be guided and protected,—alone, and hopeless of retrieving her position, even had she not scorned to consider it desirable,—she cast away the fragments of a broken chain. The world's law was no law for her mind. It was an age in which the human intellect, newly emancipated, had taken a more active and a wider range than for many centuries before. Men of the sword had overthrown nobles and kings. Men bolder than these had overthrown and rearranged—not actually, but within the sphere of theory, which was their most real abode—the whole system of ancient prejudice, wherewith was linked much of ancient principle. Hester Prynne imbibed this spirit. She assumed a freedom of speculation, then common enough on the other side of the Atlantic, but which our forefathers, had they known of it, would have held to be a deadlier crime than that stigmatized by the scarlet letter. In her lonesome cottage, by the sea-shore, thoughts visited her, such as dared to enter no other dwelling in New England; shadowy guests, that would have been as perilous as demons to their entertainer, could they have been seen so much as knocking at her door.

It is remarkable, that persons who speculate the most boldly often conform with the most perfect quietude to the external regulations of society. The thought suffices them, without investing itself in the flesh and blood of action. So it seemed to be with Hester. Yet, had little Pearl never come to her from the spiritual world, it might have been far otherwise. Then, she might have come down to us in history, hand in hand with Ann Hutchinson, as the foundress of a religious sect. She might, in one of her phases, have been a prophetess. She might, and not improbably would, have suffered death from the stern tribunals of the period, for attempting to undermine the foundations of the Puritan establishment. But, in the education of her child, the mother's enthusiasm of thought had something to wreak itself upon. Providence, in the person of this little girl, had assigned to Hester's charge the germ and blossom of womanhood, to be cherished and developed amid a host of difficulties. Every thing was against her. The world was hostile. The child's own nature had something wrong in it, which continually betokened that she had been born amiss,—the effluence of her mother's lawless passion,—and often impelled Hester to ask, in bitterness of heart, whether it were for ill or good that the poor little creature had been born at all.

> Indeed, the same dark question often rose into her mind, with reference to the whole race of womanhood. Was existence worth accepting, even to the happiest among them? As concerned her own individual existence, she had long ago decided in the negative, and dismissed the point as settled. A tendency to speculation, though it may keep woman quiet, as it does man, yet makes her sad. She discerns, it may be, such a hopeless task before her. As a first step, the whole system of society is to be torn down, and built up anew. Then, the very nature of the opposite sex, or its long hereditary habit, which has become like nature, is to be essentially modified, before woman can be allowed to assume what seems a fair and suitable position. Finally, all other difficulties being obviated, woman cannot take advantage of these preliminary reforms, until she herself shall have undergone a still mightier change; in which, perhaps, the ethereal essence, wherein she has her truest life, will be found to have evaporated. A woman never overcomes these problems by any exercise of thought. They are not to be solved, or only in one way. If her heart chance to come uppermost, they vanish. Thus, Hester Prynne, whose heart had lost its regular and healthy throb, wandered without a clew in the dark labyrinth of mind; now turned aside by an insurmountable precipice; now starting back from a deep chasm. There was wild and ghastly scenery all around her, and a home and comfort nowhere. At times, a fearful doubt strove to possess her soul, whether it were not better to send Pearl at once to heaven, and go herself to such futurity as Eternal Justice should provide.

Only the emanation of Pearl from the spiritual world has saved Hester from the martyrdom of a prophetess, which is Hawthorne's most cunning irony, since without Pearl his romance would have been transformed into a tragedy. That may be our loss aesthetically, since every reader of *The Scarlet Letter* comes to feel a great regret at Hester's unfulfilled potential. Something in us wants her to be a greater heretic even than Ann Hutchinson. Certainly we sense an unwritten book in her, a story that Hawthorne did not choose to write. But what he has written marks the true beginning of American prose fiction, the absolute point of origin from which we can trace the sequence that goes from Melville and James to Faulkner and Pynchon and that domesticates great narrative art in America.

III

Hawthorne's highest achievement is not in *The Scarlet Letter* and *The Marble Faun,* distinguished as they are, but in the best of his tales and sketches. The last of these, the extraordinary "Feathertop," sub-titled "A Moralized Legend," is as uncanny a story as Kafka's "Country Doctor" or "Hunter Gracchus," and has about it the dark aura of Hawthorne's valediction, his farewell to his own art. In its extraordinary strength at representing an order of reality that intersects our own, neither identical with the mundane nor quite transcending the way things are, "Feathertop" may be without rivals in our language.

Mother Rigby, a formidable witch, sets out to create "as lifelike a scarecrow as ever was seen," and being weary of making hobgoblins, determines to give us "something fine, beautiful, and splendid." An authentic forerunner of Picasso as sculptor, the witch chooses her materials with bravura:

> The most important item of all, probably, although it made so little show, was a certain broomstick, on which Mother Rigby had taken many an airy gallop at midnight, and which now served the scarecrow by way of a spinal column, or, as the unlearned phrase it, a backbone. One of its arms was a disabled flail, which used to be wielded by Goodman Rigby, before his spouse worried him out of this troublesome world; the other, if I mistake not, was composed of the pudding-stick and a broken rung of a chair, tied loosely together at the elbow. As for its legs, the right was a hoe-handle, and the left, an undistinguished and miscellaneous stick from the wood-pile. Its lungs, stomach, and other affairs of that kind, were nothing better than a meal-bag stuffed with straw. Thus, we have made out the skeleton and entire corporosity of the scarecrow, with the exception of its head; and this was admirably supplied by a somewhat withered and shrivelled pumpkin in which Mother Rigby cut two holes for the eyes and a slit for the mouth, leaving a bluish-colored knob, in the middle, to pass for a nose. It was really quite a respectable face.

Gaudily attired, the scarecrow so charms its demiurgic creator ("The more Mother Rigby looked, the better she was pleased") that she emulates Jehovah directly, and decides to breathe life into the new Adam by thrusting her own pipe into his mouth. Once vivified, Mother Rigby's creature is urged by her to emulate Milton's Adam: "Step forth! Thou hast the world before thee!" Hawthorne does not allow us to doubt the self-critique involved, as all romance is deliciously mocked:

> In obedience to Mother Rigby's word, and extending its arm as if to reach her outstretched hand, the figure made a step forward—a kind of hitch and jerk, however, rather than a step—then tottered, and almost lost its balance. What could the witch expect? It was nothing, after all, but a scarecrow, stuck upon two sticks. But the strong-willed old beldam scowled, and beckoned, and flung the energy of her purpose so forcibly at this poor combination of rotten wood, and musty straw, and ragged garments, that it was compelled to show itself a man, in spite of the reality of things. So it stept into the bar of sunshine. There it stood—poor devil of a contrivance that it was!—with only the thinnest vesture of human similitude about it, through which was evident the stiff, ricketty, incongruous, faded, tattered, good-for-nothing patchwork of its substance, ready to sink in a heap upon the floor, as conscious of its own unworthiness to be erect. Shall I confess the truth? At its present point of vivification, the scarecrow reminds me of some of the lukewarm and abortive characters, composed of heterogeneous materials, used for the thousandth time, and never worth using, with which romance-writers (and myself, no doubt, among the rest) have so over-peopled the world of fiction.

But the critique surpasses mere writers and attacks the greatest of romancers, Jehovah himself, as Mother Rigby deliberately frightens her pathetic creature into speech. Now fully humanized, he is named Feathertop by his creator, endowed with wealth, and sent forth into the world to woo the beautiful Polly, daughter of the worshipful Judge Gookin. There is only the one catch; poor Feathertop must keep puffing at his pipe, or he will dwindle again to the elements that compose him. All goes splendidly; Feathertop is a social triumph, and well along to seducing the delicious Polly, when he is betrayed by glances in a mirror:

> By and by, Feathertop paused, and throwing himself into an imposing attitude, seemed to summon the fair girl to survey his figure, and resist him longer, if she could. His star, his embroidery, his buckles, glowed, at that instant, with unutterable splendor; the picturesque hues of his attire took a richer depth of coloring; there was a gleam and polish over his whole presence,

> betokening the perfect witchery of well-ordered manners. The maiden raised her eyes, and suffered them to linger upon her companion with a bashful and admiring gaze. Then, as if desirous of judging what value her own simple comeliness might have, side by side with so much brilliancy, she cast a glance towards the full-length looking-glass, in front of which they happened to be standing. It was one of the truest plates in the world, and incapable of flattery. No sooner did the images, therein reflected, meet Polly's eye, than she shrieked, shrank from the stranger's side, gazed at him, for a moment, in the wildest dismay, and sank insensible upon the floor. Feathertop, likewise, had looked towards the mirror, and there beheld, not the glittering mockery of his outside show, but a picture of the sordid patchwork of his real composition, stript of all witchcraft.

Fleeing back to his mother, Feathertop abandons existence in despair of his reality, and flings the pipe away in a kind of suicide. His epitaph is spoken by a curiously softened Mother Rigby, as though experience had rendered her a more maternal demiurge:

> "Poor Feathertop!" she continued. "I could easily give him another chance, and send him forth again to-morrow. But, no! his feelings are too tender; his sensibilities too deep. He seems to have too much heart to bustle for his own advantage, in such an empty and heartless world. Well, well! I'll make a scarecrow of him, after all. 'Tis an innocent and a useful vocation, and will suit my darling well; and if each of his human brethren had as fit a one, 'twould be the better for mankind; and as for this pipe of tobacco, I need it more than he!"

Gentle and whimsical as this is, it may be Hawthorne's darkest irony. The witch is more merciful than the remorseless Jehovah, who always does send us forth again, into a world that cannot sustain us. Feathertop is closer to most of us than we are to Hester Prynne. That final dismissal of heroism is Hawthorne's ultimate legacy, glowing on still in the romances of Nathanael West and Thomas Pynchon.

CLARK GRIFFITH

Substance and Shadow: Language and Meaning in The House of the Seven Gables

In the opening pages of *The House of the Seven Gables* when Hawthorne first touches on the history of the Pyncheon family, he carefully notes how over the years the Pyncheon personality has assumed two widely varying shapes. Old Colonel Pyncheon himself typifies one distinct grouping within the family. Founder of the line and guilty of its original sin, he was a man of "iron energy," a schemer endowed with common sense "as massive and hard as blocks of granite," a practical man less interested in tradition than in providing his descendants with a "stable basis" and a "stately roof to shelter them." But while certain of his progeny have at intervals inherited something akin to the Colonel's "hard, keen sense," other Pyncheons seem bereft entirely of the foresight and tough forcefulness characterizing their ancestor. They tend to be ineffectual weaklings, "sluggish and dependen[t]," given to vagaries of thought and action. Unfitted for a life of practical affairs, they brood endlessly over the past—in particular, over the "mouldy parchments, signed with faded autographs" which represent the "dead and forgotten" claims to an enormous land grant in Maine. And although, as Hawthorne says, these traditional titles are "impalpable," signify an "absurd delusion" and a "shadowy hope," still many a later Pyncheon has dwelt upon them because he finds "nothing more solid . . . to cherish."

Basically, these descriptive comments are intended to distinguish sharply between two sorts of characters; and both the purpose and the full conse-

From *Modern Philology* 51, no. 3 (February 1954).

quences of the differentiation are matters to which we shall return. At this point, however, let us do no more than observe the linguistic, the actual word, differences contained in the passages. On the one hand, there are words like *iron, energy, massive, hard, granite, stable, stately.* Each connotes strength and vitality, the solidly real, the ponderous, the preeminently tangible. We might well refer to all of them as "substance words." Then, set over against these terms are such words as *sluggishness, mouldy, faded, dead, impalpable, delusion, shadowy.* Here the connotations suggest weakness or decay, dark unreality, the unsubstantial, the intangible. So plain, indeed, is the contrast that the second group may appropriately be designated "shadow words."

Substance words and shadow words. Throughout the remainder of the book, this verbal pattern, introduced at the outset, recurs and expands, proliferates into new terms, accumulates a greater symbolic richness. Ultimately the differences involved, extending beyond a mere contrast in human behavior, come to embrace other, more complex distinctions. By spelling out the several functions of this linguistic scheme, I hope to show that, far from being aesthetically slipshod or thematically unsatisfying, *The House of the Seven Gables* is, in the main, among Hawthorne's most effectively executed works of art, one in which exposition, symbolism, irony, drama, and meaning are alike subsumed under the far-reaching implications of substance and shadow.

I

The most readily apparent example of Hawthorne's language pattern derives from his continuing technique of characterization. In the contemporary generation which occupied the foreground of the *House,* only three authentic Pyncheons remain. Each possesses in generous measure one or another of the traits prefigured in the family's summarized history. For example, we are insistently urged to regard Jaffrey Pyncheon as the substantial Colonel's substantial counterpart: as a "weighty citizen," a "solid specimen," a man driven by a "hard, relentless will," and one made offensively massive by the "animal substance" in his face. At the opposite extreme there is the recessive Clifford, with his "indistinct shadow of human utterance," his weak facial expressions that "waver and glimmer," his naturally torpid sluggishness which suffering has intensified rather than originated. Here, also, is Hepzibah, very nearly as tremulously weak as her brother, even more given than he to feeding upon the "shadowy food" and "airily magnificent" hopes of aristocratic pretensions.

In all, these terms or close cognates are repeated dozens of times in connection with each character. Yet their frequent reappearance is neither a tedious mannerism nor a flaw in Hawthorne's creative method. On the contrary, the two clusters of purely descriptive words prove to be indispensable to the total meaning of the *House,* and, as can immediately be seen, they serve as the basic distinction out of which subtler dissimilarities—especially those of a scenic and symbolic nature—quickly emerge.

Scenically, the book is somewhat unequally divided between the interior of the house, together with the dark and decaying garden, and its exterior, principally the street running along before it. Both scenes, we soon recognize, were designed to recapitulate the distinguishing features of the characters whom they contain. Overspread by a dreary, unrelieved gloom, the inner house is little more than a collection of shadows, vaguely, almost abstractly, described. And Hawthorne's various references to it—to the chill, the stagnation, the long lapse of mortal life within—are obviously intended to complement the moral and emotional disintegration of its inhabitants. As Hepzibah and Clifford acknowledge, this ghostly interior is not simply an encircling dungeon: like an organic extension of themselves, it has come to stand for—to be—their dismal and haunted hearts. Furthermore, the scenes outside the house, though far warmer and more real, nevertheless represent Jaffrey's physical background and are made to reflect something of his solid substantiality. If Hawthorne writes at great length of Judge Pyncheon's heavy, sultry, dog-day smile, he is hardly less voluble on the subject of the hot sunlight in the streets. Occasional references to the "hard, keen" business practices of the townspeople suggest Jaffrey's "vast ability in grasping . . . and appropriating"; indeed, the entire stress upon the palpable realities without reminds us that Jaffrey, more than most, eschews "all airy matter, and never mistak[es] a shadow for a substance."

Still it will scarcely do to establish too narrowly either of these scene-character identifications. Shortly after the book opens, both the inner and the outer house acquire a metaphorical as well as a literal significance; and when this happens, the verbal scheme broadens beyond descriptive matters and is reintroduced as symbolism. Consider the street. Although we are once or twice informed that it is only a quiet lane, Hawthorne's actual descriptions, abounding in masses of heavy surface detail, generally belie this picture. In fact, the sharply etched street scenes more often suggest a place of ceaseless turmoil—of processions and tradesmen, carts and omnibuses swarming constantly past. Hence the impression grows that, while on certain occasions the street may be a secluded byway, at other times it becomes a comprehensive symbol of the brisk nineteenth-century world. Here in the midst of robust housewives and fiercely energetic railroad trains, the present is a tangible, immediately felt reality. And when, by contrast, we turn back to the inner house, it is to come at once under the dark shadow of the past.

Nor is this so solely because Hepzibah dreams of faded gentility and Clifford of his wasted youth. Rather, an explicit past is symbolically embodied in several particular shadows which Hawthorne deftly singles out from the surrounding gloom: a chair (black with age), a mirror (shaded, shadowy), a map (dim and dusty), a portrait (faded, dusky), a harpsichord (black and coffin-like). One and all, these are the worthless heirlooms of the Pyncheon dynasty, relics rooted like the moldy parchments and illegible autographs in the very origins of the family.

They are not, however, meant merely to portray the past. Just as time and guilt are closely linked throughout the *House,* so these objects, converted into time images, look backward to earlier centuries and simultaneously point up the Pyncheons' sins. The portrait and ancestral chair were properties of the old Colonel. Really an elaborate drawing of the Maine estate, the map exemplifies the Pyncheons' greed, their hereditary yearning for wealth to which they have long since lost any title. The harpsichord belonged to Alice Pyncheon, whose overweening pride typified another family trait. Out of the dim mirror there flock the ghosts of all dead Pyncheons, each stamped with the mark of personal guilt. In short, the principal shadows inside the house are associated with moral degeneracy; and making this association, we come upon the most provocative of Hawthorne's symbolic distinctions. Shadow, the past, the inner house—all combine to symbolize the tragedy of human sin, while the substantial, contemporaneous world without provides a warmly optimistic atmosphere in which it seems possible to conceal this tragedy or to banish it or to live unaware that it even exists. Such, in turn, are the outlooks, the specious outlooks, imputed to Jaffrey, Holgrave, and Phoebe.

At first glance, to be sure, any conceptual frame flexible enough to include these characters, particularly Phoebe and Jaffrey, will seem highly improbable. Nevertheless, all belong to the world outside the house and are presented in terms of its key images. Each, for different reasons, resists the profounder implications of the inner house. As he deals with their respective states of "innocence," Hawthorne's language, turned now to symbolizing moral positions, remains remarkably self-consistent. Likening Jaffrey's entire life to a "tall and stately edifice," he writes that the Judge's sin lurks deep inside, a "corpse, half decayed, and still decaying . . . with the cobwebs festooned over its forgotten door." But citizen that he is of the outer world, Jaffrey never looks inward. To him, as he bluntly reminds Hepzibah, the past is sheerest nonsense. Around his own impurity he has arrayed the most imposing of exteriors—a sunny, benevolent smile and the "splendid halls" and "high cornices" betokening a guiltless life.

Now despite the signal differences between her and the Judge, it is noteworthy that Phoebe, too, is regularly associated with images of sunlight and substantiality; and when closely examined, they turn out to be not simply the marks of her warm, generous affections. They symbolize as well the fact that her early responses to the seven-gabled house curiously parallel Jaffrey's attitude toward his life. Possessing none save the values of the outer world, Phoebe is honestly unprepared to recognize the presence of a "decaying corpse" within. Significantly, she knows little concerning the family's past, has forgotten most of what she once was told, remains profoundly incurious about Clifford's identity, Jaffrey's motives, the meaning of Maule's curse. What Phoebe's "real substance" lacks, as Hawthorne sometimes tries to show, is the modifying influence of tragic insight. While she fails as a character—fails because Hawthorne is only partially capable of demonstrating her maturation—Phoebe is, like Donatello or the bridal pair at Merrymount, an innocent whose defect is her very innocence.

To a considerable extent, therefore, Jaffrey the hypocrite and the guileless Phoebe are less representative of any particular time than they are traditional character types in Hawthorne's writing; their relation to the outer house is a part of the general symbolic plan. Holgrave, on the other hand, does personify the distinctly modern world beyond the house and, it seems likely, the easy, fallacious ethical perfectionism of the nineteenth century. Like this world of outward forms, he is a thoroughly externalized individual, a figure of many surfaces, forever "putting off one exterior and snatching up another to be soon shifted for a third." Moreover, his *social* radicalism, the subject of much critical comment, is only named, never fully analyzed; in terms of Hawthorne's imagery, it is actually the daguerreotypist's *moral* intransigency which is made to seem important. He rails not against economic injustices, that is, but against the past, that "dead corpse" which wastes the strength of the present. Loving "nothing mouldy," he deplores the old house with "its dark low-studded rooms . . . and sordidness." Were this possible, he would purify (and the verb is *purify,* not *transform*) the house with fire until only its ashes remained. The truth is that Holgrave, whose hypnotic powers imply his complete materialism, would exorcise the same shadow willfully concealed by Jaffrey and as yet unknown to Phoebe. Misguidedly intent upon abolishing evil, he is a forerunner of the materialistic purifiers at Blithedale.

Thus from simple, repetitious beginnings in the exposition of the novel,

Hawthorne's language pattern passes over into symbolism, enriches the meaning of the time sequence, defines moral attitudes, and comes full circle to shed additional light on persons and places previously described. At the same time, the two groupings of words are further enlarged through their appearance in both the irony and the drama of the narrative.

II

As much as *The Scarlet Letter,* the *House* is based upon irony. One difference, however, is that, where in the earlier book an irony of situation was emphasized (Dimmesdale's preaching to Hester, the community's celebration of Chillingworth's healing powers), Hawthorne has now turned to an irony of language, at its best more accurately termed "paradox." Again and again we encounter passages in which small linguistic byplays precisely restate Hawthorne's largest themes: Hepzibah ignores the "hard, little pellets" of Uncle Venner's advice while she builds castles in the air; Clifford's delicate soap bubbles burst against Jaffrey's massive face; the sunlight appropriated by Jaffrey for his smile also accentuates his dark depravity; his great wealth is composed of "solid unrealities." But the two richest and most effectively sustained ironies in the book work out at various places where those who take the greatest pride in their substantiality are reduced to shadows and where qualities heretofore seen as shadows are revealed as the prime realities.

In connection with the first, notice the old Colonel himself. If he thought to leave behind a stately roof, what in fact he did bequeath was a sin to "darkly overshadow [his] posterity." For all his "rough heartiness" and "great animal development," he has later come to represent merely a "dusky . . . frown . . . lingering in the passage-way." Even in his portrait the "physical outline and substance" seem "darkening away," leaving only the sinful character of the man "to be brought out in a kind of spiritual relief." And toward the close of the narrative when Pyncheon ghosts flock through the magic mirror, there comes first the Colonel, "a thing of no substance," still reenacting its old crime but doing so now with the wave of an ineffectual hand.

Quite in keeping with his resemblance to the Colonel, Jaffrey presently undergoes an identical metamorphosis. Although he never mistakes a shadow for a substance and does not "belong to the dreaming class of men," the Judge would violate Clifford's tranquillity for the sake of ancient papers which have no value and are so old and dusty that they all but crumble to the touch. Consequently, it is Jaffrey whom the moldy parchments, after all, mislead, for, as Hepzibah says, he "took hold of a dream as if it were real. He died with this delusion in his mind." Furthermore, once Jaffrey enters the house, proceeds beyond the shop door and into the inmost rooms, he does literally become a shadow, destroyed, so to speak, by the symbolic past—by Maule's legendary prophecy—and made to blend slowly, subtly, into the pervasive darkness. There is, unfortunately, rather little to be said for the tone of forced playfulness in the ensuing "wake." Yet Hawthorne's selection of details is reasonably successful when the images ironically contrast Jaffrey's love for solid forms (the ticking timepiece, the heavy cane, the references to food and wealth) with his present formlessness; when they are used to taunt the "great animal" for having fallen into an "unaccountable lethargy"; or when, at the end, they are maneuvered into showing both the sturdy, benevolent Judge and his shapeless apparition wearing a frown "as Black as the ancestral one."

What these ironic transformations suggest, of course, is that in the last analysis shadow may well outweigh substance. And since, as we have observed, shadow symbolizes sin, the case could hardly be otherwise. For evil, to repeat the oldest and truest of critical commonplaces, is the ultimate reality in Hawthorne's work, the inescapable part of every man's heritage which none can disguise or avoid or hope to argue away. Here where the initial criminal act lies buried in a dark past, so remote from the palpable present, guilt may appear to be an airy nothing. Yet it nonetheless continues and endures. If, as Holgrave protests, the past is dead, it likewise rests upon the present "like a giant's . . . body." Elsewhere Hawthorne comments on the greater ease of transmitting sin than of bequeathing tangible properties; and he dryly wonders that a "thumb's bigness" of Jaffrey's evil should overbalance in the scales as "mass of things not evil." Plainly, sin and the past and shadow symbolizing sin and the past are endowed with a power paradoxically at odds with their immateriality. In the *House* they function either to discipline the individual or, should he prove untractable, to destroy him. Out of the two processes, the superimposing of shadow over substantiality, evolves much of Hawthorne's drama.

Jaffrey, concerned to the last with external phenomena, simply becomes the decaying corpse he so long concealed. But the others symbolically identified with the exterior of the house pass inside to be instructed by its shadows. Halfway through the narrative the inner gloom touches Phoebe, disclosing to her truths deeper and more meaningful than those revealed "in broad day light or . . . in the ruddy light of a cheerful fire." Thereafter, her temperament is never again so unfailingly sunny. Her eyes look darker: their shadowiness is the token of her larger understanding. In Hawthorne's words, she is now "less girlish, but more a woman." Somewhat more plausible because better realized artistically, Holgrave's dramatic transformation is couched in a similar language. During the third long interview with Phoebe (chapter 14), the daguerreotypist's hatred for the past and for the house is strangely subdued; his hard exterior seems mellowed. Although his pledge to lend Hepzibah and Clifford "whatever aid I can" remains equivocal, he all but renounces his role as aloof spectator and moral purist. There is, he concedes, some "shallow gayety" in his own life which he has only commenced to comprehend.

Complete self-discovery is deferred until Holgrave, after coming upon Jaffrey's body, must spend a "dark, cold, miserable hour" in the house alone. Then he first perceives the terrible substantiality of guilt. Then, too, he experiences a new gush of sympathy—expressed through his now unmistakable desire to protect Clifford—and a fresh insight into Phoebe's "hope, warmth, and joy." Notably, he declares his love for Phoebe inside the house where the shadows are darkest. His later wish—so patently absurd when taken literally—that the Judge had constructed his country house of stone rather than of wood is surely to be interpreted as Hawthorne's clumsy way of demonstrating how Holgrave has accepted the unassailable reality of the past. We note, in any case, that he utters the statement while standing directly beneath Colonel Pyncheon's faded portrait, then turns in the next breath to a comment on the immutability of the Colonel's old wrong.

Properly understood, then, the inner house and all it represents will chasten the individual, teach him charity and love, impress upon him the essential fact that sin is at once indestructible and the true basis for brotherhood. But there are dangers within as well as without. To dwell exclusively among the foul shadows of human depravity is to behold only their dark ugliness, never their power for ennobling. It is a life of isolation; and by living thus secludedly, Hepzibah and Clifford have aggravated and perpetuated the original sin, set it in motion anew. Accordingly, they must seek for their redemption in the outer world. Hepzibah, having spent her life proudly denying kinship with all others, "needs a walk along the noon day street to keep her sane." Clifford, his affections eaten away, requires restoration "to the world and to himself." The attempts of these two dim shadows to reestablish contact with the solid substantiality of the streets constitutes another aspect of the dramatic unfolding in the *House*.

Though both draw strength from Phoebe's warm and tender substance, there is no lasting salvation here. In the darkening garden Clifford still watches a dreary shadow break the light of Maule's well, still turns mournfully toward the sunlight and the street and cries out for his lost happiness.

Once on a brilliantly warm Sabbath he and Hepzibah determine to leave the house for church, only to return immediately into an interior which now seems tenfold more dismal than before. Again, Clifford, shuddering and pale, is forcibly restrained from leaping through the arched window into the surging stream of life below. But following Jaffrey's death, the spell is temporarily broken. With a corpse behind them—and the image is important—the two recluses flee the house. Their flight becomes a striking instance of the language pattern translated into symbolic drama.

As if by instinct, Clifford leads Hepzibah to a train, one symbol, we noticed, of the vigorous external world and a symbol employed elsewhere in Hawthorne (particularly in "The Celestial Railroad") to express escape from sin and human responsibilities. Outside the cars, the rushing, varied landscape suggests again the panoramic street; inside, by the same token, Clifford suddenly espouses a confused jumble of theories which exactly duplicate the moral doctrines identified with that street. Like Jaffrey, he would ignore the shadow within ("Let such things slip aside. Here we are, in the world"), and the wish is intensely ironic, since this particular shadow *is* Jaffrey. In another moment Clifford echoes Holgrave, calls for the destruction of roof and hearthstone and the evil they secrete, praises mesmerism as an instrument of human reform. His remarks gradually grow more frenzied until a fellow-passenger, "bringing his gimlet-eye to a point on Clifford," impatiently protests, "I can't see through you." At just this moment, however, the train reaches a way station, dreary, solitary, standing near a "venerably black" and apparently deserted farmhouse. Impulsively leaving the coach, Clifford replies with a telling allusion: "No, I'll be bound you can't. . . . And yet, my dear sir, I am as transparent as the water of Maule's well!"

Almost certainly this ambiguous exchange is fraught with symbolic undertones. Clifford's solid opacity, so oddly out of keeping with the ghost-like qualities formerly attributed to him, is, I should judge, the mark of his having entered the real world in the wrongest possible way. Plunging abruptly out of the house, he, too, readily acquired Jaffrey's ponderous indifference and Holgrave's heavy contempt for what lay behind. For a brief time he became wholly externalized, substance untempered by shadow. But only briefly, as the succeeding references make abundantly clear. Sin and the past are inexorable, and at the height of his liberation shadow—darkness, dreariness, the black house, the shadowy recesses of Maule's well—reclaims Clifford, just as it altered Jaffrey and Holgrave, whose language he began to speak. Instantly, the "wild effervescence of his mood . . . entirely subsided. A powerful excitement had given him energy and vivacity. Its operation over, he forthwith began to sink."

Nevertheless, the excursion has not failed. Even while the train rushes away from them, Hepzibah and Clifford are, like Phoebe and Holgrave, moving toward the achievement of a proper moral balance. Here on the rain-swept platform, Hepzibah, after failing twice when confined to the house, is finally able to pray.

III

> The human heart to be allegorized as a cavern; at the entrance there is sunshine, and flowers growing about it. You step within, but a short distance, and begin to find yourself surrounded with a terrible gloom, and monsters of divers kinds. . . . You are bewildered and wander long without hope. At last a light strikes upon you. You peep towards it, and find yourself in a region that seems, in some sort, to reproduce the flowers and sunny beauty of the entrance, but all perfect.

The shortcoming of *The House of the Seven Gables* most frequently cited is, understandably enough, its plot of feud and reconciliation. Not only is this situation strained, hackneyed, and, as Austin Warren has remarked, a tiresome nuisance; much more seriously, it seems forever threatening to rob the moral drama of any slightest significance. If we are to presume that a kind of blanket amnesty is obtained through the marriage of Phoebe and Holgrave (Pyncheon and Maule), then our belief in the regenerative capacities of sin and, most especially, in a personal struggle for atonement is instantly negated. Freed by a trick, a purely mechanical plotting device, every character save the dead Jaffrey sallies forth from the dark, sin-ridden house. Guilt is painlessly transcended by the marriage vows. Hawthorne has sacrificed the moral depths of the better tales and of *The Scarlet Letter* for a trivial coincidence, a case of concealed identity, and a happy ending which would do no great credit to the sentimental novelists whom he despised.

But is this an accurate presumption, a just estimate of the book? Actually, a close consideration of the text indicates how remarkably little attention is paid to the continuing antipathies of Maules toward Pyncheons. Whether or not Hawthorne originally intended this, the specific quarrel serves as point of departure for a study of generalized guilt and then is itself thrust swiftly and decisively into the background. Always keenly aware of the Pyncheons' sins, we nonetheless tend to lose sight of their injured victims; they so far slipped Hawthorne's own mind, apparently, that he was obliged to resort to an awkward, obviously contrived flashback (chapter 13) in order to reintroduce them. Hence it seems permissible to shift away from the plot and to look for the meaning of the *House* in its pervasive symbolism rather than in its slight, superficial story. My feeling is that, far more than a suitable redress for the Maules, the crucial moral test in the book is posed by the dreary inner house.

Symbolically, this dark interior resembles the forest of temptation through which Dimmesdale wandered on his way to eventual confession. Or it is like the catacombs in *The Marble Faun,* where, as Hawthorne was afterward to write, "all men must descend if they would know anything beyond the surface and illusive pleasures of existence." Or, in what is perhaps the happiest analogy, it is akin to the figure of a heart cavern sketched out by Hawthorne in one of his journal entries. Before its door, as before the cavern, there are flowers and sunlight, seemingly substantial, but actually artificial—as artificial as Jaffrey's feigned innocence, Phoebe's untutored naiveté, Holgrave's unrealistic reforms, Clifford's wild mood in the train. Inside the house, as within the cavern, are hideous shadows of "divers kinds," terribly real, but also dreadfully distorted, even as Hepzibah and Clifford are twisted beyond all resemblance to their fellow-beings and as the roses in the Pyncheon garden are blighted by a rotting mold. But at the far end of the cavern, Hawthorne added, there lay "a region that seems in some sort to reproduce the flowers and sunny beauty of the entrance, but all perfect." And, however weakly uninspired the concluding pages of *The House of the Seven Gables* prove to be, the great bulk of the narrative would suggest that Hawthorne meant to present this region at its close.

For as we have seen, to pass into the house is necessary; yet the human heart decays when it lingers there. To pass out of the house is necessary; yet the heart is hardened when it abandons those inmost meanings which the house contains. But to pass *into* and *through* and then *out* of the house, as Phoebe and Holgrave and Hepzibah and Clifford ultimately do—herein lies the correct moral balance and, therefore, the way toward redemption. It is to see the Pyncheons' blackest weeds blossom into the flowers of Eden. It is to hear a strong note of joy struck on Alice Pyncheon's dusky harpsichord. Above all, as Hawthorne's language shows, it is to seize upon the wisdom that true reality and the truly compassionate heart are neither entirely substance nor entirely shadow but an inextricable compound of them both.

coherence, that is, remains for the most part superficial and in the execution; it only slightly impairs our view of the classical design of the action. With an eye on the action, we may reduce the plot to the following incidents:

Donatello, a young Italian nobleman of great simplicity and charm, encounters in Rome a group of visiting artists: two Americans, Kenyon and Hilda, and a beautiful dark-haired Anglo-Jewish woman, Miriam. Falling in love with Miriam, Donatello becomes aware of some mysterious event in her early private history, and of the continuing pressure exerted by a Capuchin monk, evidently a participant in the event, who now lurks menacingly on the periphery of Miriam's new life.

Incited by Miriam's fear of the Capuchin, her violent desire to be free of him, and perhaps an actual gesture of encouragement, Donatello murders him. Donatello flees Rome to his country estate at Monte Beni in the Apennines, to brood on the meaning of his act and upon his own muddled responses to it. Miriam follows him. They meet and agree that neither of them may escape the consequences of the crime. Donatello returns to Rome and gives himself up; he is last heard of in the depths of a civil prison. But the experience has transformed him into a man.

Miriam returns to give *her*self up to a life of penance, entering upon a pilgrimage to last as long as Donatello's imprisonment, which may be lifelong. Their friends, Kenyon and Hilda, having in some degree shared in the tragedy, are its survivors; and the gloom of the conclusion is faintly lit by the subdued joy of their discovery of each other and their belief—however faltering—in the value of the adventure they have all of them shared.

Thus the plot: an assortment of rather melodramatic incidents with those Mysteries-of-Udolpho overtones later complained of by Eliot. Donatello's resemblance to the marble faun of Praxiteles gave the novel its American title. *The Marble Faun* is apt enough as regards the plot; but *Transformation,* the title supplied by the English publishers, is a better index to the action; and it may be because Hawthorne knew that action only becomes realized in plot that he referred to the English publishers as pigheaded. That action is the transformation of the soul in its journey from innocence to conscience: the soul's realization of itself under the impact of and by engagement with evil—the tragic rise born of the fortunate fall. It is a New World action—my supposition is that it is *the* New World action, the tragic remainder of what Lawrence called the myth of America. It is what has to happen to "golden youth" if it is to mature; and the novel is the kind of novel which had to be written if the young literature was to mature. Donatello, though purportedly an Italian aristocrat, is nonetheless the hero of the hopeful, seen in a tragic perspective: the figure who, in approaching experience, comes up against the social world under the great, appealing illusion that (in the words of Horace Bushnell) he is "a free person [who has] just begun to be."

The outline of Donatello's personality is made known to us through the recurring imagery of Eden: imagery employed in the beginning only by Hawthorne; then, after the "Fall," by Kenyon and Hilda; and only at the last by Miriam. This progression of insight and recognition is the core of the story. To Miriam, stifled by her own enveloping history, Donatello appears as "a creature in a state of development less than what mankind has attained"; less than mankind, yet oddly more perfect; a "creature of simple elements," part animal and part child, manifesting a kinship to "that wild, sweet, playful, rustic creature" whose marble image he resembled, and manifesting, too, the unreasoning variability of animals—the docility of the pet spaniel, the tenacity of the bulldog. The action of *The Marble Faun* is the assumption of total manhood by this child-animal. The young innocent becomes entangled (in the way Bushnell predicted that, given the world, he would have to be) with the net of preexisting relationships—involvements which, like those between Miriam and the Capuchin, the hero's very character makes it impossible for him to intuit or guard himself against. The action concludes not only with the hero's assumption of manhood but with the imaginative grasp by Miriam and more uneasily by Kenyon of the meaning and the value of the sin and suffering which manhood requires.

The action has to do with the discovery of *time* as a metaphor of the experience of evil. Rome is thus the best imaginable setting; nothing in the New World could match it. What was wanted, for the maximum effect, was maximum antiquity—a symbol coexistent, if possible, with the temporal order itself; and Rome is identified in the story as "the city of all time." The seven-gabled home of the Pyncheons had reached back a century or so to the Puritan period, and Hawthorne did all he could with it. But Rome, Hawthorne remarks on the opening page of *The Marble Faun,* reaches back through a "threefold antiquity"—Christian, Roman, Etruscan. And it is in dramatic contrast to such massive age that the hero is then promptly introduced as an "Arcadian simpleton." The tension between the simpleton unconscious of time and the infinitely history-laden environment parallels the introductory tension of *The Scarlet Letter*: between Hester Prynne and the hostile community. The action in *The Scarlet Letter,* discharged by that opening tableau, follows Hester's effort to escape from the community and her eventual return into it, to spend her life there as an increasingly revered member. In *The Marble Faun,* the action unfolds from its starting point: in terms of Donatello's consciousness of the quality, the content, the pressures of time. It is thus only *after* the sin and the flight that Donatello seems to grow aware of his own ancestry—explaining to Kenyon, at Monte Beni, that his family history goes back beyond the Middle Ages to earliest Christendom and perhaps to a time before that. Donatello's family, like the city of Rome, has a multiple antiquity; and his acceptance of the burden of inheritance may be his way of coming to terms with all that Rome represents in the novel: with the world.

The degree of actual tension in *The Marble Faun* is the degree of Hawthorne's divided sympathies toward the contending factors. And he was not less ambivalent toward time than he had been toward the Puritan community. His involvement with time, always profound, had always been notably ambiguous. It was not a metaphysical interest; Hawthorne had been concerned not with the ontological status of time, but with its contents and effects: not with time as a concept, but with the coloration it lent to the things it perpetuated and with the value or the misfortune of sustained temporal relations. He had a passion for sources and beginnings, for traditions and continuities, and resented in America the scantiness of histories. Though Tocqueville was unduly impressed by the claims of the hopeful and had doubted that American poetry would "be fed with legends or the memorials of old traditions," Hawthorne never seemed able to get hold of legends and traditions enough. He wore out the few he could find; and it may have been to refurbish his stock that in 1853 he consented to go to Europe as his government's representative. In Europe, where he tripped over unchanging traditions and customs in appalling abundance, his resentment veered around toward the ancient.

"At home," Henry James remarked (1895), "he had fingered the musty; but abroad he seemed to pine for freshness." Both sides of the observation can be matched by its opposite. Even in the American days, the musty needed the fresh in the shaping of rewarding experience: this is the very formula that somewhat tamely concludes *The House of the Seven Gables*. And while, in England, Hawthorne consigned to the flames the accumulated treasures ("rubbish") of the British Museum and wondered how human aspiration could tolerate English social immobility, nonetheless in Paris he lamented fluidity and thought that nothing worth while could take root there.

Hawthorne himself had identified his generation's major ideal in the image of Adam, and he both celebrated and deplored it. The individual divorced from his racial or family past seemed to Hawthorne at once a liberated person and a lost son: an orphan, as he also had been. Such an ambivalence, the very stuff of drama, stayed with Hawthorne to the end; even in the inchoate and unfinished *Dr. Grimshawe's Secret* (posthumous,

1883), the hero Redclyffe, is an orphan cast afloat in the American world, who travels to England, motivated by "a great deal of foolish yearning for a connection with the past." Redclyffe's nostalgia is for the kind of "density" he finds in the atmosphere of an English country estate: a thickening of life and character caused by the hidden vitality of the past. In such a place, Redclyffe supposes, "the life of each successive dweller was eked out with the lives of all who had hitherto lived there . . . so that there was a rare and successful contrivance for giving length, fullness, body, substance, to this thin frail matter of human life." Yet Redclyffe stubbornly voted for America and returns there; America's homes were mere "tents of a day, inns of a night"; but, though its atmosphere was much thinner, it was also much freer. That was Hawthorne's personal conclusion, too, after a comparable meditation in Florence.

The Marble Faun was a dramatization on a large scale of these many fertile contradictions. The question of density was as relevant to art as to life. Fullness and substance for his thin, frail materials was just what the American artist needed, according to Hawthorne; and Rome offered the narrative artist every contrivance for giving such substance to the events recounted. Rome's "very dust . . . is historic," it is noted; and every fragment of church or temple is "a great solid fact out of the past." Hawthorne extended himself to exploit each indication of the past as the source of life in the present: newly built houses are "perched on the lofty delapidations of a tomb"; the Capuchin, for a Gothic moment, is confused with a legendary Wandering Pagan, lost in the Catacombs for fifteen hundred years; life feeds on death; Christianity is bolstered by paganism; the past is everywhere the exemplar or the substructure of the present. But the cumulative force of those associations, strained as some of them may be, is precisely to give maximum meaning to Miriam's cry of desperate and ebbing hope: "Is the past so indestructible, the future so immitigable?" The tension of the novel is provided by the vigor of Miriam's effort to escape the consequences of her private past and the solidity of the "fact" of the past in general.

The tension is illuminated by analogous oppositions within the field of artistic creation. Hilda, after a brief attempt at original creation, yields entirely to the work of copying the old masters; but her honesty and her heightened enjoyment of the beauty contrived by others are contrasted with the pretenses of an English sculptor who cooks up lifeless imitations of the antique and is an effete slave (Kenyon thinks) to something "whose business or efficacy in our present world, it would be exceedingly difficult to define." Miriam turns her back altogether on the art of the past, claiming to paint wholly from the self and about the self; and her self-portrait becomes an unconscious imitation of the very painting—the *Beatrice* of Guido—which Hilda is currently engaged in copying.

This is one of the major "epiphanies" in the book—one of the major moments of reversal and recognition—and a crucial event in Miriam's education. It makes possible a recognition by her of the mythic model for the adventure she has shared with Donatello; and *that* recognition is the means of accepting it, appraising the experience, and knowing what to do about it. It is Donatello who acts and is acted upon, but it is Miriam who is gifted with the perception that controls the action at last and rounds out the novel. *"The story of the fall of man! Is it not repeated in our romance of Monte Beni?"*

The value of the identification is a sudden tremendous deepening of insight. Miriam explores the analogy further: the authentic manliness of the former child-animal Donatello may, she believes, offer a clue to an ancient mystery. "Was that very sin—into which Adam precipitated himself and all his race—was it the destined means by which, over a long pathway of toil and sorrow, we are to attain a higher, brighter, and profounder happiness, than our lost birthright gave?" If the Fall was, after all, immensely fortunate, so then was Donatello's reenactment of the Fall. Miriam is saved by the analogy: by her grasp of the analogy.

And so, perhaps, is Kenyon. A little later, he confronts Hilda with the novel's concluding ambiguity: that the adventure has proved life too "deadly serious" for anyone, like Donatello, "compounded especially for happiness"; or that Donatello's adventure illustrates the fact that "Adam fell that we might ultimately rise to a far loftier paradise than his." Hilda is far too "hopeful and happy-natured" to settle for either. A small shudder runs through the final pages at the suggestion of a fortunate fall; yet the lingering, uneasy impression remains that there has been demonstrated in action what the elder James had argued in theory. Hilda, and all the world, may call Donatello's action a crime or a sin. But his fall was in many serious respects an upward step—an entrance into that true reality which, for Hawthorne, is measured by time.

Wandering through the vineyards near Donatello's country estate, Kenyon speculates on Donatello's action and the astonishing mental and moral maturity it has bred in him. In the physical scenery about him Kenyon senses an answer by metaphor to the speculations that trouble him. He looks upon the setting "with somewhat the sensations of an adventurer who should find his way to the site of ancient Eden, and behold its loveliness through the transparency of gloom which has been brooding over those haunts of innocence ever since the fall." The gloom is there, but perhaps it has a greater beauty than the original. "Adam," reflects Kenyon, "saw it in a brighter sunshine, but never knew the shade of pensive beauty which Eden won from his expulsion." The language and the response suggest that here is an adjustment to time which offers a control for life. To the eyes of the artist, the color of time was very much richer than the blankness of the original sunshine. For such was the nature of man.

LARZER ZIFF

The Ethical Dimension of "The Custom House"

Perhaps the chief interest "The Custom House" Introduction holds for the reader today is its statement of Hawthorne's theory of romance, a theory which, as many have noted, profoundly governs the form and content of *The Scarlet Letter.* What has not been as well noted is the relationship between that theory and Hawthorne's theory of the good life. The experiences surrounding Hawthorne's definition of the romance as the meeting ground of the actual and the imaginary are more moral than aesthetic, and the realization of the theory in *The Scarlet Letter* governs the moral conclusions Hawthorne would like his reader to draw as well as the subject-matter and its arrangement.

Talking of his experiences as Surveyor of the Customs at Salem, in "The Custom House," Hawthorne asserts that for the most part his colleagues are a "set of wearisome old souls, who had gathered nothing worth preservation from their varied experience of life." We can appreciate why these men are wearisome when we consider the two whom he singles out for particular discussion: one is the epitome of what he finds distasteful in his colleagues; the other is an exception who serves to underline his general observation.

The epitome of wearisomeness is the Inspector who has stored his memory with husks and thereby stunted his moral development. He has numbered in his experience three wives, now dead, and twenty children, most of them also dead. "Here," Hawthorne says, "one would suppose, might have been

---

From *Modern Language Notes* 73, no. 5 (May 1958).

sorrow enough to imbue the sunniest disposition, through and through, with a sable tinge." But this is not so. All the Inspector seems to have gained from life is a concern with the physical present. His main interest and chief topic of conversation is food—the mutton-chop he ate, the hindquarter of veal he will eat—so that he has, in Hawthorne's words, "no higher moral responsibilities than the beasts of the field," and shares the beasts' "blessed immunity from the dreariness and duskiness of age."

The exception to the moral desert which Hawthorne finds in the custom house is the old retired General who is Collector of Customs. Hawthorne sees him as noble and heroic, yet his actual contact with the General is less than with most of his other colleagues:

> He seemed away from us, although we saw him but a few yards off; remote, though we passed close beside his chair; unattainable, though we might have stretched forth our hands and touched his own. It might be that he lived a more real life within his thoughts than amid the unappropriate environment of the Collector's office. The evolutions of the parade; the tumult of the battle; the flourish of old, heroic music, heard thirty years before,—such scenes and sounds, perhaps, were all alive before his intellectual sense.

From these descriptions of character we can infer an important precept which links Hawthorne's aesthetics to his ethics. The implied proposition might be phrased as follows: "Man's inner life can be more real than his outer life." It can be applied in fiction by dealing with the thoughts and emotions of characters as well as with their actions. It is also an ethical proposition because Hawthorne obviously finds that the Collector's inner life makes him a better man than the Inspector, who is much more alive physically but does not seem ever to have reflected.

The old General, like Hester Prynne, indulges in his reveries beside a fire, and it is pertinent that the "dim glow of a coal-fire" in the Introduction is as necessary an element of the room which analogizes the romance as are the moonlight and the familiar objects. The ethical formula which precedes the aesthetic equation of the actual and the imaginary is one which characterizes the good life as a life which blends the reveries of the past with the actions of the present, which combines morality and materiality. Just as the good romance strikes a balance between the actual and the imaginary, so the man of good character strikes a balance between his inner state and the materiality of the world.

The formula is further developed in "The Custom House" when Hawthorne discusses his own moral condition. He represents himself as the descendant of a family associated with Salem ever since its founding, and he takes sentimental comfort in this genealogy. Indeed, there is the flavor of semi-conscious snobbism in his later reference to the modern aristocracy of Salem as families who can be traced "from the petty and obscure beginnings of their traffic, at periods generally much posterior to the Revolution, upward to what their children look upon as long-established rank." Hawthorne claims a moral quality for his sentiment because it has provided him with a "home-feeling with the past," a feeling which, he goes on to say, he can "scarcely claim with reference to the present phase of the town." Too much of this sentiment can be unhealthy—he is glad his children (like Phoebe Pyncheon) were born and are being bred free of a Salem in which the legacy would be weightier by another generation—but for him it is a good thing. It provides him with a background of experience, albeit vicarious, so that like the old General he can face the materiality of life with a hidden life of his own.

Instead of sitting next to the custom house fire surrounded by his memories, the Surveyor Hawthorne we are presented to pokes about the attic reading the dusty documents of New England's past—his past. The effect, of course, is similar. And just as his life has been given moral quality by its familial link with the past, so when he turns to fiction he develops an artistic link with the past. Surveyor Pue is his literary ancestor, and accounts for the century which lies between that in which the action of *The Scarlet Letter* takes place and that in which Hawthorne occupies the custom house.

The past and present, then, enter into Hawthorne's theory of experience as counterparts of the distinction between inner-state and materiality; as necessary elements of the view of life which informs the actual-imaginary view of fiction. Romance is an enrichment of the actual by the imaginary. The good life is an enrichment of the material by the inner self, an appreciation of the present through a consciousness of the past. The elements of the good life find their dramatic counterparts in the two basic elements of the romance, and such a good life is, then, the material of the romance.

For this very reason, Hawthorne professed himself dissatisfied with the total achievement of *The Scarlet Letter.* His romance seemed to him too complete an escape into the past, too much concerned with the hidden and too little concerned with the open. A better book than he has written, he tells us in "The Custom House," would be written by the man who could see the "true and indestructible value that lay hidden in the petty and wearisome incidents, and ordinary characters" which surrounded him in Salem; the man who could fathom "the deeper import" of what seemed "dull and commonplace" to Hawthorne. When reading these remarks, one thinks of William Dean Howells's description of the crowd on the boat which is taking Tom Corey and Silas Lapham to the latter's summer cottage: "In face they were commonplace, with nothing but the American poetry of vivid purpose to light them up, where they did wholly lack fire." But whereas Howells's problem was to reveal the fire that lit up commonplace characters and events, Hawthorne's was to discover the commonplace settings which would display his sense of the past's importance. His quarrel with *The Scarlet Letter* is addressed to the overbalance in that book of the half of the dualism embodying the past, the inner state, and the imaginary, so that the virtues of the present, the material, and the actual are underdeveloped. What he wishes is to be able to write about the present, although it may fictionally appear as an earlier period, giving it the values which he associates with the past, but, nevertheless, keeping the actual always in focus so that whatever his characters' dramatic reconciliations with their environment may be they are also reconciliations with materiality. He notes, at the end of "The Custom House," that if he is remembered at all in Salem he will be remembered as the historian of the town pump, the author of the little temperance piece about Salem's early source of water. He wants the contemporaneity of "A Rill from the Town Pump" to be informed with the morality of *The Scarlet Letter,* but he also wants *The Scarlet Letter* to bear a more immediate relationship to the actual than he feels it does. *The House of the Seven Gables,* for instance, can be seen as Hawthorne's attempt to fuse what he found satisfying in the aforementioned two works so as to produce a work which better balanced the past with the present.

Of course, the generally accepted opinion is that Hawthorne did in *The Scarlet Letter* achieve just such a balance between the actual and the imaginary as he talked of in the introductory sketch, so that the discontent expressed in "The Custom House" should be read merely as an expression of the artist's customary discontent with his finished product in view of the perfection he envisioned. However, if we bear in mind the ethical as well as the aesthetic connotation of his theory of romance, we can see that as sound as this opinion may be for the critic of the novel, Hawthorne could not have shared it because he refused to separate the ethics of his content from the beauty of his form. The critic is correct, of course. Hawthorne did achieve a superb balance between the actual and the imaginary in *The Scarlet Letter.* But there was an imbalance for Hawthorne because his theory of the good life did not achieve as successful an embodiment as did his theory of romance: the balancing of the actual and the imaginary should also have been the balancing of the inner state and materiality and the latter blend was not, for Hawthorne, satisfactorily composed.

This can be appreciated by considering the Puritan past which serves as the scene of *The Scarlet Letter.* It provides the characters with precisely that environment in which the secret acts of the soul are matters of public concern, in which the sin of adultery is a crime against the state, in which the scarlet letter, making public the hidden, can be worn with probability. But as aesthetically appropriate as the setting may seem, Hawthorne, in the last analysis, found it ethically inappropriate. The Puritan commonwealth might artistically stand for the actual while the superstitions and torments of its citizens might stand for the imaginary, but Hawthorne wanted his actual also to correspond to what he regarded as materiality so that when the dramatic reconciliation of his characters with their environment took place, so would the ethical reconciliation between inner state and materiality occur. This, however, is not the case in *The Scarlet Letter* because the fictional Boston is far too remote from materiality. Any reconciliation of a character's private life with its public life could hardly be viewed as an instructive achievement with obvious parallels in the nineteenth-century America which Hawthorne viewed from his window.

The idea can be illustrated with reference to Pearl who aesthetically stands so well for the meeting place of the actual and the imaginary. However, she also serves to remind us that Boston itself is a dark place. Governor Bellingham sees her at his home, a place reminiscent of old England—of the wider world—with its liveried servant, its old furniture, and its garden, which, significantly, has failed to develop after its English model but has degenerated into little more than a cabbage patch. In this setting, Pearl is a reminder for Bellingham of his "days of vanity in old King James' time." In the same scene, the Reverend John Wilson says of Pearl, "Methinks I have seen just such figures, when the sun has been shining through a richly painted window, and tracing out the golden and crimson images across the floor." He adds, "But that was in the old land."

As Pearl is the organic embodiment of the sin of her parents, that which Dimmesdale must acknowledge in the market-place, so she is also for the Puritan community the embodiment of what they attempted to leave behind when they went into the forest but what they cannot reconcile with their present life, although, to be ethically sound, they must. Boston, which aesthetically may stand for the actual, ethically partakes of the hidden half of the dualism because of its suppressed materiality.

Such a community, then, did not ultimately satisfy its creator's moral demands, for it failed to have the hearty materiality, the indulgence in the senses, which he saw in the Salem about him. He comments that the Puritans were, after all, "Native Englishmen, whose fathers had lived in the sunny richness of the Elizabethan epoch; a time when the life of England, viewed as one great mass, would appear to have been as stately, magnificent, and joyous, as the world has ever witnessed." He makes it clear that they should not have denied this heritage, and that the extravagances they have permitted themselves are, unfortunately, exceptions. Aesthetically, daily Boston might balance the secret lives of its citizens, but morally it is too much of the same. Chillingworth, for all of the dire effect he has upon Dimmesdale, opens the windows of Dimmesdale's mind to European thoughts, to what is happening in the marketplace of the world. If Hester's attempt to get to that world with Dimmesdale is ill-fated, it is not because Boston is ethically the best place, but because Hester and Dimmesdale have not yet given Boston its due meed. Pearl does so, and is no longer required to languish there but is permitted to mingle the morality which Boston has imposed upon her with the materiality which Boston unhealthily denies.

For *The Scarlet Letter* to have lived up to the theory of romance's ethical demands, then, its Boston would have to have been much more like the Salem which Hawthorne saw from his windows. He did not regret, he tells us, his initial entrance into his duties as Surveyor of Customs. Because he had worked at Brook Farm, mingled with Channing and Thoreau, and been influenced by Emerson and Longfellow, it was a healthy thing for him to get into active life. The Inspector was a necesasry antidote for Alcott. He tells us this immediately before expressing his sense of his inability to write a good book about the life around him, in order to absolve the daily activity of the custom house from responsibility for its apparent sterility, a responsibility which, he believed, actually resided in his perception of it. *The Scarlet Letter* disappoints him because the materiality of the life in it is, ultimately, too close to an objectification of the hidden lives of its characters so that his interpretation of the actual and the imaginary is not matched by its ethical counterpart.

This supposed shortcoming of *The Scarlet Letter* explains why Hawthorne's subsequent romances took the direction they did. After his first full-length work, the historical past ceases to be the scene in which Hawthorne set his work, because he wished his scene to provide more of the materiality which entered into his view of the good life than it did in *The Scarlet Letter.* The past, of course, remained an important element of that good life, and, therefore, of the romance's subject-matter, but it was subordinated to the demands of the immediate world of the work, and shaped but did not constitute it. The living are very much in control of *The House of the Seven Gables* as it reaches its resolution.

DANIEL G. HOFFMAN

"The Maypole of Merry Mount" and the Folklore of Love

One of Hawthorne's most interesting tales is "The Maypole of Merry Mount." Here, as in "The Gray Champion," "Legends of the Province House," "My Kinsman, Major Molineux," and a dozen other stories to be written later, he was guided by the aesthetic instinct that had led him to project as his earliest work a volume to be called *Seven Tales of My Native Land*. The original stories, he reports in "The Devil in Manuscript," were so disappointingly inadequate that he burned them. But the labor of their writing taught him a lesson he could learn from no one else in America at that time: how to mingle the imaginary with the actual American past so that folk traditions have the appearance of history, and history gains the heightened grandeur of legend.

"The Maypole" takes place during the final hours of the dissident colony at Mt. Wollaston, Massachusetts, where in historic fact one Thomas Morton, an anti-Puritan High-Churchman and Royalist, had established a trading-post with the Indians. "The facts, recorded on the grave pages of our New England Annalists, have wrought themselves, almost spontaneously, into a sort of allegory," writes Hawthorne in his prefatory note. But, as G. H. Orians has shown, he played rather freely with those grave pages in making Morton's dissolute band into a hedonistic cult whose object of worship is the Maypole. Q. D. Leavis and John B. Vickery have recently interpreted the tale from rather different points of view; Mrs. Leavis finds Hawthorne here

From *Form and Fable in American Fiction*. © 1961 by Daniel G. Hoffman. Oxford University Press, 1961.

to be a ritual dramatist concerned with cultural history, while Vickery takes him as a ritual anthropologist tracing religious evolution. There seem plausible grounds for both views; yet neither does full justice to Hawthorne's intentions or achievement.

His story begins with a description of Merry Mount, where "May, or her mirthful spirit, dwelt all the year round. . . . Through a world of toil and care she flitted with a dreamlike smile." The communicants of the Maypole, "should their banner be triumphant, were to pour sunshine over New England's rugged hills, and scatter flower seeds throughout the soil." But we are never permitted to forget that this colony is imperiled by the surrounding Puritans. The incipient struggle is defined in the third sentence: "Jollity and gloom were contending for an empire." After the Maypole and the mummers in animal garb dancing around it are described, these protagonists appear: "A youth in glistering apparel" has his arm about "a fair maiden, not less gaily decorated than himself." They are surrounded and crowned by roses. As we meet them they are being joined "in holy matrimony" by Blackstone, "a clerk of Oxford and high priest of Merry Mount." The ceremony has the aspect of a masquerade, although we are told that "This wedlock was more serious than most affairs of Merry Mount, where jest and delusion, trick and fantasy, kept up a continual carnival." The couple are actually participating in a double ceremony: not only are they marrying one another, but they are also Lord and Lady of the May. This is both a personal and a ritual wedlock.

At just this moment, as the "dim light" of sunset is "withdrawn" from "the whole domain of Merry Mount," some "black shadows have rushed forth in human shape" from the "black surrounding woods":

> The Puritans had played a characteristic part in the Maypole mummeries. Their darksome figures were intermixed with the wild shapes of their foes, and made the scene a picture of the moment, when waking thoughts start up amid the scattered fantasies of a dream.

Their leader, Endicott, is "the Puritan of Puritans," whose very "frame and soul seemed wrought of iron," in contrast to the "silken" revellers who now cower about him "like evil spirits in the presence of a dread magician." With his own sword he hews down the Maypole, orders stripes, stocks, branding, and cropping of ears for its captured votaries, and then turns to the newly wedded couple. "I am minded that ye shall both have a token to remember your wedding day," he threatens them. The youth, Edgar, whom Hawthorne still calls the May Lord, replies with manly fortitude:

"Stern man, how can I move thee? Were the means at hand, I would resist to the death. Being powerless, I entreat! Do with me as thou wilt, but let Edith go untouched!"

None of this courtly charity from the pitiless Puritan: "'Not so,' replied the immitigable zealot. 'We are not wont to show an idle courtesy to that sex, which requireth the stricter discipline.'" Yet even this "iron man was softened . . . at the fair spectacle of early love." Although he decrees that Edgar's "dark and glossy curls" be cropped "forthwith" he admits that "There be qualities in the youth, which may make him valiant to fight, and sober to toil, and pious to pray; and in the maiden, that may fit her to become a mother in our Israel." And so it was Endicott, "the severest Puritan of all," who crowned their marriage with "the wreath of roses from the ruin of the Maypole, and threw it, with his own guantleted hand, over the heads of the Lord and Lady of the May." No more did they return to "their home of wild mirth . . . made desolate amid the staid forest," for "the moral gloom of the world overpowers all systematic gaiety." Yet, as their garland "was wreathed of the brightest roses that had grown there, so in the tie that united them, were intertwined all of the purest and best of their earthly joys. They went heavenward, supporting each other along the difficult path which it was their lot to tread, and never wasted one regretful thought on the vanities of Merry Mount."

II

The special quality of this tale is its uncompromising equivocality of vision. Everything in it is presented from a double perspective, hence none of its statements are assertions and all have the power of imaginative reverberation. The initial presentation of the Merrymounters is as sympathetic to their enterprise as can be, yet by the end of the second paragraph their way of life has been called "dreamlike," and the invocation, "O, people of the Golden Age, the chief of your husbandry was to raise flowers!" points ambiguously toward condemnation for frivolity. the opening rhapsody soon gives way to increasing qualification, and finally to censure. The dancers at the Maypole are masqued as animals. They are in perfect sympathy with Nature, and Nature with them. "A real bear of the dark forest" joins their ring, and "His inferior nature rose half way, to meet his companions as they stooped." They are introduced as a "wild throng" of "Gothic monsters, though perhaps of Grecian ancestry"; "It could not be that the fauns and nymphs, when driven from their classic groves and homes of ancient fable, had sought refuge as all the persecuted did, in the fresh woods of the West." How ambiguous the implications! The masquers are allied with "the persecuted"—not only with Quakers and Antinomians like Roger Williams and Anne Hutchinson but with the Puritans themselves—who seek refuge in "the fresh woods of the West." But to the Puritans, later in the story, these same woods are the abode of "the fiend, and his bond slaves"—the votaries of Merry Mount. Although these "could not be" pagan spirits of the ancient world, later, when their Bacchic priest unites the Lord and Lady of the May, "a prelude of pipe, cithern, and viol, touched with practised minstrelsy, began to play from a neighboring thicket," quivering the Maypole itself with the sound. These are the antique instruments of Arcady, not those of Mt. Wollaston, Massachusetts.

How, then, are we to react to these masquers? Here they are associated with the age-old heritage of civilization itself, just as their Maypole is bedecked with a bridal wreath of roses, "some that had been gathered in the sunniest spots of the forest, and others, of still richer blush, which the colonists had reared from English seed." This wreath, the intermixture of ancient cultivation with the nurture of this new wild place, is about to be thrown over the lovers by Blackstone when the Puritans invade the scene; instead it is Endicott who so crowns their union. Sympathetically as we may tend to view the Merrymounters, we have yet to contend with their characters from another view, that of the "one stern band" who came to the New World "to pray." In a passage reminiscent of the *Anatomie of Abuse* (1583), an attack by the Puritan pamphleteer Philip Stubbes upon Maypoles, idleness, and papistry (excerpts from which Hawthorne read in the books he consulted for background), the Merry Mount contingent is described as "minstrels . . . wandering players . . . mummers, rope-dancers, and mountebanks, who would long be missed at wakes, church ales, and fairs. . . . Sworn triflers of a lifetime, they would not venture among the sober truths of life not even to be truly blest." With them came "All the hereditary pastimes of Old England": crowning the King of Christmas and the Lord of Misrule, huge bonfires on St. John's Eve. And "At harvest time . . . they made an image with the sheaves of Indian corn, and wreathed it with autumnal garlands, and bore it home triumphantly. But what chiefly characterized the colonists of Merry Mount was their veneration for the Maypole. It has made their true history a poet's tale."

Before we investigate their veneration for the Maypole we must acknowledge the opposite aspect of this "poet's tale": the Puritans. They are first introduced as "most dismal wretches," who toil with their weapons "always at hand," and come together only to hear interminable sermons and "to proclaim bounties on the heads of wolves and the scalps of Indians," both of which were members of the Merry Mount masquerade. The Puritans' whipping post is their Maypole.

Adamantine though these men "of a sterner faith" are shown to be, punitive though their actions be, we cannot, after such a qualification of the claims to our sympathy of the opposite faction, consider them merely as hateful. Although "their festivals were fast days, and their chief pastime the singing of psalms," they are yet dedicated to the ennobling conception of a moral life. Their virtues Endicott names in granting pardon to Edgar and Edith: courage, sobriety, piety. But if the Merrymounters, "sworn triflers of a lifetime," lacked the moral energy of Puritanism, the Puritans as surely lacked the spirit of love in which the Maypole had its roots. Because neither of these rival factions of mankind has the virtues of the other to compensate for its own defects, Hawthorne does not permit us to accept wholeheartedly the partial truth which either side represents. That is why the "grim Puritans, . . . each with a horseload of armor to burden his footsteps" appear just as shadowy, insubstantial, and monstrous as the masquers of Merry Mount, in whose "Maypole mummeries" they "had played a characteristic part." And that is why, in the resolution of this crisis, Hawthorne allows the heart of the ironclad Endicott to be touched by beholding love in others, and to complete the wedding begun by the priest who wore "pagan decorations" on "his holy garb." But the Puritan's heart can melt only so much: he can unbend from righteousness only to admit the newly wedded pair into Puritan life. To feel the heart's tug further earthward is beneath him; he has abjured all recognition of man's animal nature, and so, confronted by a bear who would rise to mankind, "the energetic Puritan" decrees "shoot him through the head! I suspect witchcraft in the beast." As Edgar and Edith leave the ruined Maypole forever behind them, "it was their lot to tread" a "difficult path." We are told, true, that "They went heavenward," which is to say that they sought Christian salvation within the terms laid down to them by Endicott, the terms of Puritan society. The parallel to Milton's Puritan epic of the expulsion from Eden is unmistakable:

> They, hand in hand, with wandering steps and slow,
> Through Eden took their solitary way.
>
> [*Paradise Lost,* XII.648–49]

III

So essential to this tale are religious imagery and ritual action that the suggestion was perhaps inevitable that the story be read in the terms proposed by Frazer's *The Golden Bough*. John B. Vickery—the suggestion is his—discovers that Frazer's anthropology and Hawthorne's fiction have the same theme: the "logic of religious evolution." In the Maypole story he finds "the transmutation of the phallic worship of the Maypole and the mimetic Sacred Marriage of fertility rituals into obeisance to the whipping-post, the 'Puritan Maypole,' and respect for the sacramental union of Christian marriage." This may seem plausible but ritual criticism has its dangers, as we see when Vickery goes on to propose that

> the "Gothic monsters" with "Grecian ancestry" are theriomorphic equivalents of the spirits of vegetation. The wolf, the goat, and the bear, all are emblems of the corn-spirit: while the stag, which on occasion symbolized longevity, hints perhaps at the god's ability to return to the world and to live on despite the vicissitudes to which he must necessarily be subject.

These creatures at Hawthorne's Maypole may be three corn-spirits and one longevity mummer, but curiously the first three occur together in Milton's *Comus,* which we know Hawthorne to have read. There the evil potion of the lord of lust can change the human countenance

> Into some brutish form of wolf or bear,
> Or, ounce or tiger, hog [i.e. boar] or bearded goat,
> All other parts remaining as they were.
>
> [lines 70–72]

Hawthorne, a stickler for verisimilitude, omits the beasts not native to his North American forest. His parallels in "The Maypole" are frequent enough to make credible this debt to *Comus*. The "English priest" is twice described as "the very Comus of the Crew," and Norris Yates has proposed that Milton's stage direction before Comus's first speech suggests the revels at Merry Mount, while the later directions for the breakup of his crew and the smashing of his glass may be the prototype for Endicott's destruction of the Maypole. Despite these debts to Milton where Vickery proposes anticipations of *The Golden Bough,* it is yet true that many of the elements Hawthorne took from descriptions he had read of the English folk observance of May Day do have in his tale a cultural significance similar to that which Frazer finds for them in a context of world folklore. But to apply so simplistically a scientific theory to a work of art is subversive of the tensions in Hawthorne's tale that give it dramatic power. The tale itself is designed to present something other than "the logic of religious evolution." That was one of Frazer's aims, but it is only of secondary interest to Hawthorne.

Several correspondences between "The Maypole of Merry Mount" and Frazer's second volume, *The Magic Art,* can in fact be made for the simple reason that both authors consulted the same source book for the traditions celebrating the May folk festival. All readers are familiar with Hawthorne's attribution, "The masques, mummeries and festive customs, described in the text, are in accordance with the manners of the age. Authority on these points may be found in Strutt's Book of English Sports and Pastimes." Frazer, as it happens, did not consult Strutt. But what has not been observed of Hawthorne is that in preparing "The Maypole of Merry Mount" he actually read another work on British antiquities besides Strutt's, and this one proves to be among Frazer's most frequently cited British references: *The Every Day Book* by William Hone.

Why did not Hawthorne acknowledge Hone as well as Strutt? It is true that for specific details of the May mummeries, masques, and customs, Strutt is his primary source. As Orians has noted, the stag and goat appear in the 1801 edition of *Sports and Pastimes,* as do also the salvage man with his girdle of green leaves, the grinning match, the horse collar, fool's cap and bells, the employment of the Maypole for year-round activity, and the sunset abrogation of lordly rights. Taking all these specific points from Strutt's synoptic and orderly collection, what use then did Hawthorne make of Hone?

The Every Day Book is a triple-volume product of the crazy-quilt school of antiquarian collecting, an assemblage of traditional materials of every sort in calendrical order, since almost every day was sacred to some saint or celebrated by folk observance somewhere in the British Isles. The three volumes together present seventy-five pages on May Day, its customs and its celebration in literature. Here are accounts of the setting-up of Maypoles, descriptions of the marriage of the Lord and Lady of May, the costumes of mummers and of Jack-o'-the-Green, the construction of May garlands and lovers' knots, and disquisitions on the pagan origins of May Day going back to the Roman festival of Flora. Hone quotes liberally from verses celebrating the May, for the poets "have made the day especially their own; they are its annalists." He reprints May Day selections from Browne's "Pastorals," Spenser's *Eclogues,* Langhorne's "Buchanan," Lady Craven, Lydgate, and Herrick's "Corinna's Going A-Maying." His second volume anthologizes from Chaucer (Arcite's observance to May, *Knight's Tale,* 1491–1515) and Dryden's paraphrase, a sonnet of Sannazaro, stanzas from Gay, Matthew Prior's "The Garland," the nymphs' song from *Pan's Anniversary* by Ben Jonson, and May Day sentiments by poets of lesser moment.

Besides these literary poems there are many versions of traditional Maying carols. One in particular may have attracted Hawthorne's eye, since it mentions the flower which gave his family its name. Certainly the author who in "Rappaccini's Daughter" translated his own name into "Monsieur de l'Aubépine" would have noted the carol which Hone remarks was sung "by him who has the honour to crown his lass the 'May-day queen'":

O then, my love, from me receive
  This beauteous hawthorn spray,
A garland for thy head I'll weave,
  Be thou my queen of May.

Love and fragrant as these flowers,
  Live pure as thou wert born,
And ne'er may sin's destructive powers,
  Assail thee with its thorn.

These sentiments are appropriate enough for a May Lord who is destined to become a Puritan husband.

Prose selections include a nostalgic excerpt from Washington Irving's "May-Day Customs," a picturesque account of a sumptuous fifteenth-century Robin Hood May pageant, and a quotation from Leigh Hunt:

> All this worship of May is over now. There is no issuing forth in glad companies to gather boughs; no adorning of houses with "the flowery spoils"; no songs, no dances, no village sports and coronations, no courtly-poetries, no sense and acknowledgment of the quiet presence of nature, in grove or glade.

Hunt's melancholy sounds again in an excerpt from Pasquil's *Palinodia* (1634):

Happy the age, and harmlesse were the dayes,
  (For then true love and amity was found)
When every village did a May Pole raise
  And Whitsun-ales and MAY-GAMES did abound:
And all the lusty yonkers, in a rout,
With merry lasses daunced the rod about,
Then Friendship to their banquets bid the guests,
And poore men far'd the better for their feasts.
. . . .
But since the SUMMER POLES *were overthrown*
  And all good sports and merriments decay'd
How times and men are chang'd, so well is known.

Throughout Hone's volumes appear many laments for the severity of the Puritans, who in their fanatical zeal destroyed the innocent May Day merriment of Old England. Hone prints the Puritan order of 6 April 1644 which decreed the abolition of Maypoles:

> The lords and commons do further order and ordain, that all and singular *May-poles,* that are or shall be erected, shall be taken down, and removed by the constables, bossholders, tithing-men, petty constables, and church-wardens of the parishes, where the same be, and that no May-pole be hereafter set up, or suffered to be set up within this kingdom of England, or dominion of Wales; the said officers to be fined five shillings weekly till the said May-pole be taken down.

In his third volume he remarks,

> That the excesses and lawless misrule attributed to this *Floralian* festival, by the fanatic enthusiasts of the Cromwellian age, ever existed, is indeed greatly to be doubted. It was celebrated as a national festival, an universal expression of joy and adoration, at the commencement of a season, when nature developes her beauties, dispenses her bounties, and wafts her "spicy gales," rich with voluptuous fragrance, to exhilarate man, and enliven the scenes around him.

The selection in Hone perhaps equally pregnant with suggestion for Hawthorne was a reprinting of a scarce tract by Thomas Hall, *Funebria Florae, the Downfall of May-games* (1661). This takes the form of a dialogue in which Flora, goddess of flowers, is tried by jury. Holy Scriptures, Pliny, Lactantius, Synodus Francica, Charles II, Ordinances of Parliament, Solemn League and Covenant, Order of the Council of State, Messrs. Elton and Ames, Bishop Babington, Bishop Andrews, and Ovid comprise the twelve eclectic jurors. "These," says the Crier, "with all the godly in the land, do call for justice against this turbulent malefactor."

> Judge: Flora, thou has here been indicted for bringing in abundance of misrule and disorder into church and state; thou hast been found guilty, and art condemned both by God and man,—by scriptures, fathers, councils,—by learned and pious divines,—and therefore I adjudge thee to
>
> PERPETUAL BANISHMENT

> that thou no more disturb this church and state, lest justice do arrest thee.

Thus concludes this Puritan bagatelle; its opening—the charge against Flora—is also apropos of Hawthorne's Merry Mount:

> Flora, hold up thy hand, thou art here indicted . . . for that thou, contrary to the peace of our sovereign lord, his crown and dignity, hast brought in a pack of practical fanatics, viz.,—ignorants, atheists, papists, drunkards, swearers, swashbucklers, maid-marians, morrice-dancers, maskers, mummers, May-pole stealers, health-drinkers, together with a rascallion rout of fiddlers, fools, fighters, gamesters, lewd-women, light-women, contemners of magistracy, affronters of ministry, rebellious to masters, disobedient to parents, misspenders of time, and abusers of the creature, &c.

Thus Hawthorne's probable debts to Hone are three. First is the aura attaching to the May-day customs of olden times, which the nostalgic antiquarian presents in a glow of retrospection as a golden age of carefree dance, of joy and love. This is in direct contrast to the attitude of the Puritan annalists of New England, such as Governor Bradford, who described Morton's settlement as a place of "great licentiousness . . . dissolute life . . . riotous prodigality . . . profuse excess." The idealization of the worship of the Maypole was absolutely essential to the thematic tension of Hawthorne's tale. While Strutt obliged him with descriptive accuracy, Hone's selections—especially those quoted above and Herrick's "Corrina's Going A-Maying"—gave him a richly documented sense of a golden age with a long lineage in literature and in civilization itself.

Second is Hone's association of the spirit of the May with that of poetry, not only in his eclectic anthologizing but in his statement that the poets "have made this day especially their own" and "they are its annalists." Hawthorne too would write of the Merrymounters that their "veneration for the Maypole . . . has made their true history a poet's tale." There is a special sense in which this is true of Hawthorne's story, a sense I shall explore below.

More obvious perhaps is Hawthorne's third presumed debt to Hone. In *The Every Day Book* he found abundant evidence to intensify his sense of the conflict, during Puritan times, between the forces of "jollity" and those of "gloom." This conflict was of far greater importance there than in the single New England incident at Merry Mount. Not only does Hone present the Puritans as fanatical executioners of all pleasure, but his selections reveal the long tenacity of folk observance through the twenty centuries since Roman times. They show, too, the perseverance of Maypole festivals despite the Puritans' severe punitive measures. Thus Hawthorne found a far greater warrant of probability than his Colonial sources provided for making the opposition between Maypole worship and the faith of the Puritans a central metaphor in his tale.

If we compare Hawthorne's story with the account he read in Governor Bradford's journal we can see to what extent "the facts . . . wrought themselves, almost spontaneously, into a sort of allegory":

> And Morton became Lord of Misrule, and maintained (as it were) a School of Atheism. . . . They also set up a maypole, drinking and dancing about it many days together, inviting the Indian women for their consorts, dancing and frisking together like so many fairies, or furies, rather; and worse practices. As if they had anew revived and celebrated the feasts of the Roman goddess Flora, or the beastly practices of the mad Bacchanalians. Morton, likewise, to show his poetry composed sundry rhymes and verses, some tending to lasciviousness . . . which he afficed to this idle or idol maypole. They changed also the name of their place, and instead of calling it Mount Wollaston they called it Merry-mount, as if this jollity would have lasted for ever. But this continued not long, for . . . shortly after came the worthy gentleman Mr. John Endecott . . . Who visiting these parts, caused that maypole to be cut down and rebuked them for their profaneness and admonished them to look there should be better walking.

It is apparent that what interposed between these facts and Hawthorne's allegory—his "almost spontaneity"—was a subtilization of tone, a sympathetic rendering of cultural values which "the grave pages of our New England annalists" regarded as utterly depraved. This subtilization, this sympathy with the folk customs of an antique festival of love, was in all probability suggested to Hawthorne by his reading of Hone. But Hawthorne was no antiquarian sentimentalist. He could use such suggestions for the purposes of his "moral romance" without accepting them. His own soul is in both camps, and he uses the nostalgic charm of Hone's popular traditions and romantic poetry to make more poignant his American retelling of the Puritan myth of the Fortunate Fall.

IV

What, on the other hand, did Frazer draw from Hone? In *The Magic Art* he cites from Hone descriptions of May garlands; testimony that Maypoles stood the year-round; depiction of a Maypole hung with fresh garlands and topped by a birch; and description of Jack-o'-the-Green, the mummer in a wicker cage of leafy boughs. This evidence, in conjunction with customs culled from Celtic Britain, Scandinavia, Estonia, France, Russia, and Germany, contributes to the pattern Frazer elucidates of vestigial tree-worship ultimately deriving from the mating of the Lord and Lady of May, the ritualistic union of the spirits of vegetation through whose fruitful juncture the fertility of the world is ensured.

Some of the images Hawthorne appropriated from the antiquaries were obviously vestigial symbols of ancient fertility belief. How else can one interpret the harvest doll mentioned above? Yet it will not do to ritualize everything in the story. Mr. Vickery, for instance, observes:

> [An] image of death that contributes to the midsummer symbolism of the defeated god is the figure of the "flower-decked corpse." This figure is accompanied "with merriment and festive music, to his grave. But did the dead man laugh?" The laughter and rejoicing of the Merrymounters stem from their conviction that the corpse, like the dead Adonis, would return to life. . . . In effect, the question casts doubt on the whole concept of rejoicing and resurrection. The dead man does not laugh precisely because he is a *dead man,* that is, not a man-god capable of reviving. The associations with Adonis and his Gardens of flowers are ironic and designed to underscore a contrast of major significance, that between man and divinity, mortality and immortality.

This dead man in Hawthorne's story turns up in a paragraph enumerating the frivolities of perpetual May at Merry Mount. Just after the introduction of the Puritans and their whipping-post, the tone is most critical of Merry Mount. The sentence immediately preceding mention of the corpse reads:

> Often, the whole colony were playing at blindman's buff, magistrates and all, with their eyes bandaged, except a single scapegoat, whom the blinded sinners pursued by the tinkling of the bells at his garments.

In this context a dead Adonis is gratuitous. Plainly the "flower-decked corpse" is to those who followed him "with merriment and festive music, to his grave" as the open-eyed scapegoat was to the "blinded sinners," who also followed the sound of music—"the tinkling of the bells at his garments." "Scapegoat" is an extraordinarily harsh word in the first context of a mere game; but it transfers its implications to the second procession, where the dead man, unlaughing, alone has the somber knowledge the revellers at Merry Mount deny. They do not acknowledge death; for them, life, as their priest advises, is "a dance."

Acquaintance with calendar customs reveals that the folk—especially in the Celtic regions of Britain—have for centuries confused the celebration of May Day (the Celtic Beltane) with Midsummer. Both were seasonal festivals marking the return or propitiation of fecundity, and both were celebrated with ritual marriages and bonfires. Yet Vickery suggests that Hawthorne's holding of the Maypole ritual at Midsummer "is a covert way of indicating the death of fertility cults as well as of the vegetative deity," since on the following day "the sun begins to decline in intensity and power." The succession of Puritans to Maypole votaries bears this out, since "the radically different character of [Puritan] worship suggests the destruction of [the Merrymounter's] phallic practices."

It is sufficient to the aesthetic intentions of this tale to regard Hawthorne's choice of Midsummer's Eve instead of May Eve as his recognition of the tragedy of life's transience. This recognition is not shared by the roisterers around the Maypole. To them, as we have seen, "May, or her mirthful spirit, dwelt all year round." They are living as though in the Golden Age, when time was not, or before time was. Even when death comes they do not recognize him. Hawthorne must have felt that the vernal equinox was the most poignant moment to dramatize this conflict between the ethos of Merry Mount—out of time but living a *carpe diem* hedonism—and that of the Puritans, whose thoughts dwelt on eternity but who lived this life without wasting a minute in idleness. (One thinks of the time-eternity tension in "The Artist of the Beautiful," the artist of eternity confined to a clock-shop.)

Hawthorne nowhere denies that the paganism of Merry Mount can be an efficacious faith. It does place men in sympathetic relation to Nature:

> Spring decked the hallowed emblem with young blossoms and fresh green boughs; Summer brought roses of the deepest blush, and the perfect foliage of the forest; Autumn enriched it with that red and yellow gorgeousness which converts each wildwood leaf into a painted flower; and Winter silvered it with sleet, and hung it round with icicles, till it flashed in the cold sunshine, itself a frozen sunbeam. Thus each alternate season did homage to the Maypole, and paid it a tribute of its own richest splendor.

Nature *is* the realm of those powers attributed to the Maypole, and time, in the realm of Nature, being continuous, is endless. What is in question here is not the actuality of the vegetative power the Maypole symbolizes, but the possibility of human lovers living long under its aegis. When we meet the May Lord and Lady, "Bright roses . . . were scattered round their feet, or had spontaneously grown there": they actually have the magical power of inducing fecundity in the earth with which ritual endows them. Although Merry Mount is "a continuous carnival," this ritual couple is also to be joined in actual marriage. Thus they are assuming mutual responsibilities in a community of two, the minimal society. "O, Edith, this is our golden time," cries Edgar, ". . . it may be that nothing of futurity will be brighter than the mere remembrance of what is now passing." And this is true, as it was true of Adam and Eve:

> Alas, for the young lovers! No sooner had their hearts glowed with real passion than they were sensible of something vague and unsubstantial in their former pleasures, and felt a dreary presentiment of inevitable change. From the moment that they truly loved, they had subjected themselves to earth's doom of care and sorrow, and troubled joy, and had no more a home at Merry Mount.

Then human love dooms them to time's vicissitudes, and exiles them from the merry rout.

We have seen that the marriage ceremony—as well as the ritual coupling—is performed by Blackstone, whom Hawthorne casts (unhistorically) as a bacchic renegade priest. Note that when Endicott discovers them he does not doubt the efficacy of the pagan wedding ceremony; indeed, he completes its final gesture himself, crowning them with the wreath of flowers grown from the forest's sunny floor and from richer English seeds. In the final paragraph, as the wreath drops around their heads, Hawthorne still calls them "the Lord and Lady of the May." They retain their ritual identities as well as their own. "But as their flowery garland was wreathed of the brightest roses that had grown there [at Merry Mount], so, in the tie that united them, were intertwined all the purest and best of their early joys." Their marriage, though consecrated by a stern Christian hand, was made in their "golden time," in their unfallen Eden, and if they "never wasted one regretful thought" on its "vanities," they preserved, in their heavenward journey, through "the moral gloom of the world" all that was visible of their primal innocence. Though it lead at last to heaven, the origin of love is rooted in the pagan past. The roots of love are so deeply planted in the rites that glorified the world's fecundity, the fructifying power of Nature herself, that to the very end the Christian wife and husband remain the Lady and Lord of the May. Or, to drop Hawthorne's consistent metaphor, the psychological origins of love lie too deep for the Puritan moral sense to thwart or supersede; morality may control love, but love does not originate in the denials which morality requires.

Now I have been speaking not of "phallic cults" but of love. The focus of the tale is neither exclusively the advent of a new religious dispensation, nor, as Mrs. Leavis avers, the power struggle between the Puritans and the votaries of pleasure. Obviously there *is* a succession, on the level of force, of pagan Maypole worship by Puritan piety. But, as I have just suggested, in no sense does Endicott's band succeed in hewing the roses of their May Day out of the souls of Edgar and Edith. Hawthorne's major theme is neither the supersession of religions nor of cultures; what he does here dramatize is the evolution of self-knowledge in the human soul. In "The Maypole of Merry Mount" he uses a reconstruction of an improbable historical episode to image forth a perfect objectification for the soul's progress from innocence and delight through recognition of mutability and responsibility to submission to law in order to live in the human community. The law is not perfect, the community is fallen, and though love looks not back to its origins it yet bears up to heaven itself the garland that was grown in the "fresh forest." The Lord and Lady of May are much nearer grace than is ironclad Endicott, for they never cast out of their souls their kinship with Nature, their capacity to love.

The focus of "The Maypole of Merry Mount" is then on the love of Edgar and Edith, on the fate of the Lord and Lady of May who are exiled from Paradise by the "real passion" which makes them subject to time; exiled by the mutual responsibility which makes necessary the assumption of a moral life. This is a love story, and the couple is being married on a day ever famous in folklore, in song, and in verse as a time propitious for love.

Originally this propitiousness to love did derive from the refertilization of the earth through the sacred—and impersonal—marriage of Male and Female principles. In the period with which Hawthorne and we are concerned, however, these anthropomorphic origins had long since undergone a humanization in the folk observance of the holiday. An almost universal rule of cultural change which the ritualistic critics of literature do not often remember is that forms outlast their original functions; forms persist while functions change. By the late Renaissance, although some of the forms of these ancient ceremonies remained in use among the peasantry of Europe, their significations had largely altered from the invocation of tribal or national fecundity to the casting of charms for both harvest and for love. Folklore, more flexible than its ritual origins, is ever responsive to the shaping pressures of cultural change. The traditions collected in Hone's *Every Day Book* show the direction of vestigial pagan ceremonial forms, still retained after centuries of Christianity, toward these ends: ensurance of good harvests, and love on the level of individual fulfillment. (Perhaps it is worth remembering that neither Hone nor Strutt—nor their contributors—had Frazer's awareness of the connection between folk customs and the pagan cults of Northern Europe; their ascriptions of paganism are almost invariably to the Roman past, supported by quotations from Ovid and other authors. Contributors to the *Gentleman's Magazine* a few years later in the century began to cite Druidic customs and Scandinavian practices, shoring up a foundation for the Cambridge school to build on. Hawthorne wrote too early to have absorbed ritual theory from the antiquaries available to him.) This humanization of pagan cult materials is certainly apparent in Hone's poetry selections, particularly in the Maying carol of the hawthorn and in "Corinna's Going A-Maying," which Hawthorne could have read there did he not already know Herrick's ceremonial poem of love.

V

There is yet one further dimension in which "The Maypole of Merry Mount" must be taken. Fogle has remarked that, although the Puritans are closer to reality, and all that Merry Mount possesses is but a dream,

> this dream is not merely one of coarse revelry; it is the dream of play, of art, of imagination. It is fallacious in that the dreamers leave out too much of their whole experience. . . . They imitate and abstract from life without living.

The Puritans, of course, make the opposite error, mistaking "the burden of life . . . for the whole of reality."

If I have shunted aside somewhat Mrs. Leavis's interpretation of this tale it is only because I find it more rewarding to approach "The Maypole" within other contexts in the Hawthorne canon than the political. Among these is the double context which we may term (a) his criticism of the Puritan ethic, and (b) the problem of the artist. Their combination here gives us the problem of the artist in Puritan culture, and applies as well to Hawthorne himself as to his merry mummers. The opposition of Endicott's band to the Maypole crew, it is plain, represents the punitive, repressive Puritan ethos. This spirit always attacks the imaginative freedom which attempts to participate in the aesthetic order of Nature and to imitate, reproduce, or enhance that order in masquerade, mummery, music, song, and dance. The conflict between Puritan repression of the senses and the artist's spiritual freedom is often framed by Hawthorne in these terms. The rebuke of the author's ancestors in "The Custom House" is but the climactic rendering of an obsessive theme. Their charge against the life of art is the same as that in "The Maypole": it is an imitation of life, not life itself. Hawthorne's Puritans recognize the demonic power in art, and confuse it with demonism. They are especially inimical to the artist's freedom to imitate the identity of another moral being without, it would seem, assuming the moral burdens of his model. Now Hawthorne himself was empiricist enough to know the fallacy of this Platonic moralism. His own aesthetic partakes of Aristotle's theory of artistic kinesis even while sending the artist on a transmigratory flight toward the Ideal Butterfly in a realm of Platonic Forms more pure than those in Nature. The achievement of art is itself the fulfillment of an ideal, and, as we learn in "The Artist of the Beautiful," once the transcendental ideal of perfection has been clasped, the artist is proof against the time-serving mockers of his enterprise, proof against the violent destruction of his handiwork.

In "The Maypole of Merry Mount" the votaries of the golden age, as we have seen, dwell, like Owen Warland, among the values of eternity, not those of time. From the romantic idealizations of the May by the poets and antiquaries cited in Hone, and from Governor Bradford's assertions that Morton wrote licentious verses and named his Maypole "Merry-Mount, as if this jollity would have lasted for ever," Hawthorne could see the conjunction of all the arts with a long-past time when "true love and amity was found." This is a time out of time, an unfallen time when the ideal and the real were one. Although the May Lord and his bride must be expelled from this Eden—although the Eden be destroyed—its roses are imperishably woven into the garland that unites them. The source of the dream of art, like the source of life which the votaries of the Maypole worship, is love. It is true that Merry Mount is insubstantial, a dream. But that much of Merry Mount as was not mere vanity—the dream of love, of fecundity, of the unity of man and Nature, which in their masquerades and mummings, in their songs and dances, they actually possessed—remains theirs forever. It is true that that possession was incomplete, denying as it did the necessary human obligations on which the Puritans insist. Lucky that Lord and Lady of the May, for theirs was a perfect knowledge, the sum of the two imperfections in which they lived. For them, at least, duty could be superimposed upon the artist's dream of love. They could be doubly joined in ritual and in love, doubly wedded by Bacchus and the iron Puritan, doubly rewarded by their revel at Merry Mount and by their destination in a Christian Heaven.

The folklore of love and the poetic traditions of the May which Hawthorne found in Hone and Strutt must have assumed a lasting and personal significance in his imagination. This dream of perfect love in the artist's eternity was not exhausted by its elaboration in his tale. Perhaps he liked to think of himself as the "village sport" whose honor it was "to crown his lass the May-day queen" with a hawthorn wreath. It is certain, at any rate, that when, six years later, he wrote into his journal an encomium of his wife, he called her a "twin-sister of the Spring," for "both have the power to renew and re-create the weary spirit. I have married the Spring!—I am husband to the month of May."

A. N. KAUL

The Blithedale Romance *and the Puritan Tradition*

In *The Scarlet Letter* Hawthorne had noted the utopian aspect of the Puritan migration to New England. In *The Blithedale Romance* he presents the utopian experiment of Brook Farm as an extension of the Puritan tradition. The backward glance of comparison runs like a rich thread through the pattern of the latter novel, making explicit the significance which the American romancer saw in this otherwise quixotic enterprise.

The day on which the visionaries assemble at Blithedale—to begin "the life of Paradise anew"—is bleaker and less encouraging than the day of the Pilgrims' landing as described by William Bradford. How conscious Hawthorne's narrator is of the suggested parallel we notice when, seated by the blazing hearth of the farmhouse at the end of the tempestuous journey, he reflects that "the old Pilgrims might have swung their kettle over precisely such a fire as this" and that, though Blithedale was hardly a day's walk from the old city, "we had transported ourselves a world-wide distance from the system of society that shackled us at breakfast-time." The Blithedalers are careful to distinguish the moral idealism of their motivation from the guiding principles of other contemporary communitarians. When Miles Coverdale reads the works of Fourier during his convalescence, he concludes that the world was mistaken in equating Blithedale with Fourierism "inasmuch as the two theories differed, as widely as the zenith from the nadir, in their

---

From *The American Vision: Actual and Ideal Society in Nineteenth-Century Fiction*. Yale University Press, 1963. Originally entitled "Nathaniel Hawthorne: Heir and Critic of the Puritan Tradition."

main principles." Hollingsworth, to whom Coverdale puts the case, dismisses the Frenchman in an impassioned speech which is a curious amalgam of Hawthorne and the elder James. Fourier, Hollingsworth declares, "has committed the unpardonable sin; for what more monstrous iniquity could the Devil himself contrive than to choose the selfish principle,—the principle of all human wrong, the very blackness of man's heart, the portion of ourselves which we shudder at, and which it is the whole aim of spiritual discipline to eradicate,—to choose it as the master-workman of his system? To seize upon and foster whatever vile, petty, sordid, filthy, bestial, and abominable corruptions have cankered into our nature, to be the efficient instruments of his infernal regeneration!" Since "the selfish principle" at the base of organized society is also the chief reason for the Blithedalers' withdrawal from it, in denouncing Fourier, Hollingsworth is stating by implication their own different purpose. The irony here, however, lies in the fact—which will be noted more fully later—that this criticism of Fourier remains the ultimate comment on Hollingsworth himself. The true importance of the Blithedale experiment, as Hawthorne presents it, is that it embodies the visionary hope for mankind which was coeval with the American settlement itself. Miles Coverdale puts the claim for it explicitly when he opens a later chapter, "Eliot's Pulpit," by saying: "Our Sundays at Blithedale were not ordinarily kept with such rigid observance as might have befitted the descendants of the Pilgrims, whose high enterprise, as we sometimes flattered ourselves, we had taken up, and were carrying it onward and aloft, to a point which they never dreamed of attaining."

In many ways Hawthorne was, as Mrs. Q. D. Leavis says, the unwilling heir of the Puritans. But this is far from being true with regard to the tradition of idealism which was a part of his inheritance. On the contrary, he affirmed it in the only serious way in which an artist can affirm tradition: by becoming its critic. It must be said in passing that as far as the actual experiment of Brook Farm is concerned, Hawthorne's motives in joining it were as mixed as those of his ancestors in coming to America. On the one hand, there was the practical expectation of a comfortable livelihood for himself and Sophia. On the other hand, there was a good deal of simple faith in the theory behind the venture—enough faith, at any rate, to induce him to stake a thousand dollars from his meager resources on its success. Brook Farm, as he says in the preface to the novel, was "essentially a day-dream, and yet a fact," and indeed, in the curious episode of his association with it, one finds it difficult to separate the hard-headed Yankee from the wild-eyed dreamer. Perhaps, like Coverdale, he hoped that in the long run "between theory and practice, a true and available mode of life might be struck out."

However, be his personal motivation what it may, the important thing to realize is that Brook Farm presented Hawthorne with an appropriate subject for his theme. In "Earth's Holocaust," the fantasy which describes an attempted regeneration, he had observed that it mattered little whether the attempt was made in the time past or time to come. The contours of the action were indeed hidden in the whole history of America. *The Scarlet Letter* had dealt with it at its very source in the seventeenth century. In *Blithedale* Hawthorne brought the action up to date. Here again was an embodiment of the archetypal American experience: withdrawal from a corrupt society to form a regenerate community. The basis for regeneration had of course shifted from theological to economic theory; social morality was no longer embedded in metaphysics. In this sense Hawthorne was marking realistically enough the shift in tradition that had occurred over the centuries. As I have pointed out [elsewhere], although in America, unlike Europe, the communitarian tradition developed in unbroken continuity from its chiliastic source in the seventeenth century, the experimenters of the nineteenth century were communitarians first and sectarians only in the second place—or not at all. Moreover, it was no longer confined to alien groups. Ripley's community was both native in composition and secular in purpose.

It is to emphasize the action of withdrawal and to underline the exercise of that radical choice which America was supposed to have made permanently available to mankind that the novel opens in society, with Coverdale about to take the plunge which he later compares to the Pilgrims' worldwide leap across the Atlantic. In the temporary movement of the story back to society, which occurs in the middle of the novel, we get some richly evoked scenes of Boston life. This is the most detailed body of social description in Hawthorne, and it comes very close to the best manner of European fiction. Hawthorne is not, however, a "social" novelist, and this presentation is the background rather than the milieu of the action, which explores not a social problem but the possibility of repudiating organized society in its entirety. The subject is not Boston life but rather the drama of Boston and Blithedale, or the American dialectic between actual society and ideal community. The theme is not reform but social regeneration.

While the Blithedalean visionaries acknowledge their kinship with the American Puritans of the seventeenth century, their own enterprise arises primarily from a repugnance to the principle of economic individualism, from the fact that society has come to be organized exclusively on the basis of the force which had caused the failure of Bradford's communitarian experiment but which Bradford had accepted as an inevitable factor of God's dispensation for the New World. Of course the Blithedale community has other avowed objectives, like the belief in agriculture as the true foundation of the good life. This, however, constitutes the ridiculous part of their venture, and is treated uniformly as such by Hawthorne. It is indeed the chief target of the mild but persistent comedy in which Silas Foster, together with the pigs and the manure dump, serves to point out the reality behind the masquerade, while Miles Coverdale, like Shakespeare's Touchstone, performs the function of more articulate comic exposure. Hawthorne, as much as Melville, faced but overcame the nineteenth-century temptation toward the Arcadian relapse. It is true that outdoor life helps both Priscilla and Coverdale to add sunburn to their cheeks. But, as Coverdale observes:

> The peril of our new way of life was not lest we should fail in becoming practical agriculturists, but that we should probably cease to be anything else. . . . The clods of earth, which we so constantly belabored and turned over and over, were never etherealized into thought. Our thoughts, on the contrary, were fast becoming cloddish. Our labor symbolized nothing, and left us mentally sluggish in the dusk of the evening. Intellectual activity is incompatible with any large amount of bodily exercise. The yeoman and the scholar—the yeoman and the man of finest moral culture, though not the man of sturdiest sense and integrity—are two distinct individuals, and can never be melted or welded into one substance.

Hawthorne is exposing here again the fallacy of the virgin scene: the assumption that a new and regenerated life demands the total repudiation of man's accumulated moral and material achievement, and that, as soon as the heritage of the past is abandoned, regeneration begins of its own accord. In a later chapter, while describing the exciting bustle of city life, Coverdale goes on to say how all this "was just as valuable, in its way, as the sighing of the breeze among the birch-trees that overshadowed Eliot's pulpit." When in the same chapter he observes a scene of simple domestic affection, being fresh from the discords he has witnessed at Blithedale, he reflects that he had not "seen a prettier bit of nature" during his summer in the country than the actors in that scene had shown him here "in a rather stylish boarding-house."

One should be careful, however, not to divert the ridicule that Hawthorne reserves for the Arcadia to other aspects of the community idea. As a matter of fact, though he presents Blithedale in its single corporate image, he clearly distinguishes between the different values involved in its broad spectrum. For instance, he does not debunk the issue of the equality of the sexes as he does the cult of agriculture. His attitude toward it is ambiguous in the sense that he accords to it the dignity of a serious though not one-sided argument. It is true that even the ardent feminist Zenobia gives in to Hollingsworth's view that should women ever dream of straying from their natural subservience to man, the male sex must "use its physical force, that unmistakable evidence of sovereignty, to scourge them back within their proper bounds!" But as Coverdale reflects a moment later, is such submission to male egotism a token of woman's true nature or is it "the result of ages of compelled degradation?" Together with this goes the further reflection that "women, however intellectually superior, so seldom disquiet themselves about the rights or wrongs of their sex, unless their own individual affections chance to lie in idleness, or to be ill at ease." Thus, while Zenobia's side of the case is presented as unquestionably superior to Hollingsworth's Nietzschean bombast, the whole issue of feminist reform is seen as a secondary question—an unfortunate consequence of the general distortion of human relations in society. With regard to the primary cause of such dislocations—which is indeed the cause of the Blithedalean withdrawal—Hawthorne leaves us in no doubt. Early in the novel, while commenting on the first day's assembly at Blithedale, Coverdale observes:

> If ever men might lawfully dream awake, and give utterance to their wildest visions without dread of laughter or scorn on the part of the audience,—yes, and speak of earthly happiness, for themselves and mankind, as an object to be hopefully striven for, and probably attained,—we who made that little semicircle round the blazing fire were those very men. We had left the rusty iron framework of society behind us; we had broken through many hindrances that are powerful enough to keep most people on the weary tread-mill of the established system, even while they feel its irksomeness almost as intolerable as we did. We had stepped down from the pulpit; we had flung aside the pen; we had shut up the ledger . . . It was our purpose . . . [to show] mankind the example of a life governed by other than the false and cruel principles on which human society has all along been based.
>
> And, first of all, we had divorced ourselves from pride, and were striving to supply its place with familiar love. . . . We sought our profit by mutual aid, instead of wresting it by the strong hand

> from an enemy, or filching it craftily from those less shrewd than ourselves (if, indeed, there were any such in New England), or winning it by selfish competition with a neighbor; in one or another of which fashions every son of woman both perpetrates and suffers his share of the common evil, whether he chooses it or no.

Whatever one may say of Blithedale and its members as things eventually turn out, there is no question about the force with which the vision of an ideal community is presented here. Nor is there any ambiguity about the distribution of sympathies as between the values avowed by Coverdale and those which govern the "iron framework of society." The visionaries stand—in theory at least—upon the principle of human brotherhood as against the predatory competitiveness of the established system. Blithedale itself, as we shall see, is finally judged in terms of its own professed values and not by the standards and norms of society. It is only when, and insofar as, the visionaries themselves turn out to be men of iron masquerading in Arcadian costume, that Blithedale is dismissed as humbug—as false as society but more hypocritical. But this process of criticism—of exposing the same basic drives twice over and of showing the corrupted rebel as more reprehensible than the original villain—does not lead to a reversal of values involved in the challenge. It makes for a more clear-sighted affirmation. Nor does the novelist, as distinct from the characters who are all more or less ironically presented, abandon his position with regard to "the common evil" of exploitative individualism which every person in society either suffers from or perpetrates. Hawthorne's attitude, it must be said, does not involve the repudiation of individual freedom and choice. On the contrary, like the elder James, he insists on the primacy of the moral person in all social arrangements. But the individualism he champions is not incompatible with, but rather tends toward and finds its richest fulfillment in, the human community.

Since the story is mainly concerned with the fortunes of the Blithedale community, the image of the surrounding society occupies of necessity a marginal position. Yet this is strictly true only in a physical sense. In reality, the main characters of the story, who are all communitarians, carry with themselves, more or less visibly, the outwardly repudiated social values and attitudes—like old earth clinging to tufts of transplanted grass. It is this fact which makes *Blithedale* an exploration of the dialectical rather than simply the oppositional relation between actual society and the aspiration toward a better community life. But, apart from this, one of the most remarkable feats of the novel is the manner in which the two peripheral characters—old Moodie and Westervelt—are made to suggest concretely certain sinister forces working in the depths of the social world. Although one would at first sight suppose them to belong wholly to the machinery of romance, even their connection with the central theme of *Blithedale* is close enough for one to conclude that Hawthorne's apologia in the preface with regard to the introduction of the communitarian experiment into the romance should be treated in the same light as Mark Twain's celebrated warning against finding a moral in *Huckleberry Finn*. Where Hawthorne maintains cautiously that the whole treatment of Brook Farm is "altogether incidental to the main purpose of the romance," one feels the whole romance is in reality a characteristically modulated projection of the main society-community theme.

In *The House of the Seven Gables* Hawthorne had observed that in nineteenth-century America, "amid the fluctuating waves of our social life, somebody is always at the drowning-point." This process and the consequent sense of insecurity are exemplified in *Blithedale*—more starkly and less sentimentally than in the case of Hepzibah Pyncheon—by old Moodie: the grandee of yesterday become the pauper of today; Fauntleroy turned into "a gray kennel-rat." This is a motif which recurs in a good deal of later American fiction, the career of George Hurstwood in *Sister Carrie* being a case which readily comes to mind. Hawthorne's method, however, is one of poetic, or "romantic," evocation rather than the "realistic" accumulation of minute detail, and his purpose is not so much to show the impassable gulf between classes as to point out the morally untenable nature of those distinctions which separate man from man in society. It is only in this sense that the fact of the relation between Zenobia and Priscilla becomes more meaningful than a mere contrivance of romantic plotting, for the sisterhood that is avowed at Blithedale but denied in society is not a playful masquerade as Zenobia seems to think; it is a reflection of the true nature of things.

In Westervelt, who is also connected with Zenobia and Priscilla, the projected force is one of secret power. The relation between him and the poor seamstress Priscilla is not unlike that between Ethan Brand and Esther, and mesmerism is to that extent presented as a peculiarly sinister variation of exploitative science. It makes "a delusive show of spirituality" but is "really imbued throughout with a cold and dead materialism." Westervelt represents in this sense the final degradation of the Puritan tradition. However, just as Hawthorne had explored the social implications of Puritan theology, he uses here the new psychic phenomenon to embody a sociological insight. These subtle transferences and suggested correlations are characteristic of Hawthorne's complex fictional method. Westervelt is in many ways the polished gentleman, a representative of the social type in which Coverdale sees a partial reflection of his own pre-Blithedale existence. But he is also a wizard the gold band around whose false teeth reveals him somehow as a "moral and physical humbug." Yet his power, though exerted invisibly, is real enough. In its remote control it suggests the exploitative power which technology was putting into the hands of men: the power to bring individuals into total bondage while leaving them outwardly free and untouched. Westervelt's human shape is thus "a necromantic, or perhaps a mechanical contrivance, in which a demon walked about." He, too, affirms faith in a golden future and speaks publicly of the dawning era "that would link soul to soul" in "mutually conscious brotherhood," but he speaks of it "as if it were a matter of chemical discovery." As against the brotherhood of voluntary love, which is based upon the magnetic chain of human sympathy, Westervelt's mesmeric union is enforced bondage, destructive of true individuality as well as true community.

The brotherhood of love and mutual sympathy, which is lacking or perverted in an individualist social system, is precisely what the Blithedale community has taken for the foundation of its life. It is likewise the basis of Hawthorne's criticism of Blithedale itself. What the novel finally calls in doubt is not the values avowed by the visionaries but their means, materials, and ultimately the depth and sincerity of their professions. Zenobia is a dilettante who, until she meets Hollingsworth, expects from Blithedale nothing worse than a naughty frolic and hardly anything better than a pleasant interlude in rusticity. She takes the experiment as a stage set for an unaccustomed personal role, and a curious theatricality accompanies her doings at Blithedale right up to the manner of her suicide. Coverdale is at heart a well-meaning sybarite who has joined the community out of boredom with an aimless life, although the sense of direction and purpose he develops while there is a different matter. He and Zenobia share between themselves the accusation that the Veiled Lady levels at Theodore in Zenobia's own legend: "Dost thou come hither, not in holy faith, nor with a pure and generous purpose, but in scornful scepticism and idle curiosity?" For his detachment and lack of faith Coverdale indeed suffers the same fate as Theodore does for not saving from her bondage the girl he eventually loves: he relapses into a purposeless life haunted by his lost dream. Zenobia pays for her scorn and impure motives by a gruesome death.

The one person at Blithedale who lacks neither faith nor energy is Hollingsworth. But his faith is not the faith in a regenerate community, and his energy, like that of the Puritan magistrates with whom he is explicitly compared, drives him into a moral blindness of unique opacity. Unlike the dilettantish triflers, he is in deadly earnest, and he is a true builder rather than a dreamer of schemes. What he seeks to build, however, is not a regenerate community but an enduring edifice for the treatment of criminals. His monomaniacal preoccupation with crime is the nineteenth-century equivalent of the Puritan absorption with sin. If Coverdale testifies to the ineffectuality of nineteenth-century American idealism, Hollingsworth remains a permanently frightening symbol of what happens to a visionary scheme when it is geared to an individual's ruthless egotism and overwhelming energy. As Hawthorne insists in several places, Hollingsworth's plan of criminal reform was motivated by an initially noble impulse. But he has fallen into the reformer's occupational disease of monomania—a danger which Emerson noted in "New England Reformers": "Do not be so vain of your one objection. Do you think there is only one? Alas! my good friend, there is no part of society or of life better than any other part." Hawthorne, a true visionary of the hopeful American years, had the same objection to reformist zeal; and Hollingsworth's scheme becomes truly criminal when, in pursuit of its success, he subverts the nobler purpose of total regeneration embodied in the Blithedale community, destroying in the process also the faith and happiness of its other members. The key chapter for understanding the developments which lead eventually to the failure of the community, is the one appropriately entitled "A Crisis." It is here that Hollingsworth repudiates the communitarian idea, and we realize how he has used the experiment as a covert base for his own operations. He has made arrangements with Zenobia, on morally dubious grounds, for the financial support of his reformist enterprise. Nor is he prepared to accept Coverdale's suggestion that he reveal his design to the other members of the community. On the contrary, he invites Coverdale, too, to become his collaborator and join in the subversion of the Blithedale experiment. "And have you no regrets," Coverdale inquires, "in overthrowing this fair system of our new life, which has been planned so deeply, and is now beginning to flourish so hopefully around us? How beautiful it is, and, so far as we can yet see, how practicable! The ages have waited for us, and here we are, the very first that have essayed to carry on our mortal existence in love and mutual help! Hollingsworth, I would be loath to take the ruin of this enterprise upon my conscience." To which the indomitable man replies: "Then let it rest wholly upon mine!" When Coverdale refuses to join him finally, rather than tolerate a friend who does not share his own fanatical purpose Hollingsworth repudiates the bond of personal friendship too.

This man of iron thus possesses all those attributes that Hawthorne had enumerated in *The House of the Seven Gables* as constituting the essential moral continuity between the Puritan of the seventeenth century and his descendant of the nineteenth. Like the members of that persistent clan, he is brutal in personal relations and dishonest in public ones, "laying his purposes deep, and following them out with an inveteracy of pursuit that knew neither rest nor conscience; trampling on the weak, and, when essential to his ends, doing his utmost to beat down the strong." His altruistic professions notwithstanding, Hollingsworth reveals in himself finally the same egotism, selfish principle, or ruthless individualism which the Blithedalean visionaries identified as the "common evil" of the established system. In *The House of the Seven Gables* Hawthorne had said that the truth about a public man is often best discovered in a woman's view of him, and in *Blithedale* it is indeed a disillusioned Zenobia who gives utterance to the moral obliquity of Hollingsworth's character. "It is all self!" she declares in one of the climaxial scenes of the novel. "Nothing else; nothing but self, self, self! The fiend, I doubt not, has made his choicest mirth of you these seven years past, and especially in the mad summer which we have spent together. I see it now! I am awake, disenchanted, disinthralled! Self, self, self!"

Thus, at Blithedale, too, instead of brotherhood there is selfhood, instead of faith there is skepticism, and instead of love there is fresh antagonism. It is not that, as Coverdale puts it, the Blithedaleans stand in a position of "new hostility, rather than new brotherhood" with regard to the society at large; because, as Coverdale himself adds, this could not fail to be the case so long as they were in "so pitiful a minority." Their estrangement from society is inevitable in "proportion with the strictness of our mutual bond among ourselves." The criticism of the Blithedale community therefore lies not in its hostile relation to the surrounding social system but rather in the absence of the promised bond within itself and in the divergence between its theory of mutual sympathy on the one hand and its reality of fresh antagonisms and mutual suspicions on the other. When Coverdale returns to Blithedale toward the end of the novel it has become a grim battlefield, with Hollingsworth resembling a Puritan magistrate holding an inquest of life and death in a case of witchcraft. The succeeding scenes enact Zenobia's tragedy, which, as Mark Van Doren says, is trash. But it seems to me that Van Doren misses the whole force of this calculated vulgarity, for the point is precisely that the community, built on a premise of high idealism, should resolve itself finally into the same old story of love, jealousy, and sensational suicide. Zenobia's fate only illustrates the true tragedy of Blithedale.

The great test of the experiment's human worth is of course Priscilla. It is not for nothing that Coverdale is made to put the question of Blithedale's success or failure to her avatar as the Veiled Lady in the opening chapter.

Unless the visionaries can save this daughter of poverty from her bondage, their enterprise will be a mockery of their principles. It is, indeed, Hollingsworth who declares: "As we do by this friendless girl, so shall we prosper." After vanishing from her enslavement to Westervelt, she has arisen, as Zenobia says in her legend, among this knot of visionary people to await her new destiny. What volumes of meaning this conveys with regard to the hope that was associated with the whole experiment of America! But the visionaries deliver Priscilla back to Westervelt, Zenobia being the chief instrument of her renewed bondage. A long line of critics has taken Hawthorne to task for not revealing the precise nature of Zenobia's relation with Westervelt. To me it seems that the ambiguity with which he surrounds their connection detracts nothing from, but rather adds to, the intended effect of obscure but intimate collusion. It is a collusion in which Hollingsworth is somewhat vaguely but quite unquestionably implicated, for, when Coverdale asks Priscilla in town if Hollingsworth knows where she is, the girl replies that she has come at his bidding. Coverdale himself, though honest, plays the limited role that befits his self-appointed position as chorus to the action.

Blithedale is thus not the regenerate community it professes to be. It is a company bound together, as the younger Henry James said in words that might have come from his father, rather by "its mutual suspicions and frictions, than by any successful surrender of self." It has repeated rather than eliminated the cardinal sin of the outwardly repudiated society. "Alas," the narrator says at the end of the novel, "what faith is requisite to bear up against such results of generous effort!" Hawthorne had taken for his theme the exploration of such generous effort over the whole field of American history. Faced with the corruption which inevitably overtook the visionary schemes, it is not surprising that, like Cooper, he seems to conclude that nothing like social perfection is possible upon this earth. But, like Cooper again, he knew that it was foolish to expect perfection before its time. Because his faith was matched by his historical understanding, he did not become cynical. He realized that the nineteenth century belonged to gold-toothed wizards and narrow-minded reformers, and, what is more, the visionaries were themselves imbued with the spirit of their age. Blithedale was accordingly doomed from the outset, not only to failure, but to unreality. As Coverdale says of the experiment from the perspective of his retreat to Boston: "But, considered in a profounder relation, it was part of another age, a different state of society, a segment of an existence peculiar in its aims and methods, a leaf of some mysterious volume interpolated into the current history which time was writing off."

Set out of its time and place, the community remains thus only a noble and anticipatory gesture of hope. There is, however, no unreality about the values it affirms even in failure. The true measure of these values is neither Hollingsworth nor Zenobia. They constitute the destructive element. One must look elsewhere—to Priscilla and Coverdale—for their tragic affirmation. Whatever her ultimate destiny, it is only at Blithedale that Priscilla comes into her proper heritage of freedom, happiness, dignity, and even love—such as it is. With regard to Coverdale, though his end is not very different from his beginning, we must not overlook the development that lies in between. After he sheds the more frivolous part of his skepticism together with his illness, he is reborn into a new existence. He is not, it is true, converted to the Arcadia of pigs and masquerades. Nor does he by any means abandon the serious part of his critical attitude toward the enterprise. The important change lies in the new sense of community which he acquires and which gives meaning to his otherwise empty life. He returns to Boston only because of the break with Hollingsworth and the consequent feeling of excommunication. How much he still belongs inwardly to Blithedale, however, we see from the tumultuous excitement with which he returns to it and the deep response with which he greets its distant glimpse: "In the sweat of my brow I had there earned bread and eaten it, and so established my claim to be on earth, and my fellowship with all the sons of labor. I could have knelt down, and have laid my breast against that soil. The red clay of which my frame was moulded seemed nearer akin to those crumbling furrows than to any other portion of the world's dust. There was my home, and there might be my grave." Years later the middle-aged Coverdale voices the same sentiment: "Often, however, in these years that are darkening around me, I remember our beautiful scheme of a noble and unselfish life; and how fair, in that first summer, appeared the prospect that it might endure for generations, and be perfected, as the ages rolled away, into the system of a people and a world! Were my former associates now there,—were there only three or four of those true-hearted men still laboring in the sun,—I sometimes fancy that I should direct my world-weary footsteps thitherward, and entreat them to receive me, for old friendship's sake."

To seek an affirmation of visionary hope, Cooper had read American history backward. Hawthorne, who started with the past, had moved up to his own time, and from there referred the faith in a sane community life to some possible future age. "More and more I feel that we had struck upon what ought to be a truth," as Coverdale says. "Posterity may dig it up, and profit by it."

FREDERICK C. CREWS

The Logic of Compulsion in "Roger Malvin's Burial"

In the proliferation of Hawthorne criticism over the past decade every current literary theory or methodology has had a say. A good deal of this criticism, nevertheless, has shared an assumption that the way to see to the bottom of Hawthorne is to analyze his symbolism or his recurrent motifs. Though there have been many careful studies of separate plots, and though some critics have preferred to approach Hawthorne by way of his biography or his explicit ideas, more usually he is revealed to us in terms of such symbolic categories as "the light and the dark," "the power of blackness," the Devil archetype, or the myth of man's fall. This kind of criticism can be fruitful, especially if, as in Hyatt Waggoner's case, a sense of Hawthorne's eclecticism and irony is allowed to temper the zealous pursuit of symbolic consistency. Yet there is other evidence to suggest that the exegesis of verbal patterns can subserve and disguise a critical hobbyhorse; some of the more dogmatic moral and theological readings have been couched as mere explications of Hawthorne's symbols. The rich suggestiveness of Hawthorne's language tempts the critic to ignore what is literally occurring in the plot, to iron out possible uncertainties of meaning or purpose, and to minimize the great distance separating Hawthorne from the tradition of pure didactic allegory. Such, I feel, are the shortcomings of Roy R. Male's *Hawthorne's Tragic Vision,* which, by analyzing only those symbols that can bear Biblical or sacramental glossing, succeeds in blending Hawthorne into a background of Christian moralism.

From *PMLA* 79 (September 1964).

This is not to deny that Hawthorne is both a symbolist and a moralist, but rather to suggest that criticism has tended to forget what his symbols and moral ideas are tied to—the investigations of human psychology under imposed conditions of stress. As Harry Levin acutely observes [in *The Power of Blackness*], "Fiction, for Hawthorne, is always the working-out of an improbable hypothesis. What would happen if—?" Since this is so, it ought to follow that criticism would properly begin with the motives of Hawthorne's characters and with the particular psychological experiment at hand. Not only Male, however, but most other critics as well have preferred to focus on the symbolic structure and alleged moral outcome of Hawthorne's works, skimming over the characters' motivation and therefore frequently misrepresenting it. Levin's own case is instructive, for he is extremely sensitive to psychological meaning and has no *idées fixes* about Hawthorne's world-view. What interests him, however, is not the reality of Hawthorne's characterizations but "the possibility of a literary iconology." "Thus," he explains, "while tracing configurations of symbolism, I have respected the integrity of the symbols; I have not attempted to reduce them to the literal plane, though there are points at which psychological inference can hardly be avoided." The reader will note that the "integrity" of the symbol, in this sentence, is its detachment from what it symbolizes; Levin is in effect confessing that he would rather take certain of Hawthorne's symbols, along with Poe's and Melville's, and build a theoretical construct from them than closely examine what is literally happening in any one work. The risk of this ambitious method is that the symbols may be related to their actual context only by shallow and misleading summaries of the outward plot. It is a risk that Levin, for all his brilliance and balance, succumbs to in the case of "Roger Malvin's Burial," as we shall see.

I choose this one tale to analyze because it illustrates the indispensability, and I should even say the priority, of understanding the literal psychological dramas in Hawthorne's fiction. Like all of his best tales, this one is packed with symbolic suggestions that invite a moralistic reading, and the problem it explores appears to be a problem of ethics. Yet a scrupulous examination of the main character's motives reveals that Hawthorne has approached his subject on a deeper level than the ethical—that he has not asked what someone in a certain predicament *should* do, but rather how a man may become the victim of unconscious hypocrisies over which he has no ethical control at all. Indeed, the working-out of this plot is strictly dependent, not on a religious attitude of Hawthorne's, but on an amazingly rigid logic of unconscious compulsion in the protagonist. Nor, in my opinion, is this an exceptional case. "Roger Malvin's Burial" is a particularly clear example of an amoral, problematic embodiment of a psychological theory, but in nearly all Hawthorne's tales, I would maintain, the moral "message" is a secondary element. As a recent critic has observed, Hawthorne's allusively Biblical situations are ultimately resolved on the plane of the characters' psychological maturity or immaturity, not on that of their salvation or damnation. Hawthorne's insight into human motives is frequently so penetrating as to leave us with a sense of psychological fatalism that robs the implicit or explicit "moral" of its relevance.

The story in "Roger Malvin's Burial" is as follows. Roger Malvin, an old Indian-fighter who has been seriously wounded and finds himself unable to survive the homeward journey through a forest, persuades his young companion, Reuben Bourne, to leave him to die. Reuben will thereby gain a chance to survive, whereas to remain would simply mean two deaths instead of one. After promising to return some day to bury his old friend, Reuben departs and is eventually rescued by a search party. Though he marries Roger's daughter Dorcas, he is unable to explain to her that he left her father alive, preferring tacitly to accept her belief that he has already been buried. Reuben's public character and fortunes soon begin to go awry, until finally he is forced to take his wife and adolescent son off into the wilderness to seek a new life. Yet his steps bring him, not to the intended destination, but to the clearing where he left Roger Malvin many years before. There, detecting what might be a deer behind some undergrowth, he fires his musket, only to discover that he has killed his son Cyrus on the very spot where Roger died. The story ends, nonetheless, on an affirmative and extremely pious note: "Then Reuben's heart was stricken, and the tears gushed out like water from a rock. The vow that the wounded youth had made the blighted man had come to redeem. His sin was expiated,—the curse was gone from him; and in the hour when he had shed blood dearer to him than his own, a prayer, the first for years, went up to Heaven from the lips of Reuben Bourne."

Such language naturally leads us to interpret "Roger Malvin's Burial" as a parable of atonement, for Reuben's act of manslaughter has melted his heart and enabled him to beg God for forgiveness. But forgiveness for what? It is unclear whether Reuben has atoned merely for not burying Roger or for some other failing, and critics disagree as to what he has done wrong. In Harry Levin's view, Reuben is "innocent" of Roger Malvin's death and only "inadvertently guilty" of his son's. Mark Van Doren, on the other hand, holds Reuben accountable for both the desertion of Roger and the hypocrisy of silence toward Dorcas: "he has committed a sin and he has failed to confess it when he could." A third interpretation is that of Arlin Turner, who finds that Hawthorne "relieves Reuben Bourne of any guilt for abandoning Malvin" but shows the ill effects of his failure to be honest with Dorcas. The only point of general agreement is that the slaying of Reuben's son Cyrus is accidental. For Van Doren it is "Fate" that engineers the final catastrophe, and that event strikes Levin as "one of those coincidences that seem to lay bare the design of the universe."

All of these opinions, including the unquestioned one about Cyrus's death, miss the essence of Hawthorne's story by not recognizing a difference between the feeling of guilt and the state of being guilty. Turner, to be sure, makes the point that Reuben's guilt is subjective, but in regard to the desertion scene he apparently confuses a moral absolving of Reuben by Hawthorne with an absence of guilty feeling on Reuben's part. We can see, however, in this scene and throughout the story, that Hawthorne is concerned *only* with subjective guilt as Reuben's conscience manufactures it, independently of the moral "sinfulness" or "innocence" of his outward deeds. That this is so at the end of the tale is obvious, for how could we take seriously the religious notion that a man can make his peace with the Christian God by shooting his innocent son? It is clear that Reuben has not performed a Christian expiation but simply rid himself of his burden of guilty feeling. It can be shown, furthermore, that this guilty feeling was never generated by a committed sin or crime in the first place. Once we have recognized this, the task of deciding whether Reuben has been morally absolved becomes pointless, and Reuben's own theory that his steps have been led by "a supernatural power" appears in its true light—as a delusion fostered by, and serving to cloak, a process of unconscious compulsion that is evidenced in great detail.

Everyone agrees that Reuben feels guilty after misleading Dorcas, and it seems quite evident that Reuben's behavior in that scene is governed by an inner discomfort over his having left Roger Malvin behind. But why should Reuben feel this discomfort? The scene of desertion is presented in such a way as to put every justification on Reuben's side; Roger's arguments have persuaded not only Reuben but most of the tale's critics to feel that there is only one reasonable decision to be made. Why, then, does Reuben find it so difficult to explain the true circumstances to Dorcas? The answer seems to be that in some deep way Reuben feels more responsible for Roger's death than he actually is. "By a certain association of ideas," as Hawthorne says of him later, "he at times almost imagined himself a murderer."

How could Reuben feel himself even remotely to be Roger's murderer? If there is no factual basis for the self-accusation, perhaps there is a psychological basis. The charge seems, indeed, to be true to fantasy if not true to life, for Reuben shows definite signs of looking forward to deserting Roger in spite of his comradely feeling for him. When Roger adduces the point that Dorcas must not be left desolate, Reuben feels reminded "that there were other and less questionable duties than that of sharing the fate of a man whom his death could not benefit. Nor," adds Hawthorne significantly, "can it be affirmed that no selfish feeling strove to enter Reuben's heart, though the consciousness made him more earnestly resist his companion's entreaties." This would seem to be the source of all Reuben's trouble. It is obviously advantageous as well as reasonable for him to go on without Roger, since he faces a prospect of married bliss if he survives. The contrast between Roger's altruism and his own self-seeking motives is painful to his conscience; his personal claims must strive for recognition, and Reuben feels a need to counterattack them with a redoubled dedication to remain with Roger. "He felt as if it were both sin and folly to think of happiness at such a moment." Thus we see that his feelings of guilt have already set in before he has made a final decision to leave. He feels guilty, not for anything he has done, but for thoughts of happiness—a happiness that will be bought at the price of a man's life.

The more closely we look at the scene of desertion, the more ironical Hawthorne's view of Reuben's mental struggle appears. The mention of Dorcas marks a turning-point between a series of melodramatic, self-sacrificing protestations of faithfulness and a new tone of puzzlement, self-doubt, and finally insincerity. Reuben is no longer really combatting Roger's wishes after this point, but posing objections that he knows Roger will easily refute. "How terrible to wait the slow approach of death in this solitude!" But a brave man, answers Roger, knows how to die. "And your daughter,—how shall I dare to meet her eye?" The question is already how *shall* I, not how *would* I! When this too has been answered, Reuben needs only to be assured of the possibility of his returning with a rescue party. "No merely selfish motive, nor even the desolate condition of Dorcas, could have induced him to desert his companion at such a moment—but his wishes seized on the thought that Malvin's life might be preserved, and his sanguine nature heightened almost to certainty the remote possibility of procuring human aid." There follows a grim comedy in which Roger pretends to see a similarity between the present case and another one, twenty years previously, that turned out well, and Reuben fatuously allows himself to be convinced. Hawthorne leaves no doubt that Reuben is semi-deliberately deceiving himself in order to silence his conscience. "This example, powerful in affecting Reuben's decision, was aided, unconsciously to himself, by the hidden strength of many another motive." When he finally does leave, the act is presented as a triumph of these other motives over his human sympathy:

"His generous nature would fain have delayed him, at whatever risk, till the dying scene were past; but the desire of existence and the hope of happiness had strengthened in his heart, and he was unable to resist them."

These citations from the story's first scene make it evident that Hawthorne, by having Reuben's self-seeking wishes concur with a morally legitimate but painful decision, has set in bold relief the purely psychological problem of guilt. Unlike his critics, Hawthorne does not dwell on the moral defensibility of Reuben's leaving; rather, he demonstrates how this act appears to Reuben as a fulfillment of his egoistic wishes, so that he is already beginning to punish himself *as if* he had positively brought about Roger's death. Hawthorne has anticipated Freud's discovery that (in Freud's terminology) the superego takes revenge for unfulfilled death-wishes as well as for actual murder.

Indeed, Hawthorne's whole rendering of Reuben's mind seems remarkably "Freudian." Some of Reuben's motives, as we have seen, operate "unconsciously to himself," which is to say that they have been repressed; and once this repression has circumvented conscious moral control, Reuben becomes a classic example of the man who, because he can neither overcome his thoughts nor admit them into consciousness, becomes their victim. The real reason for his inability to state the outward facts of the case to Dorcas is that these facts have become associated with the unbearable fantasy that he has murdered his friend. Guilty feeling leads to a superficially uncalled-for hypocrisy, which in turn provides further reinforcement of guilt; "and Reuben, while reason told him that he had done right, experienced in no small degree the mental horrors which punish the perpetrator of undiscovered crime."

One other inconspicuous, but absolutely crucial, element in the scene of desertion remains to be mentioned. As Hyatt Waggoner has perceptively emphasized, the relationship between Roger and Reuben is essentially that of a father to a son. Roger repeatedly calls him "my boy" and "my son," and at a certain point he turns this language to an argumentative use: "I have loved you like a father, Reuben; and at a time like this I should have something of a father's authority." Reuben's reply is interesting: "And because you have been a father to me, should I therefore leave you to perish and to lie unburied in the wilderness?" From a strictly Freudian point of view the answer to this rhetorical question could be *yes*; the "son" feels murderous impulses toward the "father" simply because he *is* the father, i.e., the sexual rival. It is unlikely that Hawthorne's thinking has gone quite this far. Yet it remains true that Reuben, in leaving Roger to die, will get to have Dorcas's affections all to himself, and we cannot say that such a consideration is not among the "many another motive" for his departure. The "father's authority" of which Roger ingenuously speaks is going to be left behind in the forest. In terms of the unconscious role he has assumed in relation to Roger, Reuben must think of himself not simply as a murderer but as a parricide.

This conclusion, which looks so speculative and over-sophisticated, receives ample confirmation from the remainder of the story. Reuben, who henceforth is occupied in "defending himself against an imaginary accusation," gradually turns his interest to his son Cyrus. "The boy was loved by his father with a deep and silent strength, as if whatever was good and happy in his own nature had been transferred to his child, carrying his affections with it. Even Dorcas, though loving and beloved, was far less dear to him; for Reuben's secret thoughts and insulated emotions had gradually made him a selfish man, and he could no longer love deeply except where he saw or imagined some reflection or likeness of his own mind. In Cyrus he recognized what he had himself been in other days." Reuben has, in a word, projected himself into his son. And what is to be the conclusive deed of "Roger Malvin's Burial"? Reuben, who harbors an accusation of having murdered a "father" and who cannot bring this accusation up to the rational criticism of consciousness, shoots and kills the boy who has come to stand for himself. In killing Cyrus he is destroying the "guilty" side of himself, and hence avenging Roger Malvin's death in an appallingly primitive way. The blood of a "father" rests on the "son," who disburdens himself of it by becoming a father and slaying his son. This is the terrible logic of Hawthorne's tale.

Thus I would maintain, in opposition to the generally held view, that the slaying of Cyrus is not at all the hunting accident it appears to be. It is a sacrificial murder dictated by Reuben's unconscious charge of parricide and by his inability to bring the charge directly against himself. He has become the accusing Roger at the same time that he has projected his own guilty self into Cyrus. These unconscious stratagems are his means of dealing with the contradictory repressed wishes (the desire to atone and the unwillingness to accept blame) that have transformed him into an irritable, moody, and misanthropic man over the course of years. The killing of Cyrus, by cancelling Reuben's imaginary blood-debt, frees his whole mind at last for the task of making peace with God; yet this religious achievement becomes possible, as Hawthorne stresses in the closing sentence, only "in the hour when he had shed blood dearer to him than his own."

There are two main obstacles to the theory that Reuben's shooting his son is intentional. One is that Reuben has no idea that his target is Cyrus instead of a deer; he simply fires at a noise and a motion in the distance.

Secondly, there is the possibility that not Reuben but God is responsible for bringing the tale to its catastrophe. The final paragraph, after all, speaks of the lifting of a curse, and Roger Malvin has imposed a religious vow on Reuben to "return to this wild rock, and lay my bones in the grave, and say a prayer over them." Both Roger and Reuben are religious men, and Reuben "trusted that it was Heaven's intent to afford him an opportunity of expiating his sin." Perhaps we are meant to read the story in divine rather than psychological terms.

The answer to this latter point is provided by Hawthorne in a single sentence describing Reuben in the final scene: "Unable to penetrate to the secret place of his soul where his motives lay hidden, he believed that a supernatural voice had called him onward, and that a supernatural power had obstructed his retreat." No one who ponders these words can imagine that Hawthorne's famous ambiguity between natural and supernatural causality is really sustained in "Roger Malvin's Burial." As for the other objection, it is certainly true that Reuben shows no conscious awareness that he is firing at his son. But does this make the act wholly unintentional? Before investigating the actual shooting we must see just what Hawthorne means by intention. His theory is evidently somewhat deeper than that of our law courts, which would surely have acquitted Reuben in a trial for murder. "Roger Malvin's Burial" discriminates from the first between surface intentions and buried ones, between outward tokens of generous concern and inward selfishness, between total ignorance and a knowledge that is temporarily unavailable to consciousness. For this last distinction we may point to the statement that Reuben cannot choose to return and bury Roger because he does not know how to find his way back: "his remembrance of every portion of his travel thence was indistinct, and the latter part had left no impression upon his mind." Yet we have just seen that Reuben will be guided by "his motives," residing in a "secret place of his soul." Furthermore, he has always "had a strange impression that, were he to make the trial, he would be led straight to Malvin's bones." We can only conclude that his unconscious does remember the route he took in that traumatic flight from the deserted comrade. The knowledge is repressed, not lost, and when Reuben finally gives himself over to the guidance of his unconscious he is led infallibly back to the scene.

In order to see the killing of Cyrus in its true light we must observe Reuben's prior behavior rather closely. Although Cyrus reminds him again and again that he is taking the family in a different direction from the announced one, Reuben keeps resuming his original course after each correction. His thoughts are obviously dwelling on something other than the relocation of his home. "His quick and wandering glances were sent forward, apparently in search of enemies lurking behind the tree trunks; and, seeing nothing there, he would cast his eyes backwards as if in fear of some pursuer." Reuben would appear to be projecting his self-accusations into multiple exterior threats to himself. The internalized Roger Malvin—the Roger Malvin created by Reuben's unwarranted self-accusation of murder—is evidently redoubling his demand to be avenged as the anniversary of his death draws near. When the fifth day's encampment is made, Dorcas reminds Reuben of the date. "'The twelfth of May! I should remember it well," muttered he, while many thoughts occasioned a momentary confusion in his mind. 'Where am I? Whither am I wandering? Where did I leave him?'" Among those "many thoughts" that have suddenly been jolted into consciousness are probably the answers to all three of Reuben's questions. Dorcas has accidentally brought to the surface, though only for a moment, Reuben's feeling that he is on a deliberate mission. Is the mission simply to bury Roger's bones? Evidently something further is involved, for in reply to Dorcas's next words, praising Reuben for having loyally stayed with Roger to the end, Reuben replies, "Pray Heaven, Dorcas, . . . pray Heaven that neither of us three dies solitary and lies unburied in this howling wilderness!" And on this foreboding note he hastens away at once. It seems to me obvious that Reuben's terribly sincere "prayer" is a response to his own unconscious urge to commit the sacrificial killing—an urge that has been screwed to the sticking place by Dorcas's unwitting irony. Like all men in the grip of a destructive obsession, Reuben hopes desperately that his own deep wishes will be thwarted; yet he rushes off in the next moment, and a few minutes later Cyrus will be dead.

We have, then, an abundance of evidence to show that one side of Reuben's nature, the compulsive side, has gained mastery over his conscious intentions. The evidence continues to accumulate as the moment of the shooting draws nearer. Reuben is assaulted by "many strange reflections," that keep him from governing his steps in the supposed hunt for a deer; "and, straying onward rather like a sleep walker than a hunter, it was attributable to no care of his own that his devious course kept him in the vicinity of the encampment." No *conscious* care, that is, for Reuben has a very good compulsive reason for his movements. Cyrus has previously set out on another deer hunt, "promising not to quit *the vicinity of the encampment*" (italics mine). Surely Hawthorne's repetition of these five words within the space of two pages is meant to strike our attention. Without quite realizing what he is doing, Reuben is stalking his son. His conscious thoughts are straying vaguely over the puzzle of his having reached this spot on this date, and he arrives at a conscious interpretation—explicitly rejected by Hawthorne, as we have already seen—that "it was Heaven's intent to afford him an opportunity of expiating his sin." The consciously accepted "sin" is that of leaving Roger Malvin unburied, but while Reuben busies himself with this lesser anxiety he is going about the business of squaring his deeper unconscious debt. Here is the deed itself:

> From these thoughts he was aroused by a rustling in the forest at some distance from the spot to which he had wandered. Perceiving the motion of some object behind a thick veil of undergrowth, he fired, with the instinct of a hunter and the aim of a practised marksman. A low moan, which told his success, and by which even animals can express their dying agony, was unheeded by Reuben Bourne. What were the recollections now breaking upon him?

These are brilliantly suggestive lines. Reuben is supposedly deer-hunting, but Hawthorne leaves no implication that Reuben thinks he has spotted a deer; he fires at a "rustling" and a "motion." To say that he does this with a hunter's instinct is slyly ironical, for of course a good hunter does not shoot at ambiguous noises, particularly in "the vicinity of the encampment"! The moan that would tell Reuben of his ironic "success," if he were sufficiently in command of himself to heed it, is said to be one "by which *even* animals can express their dying agony"—perhaps a hint that animals have not been his primary target. And finally, the question at the end serves to put the blame for Cyrus's death where it properly belongs. The repressed "recollections" of the original scene are now free to become wholly conscious because the guilt-compulsion that protected them has finally completed its work.

I have as yet made no mention of literary symbolism in "Roger Malvin's Burial." It seemed more important to establish the sequence of psychological events in the plot than to move directly to other levels of meaning. The tale is not wanting in symbolism, however. As W. R. Thompson has recently shown, the names of three of the four major characters are Biblical and suggest various parallels to Scripture. The Biblical Reuben leaves a loved one (Joseph) in the wilderness, intending to return and rescue him, but eventually lies about the whole affair. Dorcas is mentioned briefly in Acts 9:36–41 as a good, long-suffering woman, and Cyrus is the Lord's anointed soldier in Isa. 44–45. One can only agree with Thompson that these parallels must have some symbolic relevance to Hawthorne's story. But how do we arrive at an explication of the name-symbolism? Thompson, approaching the tale, as he says, "on the level of the source material," is inclined to see Reuben as an allegorical figure in the second half of the story; the Biblical Cyrus's role suggests that Reuben is no longer an individual but "a people seeking redemption and deliverance from their bondage," since Israel was to receive such redemption from the original Cyrus. Again, the Cyrus prototype "makes it mandatory that Reuben somehow achieve salvation through the medium of Cyrus Bourne." "Thus Cyrus in death leads Reuben to the only spot in creation where he can make good his pledge of so many years' standing." Now, it is evident from our tracing of the tale's literal action that these inferences are strained. Reasoning purely about the symbolism, Thompson has distorted the plot. Hawthorne leaves no implication that Reuben stands for a captive people, and it is not Cyrus, dead or alive, who leads Reuben to his fateful appointment. Nor is it at all clear that Reuben has achieved "salvation" at the end of the tale. Assuming, with other critics who have been anxious to interpret "Roger Malvin's Burial" before seeing exactly what happens in it, that the killing of Cyrus is done "accidentally," Thompson reduces Hawthorne's grim irony to a minimum and leaves the impression that the ultimate point of view behind the story is a pious one. The emphasis must be on salvation because this is what we find in Isaiah!

I suggest that a sounder procedure would be to relate the Biblical allusions to what Hawthorne has created, not vice-versa. Once we have grasped the point that the slaying of Cyrus obeys an unconscious intention, no strictly religious interpretation seems possible. Even the Abraham-Isaac parallel, which seems to me as pertinent as any other Biblical analogue, must be taken in an ironic spirit, for Reuben's "sacrifice" of his son is dictated not by God but by self-loathing. The portent of the story's ending is heretical, to say the least; Reuben's "redemption" has been earned through murder, while the guilt from which he has thereby freed himself was attached to a crime that had been committed only in his imagination. The real murder is unrepented yet—indeed, Reuben seems to show little concern for his dead son—while the fantasy-murder brings forth tears and prayer. The Biblical allusions suggesting redemption serve the purpose, in my opinion, of placing in relief the merely pathological nature of the case at hand. The idea of divine care for a chosen people is cruelly mocked by Hawthorne's plot, in which all exhortations to Heaven spring from self-delusion, and in this story the "redeemer" performs his redemptive function by unintentionally stopping a musket ball.

The other symbols in Hawthorne's story ought likewise to be considered in relationship to its essential savagery. The most conspicuous symbol is, of course, the oak sapling upon which Reuben placed a blood-stained handkerchief, partly as a signal of rescue for Roger and partly to symbolize his own vow to return. When he does return the tree has grown into "luxuriant life," with "an excess of vegetation" on the trunk, but its "very topmost bough was withered, sapless, and utterly dead." This branch, which is the one that formerly bore the emblem of the vow, falls in fragments upon the *tableau vivant* of the living and dead at the very end. The symbolic meaning is, if anything, too obvious. The sapling is Reuben, whose innocent young life has been "bent" (he bends the sapling downward to affix the handkerchief to it) to a sworn purpose and to a secret self-reproach; Reuben grows as the tree grows, becoming mature in outward respects but blasted at the top, in his soul or mind; and when the withered bough crumbles we are doubtless meant to conclude that the guilt has been cancelled and that a possibility now exists for more normal development. I would call particular attention, however, to the *excessive* vegetation and *luxuriant* lower branches. Luxuriance in Hawthorne almost always has something faintly sick about it, and the word "excess" speaks for itself. I would surmise that these aspects of the tree represent the compensatory elements in Reuben's character, the gradual accumulation of defenses against the tormenting thoughts that he has been fighting down for years. His peace of mind is partly restored at the end of the tale, but he will never again be the simple person we met in the beginning.

Finally, let us consider the symbolic value of the forest itself. Reuben's initiation into guilt, like Young Goodman Brown's and Arthur Dimmesdale's, occurs in the forest, and it is in the forest that he will bring forth what his guilty feelings have hatched. "He was," as Hawthorne says of Reuben's desire to seek a new home, "to throw sunlight into some deep recess of the forest." The forest is of course his own mind, in which is deeply buried a secret spot, a trauma, to which he will have to return. He thinks he does not know the way back, he resists the opportunity to go, but ultimately he is overruled by the strength of what he has repressed. Self-knowledge is knowledge of what lies almost inaccessibly remote in the forest of the mind, and Reuben will not be free until he has reached this point and released what lies imprisoned there. The expression and purgation of this secret will be a crime of violence, a murder which is symbolically a suicide, since the victim stands for Reuben himself.

Hawthorne's interest in the forest as a conveyer of these grave implications accounts for a good deal of the nature-description in the second half of the story. In this demonic tale it is not enough for Hawthorne to bind his characters to a "dark necessity" of one man's compulsion; he must also tease us with the possibility that God's in His Heaven after all. Hawthorne waxes lyrical as the denouement approaches: "Oh, who, in the enthusiasm of a daydream, has not wished that he were a wanderer in a world of summer wilderness?" In an expansive paragraph he fancies the possibility of a life of sheer innocence, purity, and harmony with nature. The purpose of all this is to set up an antithesis: "The tangled and gloomy forest through which the personages of my tale were wandering differed widely from the dreamer's land of fantasy." There are resemblances, to be sure, and there are moments of joy in which nature seems to echo the family's resurgent hopes. But this is near the start of the journey, when Reuben has not yet veered toward his real destination. When this happens the effect is quite different: "They were now keeping farther to the north, striking out more directly from the settlements, and into a region of which savage beasts and savage men were as yet the sole possessors." This is the "howling wilderness" that Reuben mentions in the last sentence spoken to Dorcas before the slaying; it is the wilderness of his own inner world, and his own murderous intent toward Cyrus is the savage beast that inhabits it. Though Dorcas, unaware that the killing has taken place, makes one final effort to humanize the forest by domesticating it in her imagination, the measure of her success is what she finds at the base of the rock where her father died.

The relative critical neglect of "Roger Malvin's Burial" has sprung, I believe, from the general failure to see Reuben's motivation. It is interesting that the few critics who have grasped the main outline of the tale have also been impressed by its high quality, for the apparent flaw in "Roger Malvin's Burial" is the improbability of its coincidences. If we eliminate the psychological justification for Reuben's finding his way back to the very spot where the story began, the plot of course becomes over-neat, and no talk about Fate, Providence, or "the design of the universe" can atone for the banality of it all. We have seen, however, that Roger Malvin's real "burial" takes place in what Hawthorne calls "the sepulchre of [Reuben's] heart"; in that organ the dead man lives again, directing the self-accused "killer" to perform an expiation that is not simply plausible, but absolutely necessary and inevitable.

JOHN CALDWELL STUBBS

The House of the Seven Gables: *Hawthorne's Comedy*

After *The Scarlet Letter,* Hawthorne set out deliberately to reverse himself. He had written to Horatio Bridge, "*The Scarlet Letter* is positively a hellfired story, into which I found it almost impossible to throw any cheering light." He intended *The House of the Seven Gables* to be quite the opposite. It was to be drenched with "cheering light." After the tragedy of Hester and Dimmesdale, Hawthorne proceeded to write what can only be termed comedy. Here it is useful to follow a distinction made by Northrop Frye in *The Anatomy of Criticism.* Whereas tragedy, according to Frye, often narrows a relatively free life into a process of causation, comedy tends to expand life from subjugation to a harsh or arbitrary law into greater freedom. Dimmesdale and Hester in *The Scarlet Letter* sense more and more the inescapableness of the consequences of their sin, but in *The House of the Seven Gables* the Pyncheons and the Maules move in the opposite direction, toward an eventual release from the sin committed long in the past. We should not consider *The House of the Seven Gables* to be a refutation of *The Scarlet Letter,* however. It is simply another view, and a view inherent in Dimmesdale's redemptive death at the end of *The Scarlet Letter.* In *The House of the Seven Gables* Hawthorne takes what we may call the "long view" of the consequences of sin. He sees evil in the context of a human cycle of evolution and renewal.

The difficulty with this—and let us admit that *The House of the Seven*

Gables has its difficulties—is that Hawthorne can convince us of the "truth" of *The Scarlet Letter* much better than he can the "truth" of *The House of the Seven Gables.* He can convince us of the existence of evil and its consequences by chronicling the states of mind that accompany it. But to convince us of a human cycle of renewal he has to ask us to accept, literally believe, the laws of comedy where young lovers always eventually overthrow the prohibitions of tyrannical figures. In *The Scarlet Letter* the world of the romance is measured against life; in *The House of the Seven Gables* it is measured against the conventions and expectations of comedy. There is no reason in the world why the feud of the Pyncheons and the Maules *must* be resolved in the marriage of the last descendants of each line. We have a sense that such is the way the evil *ought* to be resolved, but that is all. In *The Scarlet Letter* we begin with two facts: that Hester and Dimmesdale are social actors and that they have committed what is taken to be a sin in their community. There is a strong sense of inevitability in the way these two elements converge on Hester and Dimmesdale. Yet we need not know anything about the laws of tragedy to see that this is so. In *The House of the Seven Gables,* however, the argument of renewal does rest squarely on the idea that in Hawthorne's Illyria what *ought* to be will come to pass. All this is to suggest that the concept of artistic distance is very different in *The House of the Seven Gables* than it was in the preceding work.

Hawthorne achieved his distance in *The Scarlet Letter* by going back into the past, by playing with superstitions of the age, and by using ideal patterns to structure his work. These elements are also operative in *The House of the Seven Gables.* Hawthorne works with the action in the present as an extension from the past; he plays more broadly with the supernatural; and he patterns his action in an ideal cycle of renewal. But to this he adds the further distance of comic expectations. The work, then, depends still more on artifice than does *The Scarlet Letter.* Hawthorne seems to have recognized this fact, and he seems to have tried to exploit the idea of the artificiality of his fictional world by flagrant exaggeration.

But before we can investigate Hawthorne's use of artifice, we must have some idea of how Hawthorne presents his "long view" of sin in the human condition. He begins the romance with a comparison between man and nature. He describes the man-made house of the Pyncheons and the elm tree that grows in front of it. The house was erected by Colonel Pyncheon on land he usurped from the Maules. It represents a wrong the Pyncheons have committed, a wrong of the utmost seriousness because Pyncheon was instrumental in having Maule hung for witchcraft in order to stifle Maule's claims to the land. The house, however, exists in the world of nature. The gigantic elm tree covers the whole roof with its foliage. At one point Hawthorne says, "It gave beauty to the old edifice, and seemed to make it a part of nature." Green moss covers the gables. On the roof between two gables are the flower-shrubs of Alice's posies, which grow in the collected dirt on the roof. Behind the house is a small, weedy garden and on its sides plots of grass covered with burdock and leaves. The world of nature gradually renews itself. Thanks to the care of Holgrave and Phoebe, the garden becomes a pleasant retreat. The tree loses one branch (symbolic perhaps of the evil represented by Judge Pyncheon), but continues to flourish. A blighted red rose bush yields one perfect rose, and Alice's posies burst into bloom at the romance's end. Nature is supreme at the conclusion, when the surviving Pyncheons and Holgrave remove themselves to the country estate of the Pyncheon family. Like the cycle of nature, the Pyncheons and the Maules gradually renew themselves over the years. We see various attempts at renewal at various stages. The shopkeeper Pyncheon, who tried to break out of the confines of the aristocracy, and the old bachelor who wanted to return the land to the Maules are examples of such attempts. Also the relationship between Alice Pyncheon and Matthew Maule, a relationship half of competition of wills and half of attraction, is a step toward the eventual marriage of Phoebe and Holgrave that terminates the feud. The two worlds of man and nature come together, at least in the imagination, when Holgrave in love thinks of the Pyncheon house as a flowering Eden. Thus, Hawthorne uses the analogy of nature to point to the theme of human renewal.

The theme as I have outlined it, however, is fairly conventional material. A brief review of Requier's *The Old Sanctuary* should make this clear. Comparing *The House of the Seven Gables* with Requier's work is, of course, complicated by the fact that much of the subject matter in Hawthorne's romance comes directly from his family's past, as for instance the feud between the Hawthornes and the Englishes that was eventually ended by a marriage. Yet Requier's romance does provide us a chance to see Hawthorne's artistic shaping against a contemporary work with virtually the same kind of material. In *The Old Sanctuary* we found the symbol of the decaying building set against the self-renewing tree precisely as is the case in *The House of the Seven Gables*. The patriarchal ancestor appears in both works, and dies strikingly, flagrantly, in both. The feud of the members of the older generation is solved by the lovers in the younger generation in each work. Quite a lot of the essentials of Hawthorne's work are, then, to be found in the utterly conventional piece of popular fiction.

Where Hawthorne differs most drastically from Requier . . . is in his addition of the comic characters of Clifford and Hepzibah as a sort of middle generation between the vengeful ancestors and the lovestruck young characters. This addition is quite similar to his addition of the complex Dimmesdale between the two poles of the black Puritan and the fair Puritan in *The Scarlet Letter.* But Clifford and Hepzibah are overtly characters of parody. They burlesque the faults of their Pyncheon ancestors and the positive attributes of the young lovers as well. They shift the relatively standard materials of contemporary romance into a new mode.

The Pyncheon ancestor is presented in three guises: Colonel Pyncheon, the originator of the evil in the family line who usurped Maule's land to begin a New World aristocracy; Gervayse Pyncheon, who risked his daughter's well-being for a chance to obtain the deed to land in Maine which could lead to a European title; and Jaffrey Pyncheon, the family representative in the present who induced his uncle's death, shifted the blame to Clifford, plans to force information from Clifford about family wealth, and aspires to the governorship. These men have in common an avaricious pride by which they hope to make themselves immortal, or at least more "real" than other men, by establishing a claim as a head of some kind of dynasty. Hawthorne goes to great lengths to make clear that the claims they seek are unreal and illusory through his use of the missing deed that is granted them by Holgrave only when it is totally worthless. The deed becomes known as "an absurd delusion of family importance." Nonetheless, the Pyncheon ancestor pursues his "deed" at any cost to the rights of the people around him, with "an iron energy of purpose."

Coupled with his pride, probably another version of it, is the Pyncheon ancestor's sensual appetite. This is only hinted at in Colonel Pyncheon. In his portrait with Bible and sword, he appears to be the archetype of the black Puritan. But on the day of his house-opening, his home swells with the "Velvet garments, sombre but rich" of his aristocratic guests. And prepared for the guests is an enormous feast which Hawthorne records in great detail. A sensual opulence is present in the Colonel's life. Moreover, a certain sexual appetite is implied in Hawthorne's telling us the Colonel had "worn out" three wives. Sensual opulence becomes almost the reason for existence for Gervayse. He converts the Colonel's parlor into an apartment "provided with furniture, in an elegant and costly style, principally from Paris; the floor (which was unusual, at that day) being covered with a carpet, so skilfully and richly wrought, that it seemed to glow as with living flowers." In the corner is a marble statue of a nude woman, and by the fireplace a cabinet of ebony inlaid with ivory. Gervayse wears a flowing wig, a coat of blue velvet with lace, and a gold-flowered waistcoat. He finds American sherry too potent and prefers the more delicate wines of Italy and France. Significantly he gazes at a landscape by Claude, while Maule gains control of his daughter's mind. His act is significant because it was the lure of the aesthetic world of Europe that brought Pyncheon to agree to Maule's experiment. This sensual appetite continues in the Judge, and it becomes at times almost crude. We learn, for instance, that Jaffrey has had attacks of gout and has "limited" himself to five diurnal glasses of old sherry. One of the worst taunts Hawthorne throws at the Judge's corpse is the news that Jaffrey will miss a rich dinner with his political friends. As with the Colonel's, Hawthorne describes the dinner in detail, but here he specifically emphasizes the Judge's craving in a way he had not with the Colonel. He refers to Jaffrey's "ogre-like appetite." With polished boots, gold-headed cane, and white linen neck-cloth, the Judge seems the very model of decorum. Yet when he tried to bestow a kiss on Phoebe, she finds him a little more sensual than the occasion requires. And we learn at the end that Jaffrey was profligate in youth just as is his son. The twin strains of pride and sensuousness, then, run in the Pyncheon family. The first is parodied in Hepzibah, and the second in Clifford.

Hepzibah's experience of opening the store makes a mockery of the Pyncheon concept of pride. Hawthorne refers to the episode as "the final throe of what called itself old gentility." Hepzibah seems to continue the frown discovered on the Colonel's face when his guests found his corpse, but Hepzibah's look does not result from aristocratic severity, only from nearsightedness. Her fear of the door creaking open to admit her first cash customer, Ned Higgins, the cannibal of Jim Crows, mocks the suspense of the preceding chapter when the door swung open onto the view of the dead Colonel. Hawthorne's language changes noticeably in the chapters on Hepzibah from what it was previously. He is much more present as a commentator, and he packs his sentences with polysyllabic words and near clichés, creating a mock-heroic effect: "Our story must therefore await Miss Hepzibah at the threshold of her chamber; only presuming, meanwhile, to note some of the heavy sighs that labored from her bosom, with little restraint as to their lugubrious depth and volume of sound, inasmuch as they could be audible to nobody, save a disembodied listener like ourself." Furthermore, he views Hepzibah, from a distance, in absurd positions: "As her rigid and rusty frame goes down upon its hands and knees, in quest of the absconding marbles." But the real source of the humor in the episode is Hepzibah's fear of confronting her customers. Hawthorne describes her as one "who had fed herself from childhood with the shadowy food of aristocratic reminiscences, and whose religion it was, that a lady's hand soils itself irremediably by doing aught for bread." She can listen to Holgrave's advice that the concepts of gentleman and lady "imply, not privilege, but restriction," and she can grow angry at a lady she sees in the street for whom the world must toil "that the palms of her hands may be kept white and delicate," and yet whenever the time comes that Hepzibah must treat with her customers, her pride makes the encounter a "dreaded crisis." She is the victim of her pride and of the general ineptness that has resulted from a lifetime of prideful isolation. To be sure, Hawthorne shows much of the episode from Hepzibah's point of view, and this wins a good deal of our sympathy for her. Yet this makes her no less a mockery of the pride of the Pyncheon ancestor. Lest we miss Hawthorne's point, he compares his turbaned heroine later to the crested hens who stalk peevishly through the weedy garden of the Pyncheon house. Both Hepzibah and the hens are mockeries of the Pyncheons who would lead dynasties.

Clifford is a more complicated character. Like Hepzibah, he is an epitome of the isolation and decay of the Pyncheons, but in his attempts to break free of his isolation he brings us as close as we come to a pivotal consciousness in the work. In this study, however, we are considering him mainly as a character of parody. Clifford cuts a ludicrous figure. He affects the elegant dress of the Pyncheons, but his dressing gown of damask, faded after thirty years, is a poor substitute for the stylish dress of Gervayse and Jaffrey. He has the Pyncheon appetite. This is made clear to us when we see him first at the breakfast table. Hawthorne describes his expression: "It was a look of appetite. He ate food with what might almost be termed voracity, and seemed to forget himself, Hepzibah, the young girl, and everything else around him, in the sensual enjoyment which the bountifully spread table afforded." When he finishes, he cries like a pampered child for more. Most of all, in a half-torpid state Clifford savors the beautiful and abhors the ugly. He is governed entirely by his sense of the beautiful. He delights in Phoebe's presence, but has to turn his eyes away from Hepzibah. He enjoys the music of the street organ, but cries when he sees the ugly monkey of the organ-grinder. Because of his incapacity to bear any of the world's harshness, he virtually cuts himself off from the mainstream of life. This is demonstrated by his act of blowing delicate and beautiful soap bubbles from his arched window to passersby. This is the nearest Clifford can come to an act of communication. Certainly Colonel Pyncheon and Gervayse would disown his torpor and effeminacy, and Jaffrey is icily contemptuous of his ludicrousness in blowing bubbles from the window. But all share, in varying degrees, Clifford's sensuous desire for the world of beauty of an aristocracy. He is a lunatic version of their obsession.

Together, Clifford and Hepzibah form a pair of mock lovers. The progression of their reunion parallels the development of the love of Holgrave and Phoebe. To understand how this is so we must look first at the relatively conventional pair of romantic lovers. The love of Holgrave and Phoebe develops in three stages.

In the first stage their differences are defined. Holgrave is a radical reformer. He is a member of what R. W. B. Lewis in *The American Adam* calls "Young America" or the "party of hope." Holgrave would free the American from any dependency on tradition and the accomplishments of his ancestors and make him solely dependent on the present and his own merits. On these grounds he attacks the House of Seven Gables in particular and houses from the past in general. His attack must strike us as somewhat ironic since we have to assume he himself is caught up in the past wrong done his family by the Pyncheons. Curiosity about the past, if not the desire for revenge, must have brought him to the house. Hawthorne is explicit in his judgment of Holgrave as a reformer. He finds him too radical and too egotistical: "His error lay, in supposing that this age, more than any past or future one, is destined to see the tattered garments of Antiquity exchanged for a new suit, instead of gradually renewing themselves by patchwork; in applying his own life-span as the measure of an interminable achievement; and, more than all, in fancying that it mattered anything to the great end in view, whether he himself should contend for it or against it." But Hawthorne quickly adds that Holgrave's "faith in man's brightening destiny" is one of mankind's most important props. Without it there is little reason for man to live. Hawthorne admires Holgrave's positiveness but mocks his stiff-necked radicalism. Phoebe, with a conservatism biologically common to Hawthorne's women, also distrusts Holgrave's radicalism. "He may set the house on fire" is her first reaction when Hepzibah tells her about Holgrave. Phoebe is modern to the extent of being a good shopkeeper, but she has also a conservative strain that leads her to fear things outside the ordinary. Again Hawthorne is explicit: "The girl's was not one of those natures which are most attracted by what is strange and exceptional in human character. The path, which would best have suited her, was the well-worn track of ordinary life."

Their relationship moves into its second stage after Holgrave has read his story of Alice Pyncheon to Phoebe. Holgrave's gestures put Phoebe completely in his control in a state of semi-hypnosis. He refuses to take advantage of his control, however, and he gradually comes to realize that love for Phoebe is the source of his refusal. Holgrave speaks of a "second youth, gushing out of the heart's joy at being in love." "Could I keep the feeling that now possesses me," he tells Phoebe, ". . . the house . . . would be like a bower in Eden." And interestingly enough, he begins to mock his radicalism and think of reform through love: "Moonlight, and the sentiment in man's heart, responsive to it, is the greatest of renovators and reformers. And all other reform and renovation, I suppose, will prove to be no better than moonshine!" Only later, when Clifford notices a change in her, does Phoebe realize that she too is in love. But during the conversation with Holgrave, she admits to him that the moonlight has presented the world in a charming way which she, as a practical young woman accustomed only to the plain ordinariness of broad daylight, has never witnessed before. All that is lacking at this point in their relationship is a mutual realization and declaration of their love.

At this juncture Hawthorne suspends their development as Phoebe goes to the country, and shifts the action to the death of the Judge and to the flight of Hepzibah and Clifford. When he resumes their development at the third stage, he has removed the last obstacle to their love. Jaffrey's death wipes out the last of the dangerously avaricious Pyncheons, and Holgrave can reasonably consider himself free from the family feud. In the excitement of finding Phoebe immediately after the discovery of Jaffrey's death, Holgrave experiences a feeling of release and tells Phoebe he loves her. At this moment he is as free from the tyranny of the past as he probably will ever be, and in this situation he changes his radical position against institutions of the past. He argues now, symbolically, for a house of stone which can be altered on the inside by each generation. In other words, he argues now for a compromise between traditions of the past and changes in the present. He has come away from his unbending radical position to the more moderate version Hawthorne alluded to in his metaphor of the patched garment in his criticism of Holgrave. Phoebe too changes. She moves away from being the timid creature frightened by Holgrave's challenging attitudes. When he tells her he will be a contented man rather than a reformer, she replies, "I would not have it so!" And Hawthorne tells us she spoke "earnestly." Whether or not she has the power to control his domestication completely is immaterial. The fact is she has broadened her perspective to the extent where she can appreciate his urge to see mankind improve. Holgrave, on his side, has gained a relaxed tolerance for institutions of the past. Specifically in his case, he gains an estate and wealth with which to begin and continue a family. He accepts a place in tradition.

The Pyncheons and the Maules will be regenerated by the marriage of the young lovers, and Holgrave and Phoebe grow in stature through their relationship. These results, if left by themselves, would be utterly banal. They are the stuff of *The Old Sanctuary*. They would make up a comedy in which the forces of evil were overthrown so easily and so quickly that the work would be without substance—a *Winter's Tale* without the hardship undergone by Leontes. Fortunately Hawthorne does not let this development stand by itself; he parallels it with the relationship of Clifford and Hepzibah and gives us a counterbalancing parody of his young lovers.

When Hepzibah brings out and dreams over her miniature portrait of Clifford, she prompts Hawthorne to muse: "Can it have been an early lover of Miss Hepzibah?" After Clifford's return, Hawthorne writes of her: "How patiently did she endeavor to wrap Clifford up in her great, warm love, and make it all the world to him, so that he should retain no torturing sense of the coldness and dreariness, without!" Hepzibah is "in love" with her brother. This is not to say, however, as Frederick Crews has tried to show, that Hawthorne is treating the idea of incest. Hepzibah is too much the comic type of the old maid for us to consider her seriously in such a role. This is to say simply that the only love Hepzibah is capable of pursuing is the safely Platonic one of sister for brother. This is as near to romantic love as she can come. Her love allows her all of the sentiment of romantic love with none of the danger of its passion. In much the same way, Clifford can follow his interest in women only at a great distance from them. His distant interest in Phoebe exemplifies this: "On Clifford's part, it was the feeling of a man naturally endowed with the liveliest sensibility to feminine influence, but who had never quaffed the cup of passionate love, and knew that it was now too late. . . . Thus, his sentiment for Phoebe, without being paternal, was not less chaste than if she had been his daughter. He was a man, it is true, and recognized her as a woman. She was his only representative of womankind." Hepzibah's pursuit of Clifford, then, is the pursuit of one attenuated lover for another.

The initial block to their love is Hepzibah's ugliness. Because of his overdeveloped sensitivity, Clifford can scarcely bear to look at his devoted sister or listen to her croaking voice. She can be near him, for the most part, only when he dozes in his chair. Selflessly, Hepzibah sends Phoebe to him in his waking hours to please him. This is true until Jaffrey's death. Then Clifford, excited by a feeling of release similar to Holgrave's, offers to take Hepzibah away, presumably to begin a new life with him, Hepzibah's fondest wish. He is hardly romantic, however. "Put on your cloak and hood," he tells her, "or whatever it pleases you to wear! No matter what;—you cannot look beautiful nor brilliant, my poor Hepzibah! Take your purse, with money in it, and come along!" They set out "like children." But they are children "in their inexperience," not in Holgrave's projected state of second innocence.

On the train, Clifford, so long afraid of new elements in his love, speaks of the promise of the future as the radical Holgrave has done. He talks of human progress as an "ascending spiral curve," wants to abolish homes in favor of a nomadic existence, and puts forward a crackpot theory of electricity as "the all-pervading intelligence" by which lovers may "send their heart-throbs from Maine to Florida." Hepzibah, like Phoebe, fears the idea of leaving behind the ways of life with which she is familiar. While Clifford speaks of abolishing houses, she sees the House of the Seven Gables wherever she looks. When the pair leaves the train, Clifford feels his energy subsiding and reluctantly puts himself in Hepzibah's charge: "You must take the lead now, Hepzibah! . . . Do with me as you will!" He surrenders himself to Hepzibah in an exaggerated anticipation of Holgrave's surrender of his radicalism before Phoebe.

The rapprochement of Clifford and Hepzibah is almost a farcical representation of the love of Holgrave and Phoebe. The older couple are signally less successful than their younger counterparts. Clifford settles for Hepzibah's care because he cannot sustain the strength to push out further into life. We are told he retains some of his new energy, enough at least to make him happy in his idyllic life at the Pyncheon country seat, but we can hardly consider him to be more than at peace with Hepzibah in their seclusion with Holgrave and Phoebe. The younger couple, on the other hand, we may assume, do enter into life in the sense of beginning a marriage and a family. We get, then, a balance of the two couples. The balance is particularly noticeable because the flight of Hepzibah and Clifford is placed between the realization of love by the young characters and their declaration of the love. Hawthorne invites comparison of the two sets of couples. The modified success of Clifford and Hepzibah points out the artificiality of the complete and easy success of Holgrave and Phoebe.

The structure of *The House of the Seven Gables,* as we have now seen, depends on a rhythm of straightforward presentation counterpointed with comic inversion. The prideful building of the house is followed by the episode of Hepzibah's fear of serving customers. The section on Clifford's Sybaritism precedes the story of Gervayse's longings for the aesthetic life of Europe. And the flight of Clifford and Hepzibah comes in the midst of the developing love of Holgrave and Phoebe.

Hawthorne even balances a serious metaphorical statement of his theme against a comic inversion. The metaphor is his typical metaphor for life, the festive procession. The straightforward presentation of it involves a political parade "with hundreds of flaunting banners, and drums, fifes, clarions, and cymbals, reverberating between the rows of buildings." Hawthorne states that if the spectator sees it close up, individual by individual, he will find it "fool's play." But if he gains a wider or fuller perspective of its whole, he will sense an enormous human energy in the procession.

> In order to become majestic, it should be viewed from some vantage-point, as it rolls its slow and long array through the centre of a wide plain, or the stateliest public square of a city; for then, by its remoteness, it melts all the petty personalities, of which it is made up, into one broad mass of existence—one great life—one collected body of mankind, with a vast, homogeneous spirit animating it. But, on the other hand, if an impressible person, standing alone over the brink of one of these processions, should behold it, not in its atoms, but in its aggregate—as a mighty river of life, massive in its tide, and black with mystery, and, out of its depths, calling to the kindred depth within him—then the contiguity would add to the effect. It might so fascinate him that he would hardly be restrained from plunging into the surging stream of human sympathies.

The passage is Hawthorne's endorsement of the "long view" of life with the great potential residing in its energy. It is easily his most eloquent summary of the romance's theme. Yet it is preceded by a counterbalancing arrangement of figures in the showcase of the organ-grinder.

> In all their variety of occupation—the cobbler, the blacksmith, the soldier, the lady with her fan, the toper with his bottle, the milkmaid sitting by her cow—this fortunate little society might truly be said to enjoy a harmonious existence, and to make life literally a dance. The Italian turned a crank; and, behold! every one of these small individuals started into the most curious vivacity. The cobbler wrought upon a shoe; the blacksmith hammered his iron; the soldier waved his glittering blade; . . . all at the same turning of a crank. Yes; and, moved by the self-same impulse, a lover saluted his mistress on her lips! Possibly, some cynic, at once merry and bitter, had desired to signify, in this pantomimic scene, that we mortals, whatever our business or amusement—however serious, however trifling—all dance to one identical tune, and, in spite of our ridiculous activity, bring nothing finally to pass.

This show directly mocks the other. Whereas energy is the main attribute of the one, stasis is the chief characteristic of the other. The one is rich and mysterious; the other mechanical. The one exhibits the potential for harmonious development; the other shows "nothing finally [comes] to pass." To be sure, Hawthorne rejects the "cynical" moral of the organ-grinder's show, but he rejects it only after he has pictured it at some length. The two views—Hawthorne's and the cynic's—demonstrate the possibility of looking at the procession of life from several perspectives. Hawthorne has elected the more optimistic one and rejected the other out of hand. The fact that he gives the alternative perspective and parodies his view with a dumb show illustrates a certain arbitrariness in the work. Hawthorne has chosen to present one view, but *sotto voce* he admits there are others. This emphasizes the process of searching for meaning in the work. In the confines of the romance, we are asked to see life mainly within the comic mode, but we are made aware of other possibilities too, as Hawthorne conducts a dialectic between two voices, the voice of the *alazon* and the voice of the *eiron*.

Hawthorne emphasizes artifice in at least two other ways that are related to each other. Both involve his techniques of narration. The first is the relatively simple device of the story-within-the-story told by Holgrave. Here Hawthorne raises one of his characters just about to his own level as artificer. The story Holgrave tells has obvious thematic importance. As we have already noted, it shows us the sensual appetite of the Pyncheon ancestor. Also it presents us with a Maule in the act of controlling a Pyncheon through mesmerism. The act reveals the Maules to be almost as guilty of enforcing their will on others as the Pyncheons are. In their quest for revenge, the Maules go about as far beyond the limits of sympathetic ties between human beings as the Pyncheons went in usurping the land. Matthew Maule's destruction of Alice Pyncheon forms a contrast with Holgrave's act of sympathy and love in the present when he refuses to control Phoebe. We can measure Holgrave's progress away from the ruthlessness of his ancestors. But what is just as important, we find the levels of reality in the book are becoming blurred. Storytelling has become an integral part of the action.

The other way Hawthorne emphasizes artifice is by reducing himself just about to the level of his characters. This he does in his chapter "Governor Pyncheon" where Hawthorne taunts the dead body of Jaffrey. This scene also has great bearing on the romance's central meaning. Hawthorne very firmly links here in the Judge the sensual appetite of the Pyncheons (best shown by Gervayse) and their prideful desire for an aristocratic position (best shown by the Colonel) through the description of the political dinner where food and political power are being devoured simultaneously. Hawthorne also shows a merging of the Judge's watch time into a cyclical time of renewal. For Jaffrey time is a mere means of stringing together appointments largely for his self-gain. His day consists of appointments with Clifford, at the insurance office, at the bank, with a broker, at an auction, with a horse-seller, with a political committee to give a donation, perhaps with a widow who needs financial aid, with his physician, and at the dinner where he expects to be named candidate for governor. As his watch runs down and stops, another kind of time takes over: "Ah! The watch has at last ceased to tick. . . . But the great world-clock of Time still keeps its beat." The small meanness of the Judge's life is absorbed into a greater natural cycle of renewal, Hawthorne tells us as he develops the scene. The evil the Judge represents will be left behind as the day leaves behind the night. More interesting than the thematic relevance of the scene, however, is the way it is presented. Virtually every critic to write on *The House of the Seven Gables* has remarked on the fact that Hawthorne himself enters the work to tonguelash his villain with scornful irony. At one point, for instance, Hawthorne rails at the Judge with the rhetoric of a Puritan minister in the white heat of a damnation sermon: "Rise up, thou subtile, worldly, selfish, iron-hearted hypocrite, and make thy choice, whether still to be subtile, worldly, selfish, iron-hearted, and hypocritical, or to tear these sins out of thy nature, though they bring the life-blood with them! The Avenger is upon thee! Rise up, before it be too late!" With direct addresses like this one, Hawthorne behaves as if he were a character talking to his equal in Jaffrey. He is flouting the artifice of his work. He enters it in a way similar to the way the modern writer André Gide enters his novel *The Counterfeiters* to comment on the characters he has invented. We should note that Hawthorne enters *The House of the Seven Gables* fairly often. The scene where he presents himself in Hepzibah's chamber while she is rising is an example of this. But nowhere else does he maintain his presence in the action as long as in the Judge's death scene. In this scene he unmistakably calls attention to his presence.

So Hawthorne raises a character to the level of storyteller and reduces himself to the level of character at two instances in *The House of the Seven Gables*. In both instances we are made more aware of the figure of the artificer and the intermingling of artifice with the supposedly real world of the fiction.

What does Hawthorne try to gain by this emphasis on the artfulness of *The House of the Seven Gables*? Most obviously, he gains artistic distance from the reader and cuts down the empathy the reader may wish to feel for the characters. But this is really no more than restating the question. What does Hawthorne try to gain by distance? Certainly not the clarity of vision which he sought in *The Scarlet Letter*. Distance here depends on statement and mockery of statement, and this technique complicates more than it clarifies. Above all what Hawthorne makes us aware of is that this is *just a story,* one way of looking at life. He assures us that there are other ways. This way is merely the most optimistic. It is the comic view where all ends well. *The House of the Seven Gables* gives us life at its conceivable best. Hawthorne implies he would be well satisfied if we take it as a possibility, not a verity, against which to measure our lives. He has moved beyond verities. And that is precisely the sense he communicates through his emphasis on artifice.

NINA BAYM

The Marble Faun: *Hawthorne's Elegy for Art*

Hawthorne wrote *The Marble Faun* after a lapse of some years in his authorial career; his last completed work, it brings to a close his decade of literary prominence which had been inaugurated with *The Scarlet Letter.* The dense, rich texture of this fourth romance contrasts strikingly with the spare economies of the first; yet the mass of new symbols and metaphors derived from Hawthorne's Italian experience is manipulated to express themes and values common to all the long works. Its point of view is more unorthodox, however, and its anguish more extreme, than in any of the other romances—the author's attempts to disguise himself as a conventional Victorian moralist are therefore more than usually frantic. The result is a book that appears confused and self-contradictory. Yet despite its agitated rhetoric, *The Marble Faun* has a driving unity and a suprisingly straightforward narrative line.

As in the other three romances, the plot coheres around a character who stands a little apart from the action. Though he appears almost a bystander, the narrative is ultimately his because all events in it derive their true significance from their effect on and meaning for him. Kenyon's story is—like Dimmesdale's, Holgrave's, and Coverdale's—the story of the failed or destroyed artist. A young American sculptor of considerable promise, he goes to Rome to develop his talent. He is, however, ignorant and innocent; he does not really know either what art is or what demands it makes on the

From *The New England Quarterly* 44, no. 3 (September 1971).

artist. In Rome he becomes involved in the lives of two mysterious and beautiful Europeans—Miriam and Donatello—whose symbolic function is to teach him those things he does not know and to offer him the gift of great artistic powers if he masters their teachings. The artist's creative powers, he learns, are one with the life force that permeates nature. They rise from the subterranean depths of the self, are essentially erotic in character, and thoroughly abhorrent to society. The lesson terrifies him, and he flees backwards towards the safety represented by Hilda. Her virginal conventionality is antithetical to the disruptive sensuality of Miriam and Donatello; in his shattered, enervated panic, Kenyon gladly makes the exchange.

The book falls into three parts of roughly equal length. The first, which runs through chapter 19, introduces all the characters, themes, and symbols of the novel, and concludes with its pivotal event—Donatello's murder of Miriam's phantom persecutor. Coming to terms with this killing is, for the readers as well as the characters, the main business of the romance. The second section chronicles Donatello's struggle with the feelings of guilt that result from his crime, but its point lies less in his eventual reconciliation with Miriam (chapter 35) than in the role Kenyon plays in promoting it. Kenyon's intuitive response is to see this killing less as a willful deed than as some inevitable and unavoidable rite of passage, and less a crime than an act of heroism. Unaware of the implications of this position, he encourages a reunion of the separated couple. In the third part of the book (chapters 36–50), Kenyon goes back to Rome and suffers through the effects of his naively espoused radicalism—effects all symbolized in the loss of Hilda. He cannot absorb this loss. In order to get her back, he reverses himself, repudiates his dangerous ideas, and settles down into the mold of conventional Victorian moralism.

His turnabout much resembles Dimmesdale's. Just as Dimmesdale changes his mind when he comes out of the forest, finding the commitment he accepted so facilely there to be utterly beyond his psychic strength, so Kenyon is unequal to his expectations of himself. Outside the forest, Dimmesdale cannot sustain the idea that his act was not sinful. Kenyon, likewise, once away from rural Italy and back in Rome, finds it impossible to maintain his conviction that the murder was not a sin. The true issue is not whether this "sin" was fortunate but whether it was a "sin" at all. In all the subtle doctrinal discussion of the fortunate fall with which criticism has overburdened this romance, this crucial point has been overlooked. It is assumed that the term "fall" can be interchanged with "sin." But repeatedly, and in a variety of ways—of which the portrait of Beatrice Cenci is the most striking—Hawthorne advances the idea that one can be fallen and yet sinless.

He never doubts that Donatello has fallen through his crime, but he does not believe that Donatello has sinned.

The myth and romance allusions of the murder as Hawthorne stages it serve to depict something very unlike a crime. Miriam's innocence is asserted and reasserted. The model is made so monstrously evil, and is so much an apparition in any case, that he never acquires any human qualities. The killing is therefore brought into the tradition of fable where an imprisoned maiden is rescued from the monster, ogre, or dragon who holds her captive. No fabulous dragon-slayer has ever been considered criminal: on the contrary, they are always heroes. Five of Hawthorne's dozen Greek myths retold for children had focused on the heroic slaying of monsters—the stories of Bellerophon, Hercules, Perseus, Theseus, and Jason. Guido's archangel Michael, trampling on the fiend (to whom Hawthorne gives the model's face) is certainly not a criminal—why then is Donatello?

This, indeed, is the most important question in *The Marble Faun*. Why is this heroic deed responded to with horror and shock by all? Why is a semidivine deliverer interpreted as, and why does he feel like, a criminal beast? The question is pursued on both the psychological and social levels. On the social level, the monster Donatello has killed turns out to be a part of the social structure, a pious monk in the Holy City. The dragon is thus not the scourge of a kingdom, but its agent—or the agent, at least, of its king. Pushed further, this means that society is envisioned as institutionalized repression and persecution. This idea, though extreme, is implicit in all Hawthorne's representations of the struggle between romantic individualism and authoritarian society. This social explanation, however, is not sufficient for Donatello's case, because he is a nonsocial being and feels himself to be criminal quite independently of any social teachings on the subject. It would appear that his act has spontaneously generated its own set of guilt-feelings, and with them the desire for punishment and restraint that leads men, perhaps, to create the authoritarian institutions that repress them.

This may be Hawthorne's myth of the origins of society; in any event, there is surely some correspondence between what man intuitively feels within himself, and what the society proscribes. What, then, is this transforming and ambiguous deed, that makes man at once heroic and guilt ridden? Simply, it is a parricide. The many references to the Cenci story are utilized for this purpose—to inform us that this is a father-murder. Of course the model is neither Donatello's nor Miriam's father; nothing exasperated Hawthorne more than his readers' demands for the appurtenances of novelistic probability. The "truth" about what happens is to be found in the symbols, allusions, and references through which events are given meaning.

act out for him this most crucial of dramas. The relevance of the story of Miriam and Donatello to Kenyon comes about through Kenyon's desire to be an artist. The artist is he who draws upon the erotic, creative forces—who communicates them to his fellows through shapes of power and beauty. Unless Kenyon can accept Donatello's deed, therefore, and recognize its necessity, he cannot hope to fulfill his ambitions. He has begun his career naively believing that Victorian "ideal" art is the culmination of artistic progress through the centuries. At home he had industriously turned out a series of busts of public figures of the day, indicating for the reader's benefit that Victorian art, however it justifies itself in terms of eternal ideas, is in fact commercial and conventional, serving institutions rather than men, controlling men rather than liberating them—a tribute not to truth but the status quo.

Kenyon, to be sure, is unaware of the nature of the gods he serves. But the excitement he feels when exposed to classical art plunges him into depression and turmoil, because the true artist in him recognizes how much greater these antique works are than anything contemporary. His dilemma as a nineteenth-century artist is severe, for the classic is great in proportion to its possession of just those qualities that Victorian art prides itself on having left behind. Classical art is an undisguised, though brilliantly controlled, expression of eros, shamelessly and freely passionate, exulting in the flesh. It is "ideal" in a sense directly opposite to Victorian art. The latter "idealizes" the body by reluctantly employing it to represent a disembodied idea, while classical art makes the body ideal because it sees virtue and beauty in the flesh. The sculptor like Kenyon then cannot recreate classical greatness in his art simply by imitating classic models, because as a creature of his time he cannot honestly bring classic attitudes towards his work.

This is why Miriam opposes the sculpting of nude statues in the present age. They cannot be sculpted with a pure heart, because the sight of nakedness is accompanied by feelings of guilt and prurient discomfort. Contemporary sculptors of the body betray their uneasiness either by an excessive concern for details of costuming, as though to deny the body on which the garment is draped, or by "gilding the lily"—painting nude statues flesh-colored for example. (Hawthorne was obviously unaware that the Greeks painted their statues.) A simple, healthy acceptance of nudity is nowhere evident. The nudity of Victorian sculpture therefore conveys not the body's magnificence but its shame, and thus denies the very values art should communicate.

Generalized, the point is that the Victorian idea of art is thoroughly nonerotic. Classical art is purely erotic, or as erotic as anything shaped by a controlling intelligence can be. Midway between these two historical eras is the Renaissance, the era of the paintings Hilda so industriously copies. The great achievement of Renaissance art is its duplicity, its continued celebration of Venus in the guise of celebrating the Virgin, its strategy for preserving eros in the forms of an anti-erotic culture. This art is easily open to misinterpretation—thus Hilda is said to perfect the works she copies when in reality she is Bowdlerising them, eliminating their sensuous elements as artistic defects. Hilda is turning Renaissance masterpieces into Victorian masterpieces. Her copying is an expression of the ambivalence felt by the provincial American in the presence of art in which the erotic, though concealed, is yet sensed: she worships and emasculates simultaneously.

Much, therefore, is at stake in the question of Kenyon's development as an artist. His Cleopatra, produced in the seething excitement of exposure to masterpieces, solves certain problems peculiar to the sculptor's medium (catching life in stone, transmitting action in a reposing figure) but is especially noteworthy for its effective handling of costume and even more for its undisguised celebration of Cleopatra's anarchically erotic nature. When he begins working on the bust of Donatello, Kenyon makes yet another advance, going beyond Cleopatra's simple eroticism into something far more complex and timely. For he now perceives beauty and virtue in the very qualities of Donatello that are "fallen." The uncomplicated classical or preclassical beauty of the faun strikes him as vapid and monotonous; Donatello has become beautified and moralized precisely through his act of rebellion, an act totally outside the experience of pagan man, and therefore not represented in the features of pagan statues. Since Kenyon believes that sin cannot coexist with beauty, he is led intuitively to believe that Donatello and his Monte Beni are, though fallen, sinless. The fall of man is the story of man's growth from innocent prettiness to moral beauty, rather than from innocent beauty to sinful ugliness. This is an intuition which can make Kenyon a very great artist; it is also social heresy, but Kenyon does not begin at this point to sense its dangerous social implications. On the strength of his feelings, he begins to take an active part in his friend's drama. In the middle chapters of *The Marble Faun* he argues with Donatello, counseling him against remorse and self-indulgent repentance. This midsection of the romance centers on Donatello's conflict, but Kenyon's role in that conflict is more important for the total theme of the book than Donatello's own behavior.

Donatello's inner struggle is realized outwardly in the conflict between Miriam and the Church, Eros and Authority. The mechanism of guilt—the way in which it pushes the soul towards effacement in an authoritarian superstructure—is well demonstrated in his new obsessive Catholicism, and his fixation on the idea of becoming a monk. As a monk he will not merely be repudiating his sexuality, he will be taking on the identity and role of the man he has killed—perhaps, some day, to become Miriam's persecutor himself. Miriam, in this part of the book, is less a character than a force, an exiled part of Donatello's being. Her presence is felt all around the grounds of Monte Beni, whose rampant fertility and subtropical sunshine are associated with her. She has a shrine in the villa, a marble room where "it seemed the sun was magically imprisoned, and must always shine." To escape her influence, Donatello climbs the ancient, masculine tower which reaches away from nature and the earth, but symbolizes neither enlightenment nor freedom: cold, dark, cheerless, it is a monument to the oppressiveness of history, the weight of the church, the inevitability of death. This strange, sterile phallicism is yet another way in which Hawthorne expresses his idea that without acceptance of sexuality there is no true manliness. Separated from Miriam, Donatello is unnerved and dejected; but she, sundered from him, is likewise faded. She complains of "too much life and strength, without a purpose for one or the other. It is my too redundant energy that is slowly—or perhaps rapidly—wearing me away, because I can apply it to no use." Miriam speaks here not only as an abandoned woman in love, but as the suppressed vital principle of Donatello's own soul.

In this conflict Kenyon at first stands single-mindedly with Miriam. Alarmed at Donatello's morbidity, he tries to point out to him how he is being victimized by his guilt feelings; failing in this, he encourages Miriam to approach Donatello and strive for a reunion with him. But just at the point when a reconciliation is achieved, the sculptor imposes conditions on the renewed relationship. The scene in Perugia demonstrates certain compromises by which Kenyon expects to mediate between mutually exclusive positions. At this moment in his development, Kenyon is unaware of the fact that he is espousing two contradictory points of view; he does not realize even that he is counseling compromise. The salient features of the Perugia scene are, first, the dominant role played in it by the statue of Pope Julius, and, second, the little sermon wherein Kenyon tries to desexualize the future union of Miriam and Donatello. These are interrelated points, whose sum is that the reconciled pair must be readmitted to the good graces of the father, and that they can do so if they forego sexual fulfillment and aim instead for "mutual elevation and encouragement towards a severe and painful life . . . toil, sacrifice, prayer, penitence, and earnest effort towards right things." This formula for forgiveness, as well as Kenyon's sense that such forgiveness is necessary, indicates his fatal imaginative timidity, and foreshadows his collapse as an independent man and artist.

The staging of the reconciliation under the Pope's statue belies, or at least makes light of, the conflict between Miriam and the church, for it appears that the reunion might be socially possible, accomplished within the structure of papal authority. But this benevolent Pope is not real. He is an artist's fantasy, removed from a social context and corresponding to needs and wishes rather than realities. "No matter though it were modelled for a Catholic Chief-Priest; the desolate heart, whatever be its religion, recognizes in that image the likeness of a Father!" In chapter 18 similar homage had been paid to the statue of Marcus Aurelius, the bachelor emperor transformed by human longing into a figure of divine paternity. "'The sculptor of this statue knew what a King should be,' observed Kenyon, 'and knew, likewise, the heart of mankind, and how it craves a true ruler, under whatever title, as a child its father!'" To this Miriam responds fervently, "Oh, if there were but one such man as this!" The point is precisely that no such man exists. In Hawthorne's world, the loving father is a fantasy, the terrible father is real. The Deity in the stained glass windows appears to Donatello to be glowing with divine wrath; Kenyon, demurring, interprets the expression as divine love. But Donatello is right; subsequent events will show that he can expect only punishment from the Pope. As for the Deity, he does not exist in this romance save as he is channeled into a social structure; he therefore cannot be distinguished from the Pope.

As the pair clasp hands under the statue, Kenyon feels a sudden conscientious anxiety about their future, and he warns them against seeking "earthly bliss." The most they may hope for, and even this may not be directly sought, is a "somber and thoughtful happiness." These strictures contradict Kenyon's earlier attitudes. He had understood Donatello's sin as the inevitable fall into adulthood, an event through which all men must (or should) pass and which therefore has humanized the faun; now he sees it as something isolating and therefore dehumanizing. Then, too, he had turned to Miriam in the hope that she would lead Donatello away from remorse and guilt and sorrow, but now he is suggesting that she distort her nature so far as to abet him in a penitential life. This sudden uneasiness on Kenyon's part about what he euphemistically labels earthly bliss shows his inability to handle the full sexual implications of the reunion he has fostered, as well as the inseparable sexual element in the whole Miriam-Donatello story. It suggests his unwillingness to acknowledge the essentially sexual character of Eros. It indicates that Kenyon has deep difficulties in accepting the sexual dimension of his own creative powers.

Such difficulties are also implicit in his fierce and unreasoned attachment to Hilda, an attachment which will be the means of breaking and taming him in the last part of the book. He abjectly relinquishes his judgments and analyzes when they run counter to her narow pieties. Though a seeker and a speculative type, he praises her self-righteously proclaimed ignorance as angelic wisdom. He strives in all other matters for keenness of perception, but becomes willfully blind when it comes to scrutinizing Hilda's behavior. These facts about Kenyon are forced on our attention immediately when he returns to Rome, for he finds Hilda on her knees in the confessional, and resolutely refuses to pursue the implications of what he has witnessed. When we realize that the Catholic city in *The Marble Faun* functions precisely like the Puritan city in *The Scarlet Letter,* it will not surprise us that this self-styled daughter of the Puritans should turn to the church when she is in need. Indeed, the incident in St. Peter's represents no new development of her character. Hilda is simply changing allegiance from one set of fathers to another. She had previously been a superb copyist, obedient and self-effacing before a vision of the old masters as moral authorities. The insight she gains from witnessing the murder enables her to perceive that the old masters are not fathers at all, but rather are lovers celebrating the sensual charms of their mistresses while pretending to extoll chastity. In the light of her new wisdom their duplicity seems to her a kind of overintellectualized cleverness. Comprehending now that the authority which she attributed to them was an illusion compounded of her need and her naiveté, she seeks a replacement.

For her, as for the other characters in the romance, the conflict polarizes between art-mothers and church-fathers. Her despairing progress towards the confessional is impeded not by her Puritanism but by the restraining spirit of her mother, whose presence she feels "weeping to behold her ensnared by these gaudy superstitions." Despite Hilda's doleful and habitual lament about her motherless plight, she repeatedly and predictably rejects all the images of mothers that are presented to her. No mother is good enough for her. Her rejection of Miriam, the older sister, is the obvious example, and Hawthorne iterates the idea by showing her unavailing quest among various paintings of the Virgin (chapter 38). The point, though simple, needs stressing: Hilda imagines herself to be looking for a mother, but Hawthorne shows her looking, rather, to cast the mother off. Her reason for rejecting the mother-figure is invariably the same, and invariably applicable: the mother is not a virgin. As Hawthorne comments, "She never found just the Virgin Mother whom she needed." And no wonder.

Why is it inconceivable to Hilda that her mother be unvirgin; and how is this particular trait in Hilda's character related to the central core of meaning in *The Marble Faun*? This is surely the most difficult part of the story to encompass. Hawthorne has been analyzing all along the vicious sexual morbidity which underlies the structure of guilt, remorse, misery, inhibition, repression, and hypocrisy which is the atmosphere of *The Marble Faun*. This morbidity is at once cause and chief evidence of the social sickness of his age, and no doubt Hawthorne feels about the matter with such intensity because he shares the sickness even as he understands it. Now he is demonstrating the existence of this morbidity beneath the Victorian idealism of his pure young heroine, the idol of his culture—demonstrating, indeed, that she is the apotheosis of his culture's ills. He is risking professional destruction; surely there was psychological danger as well. At any rate, his handling of Hilda indicates simultaneous desires to pursue his dangerous course and to protect himself from its consequences.

In the resulting murk of assertion and retraction, only a few points may be firmly asserted, after which one's interpretations become conjectural. Hilda cannot cope with the idea of her mother's sexuality; in the deepest recesses of her being she believes herself to be the product of a virgin birth. (There are hints, but hints only, that Hilda even fantasizes herself as a kind of Christ figure.) As such a product, she herself is miraculously untainted by normal human sin and guilt—concepts which are interchangeable, in her mind, with the idea of sexuality. Hilda thus has created for herself a birth which frees her from sexuality. In other words, her anxiety is really for herself; she finds the notion of her *own* sexuality intolerable, and she will eliminate from her universe any persons, events, scenes, or statements that suggest the notion to her. This psychic need is the explanation of her mercilessness. She *must* cut out of her life whatever threatens this image of herself, and court whatever encourages it. She dedicates herself to the Virgin; the shrine which she tends is approached through her bedroom and the bedroom, as Hawthorne describes it, is indeed a part of the shrine.

It is ironic, but obvious, that she cannot for any length of time associate with living women. That Hilda, as well as Miriam, resembles Guido's Beatrice means no more than that Hilda, if she is a woman, must share a woman's nature. Women's nature—her sex—symbolized either by blood or by blood-red gems, is what poor Hilda through no fault of her own possesses, and what her life is dedicated to denying. Association with real women must, inevitably, develop this feared and hated part of herself. "If I were one of God's angels," she tells Miriam in chapter 23, "with a nature incapable of stain, and garments that never could be spotted, I would keep ever at your side, and try to lead you upward. But I am a poor, lonely girl, whom God has set here in an evil world, and given her only a white robe, and bid her wear it back to Him, as white as when she put it on. Your powerful magnetism would be too much for me. The pure, white atmosphere, in which I try to discern what things are good and true, would be discoloured." The defloration imagery betrays Hilda's intense sexual anxiety. Association with the fathers—with God, who has imposed this impossible demand on the unfortunate Hilda—is at once the source of the anxiety and the means by which it can be allayed. Association with the mother must inevitably lead to some perception of shared nature, producing guilt and terror and despair.

We do not know what Hilda feels as she witnesses the crime, since Hawthorne discreetly does not say, but her subsequent feelings of guilt and implication are evident. Hilda is quite right in protesting that she has not herself committed a crime, but wrong in the inference that the emotion under which she labors cannot be guilt since she is not guilty. Guilt can arise merely from having the potential to feel sexual passion. Witnessing the crime, Hilda has somehow been apprised of this potential within herself. She repudiates Miriam as a temptation to be expunged from her life, but this is not enough. She must deny not only her temptation, but her capacity to be tempted. Only the paternal institution which fosters the cults of chastity and celibacy can accept such a denial, and therefore Hilda finds relief in its conventions.

The method by which Hilda attains relief can only carelessly or hypocritically be called a confession. Criticism has made much of her sophistical attempt to receive absolution without committing herself to Catholicism, but nowhere has her far greater perversion of the confessional been noticed—her use of it to "confess" other people's sins rather than her own. The whole point of confession is to acknowledge, and be helped to bear, one's own sinful nature; Hilda's purposes are the very opposite. She does not confess, she tattles. Out of the complexities of her own anguish, she acts as an agent of the Roman government.

In general, in fact, Hilda is an agent of authority. A woman like her is, ultimately, the supreme creation of the Victorian authoritarian system (the system which is, whether it is presented as Colonial Boston or Papal Rome, Hawthorne's target). She is also the chief means by which the system is upheld. The authorities seek to preserve themselves in power by de-eroticizing men and women. The sexless ideal celebrated by Hilda makes the erotic disreputable. Innocent Miriam cannot escape suspicion and innuendo. Her passionate nature is a source of misery to her, of discomfort to men. Men seize eagerly on the cult of virginity to rationalize, legitimatize, and ultimately idealize their flight from passion. They feel threatened by Miriam's sexuality, and they fear it; yet Hilda, whose name means "battle-maiden," has the "remorselessness of a steel blade" and is the true castrator.

Once these points are grasped, the events in the last third of the book can be seen to work out, with pitiless inevitability, the destruction of Kenyon's short-lived romantic independence. The plotting here has been much criticized for its series of blatant coincidences; but to interpret the timing of episodes in the late chapters as coincidental is to miss their necessary interconnections. Hilda's disappearance coincides with Kenyon's articulation to her of some part of his new radical stance; the reappearance of Donatello and Miriam in Rome coincides with this disappearance; and finally, the restoration of Hilda coincides with the surrender of Miriam and Donatello to the authorities. Kenyon's statements to Hilda indicate his holding of a romantic view personified by the "fallen" Miriam and Donatello. This view is incompatible with that represented by Hilda, who therefore disappears, and must be given up before she can be returned to Kenyon.

These events, to be sure, have little or no relevance to the romance of Miriam and Donatello, and if one has placed the focus of *The Marble Faun* in that story one is faced with a series of discontinuities, fragments, abrupt, and unexplained shifts. There is no explanation for Donatello's renewed sense of guilt, and the linking of his return to Rome with Hilda's disappearance seems mere caprice. Miriam and Donatello are very differently treated in this last third of the book. They are much more remote, much more mysterious than they had been earlier. They invariably appear in costume, a fairly trustworthy sign in Hawthorne's works that they are figures of fantasy. In the last part of the book, I suggest, they are not "themselves" any longer, but rather are phantoms in Kenyon's consciousness. The whole phantasmagoric character of the last chapters contributes to this impression. Precisely as Miriam in the Monte Beni sequence was less a character than she had been in the book's early chapters, and more a force in or part of Donatello's conflict, so now Miriam and Donatello both are less whole characters than fragments of Kenyon's suddenly exploded psyche.

As the conflict in the Monte Beni sequence had been symbolized in the poles of Miriam and the church, so now the conflict is polarized between Miriam-Donatello and Hilda. The incompatibility of these forces had not been earlier evident; indeed, the book opens with a scene of friendship and harmony. But at that time, the crime had not yet been committed, and Hilda was misguidedly dedicated to the Old Masters. The events of the book have brought to light a conflict which cannot be resolved. Once it has surfaced, Kenyon has really no choice about which side to take, for he cannot survive without Hilda.

This is plainly seen in the mental collapse he suffers when she disappears. He is saved from madness only by the sacrifice of Miriam-Donatello. His breakdown may be attributed to the loss of Hilda's firm and shaping moral vision, on which he has depended far more than he was aware. Or it may be a crisis of guilt, brought on by his sudden awareness of how Hilda must judge his romanticism; this idea is supported by the conclusion of the book, when Kenyon once again raises his heretical ideas, this time formally to repudiate them as the price of Hilda's hand. Or it may be the surfacing of insupportable sexual anxiety, as suggested in the grotesque figures that attack him during the carnival. Whatever the cause, it is clear that Miriam and Donatello are not worth the emotional cost to Kenyon that is represented by his loss of Hilda.

The sacrifice of the couple, then, is a simple exchange for Hilda. The scene on the campagna takes its meaning from this idea. In this strangely mythic and magic episode, Kenyon is offered the choice of great artistic powers or Hilda. His choice is never in doubt. "Ah, Miriam! I cannot respond to you," he says, impatiently. "Imagination and the love of art have both died out of me." Thereupon, he is told that he shall have Hilda back. This event on the campagna, digressive though it may appear, is in many ways the novel's matrix. All its leitmotifs are employed. The scene occurs in a spot at once underground and yet in the sun, in the country away from Rome and yet within the enclosure of a Roman ruin. A magic animal leads Kenyon to what we must consider a sacred spot, and there he unearths and assembles the fragments of an exquisite antique Venus. Venus, at once the great goddess of love and the mother of Eros, is Hawthorne's archetype here for the power within and without man from which he is so profoundly alienated, and without which he is so desperately sick. The order in which Kenyon puts together the pieces of this shattered work—torso, arms, head—represents the progressive embodiment of the fundamental erotic drive in an ideal human form. This is the humanization of the life force, a paradigm of the artistic process as it should be.

No sooner has Kenyon completed his work than Miriam and Donatello appear—Venus and Eros in the flesh—and we learn that they are the original discoverers of the statue which they have left for Kenyon to put together. The interplay of these two discoveries suggests that Miriam and Donatello have acted as a part of Kenyon in making this find; they are the power within him that can grasp and create great art. But Kenyon is no longer able to use the faculty they personify. Once briefly united with them, he is now irrevocably sundered from them. He explains his sudden change, his revulsion from art and his choice of Hilda, by identifying Hilda with life and the Venus with dead marble. Frederick Crews puts it admirably: Hawthorne "seems to be saying that Kenyon's human love is supplanting his cold aesthetic taste. . . . Yet when we reflect that vapid Hilda is here dethroning a supple and lovely Venus, the surface meaning becomes exactly reversed." The "surface meaning" is no more than Kenyon's neurotic rationalization; victim of his age's malaise, he chooses the Virgin over Venus, a commitment which as Crews says is "simply a form of panic."

Yet Kenyon's panic is in a sense justified—this is Hawthorne's most bitter perception—for without Hilda he will surely go mad. In other words, Kenyon is ludicrously inadequate for the vocation he had so bravely chosen for himself. The carnival scene represents the final capitulation. Its relation to many other *Walpurgisnacht* scenes in Hawthorne's fiction is evident; indeed, Hawthorne himself witnessing his first Roman carnival must have felt much as though he were watching a dramatization of one of his own tales. The psyche in a state of anarchic turbulence throws up into the light of consciousness a myriad of horrible fears and fantasies, grotesque and terrifying figures out of the world of dreams, mostly with sexual import. The carnival fails utterly in its cathartic function for Kenyon; far from purging his nightmares, he is drowned in them. As the climax of the scene, Miriam and Donatello appear to take a ritual farewell of their friend. "Donatello here extended his hand (not that which was clasping Miriam's), and she, too, put her free one into the sculptor's left; so that they were a linked circle of three, with many reminiscences and forebodings flashing through their hearts. Kenyon knew intuitively that these once familiar friends were parting with him, now. 'Farewell!' they all three said, in the same breath." Soon thereafter Kenyon overhears a conversation implying that the pair have been arrested, and "just as the last words were spoken, he was hit by . . . . a single rose-bud, so fresh that it seemed that moment gathered." This dewy messenger signifies the end of Kenyon's feverish season in purgatory. Hilda is restored, and he is safe. At the same time, he is also hit by a cauliflower, and one is tempted to imagine that Hawthorne himself has hurled this expression of contempt for the sculptor's pitiful weakness.

One is tempted, also, if one feels any fondness for Kenyon, to imagine that Hilda like Persephone has passed a renewing season underground, and has come back humanized and warmed. But this, clearly, has not taken place. Once again Kenyon puts to her his forbidden ideas, and Hilda shrinks from him "with an expression of horrour [*sic*] which wounded the poor, speculative sculptor to the soul." Fresh from this soul-wound, and only recently recovered from his long depression, the unfortunate man cries out, "Forgive me, Hilda! I never did believe it! . . . Were you my guide, my counsellor, my inmost friend, with that white wisdom which clothes you as a celestial garment, all would go well. O Hilda, guide me home!" The idea of once again losing her is unbearable, and, lying like a frightened child to placate her, the hurt sculptor wins "the gentle Hilda's shy affection."

We cannot be certain that Kenyon will abandon his art, but we may feel sure that there will be no more feline Cleopatras or broodingly beautiful fauns. Speaking with Hilda about his loss of interest in his more ambitious productions, Kenyon had earlier said, "I should like, now—only it would be such shameful treatment for a discrowned queen, and my own offspring, too—I should like to hit poor Cleopatra a bitter blow on her Egyptian nose, with this mallet." In effect this is what Kenyon has done to his two offspring, the "glad Faun of his imagination and memory" and the "beautiful woman, such as one sees only two or three, if even so many times, in all a lifetime; so beautiful, that she seemed to get into your consciousness and memory, and could never afterwards be shut out, but haunted your dreams, for pleasure or pain; holding your inner realm as a conquered territory." It is the final act of his imagination to transform these into figures of penitence, guilt, and remorse, linked by crime. Donatello, as the artist's surrogate, is consigned to prison forever; Miriam (like Hester) is readmitted as a penitent "on the other side of a fathomless abyss" and thus made acceptable to the imagination that cannot forget her.

The gesture of the artist destroying his own works is a familiar literary motif, one that Hawthorne made in his life, and that he wrote about. The conventional moral ending of *The Marble Faun,* with Miriam and Donatello condemned and punished, Kenyon and Hilda living happily and virtuously ever after, represents in its reversals of the book's values and desires a defacing not only of Hawthorne's own ideas about great art and romanticism, but a defacing of *The Marble Faun* itself. In its evocation of the story Hawthorne would like to tell but finally cannot, of the types of human figures he would like to celebrate but dare not, of the ideas he would like to espouse but has relinquished as unworkable in his culture, *The Marble Faun* concludes with a gesture of heartsickness and despair, of hopes denied, effort repudiated. In its ending Hawthorne deals just such a blow as Kenyon proposed to aim at his Cleopatra, desecrating the things his imagination most loved, and elevating for our approval a couple whose intertwined lives represent a living death for Miriam and Donatello, "the beautiful man, the beautiful woman." *The Marble Faun* is like the Venus of the campagna, created by Hawthorne's imagination, then discolored, disfigured, and shattered by his prudence, his conscience, his fatigue, his sense of futility. Discolored, disfigured, shattered—but not finally destroyed, for one may still discern, as with the Venus, "the beautiful Idea . . . as perfect to the mind, if not to the eye, as when the new marble gleamed with snowy lustre."

LEO B. LEVY

The Problem of Faith in "Young Goodman Brown"

Few of Hawthorne's tales have elicited a wider range of interpretations than "Young Goodman Brown." The critics have been victimized by the notorious ambiguity of a tale composed of a mixture of allegory and the psychological analysis of consciousness. Many of them find the key to its meaning in a neurotic predisposition to evil; one goes so far as to compare Goodman Brown to Henry James's governess in *The Turn of the Screw*. The psychological aspect is undeniably important, since we cannot be certain whether "Young Goodman Brown" is a dream-allegory that takes place in the mind and imagination of the protagonist, an allegory with fixed referents in the external world, or a combination of these that eludes our ordinary understanding of the genre itself. The story is all three: a dream vision, a conventional allegory, and finally an inquiry into the problem of faith that undermines the assumptions upon which the allegory is based.

Whether we think of the central episode of the witches' Sabbath as a dream or a hallucination, or as a nightmarish "real" experience, it must be placed in relationship to elements of the story that are outside Brown's consciousness. His point of view is in the foreground, but it must contend with the point of view of a narrator who is not identified with his perceptions. The narrator's irony and detachment, and his frequent intrusions, are measures of the distance he places between himself and a protagonist he regards with a mixture of condescension and pity. No fewer than three

From *Journal of English and Germanic Philology* 74, no. 3 (July 1975).

attitudes toward faith emerge from the story: Brown's, the view expressed in the concluding parable, and that which by implication is Hawthorne's. The elusiveness with which the narrative moves into Brown's state of mind and then outward arises from this complex view of faith, and also from the conception of Faith as a double, who "like Beatrice Rappacini is both pure and poisonous, saint and sinner." She is at once an allegorical idea and the means by which the idea is inverted. Those celebrated pink ribbons on Faith's cap—the objects of an astonishing range of responses by critics of the story—are vital to an understanding of her metamorphosis and of Brown's desperate efforts to recover his faith.

The impression that the story hovers on the borderline between subjective and objective reality derives from Hawthorne's suggestion that Brown's experience is peculiar to him and yet broadly representative. Not until the next to last paragraph are we offered what seems to be a choice between these alternatives: Hawthorne asks, "Had Goodman Brown fallen asleep in the forest and only dreamed a wild dream of a witch-meeting?" His reply—"Be it so if you will; but alas! it was a dream of evil omen for young Goodman Brown"—is often taken to mean that we may read the story either way; but we may wonder why Hawthorne defers this question until the end. The reader may suspect that "Young Goodman Brown" is a tale in which reality is entirely subsumed by the consciousness of the protagonist; if so, his suspicion will be heightened when Hawthorne, in the sentence following his question and answer, less tentatively alludes to "the night of that fearful dream." And yet even this statement leaves the issue unresolved. This irresolution is not coyness on Hawthorne's part: if the dream theory were confirmed, it would have the effect of canceling a whole range of intimations that surround the dream but are not part of it. Through the dream metaphor the many hints of Brown's unconscious fascination with evil are communicated, but Hawthorne recognizes that our waking life and the life of dreams are bound up together—that life is like a dream in its revelation of terrifying truths. His point is that the truth conveyed in the dream—that faith may betray us—is also a truth of waking experience.

I

The story begins as a conventional allegory, creating the expectation that the characters will consistently exhibit the abstractions they symbolize. If Hawthorne intends Brown to be a pathological case, that intention is not evident in the early stages. The problem of man's journey into the mystery of evil is presented in the broadest possible terms. Faith Brown, the wife of three months, is simply "Faith," and Goodman Brown is Everyman. The bargain he has struck with Satan is the universal one, reinforced by such signs as the innocence with which he convinces himself that he can turn aside from his covenant and the assurances he offers himself of his good intentions. Initially, he is a naive and immature young man who fails to understand the gravity of the step he has taken. Though Hawthorne does not provide a transitional development, he drastically alters this picture: the early indications of Brown's immaturity are succeeded by a presumably adult determination to resist his own evil impulses. His continuing willingness to join the community of sinners coexists with a reaction against that willingness. As the task of turning back becomes increasingly difficult, confronting him with one frustration after another, his struggle takes on heroic proportions.

Far from showing himself to be "a prospective convert who is only too willing to be convinced" [David Levin], Brown displays a mounting resistance to the Devil's enticements. No sooner does he leave Faith than "his heart smote him"; he replies to the Devil's reproach for his lateness at the appointed place, saying "Faith kept me back awhile." As the two travel into the forest the Devil observes the slowness of his companion's pace and ironically offers him his staff, thereby prompting the young man to confess, "I have scruples touching the matter thou wot'st of." He genuinely wishes to escape the Devil's snare: he withstands the revelation that the deacons and selectmen of his village, and the governor himself, have preceded him on this journey; and the discovery that Goody Cloyse, the old woman who had taught him his catechism, is a witch does not affect his determination to turn back: "What if a wretched old woman do choose to go to the Devil when I thought she was going to heaven: is that any reason why I should quit my dear Faith and go after her?" He assures himself that when he returns home he will meet the minister with a clear conscience, "nor shrink from the eye of good old Deacon Gookin"; he will sleep "so purely and sweetly now, in the arms of Faith!" It is not surprising that he is "ready to sink down to the ground, faint and overburdened with heavy sickness of his heart," when he learns that the deacon and the minister are of the Devil's company. Nevertheless, he cries out, "With Heaven above and Faith below, I will yet stand firm against the Devil!"

Beyond this point, Brown calls out three times for Faith to come to his aid, and not until he sees a pink ribbon from Faith's cap that has fluttered down from the sky and caught on the branch of a tree does he abandon hope, crying "My Faith is gone." As if to reinforce the tangible evidence of Faith's desertion, Hawthorne writes that Brown "seized" and "beheld" the fateful ribbon. He now knows that Faith's voice has been mingled with the other "familiar tones, heard daily at Salem village," but now issuing from the depths of a cloud—from the company of Satan's followers sailing through the air. The most frightful episode of the tale follows: Brown becomes a "demoniac," "the chief horror" in a scene full of horrors—of terrible sounds made up of "the creaking of trees, the howling of wild beasts, and the yell of Indians." Utterly possessed by the Devil, he yields to the conviction that the world is given over to sin. But when silence falls and he enters the clearing where the assembly of the damned is gathered for the performance of its ritual, his hopes rise again because Faith, whom he expects to see, is not there. But she soon stands with him among those who are about to undergo their initiation. They are "the only pair, as it seemed, who were yet hesitating on the verge of wickedness in this dark world." They look at each other in fearful anticipation, and for the last time Brown calls out for help: "Faith! Faith! . . . look up to heaven, and resist the wicked one." But "whether Faith obeyed he knew not." The whole spectacle of the witches' Sabbath vanishes at this instant, and Brown, staggering against the rock that had formed the altar, finds himself alone in the wilderness.

It cannot plausibly be argued that Brown has all along been prone to the despair into which he is then plunged, since after abandoning himself to wickedness and turning himself into an image of the fiend he recovers his composure and calls upon Faith once more. He is alone among Hawthorne's many "demoniacs" in reversing the process of committing himself to evil. Nevertheless, the sequel shows him irrevocably fallen into gloom and despair, condemned to a long life of withdrawal and suspicion. Brown has exhibited a compulsive denial of his compact with the Devil; but when his efforts to recover his former relationship with Faith collapse, he has no recourse except despair. No effort of the conscious will can save him. And yet the story is least of all a study, like "Roger Malvin's Burial," of unconscious motivation. Instead, Hawthorne seems content to emphasize Brown's helplessness. The spiritual test to which he is submitted is conducted on terms that only demonstrate the futility of his attempts to extricate himself. Even if we suppose that he unconsciously chooses to end his dream before Faith can reply, thereby condemning himself to a lifetime of faithlessness, the fact remains that Hawthorne has caught him in a trap as diabolical as anything the Devil might invent.

The psychoanalytically oriented critics interpret Goodman Brown's helplessness in terms of the projective mechanism of the dream or fantasy, which they regard as symptomatic of mental illness. The difficulty of this approach is not the contention that the presence of the Devil and his company and the rites into which Brown is drawn are projections, but that it ignores the conflict and resistance to which Hawthorne give such explicit and emphatic attention. The projective aspect of Brown's experience is not the whole of it. His submission to evil suggests that the demands of the id have overtaken the ego; his prolonged resistance is a denial of the wishes that are the source of his projections. His conflict originates in the superego, whose task is to punish the ego for its defections and, as the voice of conscience, to repress the satisfactions of the instinctual life. Brown's recovery from the *Walpurgisnacht* episode, in which he gives way completely to the id, is made possible by the activated defense mechanisms of the ego, which cries out to be saved. If we wonder why the witches' Sabbath ends with such breathtaking abruptness, the answer might be that the ego cannot tolerate the threat of destruction that awaits it if the initiation rites take place. The sexually fraught demands of the id are put down, though at a terrible price. In psychoanalytic terms, "Young Goodman Brown" is about the defeat of the id by the ego and the superego. The result of this suppression is that Brown, despairing and embittered, belongs neither to the Devil's party nor to the only other life-sustaining cause he knows—that of the Puritan faith and the Puritan community. The withdrawal and gloom that envelop him after his return to the village come about not because he has yielded to the overwhelming vision of evil in the forest, but because he has repressed it. The ego forbids him to accept his evil impulses as his own; hence he projects them upon his wife, whose virtue he now distrusts, and upon the other villagers, in whose goodness he can no longer believe.

But this—or any other psychological interpretation—restricts our understanding of a story that is cast in religious and theological terms. We must move outside the limits of the dream or fantasy, beyond any view of the nature of the forest experience, and examine the ideas that structure that experience. A clue to the basic question raised by the story is provided by Henry James's complaint that "if it meant anything, it would mean too much." James does not identify the specific source of his objection, but the context of his remark makes it clear that he believes that behind "Young Goodman Brown" is a kind of extravagance and even irrationality that gives rise to a "magnificent little romance," as he calls it, that cannot be taken seriously. Evidently he found the image of a man pleading for faith and deprived of it with such arbitrariness baffling. The magical, supernatural, and mysterious connotations accompanying the disappearance of the witches' Sabbath and Brown's "awakening" may well have offended James's sense of fictional propriety as well as his sense of the writer's obligation to describe a moral crisis in rational terms. This development in the story originates in the Gothic idea of an irresistible and omnipresent evil. James, reacting against this vision, insists that the tale "evidently means nothing as regards Hawthorne's own state of mind, his conviction of human depravity and his consequent melancholy." However, it was not necessary for Hawthorne to literally subscribe to such a vision in order for his imagination to be powerfully engaged by it. The very excessiveness of his story is the source of its lasting impression upon those who have read it. Behind it is the motive that shapes such tales as "John Inglefield's Thanksgiving," "The Minister's Black Veil," and "The Christmas Banquet," among others, which are intelligible only on the principle that Hawthorne is dramatizing his feeling that once the commitment to evil has been made, its impact must prevail. There is no power strong enough to oppose it. In "Young Goodman Brown" the struggle is so unequal that Faith, supposedly the Devil's antagonist, is drawn into the camp of the enemy.

II

Not the least terrifying aspect of the story is the insinuation that Faith has made her own independent covenant with the Devil. There is a faint suggestion that her complicity may be prior to and deeper than Brown's. This "monstrous inversion," as Terence Martin aptly calls it, is as sinister as anything to be found in Hawthorne's writings. This development is anticipated when Faith, imploring her husband not to leave her, says that "a lone woman is troubled with such dreams and such thoughts that she's afeard of herself sometimes," and she urges him to stay with her "this night . . . of all nights in the year." In this way, her bad dreams are linked to his, suggesting that both have prepared themselves for the same experience. However, we know nothing of the circumstances that bring her into the forest except what Brown discovers for himself. When Goody Cloyse tells the Devil that she has heard that "there is a nice young man to be taken into communion tonight," he denies the report, just as he had previously assured Brown that his Faith will not come to any harm. Brown overhears a voice like Deacon Gookin's declare that "there is a goodly young woman to be taken into communion," a statement offered not as something Brown imagines but given by one who does not know that he is listening. When the converts are brought forth, Brown approaches the congregation, "with whom he felt a loathful brotherhood by the sympathy of all that was wicked in his heart." He imagines—or sees—his father beckoning him on and his mother warning him back. Here again Hawthorne blurs the distinction between actual participants and projections. However, no such ambiguity attends the identification of "the slender form of a veiled female" brought forth by Goody Cloyse and Martha Carrier to take part in the baptismal rites: "the wretched man beheld his Faith, and the wife her husband, trembling before that unhallowed altar."

There is little agreement among critics about Faith as a character or as an allegorical figure. For some, Faith is allegorically consistent: Neal Frank Doubleday takes it as a sign of Faith's benevolence that when Brown calls upon Faith to "'resist the wicked one' . . . he is released from the witch-meeting." Even those who recognize Faith's dual character argue that she retains her allegorical identity. For Roy R. Male, "almost everything in the forest scene suggests that the communion of sinners is essentially sexual and that Brown qualifies for it by his marriage." And yet Male does not regard Faith's participation in the sexuality of marriage as an indication that she is "evil" in the sense that Brown is; one wonders why the sexual union leaves her free of the stain of original sin. Daniel G. Hoffman writes that "in one sense, she *is* the forest, and Brown has qualified for admission to the witches' orgy by having carnal knowledge of her [*Form and Fable in American Fiction*]." Hoffman, too, absolves Faith of her share in the consequences of carnal knowledge: she "transcends Brown's knowledge of evil with all-encompassing love." In following Brown's corpse to the grave, "Faith remains true to him." But Hoffman's argument cannot resolve the paradox he himself describes: if "she *is* the forest"—if she too is guilty of carnal knowledge—how can she remain "the Devil's only antagonist in this tale," having "such faith in man that she can transcend the revelation that [Brown] is fallen?" After all, she too has fallen. The Devil's only antagonist, so far as the reader can tell, is Goodman Brown.

This confusion of the fictional character of Faith with the allegorical concept has its roots in the story itself. The basic thrust of the story is that faith is deficient, but the deficiency arises not from the personification of Faith as a woman and a wife but from Hawthorne's handling of the abstraction. He is not suggesting that Faith as an abstraction is susceptible to the human frailties of Everyman but somehow transcends them, even though he creates the correspondences that give rise to this misconception. His position seems to be that faith is a self-consistent principle, however unreliable and unpredictable. There is a submerged, possibly unintended, but nonetheless dreadful irony in the manner in which Faith greets Brown on his return to the village, as if she had not been present in the forest and had played no part in the terrible events that take place there. She is as she was at the beginning—except that it is impossible for Brown to see her as she was. The meaning of the story arises from this discrepancy.

Faith's most conspicuous physical characteristic consists of the pink ribbons on her cap. They are the subject of many attempts to sustain an argument about her allegorical significance and to reconcile the two Faiths, one comely, almost lightsome, and the other in complicity with the powers of darkness. The ribbons provide the symbolic continuity between Faith as an ideal of religious fidelity and as a partner in a witches' Sabbath. The most obvious feature of these interpretations is their ingenuity and their diversity. To Thomas E. Connolly the ribbons "seem to be symbolic of [Brown's] initial illusion about the true significance of his faith, his belief that his faith will lead him to heaven." Elsewhere, Connolly finds that they symbolize "illicit passion and purity." For Paul W. Miller, the ribbons "keep Faith humble and honest, and thus contribute to her ultimate preservation from the Evil One," and for E. Arthur Robinson they are "representative of woman's physical nature" and of Faith's sexual passion. Darrel Abel considers the ribbons "a badge of feminine innocence." For Paul J. Hurley, they represent "the ritualistic trappings of religious observance," and for Hyatt Waggoner they signalize Brown's immature faith. Richard H. Fogle has commented that "as an emblem of heavenly Faith their color gradually deepens into the liquid flame or blood of the baptism into sin." There is no way to choose among views that differ so in their symbolic attributions; how one interprets the ribbons obviously depends upon one's prior understanding of the story.

F. O. Matthiessen observes of the scene in which Brown believes he has visible proof of Faith's betrayal that "only the literal insistence on that damaging pink ribbon obtrudes the labels of a confining allegory, and short-circuits the range of association." He evidently means that the ribbon fails to work symbolically in an otherwise powerful depiction of Brown's inner experience. He contrasts Hawthorne's image of the ribbon to Melville's metaphor of "the ball of free will" held (and dropped) by Ishmael and Queequeg in *Moby-Dick*, remarking that "only by discovering such metaphors can the writer suggest the actual complexity of experience." But when Matthiessen adds that "we are bothered by the ribbon because it is an abstraction pretending to be something else," he fails to recognize that, on the contrary, it is because the ribbon is no more than a tangible object that its effect is "literal" rather than abstract, and for this reason cannot function metaphorically. It is simply a descriptive element, one of the realistic details that gives Faith such physical reality as she has. The ribbons belong to a fictional character described as "sweet," "pretty," and "little," more reminiscent of a genteel girl of Hawthorne's own day than a Puritan woman who might also have worn pink ribbons. She is the cheerful wife, one of Hawthorne's feminine figures, like Phoebe or Hilda, who serves as an emblem of steadfastness in a world of pollution.

David Levin argues that "Brown's sensory perception of the ribbons is no more literal or material than his perception of the Devil, his clutching of the staff, or his hearing of the Devil's statement about the fifteen-minute trip from Boston to the woods near Salem village." Approving this view, Frederick C. Crews disputes the claim that the "tangible reality" of the pink ribbons is evidence that Faith is "really" in the forest, adding that "Brown shares Othello's fatuous concern for 'ocular proof,' and the proof that is seized upon is no more substantial in one case than in the other." These critics do not perceive that whether we are looking at the story in psychological terms or in terms of evidence that Brown is beset by counterfeit images—spectres of real persons—conjured by the Devil, the literary relationships that give rise to these and other interpretations are still there, on the page and in the text. In this sense, it does not matter which critical perspective we choose to pursue. The ribbons are in fact an explicit link between two conceptions of Faith, connecting sweet little Faith of the village with the woman who stands at the Devil's baptismal font. We can legitimately disagree about the meaning of this duality; the fact remains that in proposing that Faith's significance is the opposite of what he had led the reader to expect, Hawthorne violates the fixed conceptual meaning associated with his character. This breaking of the allegorical mold is more than a technical violation of the genre: it turns the story in an entirely new direction, so that it is deprived of the essential feature of all allegory—the ability to derive an abstract truth from its unfolding.

As we have noted, Hawthorne combines the kind of allegory that depicts the interaction of characters in an external setting—a technique of "realistic" as well as allegorical narrative—with the internalization of the action in the mind of the protagonist, for the purpose of dividing the reader's perception of what is happening. The ambiguity that results has the effect of enriching the story; but when the method is applied to the ribbons, the effect is a kind of teasing. The ribbons intrude themselves upon the symbolic sphere of the story where they do not belong; they have no meaning except as a fanciful joke, a grace note woven into the solemn theme of the tale. However, they have an important dramatic function: as we see them at the beginning and end of the story, the ribbons identify the physical as distinct from the allegorical character of Faith; we have no need to see them in symbolic terms, since Faith as an abstraction is fully defined by her name alone. They are part of her adornment of dress, and they suggest, rather than symbolize, something light and playful, consistent with her anxious simplicity at the beginning and the joyful, almost childish eagerness with which she greets Brown at the end. It is only in the forest scene that the single ribbon becomes disturbing. The critics have seized upon this ribbon no less desperately than Goodman Brown himself in order to establish the continuity of the allegorical theme. But it is by means of the ribbon that Hawthorne disrupts the allegory; all that we see of Faith now is the ornament that warrants her physical presence just when her allegorical presence vanishes. The moment is dramatic in the contrast of the frivolous, fluttering piece of ribbon with the darkness, agony, and doubt that envelop the scene. It is as if Hawthorne were saying, "Yes, it is truly Faith, as you see by this ribbon, who is no longer Faith."

The psychology-oriented critics believe that they solve the problem of the ribbons by saying that they are part of Goodman Brown's dream, no more or less "real" than the rest of what his diseased mind invents out of its own necessities. This theory cannot tell us when the dream begins: does Brown dream that he bids good-bye to Faith? If so, then he may also be dreaming of his return to the village and of the despair that afflicts him, and even of his long, unhappy life and eventual death. Did he dream that he made a covenant with the Devil? Did he do so before he entered the forest to keep his appointment, waking from one dream only to fall victim to another, after a pointless evening walk? The story is constructed in such a way that questions of this kind cannot be answered; but it does make a distinction between Brown's departure and return and the period between them. We may believe that the interval is a dream, even though we cannot know when it begins. This assumption has much to be said for it; but if we follow it we must conclude that the ribbons are both in and out of the dream, that Brown is dreaming about something he is familiar with in his waking experience. It is little wonder, then, that the sight of the ribbon produces the shock that leads him to connect his dream with reality in such a devastating fashion. In emotional as well as visual terms, the world of the nightmare and the world of the Puritan community are united. This development is reinforced by the bewilderment of Brown's return to the village and its profoundly disorienting consequences. Perhaps it is not until he encounters the minister, Deacon Gookin, and Goody Cloyse, and then sees "the head of Faith, with the pink ribbons, gazing anxiously forth," that his faith is permanently shattered. The breakdown of the beliefs and assumptions that gave order and stability to his life is complete.

III

It is sometimes said that Hawthorne's purpose in "Young Goodman Brown" is to demonstrate the unresponsiveness of Puritanic Calvinism to the needs of the believer. However, Hawthorne's equation of the Puritan experience with the devil-worship that is its inversion is a form of dramatic hyperbole that should not be taken literally. The Puritan vision of evil was a dreadful one, and there can be no doubt that Hawthorne means to dramatize its excess; but this is not the same thing as drawing up an indictment of Puritan faith. Hawthorne knew that witches' Sabbaths and Black Masses were not confined to Puritan New England, and he knew that the possibility of being overwhelmed by the discovery of the power of evil was universal. He reacted strongly against the bigotry, cruelty, and hypocrisy of his New England ancestors, but that reaction does not exhaust the complex judgment he formed of them. Even the Reverend Dimmesdale, that pious hypocrite, has in his possession a larger share of the truth about the human condition—truth that derives from his faith—than the romantic and memorable rebel, Hester Prynne. Hawthorne well knew the variability of the experience of faith among the Puritans. Elsewhere he shows us that it may lead to serenity, to a dehumanizing dogmatism, or to intense suffering of spirit. Faith may also, as in "Young Goodman Brown," mysteriously abandon us.

As a form, allegory is a systematic organization of fixed beliefs; Hawthorne utilizes the form for the purpose of showing that the safety and security implicit in it are illusory. The meaning of the story is that its own simple definitions do not work. Instead, we are shown that there is no necessary connection between our critical need for faith and the responsiveness of faith. This is the larger significance of "Young Goodman Brown," not the comfortable parable that warns us against the sin of despair, which the moralistic tenor of the conclusion would have us believe can be avoided if only we listen attentively enough. The last paragraph turns Brown into an object lesson; but, as is often the case with Hawthorne's tales, a truer meaning is discovered before this point of constriction is reached. In his penetrating analysis of the problem of faith in Hawthorne's fiction, Taylor Stoehr, writing of "Rappaccini's Daughter" as well as "Young Goodman Brown," observes that "Hawthorne seems to throw the blame on his characters, while at the same time he gives them no possible means of saving themselves." Stoehr adds that "for a man who is always complaining about his characters' lack of faith, Hawthorne himself is singularly dubious about the possibilities of life and human nature."

For Hawthorne, the loss of faith is always imminent, a danger that increases in proportion to our involvement in a moral reality that is always more unsettling than we like to believe. His concern in "Young Goodman Brown," apart from describing the terrors of the Puritan struggle for faith, is with our inability to foresee the consequences of our choices or to judge the nature of the moral forces that press upon us. We can easily move past the point of return, and, like Goodman Brown, find that it is too late for what we want and need. Brown's last cry for Faith is the most poignant moment of the story, expressing his need to assimilate the experiences through which he has passed, and even his capacity to do so. The silence between dream and waking, or between the actuality of the witches' Sabbath and his ordinary life, is the silence of the void between spiritual need and spiritual sustenance. The reader is not less stunned than Brown himself, since he cannot easily resolve the paradox into which he has been led. He saw Brown at the outset abandon Faith; if that were all that he is meant to see, the tale would be very simple. But now the reader finds that Faith has deserted Brown—a distinction that may seem elusive but is nevertheless the crux upon which everything turns. Faith is originally the "good angel" to whose skirts Goodman Brown resolves to cling hereafter. To suggest that the good angel may turn herself into a demon is an insight that Hawthorne does not often risk, though there is also a hint of the diabolical in the transformations through which he takes Priscilla in *The Blithedale Romance.*

Hawthorne typically pays detailed attention to the costume and dress of his feminine characters as symbolic evidences of the stages through which they move. Except for her ribbons, Faith is pictorially a cipher, an abstraction for which Hawthorne refuses symbolic amplification, perhaps because of his sense of its precarious status. Therefore, Faith (or faith) becomes unresponsive, it disappears, and when it reappears it stands in the midst of all that it dreads. If, awaking at midnight, Goodman Brown shrinks from the bosom of Faith, it is because he has taken the full measure of her duplicity. "Such loss of faith is ever one of the saddest results of sin," Hawthorne says of Hester Prynne, and in *The Scarlet Letter* he castigates "the Fiend" for leaving nothing "for this poor sinner to revere." But in "Young Goodman Brown" it is Faith, not Satan or the sinner, whose defection is at issue.

SHELDON W. LIEBMAN

Hawthorne's Romanticism: *"The Artist of the Beautiful"*

In the concluding paragraphs of "The Christmas Banquet" Roderick Elliston asks his wife Rosina to comment on the story he has just finished reading to her. "Frankly," she says, "your success is by no means complete. . . . It is true, I have an idea of the character you endeavor to describe; but it is rather by dint of my own thought than your expression." This is not to say, however, that the story really fails, at least for the reason Rosina gives. Having learned something about "the gloomy mysteries of the human heart" from his experience in "Egotism; or, the Bosom Serpent," Roderick has chosen to convey the lessons he has learned by implication. As his friend the sculptor says, Rosina's imaginative participation in the tale was "unavoidable" since the personality of its central character is "negative."

The point is worth making because Hawthorne's readers often find themselves in Rosina's dilemma. Most of his successful tales deal with characters like Roderick's Gervayse Hastings: "moral monsters" who have a "deficiency in [their] spiritual organization." In such stories as "Young Goodman Brown" and "My Kinsman, Major Molineux," readers must try to determine the author's moral vision on the basis of characters whose words and deeds contradict it. They must infer the positive from negative examples.

In view of this problem, "The Artist of the Beautiful" is a good starting point in studying Hawthorne's fiction. Its principal character is not a moral

---

From *ESQ: A Journal of the American Renaissance* 22, no. 2 (1976).

failure like Robin Molineux or Goodman Brown. He is ultimately a heroic figure who, like Roderick Elliston, comes to terms with his spiritual deficiency in the process of growing from innocence to experience. And both the course and consequences of his transformation tell a great deal, directly and explicitly, about Hawthorne's beliefs. Furthermore, though he always deals with the relationship between man and nature, man and God, and man and man, Hawthorne treats the subjects far more extensively in this story than he does elsewhere in his fiction. He traces the artist's development not only in terms of aesthetic questions but in terms of moral and metaphysical issues as well. Thus, "The Artist of the Beautiful" offers the unusual opportunity of assessing Hawthorne's view of the human condition on the basis of a character whose thoughts and actions represent a careful examination of important philosophical problems and who eventually learns to think and act in accord with the main tenets of Hawthorne's moral vision.

Owen Warland, the Artist of the Beautiful, is the traditional protagonist in the classic struggle between the artist and the world. His tale is told, however, not in the language of traditional philosophy but in the special vocabulary of the Romantic Age. It focuses on the most important issues of the period: the ontological status of subjective perceptions and experiences, the relationship between beauty and use, and the respective claims of the natural and the mechanical. Thus, the central figure in the story is not just an artist but a *Romantic* artist, caught between the antitheses of ideal and real, spirit and matter, imagination and understanding, and art and criticism.

Despite the clarity of its issues, though, "The Artist of the Beautiful" is as difficult to interpret as any other Hawthorne story. And despite the directness of its method and the explicitness of its language, it has drawn a variety of critical responses. Is the story a glowing defense of Romanticism? Or is it an ironic condemnation of the artistic and philosophical ideals of the early nineteenth century? These questions have arisen because the artist himself is not an easy character to define. And this is so primarily because he passes through three distinct phases of development, each one of which could provide the basis for a different reading of the story.

First, Owen Warland is set against a trio of characters—Peter Hovenden, his former master in the watchmaking trade; Annie, Peter's daughter; and Robert Danforth, a blacksmith and later Annie's husband—who, despite their differences, actually constitute one antagonist and represent a single point of view. As their philosophical opponent, Owen is as different from them as his nineteenth-century Romanticism is from their eighteenth-century rationalism. As the story progresses, however, the similarities between Owen and the trio become increasingly evident, and Owen's position is shown to be as narrow and his defense of it as dogmatic as are those of his opponents.

Revealing the duality in his own nature, the artist vacillates between the idealist he would like to remain and the skeptic he is tempted to become. Finally, having assimilated the contrarieties of his experience, reconciled the conflicts in his own personality, and in a sense transcended the seeming contradictions both within and without, he emerges as the consummate artist—but only after and *as a result* of an arduous spiritual pilgrimage.

In the early pages of the story, Hawthorne focuses on the conflict between artist and public and the philosophical issues which divide them. Unlike Peter Hovenden, who believes only in what he can touch—"the densest matter of the physical world"—and unlike the blacksmith, who "spends his labor upon a reality," Owen believes in things of the spirit inaccessible to the senses and untranslatable by brute force. Ideas are "real to him for the instant, without the toil, and perplexity, and many disappointments, of attempting to make them visible to the sensual eye."

Owen is capable of seeing the ideal and spiritual through the power of imagination. Because he finds his reality within himself he "copie[s] from the richness of [his] visions" rather than from the commonsense world available to him through ordinary perception. His passion for things unseen is so powerful that "[i]t seemed, in fact, a new development of the love of the Beautiful, such as might have made him a poet, a painter, or a sculptor, and which was . . . completely refined from all utilitarian coarseness." In this respect, "[t]here was nothing so antipodal to his nature as [Peter Hovenden's] cold, unimaginative sagacity," which "saw so distinctly what it did see, and disbelieved so uncompromisingly in what it could not see."

Seeking the beautiful everywhere and finding it imaginatively only in nature, Owen becomes a student of the grace and motion of the natural world. "He wasted the sunshine, as people said, in wandering through the woods and fields, and along the banks of streams. There, like a child, he found amusement in chasing butterflies" rather than in working for the "dusty [prize] along the highway" recommended by Peter Hovenden and his friends. As a child, he looked at a steam-engine, "turned pale and grew sick, as if something monstrous and unnatural had been presented to him." Even the smallest of God's creatures is far more beautiful to him than the greatest works of man: people "sometimes saw reason to suppose that he was attempting to imitate the beautiful movements of Nature, as exemplified in the flight of birds or the activity of little animals."

Because he is drawn to the eternal and infinite, as well as to the beautiful, Owen is naturally the enemy of time and space, especially as they are represented by the clocks in his shop and the less tangible but more onerous limits his business imposes on him. Having suffered from Peter Hovenden's belief that "life should be regulated, like clockwork" and his master's attempt "to restrain his creative eccentricity within bounds," he defines time in his own way. As Annie suggests, he "is inventing a new kind of timekeeper," expressive of the quality and intensity of life rather than predetermined according to arbitrary and rational standards. He "cared no more for the measurement of time than if it had been merged into eternity" because for him it *is* merged into eternity. He makes music of the harsh sounds of ordinary time so that "each flitting moment fall[s] into the abyss of the Past," made beautiful and harmonious for the present and then forgotten. To emphasize the spiritual significance of time, he "arrange[s] a dance of funeral procession" on old clocks, "representing twelve mirthful or melancholy hours."

If this contrast between the points of view of Owen Warland and Peter Hovenden constituted the whole story, one could call it, as some critics have, a celebration of Romanticism. In finally creating the beautiful Owen stands up to "the bitterness of worldly criticism" and successfully defies all those who question his purpose and scorn his efforts. In this view—and in terms of the commonplaces of Romantic critical theory—Hawthorne depicts the triumph of the imagination over the understanding, the spiritual over the material, and the aesthetic over the utilitarian.

"The Artist of the Beautiful" is not so simple, however. For although Hawthorne insists on the opposition between these two sets of ideas, he insists as much that the artist, in order to succeed in his life and work, must resolve this conflict and deal directly with the "thwarting influences" that beset him. After all, "the absorbing dream of [Owen's] imagination" is not only to *see* the beautiful but also to *create* it. He feels "the impulse to give external reality to his ideas" and wants to produce "a beauty that should attain to the ideal which Nature has proposed to herself, in all her creatures, but has never taken pains to realize." And *because* he "strive[s] to put the very spirit of Beauty into form, and give it motion," he must ultimately deal with the reality he denies, the practical world, as well as the limits of his powers and the constraints of form.

Indeed, most of its readers consider the story an attack on Romantic art and the life of the Romantic artist because they do not see that Owen comes to terms with these inevitable obstacles to his success. And for most of the tale they are right; he is not an artist in fact but an artist *manqué,* sensitive, lonely, absorbed, and at least a problem to himself if not a danger to those around him.

With "his pale face bent earnestly over some delicate piece of mechanism, on which was thrown the concentrated lustre of a shade-lamp," Owen evidently labors in a sphere as narrow as it is intense. He becomes "more and more absorbed in a secret occupation" which requires him to work at night because he is totally committed to "intellectual activity." "Daylight, to the morbid sensibility of his mind, seemed to have an intrusiveness that interfered with his pursuits." He prefers cloudy days which allow "his sensitive brain" to lose itself in "indefinite musings" and give him an "escape from the sharp distinctness with which he was compelled to shape out his thoughts."

What Owen lacks is something to balance "the absorbing dream," a deeper vision encompassing more than his own reality and a more human labor drawing on other resources in his nature. He is capable of "los[ing] himself in contemplation," but he is somehow unable to embody his vision in appropriate form. And, more important, like all those "with human yearnings, but separated from the multitude by a peculiar lot," he is "insulated" from his fellows and "moral[ly] cold"—an isolation which could lead, as it does in "The Prophetic Pictures" and "The Birthmark," to greater delusions and even madness.

Given this imbalance in his artistic pursuit, Owen is doomed to fail. He turns the clocks in his window away from the street not indifferently but "churlishly." And because his feelings are "easily disturbed," he can tolerate no interruptions. When Annie visits him, he is "seized with a fluttering of the nerves, which made his hand tremble too violently to proceed with such delicate labor." He shrinks from the blacksmith's hearty laugh as readily as he does from the watchmaker's scornful remarks because he is "full of little petulances." His sensitivity is so extreme that he is completely defeated by any intrusion. And his dedication is so pathological that when Annie upsets his work "the artist seize[s] her by the wrist with a force that [makes] her scream aloud," and he convulses in an "intense rage and anguish that writhe[s] across his features."

In every respect Owen's inadequacies contrast with those of his opponents. Just as Peter Hovenden lacks his spiritual power, Owen lacks the physical "firmness" which Peter respects so much. It is therefore a quality he depends on others for. "And what a help and strength would it be to him, in his lonely toil, if he could gain the sympathy of the only being whom he loved!" "I yearned for sympathy," he says to Annie, "and thought . . . that you might give it me." But the strength he needs must come from within: "It is requisite for the ideal artist to possess a force of character that seems hardly compatible with its delicacy; he must keep his faith in himself, while the incredulous world assails him. . . . [He] must stand up against mankind."

Owen, however, not only depends on Annie for encouragement and sympathy, but, regarding her rather than his work as the fulfillment of his dreams, virtually worships her. "Anything for your sake, Annie," he says to her, "anything, even were it to work at Robert Danforth's forge." His entire effort is "for [her] sake alone" because she is "the visible shape in which the spiritual power that he worshipped . . . was made manifest to him." And he "persist[s] in connecting all his dreams of artistical success with [her] image." Thus, Owen is not even his own man, and his labor is something less than the ideal pursuit he thinks it is. Everything is subordinated to his love for Annie. And as long as he continues to see her as the embodiment of his dreams, they will remain "vague and unsatisfied"—and they will leave him "spiritless."

The problem is that the artist's imagination is as unreliable as Peter Hovenden's understanding. Owen goes so far as to believe that Annie is capable of loving him, and he is as deluded about the nature of her affection as he is about the dimension of her understanding. He thinks "that this young girl possessed the gift to comprehend him, better than all the world beside." And he continues to believe, despite his disappointments, that she is "imbued . . . with a finer grace, that might enable her to be the interpreter between Strength and Beauty." Like the artist in "The Prophetic Pictures," he makes the object of his perception "as much a creature of his own" as his other imaginary creations: his "inward vision" works independently of external facts. Like Aylmer in "The Birthmark," he simply fails to see the object of his affection as an ordinary human being.

At the same time, and like his own worst enemy, Owen finds the hindrances to his success everywhere but in himself. Whenever he responds irritably to even a friendly visit and destroys his work as a result, he blames someone else. "I am ruined!" he cries again and again. Though he calls Peter Hovenden his "evil spirit," however, it is clear that the antagonist is also, if not entirely, in Owen himself. When he hears of Annie's engagement, he stifles a cry of agony "like a man holding down an evil spirit." And when he releases his rage and anguish, he ruins his work by his own hand. He is incapable of taking the responsibility for his failure because he believes he is destined to do great things. And this makes him as dogmatic in his way as Peter Hovenden is in his. But for this kind of interference, he says, he would "long ago have achieved the task that [he] was created for." Thus, he acts "as if his fate were embodied" in the mechanism he so intently labors at, just as the old watchmaker thinks that his undoing will be brought about by his work.

Owen's capacity for evil is suggested in his attitude toward time. As Peter Hovenden says, his ingenuity "spoil[s] the accuracy of some of the best watches in my shop" and might even "turn the sun out of its orbit, and derange the whole course of time" if it could. He is therefore "unfit . . . to lead old blind Father Time along his daily course," for he despises "the harsh dissonances of life," the metallic tones of ordinary time. He turns the faces of the clocks in his window away from the street, as if he were "disinclined to inform the wayfarers what o'clock it was." When he gives up the business in the summer he "permit[s] Father Time . . . to stray at random through human life, making infinite confusion among the train of bewildered hours." Ironically, this is precisely the effect that others, with their rigid insistence on clock time, have on him. When Robert Danforth sounds the iron accents of common time, he "darkens and confuses the spiritual element within [Owen]."

What the artist forgets or has yet to learn is that between his sense of time, residing in both the present and the eternal, and Peter Hovenden's sense of time, residing in the past and the future, stands the time expressed by "ancient clocks that have grown nearly allied to human nature, by measuring out the lifetime of many generations"—and representing both life and death, the joys of time present and eternal as well as the terrors of time passing from past to future. It is human and natural time, expressing both motion and stasis and measuring the long and immortal process of growth and decay which embraces all things.

Depending as he does on dreams, illusions, and imaginations, Owen is similar to the other artists, scientists, reformers, and clergymen in Hawthorne's fiction who represent a real threat to the order of things. Though as an artist he can do little real damage in the world of actuality, he is nevertheless related temperamentally and morally to those whose work enables them to destroy either themselves or others. Owen thus stands for the dangers of idealism untutored by experience: the tyranny of the imagination, the spirit's ethos of manifest destiny, the mind's ruthless conquest of a universe otherwise subject to its own laws and bound by the covenants of its own nature. As long as Owen refuses to accept the regular processes of nature herself, he must fall far short of his goals.

Hawthorne probably based his portrait of the Romantic artist on the popular conception of the type, particularly represented by Keats, Shelley, and Byron—not necessarily as they were but as they were portrayed in the literary quarterlies of the early nineteenth century. With his many negative traits, Owen is a member of the *genus irritabile vatum,* a *kind* of Romantic artist originally defined by Horace and the subject of critical comment by many of the Romantic poets themselves, most notably Coleridge. In the second chapter of *Biographia Literaria,* devoted to the *"Supposed irritability of men of Genius,"* Coleridge challenges the notion that artists are inevitably either cold-blooded fanatics or thin-skinned enthusiasts. "The sanity of the mind," he says, "is between superstition with fanaticism on the one hand, and enthusiasm with indifference and a diseased slowness to action on the other."

Coleridge's two types appear in "The Artist of the Beautiful" as Peter Hovenden and Owen Warland. The former type is noted for a "debility and dimness of the imaginative power, and a consequent necessity of reliance on the immediate impressions of the senses." He has "a deficient portion of internal warmth" and lacks the "foundation" in his own mind for what he believes. The result is fear and anger: "Experience informs us that the first defence of weak minds is to recriminate." The latter type is known for the vividness of his idea: "the mind is affected by thoughts, rather than by things; and only then feels the requisite interest even for the most important events and accidents, when by means of meditation they have passed into *thoughts*." While moderate in peaceful times, "in times of tumult they are the men destined to come forth as the shaping spirit of Ruin, to destroy the wisdom of ages in order to substitute the fancies of a day." In this light, the artist and his antagonist represent twin evils in Hawthorne's story. And as long as Owen remains as far from "things" as Peter is from "ideas," he continues to be a half-person incapable of creating even the humanly possible.

As often as not, Hawthorne leaves his artists and scientists at the point at which Owen has arrived about midway thought the story: still committed to the ideal, still absorbed in the attempt to make it real, and still overwhelmed by the inevitable obstacles to his success. Sometimes, like Aylmer and Giovanni, they continue in their pursuit of perfection, as Owen does for a time, and are led to destroy another human being. Sometimes, like Goodman Brown and Ethan Brand, they give up their quest, as Owen does later in the story, and simply destroy themselves.

The Artist of the Beautiful is unique, however, because his attempts at symbolic murder and suicide are temporary. His life as an artist *manqué* is at last merely a point of departure from which he emerges as an example of the supreme artist and a model against which Hawthorne's other idealists may be compared—unfavorably. By the end of the tale Owen has become the only major figure in Hawthorne's fiction to attain the idealistic goals he originally set out to pursue. And this is the point which most readers of the story have failed to understand. Focusing as it does on the artist's *transformation,* the tale reflects the theme of spiritual regeneration which is prominent in some of the greatest works of the Romantics: Coleridge's *Rime of the Ancient Mariner,* Wordsworth's "Intimations of Immortality," and Carlyle's *Sartor Resartus.*

Before his final change, however, Owen swings back and forth between the two extremes defined in the story. And in doing so he experiences both dimensions of self he needs to know in order to become the complete person he wishes to be. After the blacksmith's visit he falls into "despair" and "darkness." When he appears to the world again his face shows "a cold, dull, nameless change," and he returns to work "with dogged industry" and "obtuse gravity." He wishes to be "delivered" from the imprisonment of his spirit, but with Peter Hovenden's visit he is "thrown back into the state whence he had been slowly emerging." Then rededicating himself to his secret task, he is interrupted again, this time by Annie. Ruined once more and "having lost the steadfast influence of a great purpose," he turns to drink and revelry. Hawthorne explains: "when the ethereal portion of a man of genius is obscured, the earthly part assumes an influence the more uncontrollable, because the character is not thrown off the balance to which Providence had so nicely adjusted it." Owen finds his life shrouded in gloom and the gloom filled with "spectres that mocked at him."

Owen recovers yet again only to be interrupted for the last time by Peter Hovenden's announcement of Annie's engagement. Now, Owen's loss is total. And he has arrived at the point to which Robin Molineux and Goodman Brown have come at the same juncture in their respective stories, similarly haunted by spectres and bewildered by their experience. Because "the angel of his life [has] been snatched away," the artist must either give up his quest altogether or learn to rely entirely on his own resources.

Appropriately, after the darkness inspired by Robert Danforth, the despair initiated by Peter Hovenden, and the disease inflicted by Annie's departure, Owen becomes the mirror-image of the infant who will eventually destroy his work. With a new "childishness" in his aspect he has acquired an "obtuser garniture of flesh," and "his delicate little hand" has grown "plumper than the hand of a thriving infant." He acts "as if the spirit had gone out of him" and loses faith in everything he once believed in. The "marvels of mechanism" are now "absolutely fabulous." The mysterious accounts of Albertus Magnus and Friar Bacon are now "mere impositions." And he no longer believes it possible "to spiritualize machinery." He has, as he claims, "acquired a little common sense," and he is inclined to laugh at his past follies. In short, "he had ceased to be an inhabitant of the better sphere that lies unseen around us. He had lost his faith in the invisible, and now prided himself . . . in the wisdom which rejected much that even his eye could see, and trusted confidently in nothing but what his hand could touch." In all things he has become indistinguishable from his antagonists.

Yet, when his spirit awakens from its slumber, Owen is an entirely new person, as different from Peter Hovenden as he is from his former self. He has passed through a spiritual crisis and has implicitly acknowledged the inevitable disappointments of earthly life. And he has acquired a larger vision and a larger creative capacity as a result. Encircled by a radiant halo, his creation is a sacred object born of the wedding of ideal and real. It is a "bridal gift" which celebrates as much the marriage of opposites in his own nature as his reconciliation to the limits of the material world. Alive with the artist's *own* spirit, the mechanical butterfly embodies the beautiful, the ethereal, and the ideal, as it could not before. As Owen says, "it may well be said to possess life, for it has absorbed my own being into itself; and in the secret of that butterfly, and in its beauty—which is not merely outward, but deep as its whole system—is represented *the intellect, the imagination, the sensibility, the soul* of an Artist of the Beautiful" (emphasis mine)—*the entire being* of the artist who, unlike his brethren of the *genus irritabile,* now labors in the service of all his faculties.

Like the characters Hawthorne describes in "The Christmas Banquet," Owen has passed "that dreary point in life, where Folly quits us of her own accord, leaving us to make friends with Wisdom if we can." He is one of those "initiated souls to whom sorrow had been a talisman, admitting them into spiritual depths which no other spell can open." And in his life, as in theirs, "[s]*ometimes, out of the midst of densest gloom, there flashed a momentary radiance,* pure as crystal, bright as the flame of stars, and shedding such a glow upon the mysteries of life, that the guests were ready to exclaim, 'Surely the riddle is on the point of being solved'" (my italics). With this wisdom, unlike the unhappy attendants of the Christmas Banquet who fail to believe in the radiance enough to be able to recreate it, Owen is able to create "Nature's ideal butterfly . . . realized in all its perfection," the "incarnation of his idea," the result of "converting what was earthly to spiritual gold."

Because he has learned that the ideal and the real have their respective claims, Owen understands that "the reward of all high performance must be sought within itself, or sought in vain." He realizes now, as he did not before, "that ideas which grow up within the imagination, and appear so lovely to it, and of a value beyond whatever men call valuable, are exposed to be shattered and annihilated by contact with the Practical." He is unmoved when his butterfly is crushed because "[h]e had caught a far other butterfly than this. When the artist rose high enough to achieve the Beautiful, the symbol by which he made it perceptible to mortal senses became of little value in his eyes, while his spirit possessed itself in the enjoyment of the Reality." He has learned to see his labor as an end in itself, its source in the realm of the spirit as immortal and its result in the domain of the material as subject to the limits of mortality.

Clearly Owen has accepted the limits of time and space in realizing that death is often "untimely" and sometimes leaves man "without [the] space" he needs to complete his life's work. In making the butterfly he defies these boundaries, however, if only for a short time. He has brought back to life the spirit of all the "child-angels" and "departed infants" who once chased butterflies "across the meads of Paradise," and he has created a thing of such "perfect beauty" that "the mind could not have been more filled or satisfied." Yet his achievement has been made possible by his acceptance of the limits that ultimately prevail. When the butterfly tries to return to him after touching the ceiling—"that earthly medium"—he says, "Thou hast gone forth out of thy master's heart. There is no return for thee."

Through his struggle Owen gains the strength which his project requires and the confidence necessary for its completion. Anxious "lest death should surprise him in the midst of his labors" he is no longer either hopeless or fearless but possessed of both a "sense of insecurity" appropriate to one who has acknowledged the fact of mortality and a "vital faith in [his] invulnerability" appropriate to one who knows, as Hawthorne says in "The Christmas Banquet," that "mortal griefs are but shadowy and external; no more than the sable robes, voluminously shrouding a certain divine reality, and thus indicating what might otherwise be altogether invisible to mortal eye." And having transcended both the deluded hopes of his earlier days and the equally vain fears induced by his critics, he is able to create something valuable to himself and to the world as well. His judgment equal to his genius, he is capable of journeying, like the child pictured on his jewel box, from earth to heaven, and, like the Danforths' child "who had come mysteriously out of the infinite," from heaven to earth again.

Thus, in the face of even Annie's scorn, Owen remains composed and unaffected: "in the latter stages of his pursuit, [he] had risen out of the region in which such a discovery might have been torture." He explains "calmly" to his friends that the butterfly is doomed "[i]n an atmosphere of doubt and mockery," which he now regards as inevitable. And "he look[s] placidly at what seemed the ruin of his life's labor, and which was yet no ruin." Having traversed the course of development which Wordsworth describes in "Intimations of Immortality"—wandering innocently through woods and meadows, feeling the bliss of blessed creatures, celebrating in an imaginary dance and funeral the mirth and melancholy he little understands, and finally watching the once-bright radiance fade away from him—he admits that the "butterfly is not now to [him] what it was when [he] beheld it afar off, in the daydreams of [his] youth." And he is touched with the melancholy of Wordsworth's final stanza: "with a momentary light of triumph in his eyes and a smile of sunshine, yet steeped in such depth of thought that it was almost sadness."

Owen becomes at last the artist in "*ideal* perfection," as Coleridge describes him, bringing "the whole soul of man into activity, with the subordination of its faculties to each other, according to their relative worth and dignity." By reconciling the artist and the critic in his own nature, he is able to balance idea and image, novelty and familiarity, and enthusiasm and self-possession. He is able to do so, however, only after he has undergone a "severe, but inevitable test." Ideas are "real to him . . . without the toil, and perplexity, and many disappointments" of trying to make them real to others only as long as he "content[s] himself with the inward enjoyment of the Beautiful." Yet, again, it is inevitable that he "chase the flitting mystery beyond the verge of his ethereal domain, *and crush its frail being in seizing it with a material grasp!*" (my italics).

In this way Hawthorne shows that both effort and failure are unavoidable steps in the creative process. And the plump, sagacious child who is both spirit and matter, skeptic and believer, is at once a given in the moral universe and an extension of the now plumper and more sagacious artist who ultimately bears full responsibility for both the life and the death of his creation. His fall into doubt and despair is thus an "inevitable change" because he must lose the illusion that the enemy lies outside himself and that the limits of art are imposed by something other than its own nature: "This so frequent abortion of man's dearest projects must be taken as a proof, that the deeds of the earth, however etherealized by piety and genius, are without value, except as exercises and manifestations of the spirit." Like Carlyle's Diogenes Teufelsdröckh, Owen must leave his apprenticeship, love and lose a beautiful young maiden, pass through the Centre of Indifference, that is, the loss of hope and fear, recognize his own inadequacies, and accept the temporal and spatial boundaries of the material universe, before he can attain this wisdom.

The dominant image of "The Artist of the Beautiful," the butterfly which represents at once the artist, his inspiration, and his creationa, is a common metaphor in the works of the Romantics. Hawthorne could have found examples of it in two of Wordsworth's early poems, both entitled "To a Butterfly," in which the butterfly calls forth memories of childhood. In both poems, it reminds the poet of chasing butterflies long ago and innocent summer days of sunshine and song. It is the "Historian of [his] infancy" because it revives "dead times." As an image of the poet's soul, the butterfly appears in Coleridge's "Psyche," where it is "The butterfly the ancient Greeks made / The soul's fair emblem." In *Biographia Literaria* it stands for "the philosophic imagination" which bridges the gap between ideal and actual:

> They and they only can acquire the philosophic imagination, the sacred power of self-intuition, who within themselves can interpret and understand the symbol, that the wings of the air-sylph are forming within the skin of the caterpillar; those only, who feel in their own spirits the same instinct, which impels the chrysalis of the horned fly to leave room in its involucrum for antennae yet to come. They know and feel, that the *potential* works *in* them, even as the *actual* works on them!

In this context, it is easy to understand what Hawthorne means when he says that Owen has represented "a lofty moral by a material trifle." As Wordsworth says, "The commerce between Man and Maker cannot be carried on but by a process where much is represented in little, and the Infinite Being accommodates himself to a finite capacity."

Similarly, in *Sartor Resartus* the butterfly is a symbol of the process by which man becomes more fully human. "Wilt thou know a Man, above all a Mankind," asks Teufelsdröckh, "by stringing-together bedrolls of what thou namest Facts? The Man is the spirit he worked in; not what he did, but what he became." Carlyle comments, "The imprisoned Chrysalis is now a winged Psyche: and such, wheresoever be its flight, it will continue." The butterfly's slumber is evidently the "healing sleep" of the soul's nadir, at the Centre of Indifference, which precedes its awakening to "a new Heaven and a new Earth." And after his self-annihilation, the man of genius is ready to acknowledge, in Teufelsdröckh's words, that "the Ideal is in thyself, the impediment too is in thyself: thy Condition is but the stuff thou art to shape that same Ideal out of." Finally, like Owen Warland, having passed "through the various successive states and stages of Growth, Entanglement, Unbelief, and almost Reprobation," he is ready to enter "a certain clearer state of what he himself seems to consider as Conversion."

The idea of transformation which the butterfly represents is not, of course, the exclusive property of the Romantics. It is the central theme of Hawthorne's favorite writers, especially Milton, who along with the Romantics are distinguishable from the "neoclassicists" of the seventeenth, eighteenth, and nineteenth centuries not only by their emphasis on self-transcendence but also by their view of art as the highest human endeavor and their view of the creative process as an expression of the whole soul of man. They define it not as Johnson, Kames, Campbell, Blair, and their predecessors do, as an act which makes use of two distinct and specialized faculties, imagination and understanding, but as an act in which genius and judgment combine to form a wholly new faculty or, better, in which all emotional and intellectual resources work together as one. And the whole is greater than the sum of its parts. In this view the creative act is simply a recapitulation of the artist's self-transcendence. In other words, the protean imagination which is the source of his creativity is also the product of his moral and psychological transformation. And his artistic labor and its result are thus the final manifestation of his metamorphosis.

This theme is prominent throughout Hawthorne's work, most obviously in many of his sketches, and in most of his stories about young couples. Such essays as "The Haunted Mind," "Sights from a Steeple," and "Night Sketches" follow the pattern of "The Artist of the Beautiful" in their movement from naive optimism to equally naive pessimism and finally to a vision of redemption. And the same may be said of "The Maypole of Merry Mount," "The Canterbury Pilgrims," and "The Great Carbuncle." These works are modeled on the three-part structure of Wordsworth's "Intimations" and "Tintern Abbey" and Coleridge's *Ancient Mariner* and "Frost at Midnight." Though Hawthorne appears to be anti-Romantic in most of his major stories, he is critical even there not of the Romanticism which has its roots in Spenser, Shakespeare, and Milton but of its more extreme representatives of the early nineteenth century, the origins of which are more narrowly either Platonic or skeptical. In "The Birthmark," "Rappaccini's Daughter," "The Gentle Boy," "My Kinsman, Major Molineux," and "Lady Eleanore's Mantle," Hawthorne challenges the unreproved idealism of the Concord Transcendentalists, and in "The Prophetic Pictures," "Ethan Brand," "The Minister's Black Veil," and "Young Goodman Brown," he objects to the unredeemed melancholia of the satanic school. With Carlyle he would have his readers put away their Byron and read Goethe. And with Coleridge he would have them forget the Neoplatonists and take up Kant.

RICHARD BRENZO

Beatrice Rappaccini: A Victim of Male Love and Horror

Critics have been fascinated by Nathaniel Hawthorne's "Rappaccini's Daughter," a tale which has proved as elusive, ambiguous, symbolic, and intimidating as Beatrice Rappaccini is in the eyes of Giovanni Guasconti. Roy R. Male sees the story as an allegory, rich in ambiguity, about a conflict between "idealistic" faith "and materialistic skepticism," with Beatrice symbolizing the first, Baglioni the second, and Giovanni caught between the two. Frederick C. Crews emphasizes the psychosexual elements of the tale, characterizing Giovanni as "another Hawthorne protagonist who regresses to juvenile nausea over female sexuality." Other scholars view the tale as an allegory of corrupted and pure nature, or emphasize the attack on single-minded scientific inquiry, represented by Doctor Rappaccini. These interpretations have validity, especially Crews's stress on the sexual quality of Beatrice's allure. However, what I find striking is the story's concern with the relationship of three men to a woman, who, though she never deliberately harms any of them, and though the men profess to have her good in mind, is nevertheless destroyed by them.

The tale is a partial allegory; Beatrice's poisonous nature as well as the garden and its contents are to be understood symbolically, and the relationship of the woman with her lover, her father, and to a lesser extent her professional rival, Baglioni, are typical male-female pairings. Yet the characters must exhibit credible attitudes, motives, and responses if the story's ethical content is to have any validity. For this tale, like *The Scarlet Letter,*

From *American Literature* 48, no. 2 (May 1976). © 1976 by Duke University Press.

"The Birthmark," and "Ethan Brand," concerns the exploitation of one person by another, for love, for revenge, for science, or simply for curiosity.

In "Rappaccini's Daughter" this exploitation is carried on for a different reason by each of the male characters. All their motives are based on Beatrice's *femaleness,* although her *sexuality* is the prime motive only for Giovanni. She becomes a focus for these men's fantasies, fears, and desires, and is credited with (or at least punished for) various evil intentions which in fact spring from within the minds of the three men. In the language of psychology, Giovanni, Rappaccini, and Baglioni "project" upon Beatrice impulses they are unwilling to acknowledge as their own. Ethan Brand finally learns that the greatest sin lies in the human heart, in fact, in his own heart. But neither Giovanni, Rappaccini, nor Baglioni ever gains a similar insight.

The central symbol of the tale is not Beatrice, the garden, or the gorgeous flower, but the poison which pervades all three. Poison usually symbolizes death, but here the effect seems more fearsome because more subtle, rendering the victims contagious to others without killing them. However, the poison causes a death of sorts, since it isolates its victims from most previous or future human relationships. This isolation is precisely what causes Beatrice her greatest sorrow.

Yet the poison itself is introduced by a man, her father; it is not inherent in the woman. This extremely important point is underlined by the tale Baglioni relates to Giovanni of how an Indian prince sent a woman as a gift to Alexander the Great. This beautiful woman had been "nourished with poisons from her birth upward." The prince had expected Alexander to be poisoned when he had relations with the woman. "'With that rich perfume of her breath, she blasted the very air. Her love would have been poison!—her embrace death! Is not this a marvellous tale?'" The Indian prince, like Rappaccini, is obviously responsible for impregnating the woman's system with poison; yet he is mentioned only once, while Baglioni's retelling dwells on the woman's beauty and deadliness. Although Baglioni knows, and Giovanni eventually learns, who is responsible for Beatrice's envenomed body, their efforts to thwart Rappaccini's power are aimed at his innocent daughter, who stirs their imaginations far more than does her father.

The inclusion of this tale by "an old classic author" also universalizes the significance of Hawthorne's allegory. "Rappaccini's Daughter" is his variation on the "femme fatale" legend, one of the most prevalent myths of literature and folklore. She is the woman whose embrace is death, who destroys, degrades, devours, and enslaves her lovers. But neither Beatrice nor the Indian woman is this kind of female, essentially malignant, deliberately harmful to men.

Let us first look at Giovanni's behavior, since his relationship with Beatrice forms the main plot of the story. The young man is infatuated with her from the moment he first sees her in the garden below her window. Yet he immediately senses something dangerous about her, especially because of her resemblance and immunity to the purple-flowered plant which her father carefully avoids. "Flower and maiden were different and yet the same, and fraught with some strange peril in either shape." Significantly, this feeling comes to him in a dream, showing how Giovanni's own fancy begins almost immediately to influence his idea of the woman. Moreover, other imagery suggests that maiden and flower are not only sisters but lovers, adding a sense of perversion to Giovanni's sexual fear of Beatrice.

Since Giovanni's imagination is provoked by his very first observance of Beatrice and her surroundings, it is difficult for him to focus on the reality of who and what she is. In the following passage, notice how his thoughts quickly move away from the actuality of Beatrice to metaphors created by his mind.

> "Here am I, my father! What would you?" cried a rich and youthful voice from the window of the opposite house; a voice as rich as a tropical sunset, and which made Giovanni, though he knew not why, think of deep hues of purple or crimson, and of perfumes heavily delectable. . . .
>
> Soon there emerged from under a sculptured portal the figure of a young girl, arrayed with as much richness of taste as the most splendid of the flowers . . . with a bloom so deep and vivid that one shade more would have been too much. . . . the impression which the fair stranger made upon him was as if here were another flower, the human sister of those vegetable ones, as beautiful as they . . . but still to be touched only with a glove, nor to be approached without a mask.

The association of Beatrice with the plant is only partially correct. Although both are beautiful, rich, and perilous, Beatrice has human qualities which make her more than Giovanni's fantasies. She loves beautiful things, she wants to love, she is able to laugh, to think, and to sacrifice herself, as the reader later discovers. The two words used most frequently to describe her are "rich" and "deep," both indicating an abundance of character, beauty, and knowledge, not all of which, however, may be apparent on first view.

The next time Giovanni watches Beatrice, he notices with horror that an insect buzzing near her suddenly falls dead, and that a bouquet he tosses her seems to wither as soon as she catches it. Giovanni avoids the window for several days, yet cannot bring himself to vacate his chambers or get used to Beatrice's daily routine. Hawthorne brilliantly describes the emotions she has aroused in the young man.

> Whether or no Beatrice possessed those terrible attributes—that fatal breath—the affinity with those so beautiful and deadly flowers—which were indicated by what Giovanni had witnessed, she had at least instilled a fierce and subtle poison into his system. It was not love, although her rich beauty was a madness to him; nor horror, even while he fancied her spirit to be imbued with the same baneful essence that seemed to pervade her physical frame; but a wild offspring of both love and horror that had each parent in it, and burned like one and shivered like the other. Giovanni knew not what to dread; still less did he know what to hope; . . . Blessed are all simple emotions, be they dark or bright! It is the lurid intermixture of the two that produces the illuminating blaze of the infernal regions.

Giovanni's dreads are indefinable, yet potent and monstrous; his "love and horror" are reactions to the "embrace" and the "death" he associates with the sexuality of Beatrice. The passage makes it clear Beatrice is not trying to seduce Giovanni in any sense. He "fancies" her spirit is full of a "baneful essence" because the vague evidences of her poisonous system are seized upon and magnified by fears already present in his psyche.

Giovanni's first meeting with Beatrice, which occurs after he has admired her for some time, shows his continual difficulty in separating his image of her from reality. His two talks with Baglioni have also contributed to his feeling that there is something sinister about Rappaccini and his daughter, without giving him much of a clue as to why they are threatening. Significantly, Beatrice warns him almost at once to "'Believe nothing of me save what you see with your own eyes.'" Since what Giovanni has seen with his own eyes has only confused him, he responds with "'Bid me believe nothing, save what comes from your own lips.'" Her reply goes straight to the heart of the story: "'I do so bid you, Signor!' she replied, 'Forget whatever you may have fancied in regard to me. If true to the outward senses, still it may be false in its essence. But the words of Beatrice Rappaccini's lips are true from the depths of the heart outward. Those you may believe!'" Giovanni is deeply impressed by this statement. "He seemed to gaze through the beautiful girl's eyes into her transparent soul, and felt no more doubt or fear." For a moment, her mystery, on which his imagination feeds, disappears, although she does not seem thereby shallow or less intriguing. As they talk, Giovanni notes that her thoughts seem to come "from a deep source"; the young man is surprised that the woman "whom he had idealized in such hues of terror" should turn out to be "so human and so maidenlike. . . . the effect of her character was too real, not to make itself familiar at once."

For Beatrice the conversation is also a milestone, since Giovanni's presence makes her forget the shrub with purple blossoms for the first time. Despite her many virtues, her personality is incomplete, since her love has been directed towards a plant, not a human being. She immediately demonstrates her concern for Giovanni's welfare; when he reaches to pluck one of the purple flowers, she warns him away: "'Touch it not!' exclaimed she, in a voice of agony. 'Not for thy life! It is fatal!'" Giovanni later forgets this concern for his safety.

After he returns to his room, Giovanni's thoughts of Beatrice are a mingling of his imaginings with the reality he has experienced.

> The image of Beatrice came back to his passionate musings, invested with all the witchery that had been gathering around it ever since his first glimpse of her, and now likewise imbued with a tender warmth of girlish womanhood. She was human: her nature was endowed with all gentle and feminine qualities; she was worthiest to be worshipped; she was capable, surely, on her part, of the height and heroism of love. Those tokens, which he had hitherto considered as proofs of a frightful peculiarity in her physical and moral system, were now either forgotten, or, by the subtle sophistry of passion, transmuted into a golden crown of enchantment.

Now Giovanni idealizes her, and his idealization ignores the real, though not willful, perils in her "physical system." Swinging between the two classic extremes of viewing woman as demon or as saint, he never finds a basis in reality for his feelings about Beatrice. Hawthorne hints that Giovanni feels only a "cunning semblance of love which flourishes in the imagination, but finds no depth of root into the heart."

Giovanni continues to meet Beatrice, now with her full approval, and even at her insistence. All "appreciable signs," such as their looks and words, indicate they are in love. Yet there is a distance between them; their love has no sexual dimension, "no seal of lips, no clasp of hands, nor any slightest caress, such as love claims and hallows." Giovanni wants this physical intimacy, yet when he seeks it, Beatrice gives him "such a look of desolate separation" that he gives up his attempts. If we understand the story literally,

Beatrice avoids this contact because she fears contaminating him. But is there a deeper meaning behind her avoidance of physical contact?

Giovanni's reactions provide a clue. Beatrice's reluctance causes "horrible suspicions that rose, monster-like, out of the caverns of his heart, and stared him in the face; his love grew thin and faint as the morning-mist." Giovanni has not really shed his mistrust of Beatrice. The strength of his love decreases when she appears sad and increases when she appears happy; it has no firm roots in his heart. Love may "hallow" kisses, caresses, and deeper sexual contact, but Giovanni's love is limited and unhallowed. Unless he can free himself from the "horrible suspicions" which arise when Beatrice avoids his touches (suspicions which indicate his inability to look past her "physical system" to her "moral system") he is not prepared for the risks and commitments of sexual love.

His "horrible suspicions" seem related to fear of the "embrace of death," symbolized by the poison in Beatrice's system. There is no suggestion that Giovanni feels "castrated" or inadequate because she has rejected his sexual advances. Rather, he seems to desire sexual union, while fearing its dangers. Ironically, Beatrice's reluctance itself brings about his suspicions that there must be something deadly in her, which could be unleashed upon him if he has relations with her. For Giovanni, sexual commitment to Beatrice means "death" in the sense of being dominated by a woman, being robbed of his independence, and having his personality swallowed up. Beatrice actually makes no attempt to bind him to her; actually, she professes to want "'only to love thee, and be with thee a little time, and so to let thee pass away, leaving but thine image in mine heart.'" It is hard to believe this statement could reflect Beatrice's deepest feelings, of which she may be unaware. "Pass away" may also have two meanings, although I doubt we should assume Beatrice expects Giovanni's death. In this matter, his insight seems deeper than hers; he knows his involvement with Beatrice must be permanent, while she, ignorant of the power of her sexuality, underestimates the difficulties of separating her destiny from Giovanni's. In fact, Giovanni has a real compulsion to possess Beatrice, to change and control her, a compulsion revealed by his attempts to know her sexually, and by his persistent desire to shape her into his personal image of the divine woman.

The great proof of the instability of Giovanni's love and of his wish to possess Beatrice comes when he decides to test her by observing whether her breath wilts a bouquet he plans to give her. His third conversation with Baglioni has driven him to this trial, since Baglioni has warned him that he may be the subject of an experiment conducted by Rappaccini, with his daughter's unwitting assistance. "'The fair and learned Signora Beatrice would minister to her patients with draughts as sweet as a maiden's breath. But woe to him that sips them!'" Baglioni gives Giovanni an antidote which he maintains will cure Beatrice's poisonous nature and foil Rappaccini's schemes. Giovanni, whose latent suspicions are once again aroused "like so many demons," defends Beatrice's honesty and virtue, but he cannot refute Baglioni's claim that she is "poisonous as she is beautiful!" Therefore, he buys the flowers for the test, and also accepts the antidote. In doing so, he ignores Beatrice's earlier instructions not to believe what he sees, but only what she tells him.

Just before Giovanni leaves to test Beatrice, he looks vainly in his mirror, an action displaying "a certain shallowness of feeling and insincerity of character." His shallowness contrasts with earlier descriptions of Beatrice's depth. Unsuspecting, he admires his overhealthy complexion, and thinks "'her poison has not yet insinuated itself into my system. I am no flower to perish in her grasp!'" Immediately thereafter, he discovers that the flowers have withered in his own hand, apparently from the poison in his own breath. With his worst fears confirmed, he hears Beatrice calling him, and mutters, "'She is the only being whom my breath may not slay! Would that it might!'" Here is proof that the deadly intent he attributes to her is within himself as well.

Although Giovanni has been repeatedly warned that Rappaccini is using Beatrice to harm him, and although he has continually observed Rappaccini spying on him and his daughter, still the young man's fascination and fear are always focused on Beatrice, not on her father. In their last meeting Giovanni accuses her: "'Yes, poisonous thing! . . . Thou hast done it! Thou hast blasted me! Thou hast filled my veins with poison! Thou hast made me as hateful, as ugly, as loathsome and deadly a creature as thyself . . . . let us join our lips in one kiss of unutterable hatred, and so die!'" The motives he attributes to her are really his own, as noted previously. Giving her the antidote is his attempt to remake her into his ideal woman. Only he feels "unutterable hatred." More generous than he, Beatrice tells him to wait before drinking the antidote, so he can first observe the effects on her body. Although she is willing to sacrifice her life for him, he is willing to sacrifice nothing for her. Giovanni has respect neither for what little independence Beatrice has, nor for her personal integrity, where both virtues and faults are inextricably entangled, as they are in everyone. His "love" requires a woman who will gratify his ego and conform to his fantasies. Beatrice makes no such demands on him and is unaware until their last meeting that he has become poisoned. Therefore, she is entirely correct when she asks him, "Oh, was there not, from the first, more poison in thy nature than in mine?" The poison in her "physical system" is far less deadly than the venom in his "moral system."

Although Baglioni acts with more deliberation than does Giovanni, his attitudes and behavior resemble those of the young man. Superficially, Baglioni appears a benevolent character, concerned with the welfare of his old friend's son, and intent on exposing and frustrating the schemes of Rappaccini. Yet although Baglioni realizes Rappaccini is the source of the evil, Beatrice is the target of his attempts to combat this evil. In fact, he sees her as a real danger to his position at the University, telling Giovanni, "'she is already qualified to fill a professor's chair. Perchance her father destines her for mine!'" That this fear is groundless is proved by Beatrice's subsequent denial. "'Do people say that I am skilled in my father's science of plants? . . . No; though I have grown up among these flowers, I know no more of them than their hues and perfume; and sometimes, methinks I would fain rid myself of even that small knowledge.'" Clearly, she is not happy with the life her father has forced upon her.

Baglioni, not Beatrice, seeks academic triumph and status. He wants to discredit Rappaccini, about whom he has mixed feelings; he fears and envies, yet also admires the doctor. Perhaps Baglioni suspects that Rappaccini possesses a greater knowledge of medicine and botany than he himself does. He acknowledges only grudgingly that Rappaccini has had success treating the sick with his medicines, whose "'virtues are comprised within those substances which we term vegetable poisons.'" Later, Baglioni warns Giovanni that "'for some purpose or other, this man of science is making a study of you. I know that look of his! It is the same that coldly illuminates his face, as he bends over a bird, a mouse, or a butterfly, which, in pursuance of some experiment, he has killed by the perfume of a flower;—a look as deep as Nature itself, but without Nature's warmth of love.'" Baglioni's callous manipulation of Giovanni and Beatrice later on shows how well he fits his own description of Rappaccini. That his hatred of the doctor is mixed with genuine admiration is shown by his remarks after he gives Giovanni the antidote (itself a poison). "'Let us confess the truth of him, he is a wonderful man!—a wonderful man indeed! A vile empiric, however, in his practice, and therefore not to be tolerated by those who respect the good old rules of the medical profession.'"

After their first meeting, Giovanni avoids Baglioni, afraid that the professor may detect his secret passion for Beatrice. However, Baglioni stops him in the street, warning him that Rappaccini has taken a sinister interest in him. When Giovanni leaves, we discover Baglioni's motives are not simply benevolent, but are instead a complex mixture of friendship, envy, professional rivalry, and fear of Beatrice's threat to his academic chair: "'This must not be. . . . The youth is the son of my old friend, and shall not come to any harm from which the arcana of medical science can preserve him. Besides, it is too insufferable an impertinence in Rappaccini, thus to snatch the lad out of my own hands, as I may say, and make use of him for his infernal experiments. This daughter of his! It shall be looked to. Perchance, most learned Rappaccini, I may foil you where you little dream of it!'" Possessive of Giovanni, Baglioni observes and fears the same possessiveness in Rappaccini. The young man's instincts are correct in making him avoid Baglioni, for the latter makes Giovanni his tool for destroying the Rappaccinis. If Baglioni feels threatened by Rappaccini, then the thought of a woman being his intellectual superior and displacing him from his position must be doubly frightening. To be outdone by Rappaccini would be "insufferable"; to be outdone by Beatrice would be utterly disgraceful.

Thus, Baglioni's self-righteous denunciation of the doctor at the very end of the tale is not really a moral judgment, but primarily the gloating satisfaction of an academician exposing the error of a colleague. "Baglioni . . . called loudly, in a tone of triumph mixed with horror, . . . 'Rappaccini! Rappaccini! And is *this* the upshot of your experiment?'" Why "mixed with horror"? Perhaps we are to believe Baglioni has not anticipated that Beatrice would die, only that the antidote would thwart Rappaccini by disenvenoming his daughter, thus releasing her from her father's control. If Baglioni has miscalculated the drug's effect, perhaps his knowledge is not as great as he pretends. Or perhaps Baglioni, like Rappaccini, is conducting an experiment, testing on Beatrice a drug of whose effect he is unsure. Thus, the horror may be inner-directed, since Baglioni's final question could be asked of himself as well as of Rappaccini. And if Baglioni knows the antidote will be fatal, he is a murderer.

When considering Rappaccini's relationship with his daughter, it is important to look first of all at the story's title. While apparently merely descriptive, it emphasizes that Beatrice is her father's creation; she springs from him. She is dependent on him, and is his unwitting tool. We cannot judge the daughter without looking past her to her father.

Rappaccini is a difficult man to judge, however, since so much of our information about him comes through the deeply biased Baglioni. Nevertheless, Baglioni is right about certain things. Rappaccini is a schemer; he does have sinister plans for Giovanni. He is also arrogant, ruthless, and cunning, but above all he is obsessed with power, the power to intimidate and the power to control. True, Baglioni accuses him of sacrificing "'human life, his own among the rest, or whatever else was dearest to him, for the sake of adding so much as a grain of mustard-seed to the great heap of his accumulated knowledge.'" Yet Rappaccini's statements at the end of the tale show clearly that this quest for knowledge is in turn subservient to his need for power. The exact nature of his schemes is unclear; are Giovanni and Beatrice to be his agents in a play for some sort of social or even political power? However, Rappaccini is a plotter and activator, not a doer. Therefore he needs Beatrice as his instrument.

Rappaccini is gratified when he learns Giovanni is also envenomed, so that he and Beatrice can pass "'through the world, most dear to one another, and dreadful to all besides!'" Suspicious and isolated himself, he cannot understand why his daughter mourns her loneliness and spurns the power his science has given her. Like Giovanni and Baglioni, he projects his own selfish desires onto Beatrice, and therefore blames her, not himself, when she refuses to go along with his scheme. "'What mean you, foolish girl? Dost thou deem it misery to be endowed with marvellous gifts, against which no power nor strength could avail an enemy? Misery, to be able to quell the mightiest with a breath? . . . Wouldst thou, then, have preferred the condition of a weak woman, exposed to all evil, and capable of none?' 'I would fain have been loved, not feared,' murmured Beatrice."

Supremely ironic is Rappaccini's rhetorical question about whether Beatrice would prefer to be a "weak woman." By isolating her, he has kept her ignorant, dependent on him, and therefore weak. He needs a weak daughter, weak enough to let him experiment on and through her. Moreover, although Rappaccini claims the poison will benefit Beatrice, it is really a punishment. He does not expose himself to it, after all. We may assume that if he approaches the plant with a mask and heavy gloves, he must also approach Beatrice in the same cautious manner. His experiments have created a daughter towards whom his attitude, like Giovanni's, must be essentially fear, covered by only a "cunning semblance" of love. The power Rappaccini has given his daughter is ultimately for his own use, not for her protection. Ironically, her poison makes her vulnerable to the power of the outside world in a way Rappaccini has not anticipated. Beatrice most needs protection from her father, who is her worst enemy, and the one person whom his science cannot prevent from harming her.

Ultimately, the poison in the natures of Giovanni, Baglioni, and Rappaccini represents their own fears, obsessions, ambitions, and unhealthy desires. The poison they see (and fear) in Beatrice is actually the evil they cannot admit is in themselves. This idea is dramatized by Rappaccini's deliberate poisoning of his daughter, an act which makes her dangerous to himself and others. Having poisoned her, they cannot bear the thought that she may poison (control, displace, rebel against) them. Even though each man knows, intellectually, that she is an unwitting tool, each has psychological needs which must find a victim, a target, or a vehicle.

Giovanni has a destructive need to dominate and possess Beatrice; this is precisely the quality he finds most threatening in his idea of her. Baglioni imagines Beatrice is about to make a conquest of his academic chair; in fact, he desires to score a triumph over Rappaccini by neutralizing his daughter. He plans to discredit Rappaccini's experiments by performing equally reprehensible experiments himself. Her father, whose experiments with poisons are intended to make others fear him, assumes Beatrice is also moved by a wish to be feared. The poison he loves and fears in her is really the destructive impulse in his own being. All three men are right, of course, in mistrusting each other and even fearing Beatrice. But their sin lies in taking their revenge on Beatrice, instead of directing their enmity at each other or better still, trying to heal themselves.

As I have said, the men's motives and the story's meaning depend on Beatrice's femaleness. Each man represents a typical male role, and the story examines how men playing each role might find a woman threatening, and might therefore try to destroy her. Giovanni, her lover and almost-husband, desires her sexuality, yet fears its power to dominate and destroy him. Baglioni, her professional rival, feeling insecure about his university position, tries to neutralize her by diverting her energies to woman's proper sphere, marriage. Her father wants her beautiful enough to win a husband, dependent enough to remain in his home, obedient enough to do his bidding, and compliant enough to be molded to his standards. None of these men could have been portrayed as feeling these same fears, with the same intensity, about a man. Notice, for example, that Baglioni views his struggle with Rappaccini almost as a game, with a rather gentlemanly tone. Only with Beatrice does he play for keeps.

And the fate of Beatrice anticipates the fates of later women in literature, in *The Awakening, The Bell Jar,* even in *A Streetcar Named Desire*. Educated for a life of sacrifice, Beatrice can respond to the irrational fears of men only with one more sacrifice. It is unclear whether she knows that drinking the antidote will be fatal, but the "peculiar emphasis" she puts on the words "'I will drink—but do thou await the result'" indicates that she suspects it will be deadly and accepts her death quite happily while saving Giovanni's life at the same time. The final irony is the reversal of Baglioni's story of the Indian woman. As Hawthorne suggests, one must look beyond such femmes fatales to the hommes fatals who make them deadly. Giovanni, Rappaccini, even Baglioni, have professed a desire to help Beatrice, while secretly fearing her "embrace of death." Consequently, they have embraced her—offer her help—in their own selfish, vengeful, scientific ways, and for her their embrace has meant—death.

RICHARD H. BRODHEAD

New and Old Tales: The Scarlet Letter

This news, which is called true, is so like an old tale that the verity of it is in strong suspicion.
—*The Winter's Tale*

The Scarlet Letter is at the same time Hawthorne's debut in a new artistic medium and a kind of restrospective exhibit of his work. No other of his novels is so close to the preoccupations of his tales. His choice of chronological setting aligns the book with all his studies of the historical past, and in particular with his explorations of the energetic restrictiveness of the Puritans in tales like "The Maypole of Merry Mount" and "Endicott and the Red Cross." The dramas that Hawthorne enacts in this setting are also familiar ones. Dimmesdale's experience exhibits the self-destructive operations of concealed guilt and the obsession with sin portrayed in "Roger Malvin's Burial" and "Young Goodman Brown"; Roger Chillingworth's passionate intellectual curiosity looks back to Ethan Brand's, and he shares Brand's experience of willed violation of others and the unwilled dehumanization of the self. In composing *The Scarlet Letter* Hawthorne seems purposely to gather together the themes—historical, moral, psychological—that have given his work its distinct identity; then, by integrating them and projecting them onto a larger canvas, he manages to eclipse his earlier achievements exactly by fully realizing their subjects' interest and potential.

When *The Scarlet Letter* is approached through Hawthorne's tales its

---

status as an almost self-conscious culmination of his artistic career is the first thing that is striking; the second is the confidence with which Hawthorne proceeds to execute his larger design. The rightness of the opening scene as a suggestive introduction to the novel's major concerns; the gradual but steady unfolding of its action, in which Hawthorne unobtrusively scores in part after part; the firm balance of continuing action and authorial exposition—all demonstrate his assured artistry as a novelist and serve to announce, in an understated way, his mastery of his new craft.

The first scene of *The Scarlet Letter* involves the punishment of the convicted adulteress, Hester Prynne, by public exposure on the scaffold in the Boston marketplace. The scene unfolds with a slow and deliberate pace. Before he allows Hester to appear, Hawthorne focuses our attention on the prison door, meditating on it in such a way as both to localize it in a specific time and place and to see in it a dark exigency, a "black flower of civilized society." Then he allows the point of view to pass over to other observers of this scene, a group of Puritan women. In their comments—ranging from a legalistic, punitive desire to brand or execute the adulteress to a softer voice that recognizes the anguish of the victim of punishment—Hawthorne affords us a series of vantage points by which to frame our own initial response to Hester. But in offering possible attitudes in this way the women do not cease to be participants in a specific scene. They are part of the audience before which Hester is to be exposed, and by surrounding Hester's emergence with their reactions Hawthorne makes us see the experience of his main characters from the first as being bounded by, as well as the affair of, a larger society. His own commentary emphasizes the nature of the community the women represent. By placing them near the age of "man-like Elizabeth" and contrasting them with the paler women of his own day he sees their coarseness of body and speech in relation to a specific moment in a historical evolution. Their sentiments are understood historically as well, as exemplifications of "the early severity of the Puritan character." In their concern with the rigid administration of punishment to a criminal and sinner they exhibit the special outlook of "a people amongst whom religion and law were almost identical." Through them we recognize the values by which their society defines itself and also the quality of private feeling that upholds those values, "the general sentiment which gives law its vitality."

By choosing the punishment of Hester as his first scene Hawthorne is able to reveal the Puritan community in what seems to him its most essential aspect, enacting its deepest social and religious values. The scene is typical of his handling of the Puritans in *The Scarlet Letter* in its focus on their celebration of their community's own special nature and its bonds of authority. We see this again in the Election Day scene which balances this one at the book's conclusion. In both cases he is unusually attentive to what he calls "the forms of authority," the ceremonious behavior through which they act out their values. The comments of the chorus of women end when the prison door opens and the town beadle emerges, "with a sword by his side and his staff of office in his hand."

> This personage prefigured and represented in his aspect the whole dismal severity of the Puritanic code of law, which it was his business to administer in its final and closest application to the offender. Stretching forth the official staff in his left hand, he laid his right upon the shoulder of a young woman, whom he thus drew forward.

The action here has the stylization of a ritual. The beadle submerges his individual personality into his role as agent of justice, identified by appropriate emblems. He acts out that role in his ceremonious gesture, converting Hester's emergence into a carefully contrived visual allegory of civil and spiritual righteousness: "A blessing on the righteous Colony of Massachusetts, where iniquity is dragged out into the sunshine!"

But his ritual is disrupted. Hester pushes his staff aside and walks forward "as if by her own free-will." This is Hester's first act, and its resonance is amplified by the next detail Hawthorne presents: "On the breast of her gown, in fine red cloth, surrounded with an elaborate embroidery and fantastic flourishes of gold thread, appeared the letter A." The Puritan pageant casts Hester as Iniquity; the A they impose on her is the symbolic badge of her office, that of Adulteress. Their strict symbolism moves to rigidify experience into formal categories of virtue and sin, and they conceive of their symbols as having sanction for their meaning in divine principles of good and evil. As Hester rejects their pageant she also rejects the code on which it is based. She converts the spectacle of "iniquity dragged forth" into an act proceeding from her own free choice. She accepts the designation of adulteress, but on her own terms; her embroidery of the scarlet letter turns it into a more complex symbol, one that does justice to the inseparable conjunction of something guilty and something vital and fertile in her passionate nature. And while the art of the Puritans' A has the sanction of divine truth, her personalized letter is presented as an act of creative self-expression, a product of her own imagination that has its meaning in terms of her own knowledge of herself.

Hester's rejection or modification of the pageant prefigures the conflict between her and her society, but it also suggests a larger conflict in *The*

Scarlet Letter of which this is only one version, a strife between two modes of experience and understanding: one that tends toward restriction, fixity, and orthodoxy, and one that tends toward a freer expression and recognition of the self's desires, needs, and powers. The moment marks, as well, a turning point in the scene from a social and historical perspective to an individual and psychological one. As Hester mounts the scaffold Hawthorne adopts her point of view, measuring the nature of the assembled crowd now by registering its presence to her consciousness. As he notes her urge to reckless defiance, her anguished shame, and her peculiar defenselessness against the solemnity of the occasion, he qualifies her initial assertion of freedom, enabling us to see the power the community holds over her emotional life. The freedom she does attain here comes through the reveries of her past life that intervene between her and the crowd's awful gaze. At the same time, her daydream finally destroys its own value as a means of escape; as she watches her life unfold she is led back inexorably to the present moment and the present scene.

In presenting Hester's reverie Hawthorne skillfully observes both her psyche's instinctive mechanism of self-protection and her own coming to an awareness that her position on the scaffold is the inevitable outcome of the whole course of her life. His observation here gives us our first glimpse of the exquisite shorthand by which he records the processes of consciousness throughout the novel. In addition to demonstrating his skill as a psychological analyst Hester's reverie also illustrates Hawthorne's more basic craft as a storyteller. *The Scarlet Letter* emphatically opens in the middle of an action, and through this vision he is able to sketch in, in two paragraphs, the past that has led up to this action. Further, Hester's momentary recollection of her husband, "a man well stricken in years, a pale, thin, scholar-like visage . . . with the left shoulder a trifle higher than the right," serves to prepare us for the immediate future. Exactly as Hester's reverie comes to a close we look back out at the scene and recognize, at the edge of the crowd, the figure whom Hester has just seen.

As Hester recognizes her husband her relation to the crowd changes. Their gaze now becomes a "shelter" from the intenser gaze of Chillingworth and from the more specific shame and guilt that she feels before him. The appearance of Chillingworth marks a subtle shift in the action of the scene. The dramatic conflict between Hester and the Puritans gives way to a more private drama involving the characters most intimately connected with the fact of adultery. Thus it is appropriate that in the next scenic transition, to the injunctions of the Puritan magistrates and ministers, what is ostensibly a cut back to the Puritans is actually the occasion for Hawthorne's first introduction of Dimmesdale. The role that Dimmesdale must play in this scene, again, implicitly suggests the whole ambiguity of the position of this "remorseful hypocrite." In urging Hester to reveal the name of her child's father he speaks as the voice of community authority and righteousness. At the same time, the combination of his equivocation—"If thou feelest it to be for thy soul's peace"—and his impassioned appeal that she ease her accomplice of the burden of his secrecy hints at his own part in the plot, reflecting his dread of being, as well as his desperate longing to be, revealed in his true position.

The characters who belong together are now assembled, placed in the suggestive grouping around the scaffold that they will form again in "The Minister's Vigil" and once again when the true relations that that grouping embodies are revealed in the book's final scene. And as it gathers together the characters of this private drama, so too this scene engenders the energies of that drama. Dimmesdale, poised with his hand upon his heart, is seen protecting his secret; Chillingworth's resolution—"He will be known!"—already incarnates his fierce purpose to expose that secret.

A consideration of this much of *The Scarlet Letter* may be enough to demonstrate the remarkable skill of Hawthorne's narrative exposition. Everything that he tells us contributes to our understanding and visualization of this highly charged scene. And without ever going outside that scene in these chapters he manages to establish all the characters, motives, and thematic conflicts that will animate the rest of the book. These chapters serve as well as any others to reveal a persistent feature of Hawthorne's art of the novel, his strict economy.

If the first scene is typical of Hawthorne's artistry, it also exemplifies the sort of fictional world he creates in *The Scarlet Letter.* This world possesses, first, a dense social and historical reality. The feelings and forms of behavior of the Puritan characters are linked to the outlook of a particular group set in a particular moment in time. The prison and the scaffold, located in accordance with the actual topography of early Boston, are also understood as extensions of the Puritans' care for lawful authority and punishment. Hawthorne's concern for accuracy of historical detail is evident throughout the book, but his interest is never merely antiquarian; all his descriptions of physical settings work to exhibit the nature of the society that creates them. This is true even of his minute account of the architecture, furnishings, and garden of Governor Bellingham's hall in the seventh chapter, which seems at first like the one point in the book where he aims at a purely factual description of place. The overbearing defensive outer wall and Bellingham's suit of armor suggest once again the stern militance of the Puritans.

The glass of ale on the table, the comfortable furnishings, and the evidences of a failed attempt to create an English garden show a kind of counterimpulse, an inclination toward a more pleasurable way of life out of which these men of iron try to re-create what they can of the more commodious civilization they have left behind. By the time he finishes his description of the hall Hawthorne has revealed, through the details of the scene, a complex image both of the Puritans' temperament and of the historical situation that gives rise to that temperament, their situation between Elizabethan England and America's hostile and barren strand.

In addition Hawthorne's world possesses a dense psychological reality. He endows his characters with their own individuating tempers and desires, then watches their peculiar consciousness responding to their situations and to one another. If he describes the interior of a house in "The Governor's Hall," much more often he turns to sift the contents of "the interior of a heart." His brief account of Hester's feelings on the scaffold prepares the way for chapters like "Hester at Her Needle," "The Interior of a Heart," "Another View of Hester," and "The Minister in a Maze," chapters which have as their only actions Hawthorne's minute dissections of his characters' inner worlds—their responses to their daily positions before the community, their continuing desires, and the new forms that their desires take under the pressure of their circumstances.

The first chapters also illustrate how Hawthorne animates the social and psychological realities he creates and gives them the forward motion of an action. There are three levels of interaction here, the public one involving the Puritan community, the internal one of feeling, thought, and psychic struggle, and the private drama of interaction among the main characters. Hawthorne's subtle modulations among them prefigure the larger movements of his narrative, which alternates in the same way among communal scenes, introspections of characters seen in isolation, and dramatizations of their personal encounters. Each level generates its own conflicts, such that the initiative of the action can pass back and forth among them. Thus for example the public exposure of Hester rebounds on the nature of Chillingworth in such a way as to generate the jealous and revengeful passion to know that governs his action throughout the story; Dimmesdale's private obsession with penance leads him onto the scaffold at night; and Hester's recognition of his feebleness in their encounter here in turn generates her desire to make Chillingworth known to him and to propose their mutual escape.

The world Hawthorne creates in *The Scarlet Letter* is the final product of the inspiration that he dramatized in "The Custom House," and the nature of this world enables us now to understand more precisely the relation of his inspiration to his process of fictional creation. The scarlet letter comes to him streaming with revelation. But this revelation is peculiarly inarticulate; the "deep meaning in it, most worthy of interpretation" communicates itself to his sensibilities, but it evades "the analysis of my mind." Further, while the letter itself is full of fixating power, the story that accompanies it—the dingy roll of paper pertaining to Hester Prynne—is at this point lifeless and uninteresting to him. In the moonlit room he attempts to spread out his intuited revelation into imagined characters and scenes, to transfer the burning heat of the symbol into a warmth that will animate the participants in his story.

The Scarlet Letter illustrates how Hawthorne does this. He converts the isolated symbol into a badge fashioned by a historical community. The A becomes the Puritans' A, the emblem through which they impose their judgment on a violator of their communal values. The letter thus brings the book's social and historical stratum into being, and by meditating on their use of the symbol Hawthorne can analyze the peculiar nature of the Puritans—their devotion to law and religion, their addiction to formalized behavior, the imaginative outlook inherent in their orthodox symbolism. At the same time the A is a badge for individuals, a token of their act of adultery and the passions that have led to that act, and a mark as well of the complex system of guilt and responsibility that ensues from that act. In this aspect the scarlet letter becomes the focal point of the characters' daily experience and the center of their attention. Chillingworth's vengeful inquiry reaches its first climax when he discovers the letter on Dimmesdale's chest. Dimmesdale's obsession with his guilt is most clearly revealed in his compulsive visions of the letter in the world outside his mind. Hawthorne presents Hester's life as an outcast by recording the variety of responses she feels as others look at her scarlet letter, and he measures her efforts at creative resistance by showing her various modifications of the letter into tentative expressions of a complex truth. He passes his own experience of fixation before the scarlet letter on to his characters; their need, like his own, is to find out or express the meaning of the symbol even as they live out that meaning, if they are to free themselves from its purely obsessive power. As he grounds the letter in his characters' experience and observes their motives and modes of passion before it, the symbol evolves into the dense web of psychological and dramatic relationships in his novel.

By composing a narrative in this way Hawthorne overcomes the tensions within his own creative vision. The symbol and the ingredients of a story come together in a seamless unity in which each manifestation of the letter illuminates an aspect of the characters' or the community's evolving experience. He overcomes, as well, the initial gap between what he calls his sensibilities and his conscious mind. By calling forth dramatic scenes and then analyzing the implications of their actions he achieves a synthesis in which imagining and understanding are continually changing into each other. And there is no sense of a gap here between what he calls the Actual and the Imaginary. He freely draws on both social history and psychic activity, creating his novel's world by engaging the two in a process of dynamic interchange.

The reconciliation of opposites is what gives *The Scarlet Letter* its singular intensity and its consistent formal poise. It also helps to account for some of the characteristics that set this novel apart from the other books I [discuss in *Hawthorne, Melville, and the Novel*]. The world of *The Scarlet Letter* has, for all its complexity, a more uniform reality than do the other novels. It is more generous in the amount of individual life with which it endows its characters, and it adheres more closely to the texture of their experience of themselves and their world. Hawthorne and Melville wrote other books that are as powerfully tragic as this one, but none that has its interest so simply as a moving human drama—"a tale of human frailty and sorrow." One reason for this is that the position of author and reader as imaginative creators is less pronounced and problematic here. In telling his story Hawthorne assumes the role of a concerned yet dispassionate observer, one whose knowledge of the past and skill in the science of the heart enable him to follow the implications of his drama's turns of events with maximum lucidity. He implicitly invites us as readers to join him in accepting his imagined world as real and in bringing to bear on that world a concerned yet finely discriminating attention. Another, related reason is that *The Scarlet Letter* has a more coherent and uniform narrative manner than the other novels. It is significant, for example, that this novel alone does not contain a tale within a tale. Coming to *The Scarlet Letter* from Hawthorne's next two books, with their curious mixtures of modes, or from Melville's fragmented and fictively exuberant novels, we must be struck by its sustained style and tone, its symmetrical structure, and its spare, linear plot. Henry James is right to ascribe to *The Scarlet Letter* "a sort of straightness and naturalness of execution." This is the one case in which the author seems to feel able to do everything he wants to do by embracing the storytelling procedures of the novel in a straightforward way.

These are some of the features that make *The Scarlet Letter* seem to belong, as no other novel of the American Renaissance does, to the mainstream of nineteenth-century fiction in England and Europe. The resemblances go beyond formal practice to include as well the vision of life that form is in the service of. The central place that Hawthorne gives to the presentation of individual life as lived within the context of a particular social group and historical moment and to the dramatization of a struggle between social restraint and the impulse toward self-fulfillment links *The Scarlet Letter* to such far-flung cousins as *The Red and the Black, The Mill on the Floss,* and *Anna Karenina.* Nicolaus Mills has demonstrated its especially close thematic affinities with *Adam Bede.* Both books use a sexual transgression as a center from which to study the conflict between community morality and individual desire. Both focus not on the act of transgression but on the movements of remorse, repentance, and revenge that are its consequences. And they do so because both Hawthorne and Eliot are interested in social and psychological phenomena from a point of view that is finally ethical.

The links that make *The Scarlet Letter* seem closer in form and theme to a work like *Adam Bede* than to a work like *Moby-Dick* are genuine and important. At the same time, as soon as it is compared to a novel in the European realistic tradition its own peculiar features come into high relief. Eliot's novel has a plenitude next to which *The Scarlet Letter* seems compact or even niggardly in its presented life. Eliot is willing to give such minor characters as Reverend Irvine, the Poysers, Lisbeth Bede, and Bartle Massey a fullness of realization beyond what their function for the plot requires. Because her world is so densely peopled her main characters are always seen within a large web of relations, and their actions are seen as having consequences not just in their own lives but in the lives of many others as well. By contrast Hawthorne confines his lesser characters to walk-on parts, reserving a fuller dramatization exclusively for his major characters. This has the effect of making them seem detached from and larger than the figures of the background, and of focusing attention not on the whole round of their lives but on their urgent reactions to the fact of adultery. Eliot also works against a sense of central effect by enveloping her main action in a multitude of scenes of more leisurely and ordinary life. Hawthorne concentrates instead on scenes of crisis and major encounter. What makes the descriptive sketch in "The Governor's Hall" stand out from the rest of *The Scarlet Letter* is that it is the only point at which Hawthorne seems to be describing daily life simply for its own sake. But even here description gives way to significant action, to Hester's defense against the Puritans' desire to take Pearl, the product of her sin, away from her. Where Eliot's novel seems to overflow with a fullness of represented life Hawthorne's has an intense and almost exclusive preoccupation with the conflicts directly embodied in the scarlet letter. He himself notes the sort of tautness and single-mindedness his work possesses when, in a letter, he describes *The Scarlet Letter* as "keeping so close to its point . . . and diversified no otherwise than by turning different sides of the same dark idea to the reader's eye."

This phrase suggests another way of accounting for the singular intensity of *The Scarlet Letter.* It is not just that Hawthorne does not include an abundant record of variegated life, but that the details he does include are so intimately bound together as "sides of the same dark idea." Part of what works against a sense of openness and free life in the novel is its marshaling of its components into strong patterns of interrelation. Thus we see the scaffold as a physical object, and also as a social creation; but our sense of its meaning is also shaped by its appearance in Hawthorne's figurative language. He says of Dimmesdale:

> it would always be essential to his peace to feel the pressure of a faith about him, supporting, while it confined him within its iron framework.

He uses a related image to describe Hester's emotions on the scaffold:

> The very law that condemned her—a giant of stern features, but with vigor to support, as well as to annihilate, in its iron arm—had held her up, through the terrible ordeal of her ignominy.

The framework that both supports and confines recalls the actual pillory on the scaffold, and the resonance between the object and these images suggests a complex relation between things and inner experience. It links the actual forms the Puritans construct as instruments of their law on the one hand to the individual psychic needs that make law strong and on the other to the individual psychic experience produced by the law's implementation. The sort of complex link between public and private that this cluster of images establishes is a recurrent feature of *The Scarlet Letter.* To choose another example, Hawthorne tells us in "The Prison-Door" that every community contains a prison and a graveyard. The novel begins outside an actual prison and ends in contemplation of an actual grave. But between these points we see them in other forms: the Dimmesdale who keeps the truth of his life secret is called a "prisoner" in the "dungeon of his own heart"; when Hester allows her continuing love for Dimmesdale to surface into her conscious mind she hastens "to bar it in its dungeon." Both the town and the mind contain dungeons, and both the Puritans and the main characters are jailers; their private and psychic acts of repression repeat the public and social one. What makes Hawthorne's dramatization of the conflict between untamed desire and repressive restraint interesting is his sense that the self contains its own version of the parties to this conflict within itself. Some of the most moving passages of analysis in the whole novel are those in which he shows how his characters, under the burden of their situation, come to dehumanize themselves even more thoroughly than their oppressors do. His images of the dungeon are the means by which he shows the dynamic interaction between the external and the internal versions of this conflict.

The cross-linking of things and images that these two examples illustrate takes place constantly in *The Scarlet Letter.* The novel's world obeys a rigid law of conservation, such that whatever appears in its physical world is bound to reappear, before long, in the figurative language describing its mental world. This rule holds true for its obvious symbolic objects—the red rose and the black flower that appear in the first scene reappear as metaphors by which Pearl is linked to the wild vitality of nature and by which Chillingworth expresses his dark determinism. But it holds true as well for relatively less significant objects. Chillingworth's freethinking is as a "window . . . thrown open" to Dimmesdale, and shortly after this is said the two men look out of an actual open window and see Hester and Pearl. Hester embroiders robes for occasions of state, and official ceremonies like the Election Day pageant are called the "brilliant embroidery to the great robe of state." It is all but impossible to isolate an item in *The Scarlet Letter* that does not make both physical and metaphorical appearances.

The system of cross-reference that this kind of repetition establishes is obviously one of the major ways in which Hawthorne suggests and controls meaning in *The Scarlet Letter.* But what is more important for our discussion here is the effect that this system has on the texture of reality in the novel. It makes that texture an insistently patterned one; and the participation of each of the novel's details in such larger configurations of elements works against their functions as simply aspects of a representation of actual life. Further, it works against a clear distinction between mental and physical reality. The supportive framework and the area of repressive confinement float between the two, making themselves manifest now as parts of an actual scene, now as features of the mind. The forest in which Hester meets Dimmesdale is both a topographical fact and an image of "the moral wilderness in which she had been so long wandering"; the sunshine that brightens and fades in strict accordance with their emotions of joy and despair makes the forest appear both as a natural place and as an externalization of their mental states, a product of the process Harry Berger describes in *The Faerie Queene* by which "psyche is . . . unfolded into an environment." Our experience in the world of this novel is akin to Hawthorne's own in the moonlit room. Ordinary boundaries become fluid, such that things are both seen as things and felt as thoughts. Above all Hawthorne's world is governed by the moonlit room's sense of haunted interconnectedness. It is not enough to describe it as economical or compact; its fluid interrelatedness of parts and its supersaturation with significant patterns give it the quality of overdetermination that Freud ascribes to dreams.

This double sense of distinctness of individual outline and dreamlike interconnectedness is exactly the effect produced by the item that reappears most insistently in the book, the scarlet letter itself. Hester's A is almost always before us, and it has a curious power to replicate itself in a series of visual variants. It is reflected in suits of armor, pools, brooks, and eyes; it is repeated in Pearl's clothing and in her seaweed creations; it shines forth in the midnight sky; it burns itself onto Dimmesdale's chest. In each of its manifestations the letter has an analyzable meaning in terms of the characters' and the community's experience. But at the same time the various letters keep returning our attention to something prior to its specific embodiments, to the fact of the scarlet letter itself. Its continual presence makes us feel in reading the novel as Miles Coverdale does during his troubled dream on his first night at Blithedale:

> During the greater part of it, I was in that vilest of states when a fixed idea remains in the mind, like the nail in Sisera's brain, while innumerable other ideas go and come, and flutter to-and-fro, combining constant transition with intolerable sameness.

Images combine, separate, and recombine, the action accelerates and slows down, the characters come together and move apart—but while all of this is happening, infusing it and linking its parts to one another and to itself is the scarlet letter.

I noted earlier that *The Scarlet Letter* differs from *Adam Bede* in its single-minded focus on its characters' experience of the consequences of adultery. This is a difference of emphasis; but the features we have just been considering point to a more fundamental difference, to something that distinguishes this novel from the rest of its European relatives as well. In none of these is the drama so pervasively haunted by an autonomous symbol. As Hawthorne turns his symbol into a story he gives its revelation a specific human content, ground it in the reality of his characters' and their society's experience. But as he does so the symbol does not evaporate; its insistent presence within the novel indicates that it retains a residue of its original power. The effect of this can be seen in the existence in the novel of narrative structures somewhat separate from the dramatic one, structures by which

Hawthorne encourages us to perceive the letter more nearly in its original form *as* a symbol.

An illustration of this can be found at the end of "The Governor's Hall." Hester has come to challenge the community's right to deprive her of Pearl, and Hawthorne painstakingly sketches in the furnishings of the room in which she waits. But suddenly the furniture yields up a revelation: Hester sees herself mirrored in the suit of armor, and on its curved surface she is reflected in such a way that her badge of sin becomes disproportionately large, and her human figure disproportionately small. The meaning of this revelation is enacted dramatically in the ensuing scene, in which she must struggle to defend her own human desires and needs against the reductive and distorted view of her as "a scarlet woman, and a worthy type of her of Babylon" that the Puritan men of iron assume. Indeed the conflict is so fully realized within the dramatized interaction of Hester and the Puritan leaders that the moment of reflection in the armor is in a strict sense unnecessary to the scene's significance. What it enables us to do is to perceive the outlines of the scene's conflict in advance, in a static and symbolic, rather than dynamic and dramatic, form.

The kind of double presentation that takes place here is a common feature in *The Scarlet Letter*.. Curiously, Hawthorne follows this procedure even in the midst of his book's most intense encounters. The nineteenth chapter, "The Child at the Brook-Side," offers an example of this. Hester has just made the identity of Chillingworth known to Dimmesdale, and the two have resolved to flee together. In the surge of joy with which they cast aside, for a moment, the perplexity and pain of their seven years' suffering, they turn their attention to the third member of their family, little Pearl. The scene that follows is a beautiful instance of Hawthorne's dramatic art. He circles among his characters, briefly noting their reactions in this tense moment: Dimmesdale's timid hopes and his nervous dread of exclusion; Pearl's anger and jealousy at seeing Dimmesdale usurp her place at her mother's side, and her incomprehension of her mother divested of her letter; Hester's feelings of estrangement from Pearl, and the troubled sense of shame and resentment with which she resumes her badge. But, strangely, planted in the middle of this dramatic moment is another version of the scene, an intricate visual tableau. Pearl, dressed as the scarlet letter, stands beside the brook, and her reflection in it is said to be a "more refined and spiritualized" version of her "reality," which "seemed to communicate somewhat of its own shadowy and intangible quality to the child herself." On the other side of the brook is the discarded scarlet letter, and it too is reflected in the brook, so that as Pearl points at Hester her reflection points at the letter.

Why does Hawthorne insist on doubling and redoubling in this way? It is obvious that, as in "The Governor's Hall," the scene could function effectively enough without this complication. To see what it would look like without reflections, as a simple presentation of a child's jealous and insecure response to her mother's lover, we can turn to the scene in *The Rainbow* in which D. H. Lawrence, apparently drawing on Hawthorne, shows Anna Lensky's reaction to Tom Brangwen. Hawthorne's treatment at the dramatic level is, if anything, subtler than Lawrence's; the problem, then, is not that he cannot render psychological drama, but that even as he does so he insists on including another articulation of his scene as well. In the fourfold reflection the scarlet letter itself becomes, in effect, a character, insisting upon itself as the reality of the characters' lives and the condition of their relationships. Hawthorne's technique forces us to observe the action from a double perspective. At one level we are involved with the characters, sympathetically observing their experience of the letter and of one another; at another level we are distanced from them, watching the letter itself express as meaning what they are experiencing as action. Here again an interaction of complex characters and an exercise in symbolic perception meet and mingle without quite coalescing.

The modulation between symbolic and dramatic in "The Child at the Brook-Side" is in part a function of the peculiar status of Pearl in the novel; and a look at Pearl shows that the tension between two kinds of vision and realization in Hawthorne's scenic art extends to his art of character as well. Some of the details of Pearl's wild and wayward playfulness are taken from Hawthorne's notebook observations of his daughter Una, and this illustrates the sort of fidelity to life that he aims at in creating his elf-child. In both the notebook and the novel he is particularly interested in the succession of games by which the child both acts out her imaginative freedom and, unconsciously, prepares herself for a mature life. Some of the finest passages in *The Scarlet Letter* are those in which Hawthorne describes the imaginative counterworld Pearl establishes in her play, in an effort to gain control over her hostile and baffling environment—her savage uprooting of the weeds that represent the Puritan children to her, for instance, or her re-creation of the mysterious scarlet letter in seaweed. These serve as well to show forth the modification of her nature by her specific situation. Her alternate moods of hostility and affection, of perverse glee and anxious brooding over her origin and separateness, mark her as the child who has grown up in the shadow of her mother's isolation, rebelliousness, and despair.

Hawthorne thus presents Pearl as having a complex psychological nature with its own origins in her environment, but this is only one version of her character in the novel. At other points she is seen not just as Hester's child but as an externalization of her repressed character; thus in the Election Day scene Pearl acts out the impulses that her mother stifles in herself. Her "trait of passion," her luxuriance of imagination, the natural wildness in her that refuses to comply with rules and restraints link her to the aspect of Hester that has found expression in her crime. These qualities are what lead Hester to identify Pearl with the scarlet letter; and to a surprising extent Hawthorne accepts the simile she creates as indicating a true identity: Pearl *is* the scarlet letter. She is, thus, the "emblem and product of sin," a "living hieroglyphic," now acting like a perverse or bewildered child, now serving an allegorical office of embodying the complex of traits that the letter stands for or reminding others of the power of the symbol when they try to ignore it.

The problem that Pearl presents to us as readers is that these two roles coincide at so many points without ever coalescing. And again, it is not as if Hawthorne were incapable of rendering her compellingly in one or the other of these modes of being; nor is he simply confused in his perception of her. With the character of Pearl as with the drama of his scenes he deliberately chooses to adopt the procedures both of a realistic fiction and of a frankly symbolic mode. In doing so he chooses in effect to exploit the tension between his symbol and his story, and he does so for the sake of producing a specific effect. He complicates our relation to his presented materials, making us succumb to his illusion and accept his world as a complex reality unfolding itself dramatically but at the same time holding us back and encouraging us to understand his drama's emerging meaning through the clearer exposition of a symbolic design.

One of the most interesting moments of symbolic experience in *The Scarlet Letter,* and one that best shows how Hawthorne complicates our relation to his fiction, is found in "The Minister's Vigil." In this chapter Dimmesdale goes to the scaffold at midnight to do public penance for his sin. But even as he does so he is half-aware that his act, like the rest of his rituals of self-scrutiny and self-torture, is a "vain show of expiation." By going through the forms of penitence without actually revealing his guilt Dimmesdale only succeeds in renewing his sin of concealment. Each renewal reinforces his imaginative allegiance to the law that condemns him—thus Hawthorne notes that his sin has the effect of binding him more tightly to the categories of Puritan orthodoxy—so that the fact of his own untruth becomes his only reality and his only identity. "The Minister's Vigil" provides an extreme close-up of the processes of Dimmesdale's mind. Its noting of his masochistic fantasies of exposure before the townspeople, of his involuntary and perverse attempts to betray himself by laughing and shrieking, and of his recoils of dread from the prospect of discovery gives us the book's richest realization of the compulsive fantasy life in which Dimmesdale's obsession with his guilt imprisons him. In the midst of these fantasies he gains for a moment an opportunity to escape from his unreal world. He stops Hester and Pearl as they pass through the marketplace, making them stand with him on the scaffold. As he joins hands with them he feels "a tumultuous rush of new life, other life than his own," an "electric chain" of vital relatedness. But he refuses to embrace the possibility for release that this moment offers. When Pearl asks him when he will stand with them publicly he replies: "At the great judgment day!" And exactly as he states his refusal a version of the judgment day takes place: the sky is illuminated as if by "the light that is to reveal all secrets."

At this point Hawthorne does not trouble us unduly about the nature of this light, allowing us to accept, if we like, the plausible explanation that it is "doubtless caused by one of those meteors." Doubtless. But to Dimmesdale the light looks like a scarlet A, and in the brief scene that concludes the chapter the sexton informs us that many of the townspeople saw the same thing. The scarlet letter makes, here, its most audacious appearance. And its appearance works here, as in "The Governor's Hall" and "The Child at the Brook-Side," to reverse the direction of our perception. We have been reading a psychological novel, observing the course of a character's perceptions and emotions; even when we watch Dimmesdale seeing the portent we are still considering the symbol in terms of a character's mental experience of it. But with the sexton's second sighting Hawthorne gives the symbol an independent reality and makes us observe the characters under its aspect as it announces itself as an imperious necessity. Under its aspect the relationships that the characters must live through in the book's dramatic plot are revealed, in an instantaneous vision, in their essential nature. Dimmesdale, Hester, and Pearl stand joined together in the place of punishment, and Chillingworth, looking like the "arch-fiend," looks on. And above them, including them all in its light, is the scarlet letter.

Was it a vision, or a waking dream? Hawthorne does everything he can to make his letter in the sky unsettling for his readers, but correspondingly he does everything he can to afford us ways of coping with it. We might take it as a naturalistic fact, a somewhat oddly shaped and colored meteor. Or we might treat its apparent supernaturalism as really a psychic projection of Dimmesdale's guilty mind; by refusing to pass judgment on himself he compulsively sees that judgment as being passed on him by the world. Or we might join the Puritans, who unblinkingly accept the supernaturalism of the A and read it as a divine message to their community, announcing the accession of Governor Winthrop to the status of Angel. The inclusion of the Puritans' interpretation here clarifies the peculiarity of Dimmesdale's own. He shares their habit of finding symbols latent with divine meaning in nature, but he perverts that practice by finding "a revelation, addressed to himself alone" rather than to the whole of God's chosen community. In the morbid egotism of his guilt he assumes that "the firmament itself should appear no more than a fitting page for his soul's history and fate." His is a further way in which we might read the celestial sign.

As the last paragraph indicates, "The Minister's Vigil" concludes with a drama of interpretation. We see how the characters understand the letter, and we see their understandings as proceeding from a whole way of making sense of experience. But what is most interesting about this drama is that we are implicated in it. For finally, when the characters are done with it, we have the fact of the A in the sky left over, unexplained. Hawthorne in effect withdraws his narrative's mediating veil and makes us undergo his own and his characters' central experience of direct and unaided encounter with the flaming symbol. And as we are forced to decide what to make of it the characters' modes of vision become the matter not of detached observation but of our own urgent choice. We are left alone to complete the episode's reality and meaning as we may, and as we do so, Hawthorne's demonstration of the implications of the available options ensures that we will be highly self-conscious about our own procedure as an imaginative act of a certain sort. A final purpose of the symbolic mode of *The Scarlet Letter,* therefore, is to complicate our perception of the story in such a way as to turn it in on itself.

An episode like this one illustrates the most important difference between *The Scarlet Letter* and the realistic novels with which it shares some features. Hawthorne includes all the interacting facets of individual and social life that compose their presented reality, but he refuses to exclude from his novel the presence of a magical or supernatural order. This order is seldom entirely absent even in more strictly realistic fiction. Adam Bede's premonition of his father's death and Anna Karenina's prophetic dream of the train are incidents marvelous enough from the point of view of everyday causality. But Hawthorne is unique in the central place he gives to this mode of experience and in the way he engages his readers' perception of it. He strives to make the celestial A not plausible but as spooky as possible; and at the same time, he uses it to worry us, to render the nature of reality problematic and to make us aware of our own assumptions about that nature.

Supernatural magic plays a role throughout *The Scarlet Letter.* The novel contains within it the materials for another novel, the Puritans' version of its characters, events, and significance. Their version is a lurid romance. Pearl is, to them, a demon offspring; Hester's letter emits an infernal light and heat; Dimmesdale is an angel, and Chillingworth a "diabolical agent" who, like Satan in the Book of Job, "had the Divine permission, for a season, to burrow into the clergyman's intimacy, and plot against his soul." The phrases "there was a rumor" and "some averred" with which Hawthorne introduces these details are reminiscent of the "some will say" and "some maintain" in Wordsworth poems like "The Thorn" and "Lucy Gray." Both authors include the ghostly surmises of superstitious rumor in their narratives as a way of regaining access to a suppressed stratum of imaginative experience. Hawthorne's surmises help him to show the workings of the Puritan imagination from within. They see their world as a strife between supernatural and subterranean powers of good and evil, and they see this strife as governed by a providential order. At the same time, Hawthorne consciously distances himself from their raw magic, accepting it as indicative of a psychological, not theological, truth. Rather than rejecting outright the notion that the A burns Hester with infernal fire, he notes that it does indeed sear her bosom, with shame. Similarly he suggests that Mistress Hibbins, rather than being an actual witch, may simply be mad, and at another point he speculates that insanity may be the psychological equivalent of damnation, "that eternal alienation from the Good and True."

Hawthorne's invocations of the magical formulas of a more primitive and archaic sort of fiction and his conversion of their significance into psychological terms is part of a larger effort in *The Scarlet Letter,* an effort to resuscitate something like the Puritans' ideas of evil, sin, and damnation as serious concepts that can be used in a more secular treatment of human experience. His extremely self-conscious experiments in qualified credulity illustrate the feature Geoffrey Hartman in the Miltonic and Romantic revival of romance, a "freer attitude of the mind toward the fictions it entertains." Hartman's description of "L'Allegro" fits *The Scarlet Letter* perfectly:

> Thus psyche emerges from the spooky larvae of masques and moralities like a free-ranging butterfly. Though still in contact with the world of spirits, it is no longer coerced or compelled.

But, as "The Minister's Vigil" shows, Hawthorne does not always make the demystification of the supernatural so easy for himself and his readers, nor does he always maintain the same self-conscious distance from the extravagant romance of the Puritans.

Consider, for a moment, the character of Chillingworth. The Puritans believe that the fire in his laboratory is brought from hell, and just after he records this rumor Hawthorne himself adopts a closely related image.

> Sometimes, a light glimmered out of the physician's eyes, burning blue and ominous, like the reflection of a furnace, or, let us say, like one of those gleams of ghastly fire that darted from Bunyan's awful door-way in the hill-side, and quivered on the pilgrim's face.

The "let us say" implies a degree of detachment in this invocation of the Puritans' demonic imagery. But what is curious about the characterization of Chillingworth is the extent to which Hawthorne makes use of the Puritans' imaginative mode in presenting him. When he meets Hester at the seaside "there came a glare of red light out of his eyes; as if the old man's soul were on fire." The vulgar are not alone in seeing him as Satan's emissary; Hester, Pearl, and Dimmesdale all associate him with the Black Man, and he appears as the arch-fiend in the last two scaffold scenes.

There is, of course, a psychological truth contained in this diabolical imagery. "In a word, old Roger Chillingworth was a striking evidence of a man's faculty of transforming himself into a devil, if he will only for a reasonable space of time, undertake a devil's office." Giving himself up completely to his one evil purpose, Chillingworth brings about his own dehumanization and makes himself "more wretched than his victim." And his malignity is not motiveless. His character has, as have the others, a psychological complexity and etiology of its own. Frederick C. Crews insists on this:

> We cannot conscientiously say that Chillingworth *is* a devil . . . when Hawthorne takes such care to show us how his devilishness has proceeded from his physical deformity, his pense of inferiority and impotence, his sexual jealousy, and his perverted craving for knowledge.

But the real question is not whether Chillingworth is plausibly motivated, as he surely is, but whether or not he is offered to us as a character possessing the sort of realistic psychological density that Crews's insistence on motive implies. And in this respect we must conscientiously say that he is a devil. As with some other villains—Richard III or Iago or Milton's Satan—what pass as his motives seem at times results rather than causes; his deformity, for instance, is seen steadily developing as his evil intent strengthens, as an outward expression of his inner condition. As the novel progresses his dark face, his disfigured body, the hideous glares in his eyes, his lurid satanic speech—these become the central features of his character. Whereas a novelist like Eliot, in dealing with a similar figure—Casaubon, in *Middlemarch*, is another impotent scholar-husband, one who has so completely channeled his vital energies into his intellectual researches that his belated marriage can be only a betrayal of a passionate woman's "budding youth into a false and unnatural relation with my decay"—fills out her type with an abundance of detail and many-sided analysis, Hawthorne purposely makes his character less and less complex, more and more the rigidified villain of raw romance. In presenting Chillingworth, rather than distancing himself from it, Hawthorne adopts the sort of fiction that he associates with the Puritans and allows it to bring a part of his created world into being.

Leslie Fiedler notes that "one of the major problems involved in reading *The Scarlet Letter* is determining the ontological status of the characters, the sense in which we are being asked to believe in them." The characterization of Chillingworth shows why this is so: ontology is a problem because the characters in the novel are endowed with radically different sorts of reality. Hester's mode of existence is at the furthest extreme from Chillingworth's. We have already seen some examples of her ability to attenuate or complicate the implications of the forms the Puritans seek to impose on her. When she does accept Puritan designations she does so out of a process of mind that belies their meaning. Thus in the beautiful chapter "Hester at Her Needle" Hawthorne observes with fine tact the process by which she comes to reject the pleasures of her art as sinful. She senses that her art might be a way of expressing, and thus of soothing, her repressed passion, and in order to protect her love she rejects—and labels as sin—whatever might help her to sublimate it. Here she employs Puritan terminology in a most un-Puritan strategy of consciousness, using it to perpetuate an inner need which she is unable to act out and unwilling to relinquish. Her effort to retain her passion intact leads her, in the chapter "Hester and Pearl," to commit a conscious deception. In the face of Pearl's earnest questionings Hester senses that Pearl might be capable of becoming a confidante, a friend, and thus of helping her to "overcome the passion, once so wild, and even yet neither dead nor asleep." In telling Pearl that she wears the scarlet letter for the sake of its gold thread she is not true, to Pearl, to her badge, or to herself. But her falseness here is another strategy by which she attempts to maintain all the elements of her true self in suspension. She cannot achieve in her life the full expression of her complex self that she has wrought into her symbol, but she instinctively and covertly moves to keep this alive as a possibility.

Hawthorne writes that "the tendency of her fate and fortunes had been to set her free." Her freedom is a mixed state of lucidity and self-deception, integrity and falsehood, love and hate: she experiences herself as being, like her letter, a "mesh of good and evil." What is most exciting about Hester is her openness to all the varieties of experience—intellectual, imaginative, emotional—that the continuing emergency of her life brings to her. When she meets Chillingworth at the seaside she has a clear vision of what he has become; she perceives her own share of the responsibility for his transformation; she desperately insists on the possibility of a free act of forgiveness; and she recoils with bitterness from his grim refusal. No other character in the book is capable of this range of feeling. When she decides to go to Dimmesdale's aid she is prompted by her love, by her perception of his weakness, and by her recognition of the responsibility she has incurred for his destruction by promising to keep Chillingworth's identity secret. In defining a duty for herself she generates an ethical imperative out of a clear insight into the whole range of contradictory desires and obligations that confront her. Again, no other character in the book is capable of the adventure of free ethical choice that Hester undertakes here.

Hawthorne lavishes on Hester all of the psychological analysis that he deliberately withholds from Chillingworth. He endows her with the complex reality of a whole self as he becomes increasingly content simply to present Chillingworth's diabolical face. This is what creates the discrepancy between their ontological statuses, and it should be obvious by now that this discrepancy is neither careless nor purposeless. The way in which we are asked to believe in them as characters is a function of the way in which they believe in themselves. Chillingworth relinquishes his own freedom and adopts, in a perverted because atheistic way, the deterministic outlook of the Puritans. A dark necessity, he tells Hester, rules their fates: "Let the black flower blossom as it may!" As he does so he gives up his complexity of being and becomes a rigidified figure of diabolical evil, a character in the sort of providential romance that the Puritans imagine. Hester is allowed the freedom and variegated selfhood of a character in a more realistic mode because she first opens herself to the full complexity of her existence. It is as if in deciding how they will understand themselves and their world the characters also get to decide what sort of literary reality their author will let them acquire; the different fictional modes in which they are realized become explicit reflections of their own imaginative outlooks.

Charles Feidelson notes that Hawthorne carefully sets *The Scarlet Letter* at the historical watershed between the medieval and the modern, and that the novel presents the interaction of these ages as a conflict between two ways of creating and perceiving meaning. One of these sees experience as having meaning within a context of divine truth; within this context its symbolism tends toward fixity of significance, and its moral perception similarly moves to fix the value of characters and acts within rigidly separated categories of good and evil. The other is more secular and indeterminate. It sees meaning and value as generated from within human experience itself, so that its symbolic expressions and moral discriminations are valid to the extent that they emerge from a recognition of the whole complexity of life, including its inseparable mixture of good and evil. The contrast between Chillingworth's determinism and Hester's openness is only one version of this conflict; we see it again in the contrast between the A the Puritans impose on Hester and the A she creates, and between the sense of duty implicit in the Puritan's legal and religious forms and the sense of duty that leads Hester to go to Dimmesdale's rescue.

In its use of different fictional modes *The Scarlet Letter* also reenacts this conflict in its form. By using in his own right the romance form he associates with the Puritans Hawthorne makes us experience Chillingworth as fixed to his role in a drama of angels and devils; his inclusion of magic throughout the novel encourages us to participate in the imaginative experience of a supernatural conflict between good and evil. The more realistic—in Hawthorne's terms, novelistic—mode of the bulk of his narrative forces us to make sense of the novel's world in another way. Here our understanding emerges gradually, from a careful observation of the twists of motive, thought, and emotion that make up the characters' lives. And our judgments here must always be tentative and open-ended, coming nearer to truth to the extent that they are faithfully responsive to the quality of the characters' whole experience. In effect the book itself illustrates a newer way of imaginatively conceiving of human existence emerging from an older way.

The inclusion of radically incommensurate fictional modes in *The Scarlet Letter* is a final way in which Hawthorne complicates his book's world and our relation to it. Like the inclusion of symbolic and dramatic articulations, it makes us perceive that world alternately under different aspects; and here again Hawthorne's double procedure also works to heighten our awareness of our own activity of perception. As they play against each other in the novel we become aware of each mode as a kind of fiction, as a specific form of imaginative representation. Hawthorne draws our attention to his own art of illusion, and he does so in order that we will be aware of the views of experience we are subscribing to as we accept his illusion as reality. In doing this he does not destroy the illusion his fiction creates or undermine its value; but he does keep its validity from being assumed too readily. Having understood the Puritans' sense of reality as a function of their scheme of perception, Hawthorne cannot but be aware that whatever he creates must be a function of another such scheme. This does not mean that he sees all representations of reality as simply illusory. But it means that their validity is conditional on a clear awareness of the outlook through which we make sense of reality. Thus he allows us to participate in both versions of his novel's experience, and also frankly to recognize each *as* a version, so that we may decide within the context of that recognition in which terms that experience is better understood.

The peculiarities of fictive form that I have been discussing are all present in the last scene of *The Scarlet Letter.* The chapters leading up to "The Revelation of the Scarlet Letter" are superb examples of Hawthorne's narrative art. Everything that has appeared in the book is gathered together in preparation for a fateful climax. The descriptions of the crowd, of the procession, and of Dimmesdale's sermon and its effects are among the most beautiful and thorough passages of social observation in the book, and at the same time we never forget that this public spectacle is postponing a critical event in the book's private drama. As the ministers and the magistrates leave the church the action becomes genuinely suspenseful. Everything is done in slow motion. Dimmesdale totters; he rejects Reverend Wilson's aid; he advances to the scaffold; Bellingham comes forward to assist him, but he is warned back by Dimmesdale's look. The martial music plays on, but Dimmesdale pauses. And now, with grim theatricality, he stages a ceremonious spectacle of his own, the spectacle of exposure of sin that he has acted out in his mind and on the scaffold at night. Supported by Hester, and with Pearl between them, he acts out a scene in which he is both avenger and sinner, exposer and concealer, agent and victim of God's wrath.

In this scene a dogmatic and theological and a secular and humanistic imagination come into passionate conflict one last time. Dimmesdale's outlook here is that of the Puritans raised to a ghastly pitch. He sees Chillingworth as the tempter and fiend; he speaks of the lurid gleam of Hester's letter; he sees the drama of his own life as a strife between God and the Devil, and his revelation as a "plea of guilty at the bar of Eternal Justice." Set against his grim exultation and the narrow fixity of his orthodox interpretation are Hester's despair and her desperate attempts to broaden and thus deny the categories of his thought: "Shall we not spend our immortal life together? Surely, surely we have ransomed one another, with all this woe!" Their debate is fully dramatic. Behind each of their claims we are aware of the personal psychic processes that inform their attitudes. We realize that Dimmesdale's orthodoxy, here as before, is perverted in the image of his own guilt-obsessed mind. He is as masochistically obsessed with passing a self-destructive judgment on himself as he was in "The Minister's Vigil."

And his is here, as it was there, an egotistical interpretation of the providential design: "behold me here, the one sinner of the world!" We also realize that Hester is giving expression to her own guilty fantasy of a heavenly consummation, and that her affirmation that human love provides its own sanctifications and ransoms, like her bold claim in the forest that their love had a consecration of its own, is a desperate one, and one that does not square with the full complexity of the aftermath of their adultery. Each one's version of what their experience means is qualified by our awareness of his character, but these versions are allowed to stand side by side, without further comment. The narrator refuses to press the question of the truth or falsity of their statements beyond what they themselves have attained. If we try to do so we must return to Hester's answer: "I know not! I know not!"

Dimmesdale concludes his confession with a fierce shriek:

> "He bids you look again at Hester's scarlet letter! He tells you, that, with all its mysterious horror, it is but the shadow of what he bears on his own breast, and that even this, his own red stigma, is no more than the type of what has seared his inmost heart! Stand any here that question God's judgment on a sinner? Behold! Behold! a dreadful witness of it!"
>
> With a convulsive motion he tore away the ministerial band from before his breast. It was revealed!

But no sooner does he make his revelation than the author draws the curtain before our eyes: "But it were irreverent to describe that revelation." And, having dismissed the ghastly miracle, he continues with his narration of the scene.

By now we have grown accustomed to seeing the scarlet letter announce itself as a symbol in the middle of a fully dramatic scene. But this demurrer on Hawthorne's part is nonetheless startling. It is hard to say which is more surprising: the fact that he insists on including as the climax of his scene such a strange and wondrous revelation, or the fact that, having done so, he then refuses to show it forth. Why should he so carefully arouse the sort of curiosity that he does here and then so pointedly cheat it out of its gratification?

This final scene brings to a head a conflict of narrative methods that has run all through the book. Dimmesdale's uncovering of his red stigma stands as the culmination of a carefully cultivated line of suspense—Hawthorne has teased and teased us with allusions to this mystery. In constructing his plot around the concealed presence of this physical sign he gives the book the shape of a ghostly romance; it operates by a magical order of causal determinism in which internal conditions are externalized as physical appearances. This line of suspense is the narrative's equivalent to the fictional mode in which Chillingworth is envisioned, and again Hawthorne associates this mode with Puritan mental fictions. As Dimmesdale presents it the symbol is fraught with providential significance, a wonder-working token to God's justice to sinners. And just as Chillingworth's fictional mode plays against Hester's, so too another kind of suspense is set against that of Hawthorne's romance plot. This interests us not in supernatural manifestations, or in what God has wrought, or in anything that admits of a determinate meaning, but rather in what choice Dimmesdale will make, what role his decision will play in his own psychic life, and what effect his choice will have on the other characters. This is the suspense of a more realistic novel; it invites us to see the story's meaning in its drama, in the texture of the characters' experience and in their exercise of their human freedom.

Hawthorne can and does give us the sort of scene that the latter kind of interest demands, but he insists on including a more mysterious and magical drama as well, and he refuses to make it easy for us to ignore it. As in "The Minister's Vigil," when the dramatic scene is completed the appearance of the scarlet letter is still to be explained, and here again Hawthorne uses its problematic status to engage us in a self-conscious act of interpretation. In returning to Dimmesdale's revelation in his last chapter he offers no explanation of his own for his story's omitted climax. Instead he reports the explanations of various spectators—that the letter on Dimmesdale's chest was the result of self-inflicted penitential torture, that it was magically produced by Chillingworth's potent necromancy, that it was the work of "the ever active tooth of remorse, gnawing from the inmost heart outwardly." There is a fourth account as well, that of certain "highly respectable witnesses," according to whom there was no scarlet letter and Dimmesdale had no hidden personal guilt to conceal. To these witnesses Dimmesdale stood on the scaffold with the adulteress and her child to express in parabolic form the lesson that "in the view of Infinite Purity, we are all sinners alike."

Hawthorne releases us from his narrative authority and allows us to choose among these, or to adopt whatever other explanation we like. And while at first his multiple choice seems simply to make the meaning and even the factuality of Dimmesdale's revelation ambiguous, the dimensions and the point of the ambiguity are not at all imprecise. Each of these choices gives the scene significance in terms of an implicit view of the nature of human guilt and evil. By absconding with his book's climax and providing these alternate versions of it instead, he allows us to construct our own conclusion, to see something or nothing on Dimmesdale's chest, but either one on the condition that we be aware of the nature of the vision that will make what we see meaningful to us. Our final moment of direct confrontation with the scarlet letter has the same purpose as the earlier ones did, but now that purpose is more obvious: it leaves us alone to complete the novel by determining its reality and its meaning as we think best, and to be conscious of our imaginative procedure as we do so.

Finally Hawthorne's multiple choices provide one last clue to the purpose of his use of romance in *The Scarlet Letter.* From what we have seen of the Puritans in the novel the fourth choice sounds less like their reaction than like that of highly respectable readers of a later age. In its unwillingness to admit mysteries like Dimmesdale's letter to its consciousness it partakes of what Hawthorne calls "our modern incredulity." And in ceasing to believe in any form of magic it also ceases to adhere to a concept of sin as anything more than a comfortably universal phenomenon, lacking individual manifestations. In its light we see what the first three views have in common. They are all willing to accept the mysterious letter as a reality, and they all accept as a reality the "deep life-matter" of guilt or evil from which they see it as springing. Hawthorne's own willingness to enter into the enchantments of romance and his eagerness to make us experience romance's magic all through *The Scarlet Letter* is a form of resistance to the trivializations latent in the secularism of an age that places "gilded volumes on the centre-table" where the Puritans placed more serious literature and an age that makes adultery a matter of "mocking infamy and ridicule." It is his way of regaining access to the mysteries of the psychic life, the reality of which both the Puritans and his own more secular fiction attest to in their own ways.

KEITH CARABINE

"Bitter Honey": Miles Coverdale as Narrator in The Blithedale Romance

It is perhaps not surprising that Miles Coverdale is so distrusted and maligned a figure in *The Blithedale Romance,* since Hawthorne, by making him constantly expose his own limitations, could almost be thought to be disowning him. Critics have settled on three main charges. First, Coverdale is a "literary snoop," suffering from "a merciless inquisitiveness," who treats the feelings of his friends as a game, and thus loses their "confidence" and dehumanizes himself. Both Coverdale's own fear that "the cold tendency . . . which made me pry with a speculative interest into people's passions and impulses, appeared to have gone far towards unhumanizing my heart," and Zenobia's forthright denunciation of "your game, groping for human emotions in the dark corners of the heart" are taken to confirm this charge. Second, Coverdale is not to be trusted. Philip Rahv's argument that Coverdale is lying when he confesses at the end "I—I—myself—was in love—with—PRISCILLA!" because "it is evident on every page that the only genuine relationship is that of Coverdale to Zenobia," is the bluntest expression of this distrust. Third, Coverdale is treated ironically by Hawthorne throughout the narrative. Not only does Coverdale spend most of his time trying to catch up with his own narrative, but, more importantly, he is, ironically, unable to understand it; and is, therefore, incapable of either self-awareness or moral or artistic maturity. Thus for J. C. Stubbs it is evident "real people capable of real suffering exist just beyond the comprehension of the witless narrator"; for James H. Justus, "If there is a tragedy attendant upon Zenobia's fate it takes shape, outside and beyond the range of Coverdale's perception," and for Nina Baym, "Art is passionate and it celebrates passion; rejecting this truth, Coverdale is incapable of mature artistry and must remain a childish man, an ineffectual 'poetling.'"

Such readings are altogether too simple. Coverdale allows Hawthorne to dramatize his own troubled, ambivalent perceptions of the artist's role and function. Indeed *The Blithedale Romance* is organized so that the apparent subject matter (the love quartet, the Blithedale community experiment itself, the issue of possession) and the major metaphors (veils and masquerades, mesmerism and clairvoyancy) are all made to bear on this central concern. I will concentrate on the changing status of the narrative; on Coverdale's developing relation to the characters whose story he tells, and upon the paradox at the heart of his final accession to authority. Only through these approaches, in my judgment, can Coverdale properly receive the sympathetic hearing his problems demand.

II

It is characteristic of Hawthorne's craft in *The Blithedale Romance* that the opening chapter hints how we are to read the narrative, and alerts us to the extraordinary relation of Coverdale to his own narrative, and why that relation is significant. Also, in retrospect, we see how Hawthorne has worked for suggestive analogies in "The Veiled Lady," and in the association of both her exhibitor and his victim, with the exhibitor of the romance itself.

The wonderful exhibition of the veiled lady "under such skilfully contrived circumstances of stage effect, . . . which at once mystified and illuminated" her "remarkable performances" is a triple image: of the very form of the story—a "skilfully contrived" masquerade; of the reader's position—"mystified" and awaiting "illumination"; and of a judgment upon the Blithedale experiment itself as another form of "mock life."

Westervelt as the "exhibitor" of Priscilla works both as an analogy with and a contrast to Coverdale who is himself an "exhibitor" of "three characters who figure so largely on my own private theatre." Unlike Westervelt we are continually made aware that Coverdale is not in charge of affairs. He is obliged for much of his narrative, as with Moodie in the first chapter, to "arrive" "only through subsequent events," "at a plausible conjecture as to what his business could have been." In fact, his stance is extraordinary: writing twelve years after the events he describes he still "conjectures" as to "Zenobia's whole character and history; . . . her later purposes towards Hollingsworth." He confesses he is "a secondary or tertiary personage" in his own narrative, and, characteristically, he is either a distant observer of the action, or he stumbles upon an event, such as Zenobia's "trial" (chapter 25), thirty minutes after it is over. Moreover, unlike Westervelt, the manager of "the phenomenon in the mesmeric line" who keeps Priscilla under a spell "enshrouded with the misty drapery of the veil" insulated from "the material world, from time and space," Coverdale does not *possess* the "subjects" of his theater. In fact, it is precisely because Coverdale's characters are not puppets, and can, like Moodie, continually interrupt and surprise his bewildered speculations, that Coverdale avoids "the cold tendency" which is truly embodied in the "unhumanized" heart of Westervelt.

Coverdale's remarkable position in relation to his own narrative, and the consequences of that relation with regard to how his story will be told, are captured in his response to "the Veiled Lady's" "Sibylline" prophecy: he is left "turning" a "riddle in my mind, and trying to catch its slippery purport by the tail." Unlike Westervelt who deals in spells, Coverdale is still, at the time of writing, probing a mystery. And we are invited to share both the process of his discoveries and his struggle to establish his authority over the "slippery" meanings and the consequences of the tale he has to tell.

It is the analogy with Priscilla which established that, though Coverdale may not be the artist as mesmerist, he *is* the artist as clairvoyant or medium, flickeringly aware of the future, and responsive, like Priscilla to Westervelt, to the moods and demands, to the *influence* of his characters. Thus during his first night at Blithedale, Coverdale's "half-waking dreams . . . anticipated several of the chief incidents of this narrative including a dim shadow of its catastrophe." As Coverdale recognizes, he is, willy-nilly, "something like a mesmerical clairvoyant" who operates through "a species of intuition" which renders him subject to being taken over, like Priscilla, by forces he cannot control. I take this to be the meaning of the curious moment when Coverdale, high in his hermitage, is visited by "a mood of disbelief in moral beauty or heroism, and a conviction of the folly of attempting to benefit the world." It is only when Westervelt hoves into view that Coverdale recognizes it was "chiefly . . . this man's influence" that had sponsored the skeptical and sneering view which "had filled my mental vision in regard to all life's better purposes."

It is surely apt that Coverdale first meets the woman he loves under the "management" of a mesmerist. That it is his fate to love a woman who is always free to be someone else's possession, who is always a medium for others' designs, ironically mirrors the position of the artist in relation to his own creations, of man in relation to his fellows, and of his fellows in association with each other. These issues are illuminated in the sequel to the first chapter, namely Coverdale's second visit to see "the Veiled Lady" in "A Village Hall" (chapter 23).

Coverdale's involuntary intuition in his "hermitage" prepares us for his "horror and disgust" as he realizes that if the mesmerist's claims "of the miraculous power of one human being over the will and passions of another" are true, then "the individual soul was annihilated . . . and . . . the idea of man's eternal responsibility was made ridiculous, and immortality rendered at once, impossible, and not worth acceptance." Furthermore, that Westervelt imbues Coverdale with "a sneering view" ensures that Coverdale can recognize "the smell of corruption" in the latter's talk of "a new era that . . . would link soul to soul, and the present life to what we call futurity" and "finally convert both worlds into the great mutually conscious brotherhood."

The implications of Coverdale's noble judgment are threefold. Firstly, as Coverdale is aware, for the artist to mimic the mesmerist is both to annihilate the individual soul of his creations, to deny his "responsibility," and, therefore, to damn himself. The consequence is that his characters must be "free" to decide their own fates; thus ensuring the writer's authority is provisional. Secondly, if the author as man responds similarly to the integrity of his fellows, and does not act (as Hollingsworth does in this scene when he takes Priscilla away from Westervelt) he must remain a perennial observer experiencing life, like Coverdale, as both alienation and loss. Coverdale suffers the mortification of watching Priscilla's rescue from Westervelt, "her deadliest enemy," to land "safe forever!"—in the equally possessive arms of Hollingsworth. Thirdly, and even more importantly, Coverdale's recognition that Westervelt's aims express a "cold and dead materialism," masquerading as brotherhood, enables Hawthorne to establish the authority of his narrator. After all in losing Priscilla "forever" he learns the hard way that Westervelt's ideal "brotherhood" operates as a black parody of Blithedale's aims for a better world. Both systems indeed are not "new sciences" but the revival of "old humbugs" which deny the possibility of new sympathetic forms of human relations.

III

Coverdale's responsiveness as medium, his perceptions as clairvoyant, and his doubts about both, are essential, initially, to an understanding of his function. Even his "hermitage," which he ironically confesses "was my one exclusive possession, while I counted myself a brother of the socialists," and which is commonly regarded as proof of his fundamental disaffection from the aims of Blithedale, is less self-serving and defensive than it appears. His "hermitage" is in fact at once an embodiment and an outcome of a series of devastating perceptions. Indeed, he only retreats to it after recognizing "the presence of Zenobia caused our heroic enterprise to show like an illusion, a masquerade, a posture, a counterfeit Arcadia"; after he discerns that Hollingsworth "had come among us, actuated by no real sympathy with our feelings and hopes"; after he grimly divines that "for a girl like Priscilla and a woman like Zenobia to jostle one another in their love of a man like Hollingsworth, was likely to be no child's play"; and still more importantly, after he recognizes "my own part in these transactions was singularly subordinate. It resembled that of Chorus in a classic play."

Coverdale's retreat is also a necessary step because unlike his fellow medium, Priscilla, he questions his "species of intuition" and lives in terror that the source and consequences of his clairvoyance may be demonic—thus rendering him susceptible to confusing "a spiritual lie" and "a subtle recognition of a fact." Coverdale's wise awareness of this danger saves him not only from Westervelt's demonism, but, too, from "the spiritual lie" which Hollingsworth unwittingly lives. Thus, whereas the latter wastes "all the warmth of his heart" on his "philanthropic theory!" which turns into "a cold spectral monster which he had himself conjured up," Coverdale recognizes that too exclusive a devotion "to the study of men and women" risks fashioning "a monster" which "after all . . . may be said to have been created mainly by ourselves." Coverdale, therefore, withdraws from Hollingsworth not because of "his reticence to commit himself humanly to others [as James H. Justus says,]" but because his friend's "spiritual discipline" masks egotistic designs like Westervelt's which violate the very spirit of Blithedale and enslave the wills of Priscilla and Zenobia. Hollingsworth in his treatment of Priscilla fails therefore the victim figure who, as he recognizes, will prove *a test case of Blithedale values*: "as we do by this friendless girl so shall we prosper."

As refractions of the artist's problems, then, Westervelt and Hollingsworth establish that it is to Coverdale's credit that he is aware of the risks of "demonism" and self-conjured "spectral monsters." It is, however, Priscilla who is oblivious to such dangers, who is the major key to Coverdale's authenticity as an artist and his limitations as a man. As Priscilla is not free of Westervelt when she is brought to Blithedale, and experiences only another form of possession (which she accepts unquestioningly), so Coverdale discovers that he cannot, either in his hermitage or in Boston, avoid the responsibilities of his "sympathies"—root meaning "having a fellow feeling"—sponsored by his commitment, no matter how consciously ambivalent, towards the Blithedale experiment, or, more importantly, by his "species of intuition," which ties him, irrevocably, in ways he had not anticipated, to his friends. Thus even though he leaves Blithedale for Boston after "the tragic passage-at-arms" with Hollingsworth, and after Zenobia's stagy rejection of his counsel ("It needs a wild steersman when we voyage through chaos! The anchor is up! Farewell!"), "they first" begin to "encroach upon" his "dreams" and then, again, press back into his life as he looks out of the back window of his hotel only to see Priscilla, Westervelt, and Zenobia together in "a rather stylish boarding house." In one of the central passages in the romance he reflects:

> There now needed only Hollingsworth and old Moodie to complete the knot of characters, whom a real intricacy of events, greatly assisted by my method of insulating them from other relations, had kept so long upon my mental stage, as actors in a drama. In itself, perhaps, it was no very remarkable event that they should thus come across me, at the moment when I imagined myself free. Nevertheless, there seemed something fatal in the coincidence that had borne me to this one spot . . . and transfixed me there, and compelled me again to waste my already wearied sympathies on affairs which were none of mine, and persons who cared little for me. . . . After the effort which it cost me to fling them off—after consummating my escape, as I thought, from these goblins of flesh and blood and pausing to revive myself with a breath or two of an atmosphere in which they should have no share—it was a positive despair, to find the same figures arraying themselves before me, and presenting their old problem in a shape that made it more insoluble than ever.
>
> I began to long for a catastrophe. If the noble temper of Hollingsworth's soul were doomed to be utterly corrupted by the too powerful purpose, which had grown out of what was noblest in him; if the rich and generous qualities of Zenobia's womanhood might not save her; if Priscilla must perish by her tenderness and faith, so simple and so devout;—then be it so! Let it all come! . . . I would look on, as it seemed my part to do, understandingly, if my intellect could fathom the meaning and the moral, and, at all events, reverently and sadly. The curtain fallen, I would pass onward with my poor individual life, which was now attenuated of much of its proper substance, and diffused among many alien interests.

It is Priscilla's fate to be pursued by two figures she never recognizes as "goblins of flesh and blood." Westervelt exploits her for her clairvoyance and Hollingsworth for her money. Her "faith, so simple and devout" ensures she does not realize at the end that the "vindicative shadow" of Zenobia—another "goblin of flesh and blood"—"dogs the side" of Hollingsworth "where" she "is not." Yet as Coverdale ruefully acknowledges her "fine heart" has found in the broken, "child like" Hollingsworth "its proper substance," whereas his own "life" is indeed "attenuated." His fate, as a human being, in contrast to Priscilla's, as he now courageously and honestly acknowledges, is to be an onlooker, wasting "his weary sympathies on affairs which were none of mine and persons who cared little for me." Coverdale's "let it all come" is not, as [Frederick C.] Crews argues, "a vengeful daydream," nor is it merely fatalism; he is beginning to learn that he cannot change the role he must, ineluctably, play of "Chorus in a classic play." In fact *The Blithedale Romance* is, in part, about the education of Coverdale, into an acceptance of the role of the artist as sympathetic observer who misses out on life.

The "goblins of flesh and blood" who will not be flung off and who present "their old problem in a shape . . . more insoluble than ever" tempt him as an artist in ways Priscilla can never know. Zenobia, Hollingsworth, and Priscilla are, to paraphrase Pirandello, "three characters in search of an author." Their search, as Coverdale recognizes, involves the artist in a paradox. An attempt to understand and solve "their old problem" involves the artist both as medium and as diagnostician: and both functions involve the artist's recognition that his characters are "goblins of flesh and blood." They are "goblins" in the precise meaning of the term: "ugly and mischievous demons" who fly about the world deceiving folk. Their need to have their story told and their "old problem" understood tempts Coverdale to commit the unpardonable Hawthornian sin of violating their "flesh and blood" by restricting them to his "mental stage" and thus surrendering like Westervelt to "the miraculous powers" of demonism. Furthermore the artist cannot refuse them because they are, too, "of flesh and blood," they are his friends, able at once to "encroach" upon his "dreams" and to solicit his essentially unwearying sympathies. Yet, simultaneously, as goblins, eager to damn him, they unavoidably stimulate the arrogance resident even in sympathy and proceed to induce Coverdale and Hawthorne to produce yet another version of "mock life" masquerading this time as sympathy and accordance.

The paradox heightens, because as the passage I have quoted illustrates, as Coverdale must distance himself to understand the problem of his characters, so Hawthorne must distance himself in order to use and to understand his chosen narrator, Coverdale. Hence both the coolness and the comedy in Hawthorne's relation to Coverdale. The latter's rather calculating remarks at the beginning of the passage reflect Hawthorne's typical self-referentiality: the "method," the use of "the knot of characters" is *his* way of ensuring that the inherent duplicity of his romance works. Hawthorne's "theater," his masquerade, is not as much of "a fancy-sketch" as he would have us believe in his Preface. Nor clearly is his "whole treatment of the affair" of Brook Farm "incidental to the main purpose of the romance." The "old problem" which Coverdale accepts as his business to solve involves an estimation of why the oldest story of all—unrequited love—seems to embody the reasons for the failure of the Blithedale experiment. Coverdale's analysis reveals that "their old problem" like the Blithedale community's efforts to change the relation between the sexes, to strive for brotherhood and to escape from individualism and ego, stumble inexorably against the stubborn fact of "the self."

That Hawthorne distances himself from Coverdale who feels estranged from his own narrative is entirely unsurprising. As Mark Kinkead-Weekes remarks, . . . we confront, even in *The Scarlet Letter,* "an authorial *persona,* persistently interposing a highly artificial style between us and what we see"—and, one might add, receive. Of course Hawthorne treats Coverdale on occasion as a comic figure. Coverdale's earnest protestations that he thought he had escaped these "goblins of flesh and blood" involves a ludicrous, even surrealistic aspect (never entirely missing in Hawthorne's fiction) which will wax larger when Coverdale is chased by "chimeras." Further, Coverdale's sober projection of an anticipated stance ("The curtain fallen, I would pass onward, with my poor, individual life") is slightly in excess of its occasion, and thus again works ironically at his expense. Again Hawthorne is quite capable of burlesquing his narrator's "curiosity" (and incidentally the conventions of the first-person novel) when he places his narrator in his hermitage straining to hear what Westervelt and Zenobia have to say. Coverdale is obliged to confess mournfully (and therefore comically), "I could hardly make out an intelligible sentence on either side."

I think it is a mistake, however, to think that, because Coverdale is treated in part as a comic figure, who is reluctant even to tell the story, and who doubts his fitness for the task, that therefore he is not to be taken seriously. Rather I would stress that Hawthorne has also invested in Coverdale (in his only novel which grew out of a shared experience with friends and associates) his deepest feelings and perceptions concerning the place and responsibility of the artist in relation to his fellow men and to society at large. Through Coverdale he ponders the right of the artist to treat and remold communal human experiences.

Coverdale's position is even more treacherous than Holgrave's in *The House of the Seven Gables,* another Hawthornian artist and analytical observer. Holgrave, the descendant of a wizard, recognizes (like Coverdale) that "A mere observer like myself . . . is pretty certain to go astray." After seeing Judge Pyncheon's corpse, however, he can turn to Phoebe, the woman he loves, and confess his bewilderment: "I am all astray, and need your counsel." Priscilla, in contrast to Phoebe, is perpetually beyond Coverdale's reach and he, unlike Holgrave, is pursued by "goblins of flesh and blood." Yet, it is his unrequited love for her, his recognition of the essential value of her "true heart," which ensures he is not possessed and destroyed as both man and artist by the "goblins" who seek him out. We may grin at his putative stance but it reveals he possesses a complex sense of both the issues and the costs of authorship. His awareness of the risks confirms that he is ready to play his part "reverently and sadly," and with increasing authority, as events move steadily towards the "catastrophe" he increasingly envisages.

IV

The last third of the romance confirms that Coverdale's quest for artistic authority involves him in a continual struggle to balance the competing claims and dangers of both his analytic detachment and his sympathetic involvement.

Early in chapter 19 Coverdale honestly and painfully acknowledges his "keen, revengeful sense of the insult inflicted by Zenobia's scornful recognition, and more particularly by her letting down the curtain" but he asserts nonetheless his fitness as "chorus."

> She should have been able to appreciate that quality of the intellect and the heart, which impelled me (often against my own will, and to the detriment of my own comfort) to live in other lives, and to endeavour—by generous sympathies . . . and by bringing my human spirit into manifold accordance with the companions whom God assigned me—to learn the secret which was hidden even from themselves.

Hawthorne is dramatizing here his own, as well as Coverdale's, sense of the arrogance of the artist who wishes "to learn the secrets . . . hidden even from themselves." Both author and narrator escape demonism on the one hand and loss of self on the other, because they struggle to bring their "human spirit into manifold accordance" (root meaning "to bring heart to heart") "with the companions . . . God assigned" them. *They both strive in their art to fulfil the aims of Blithedale.* The quest for "accordance" is in diametrical opposition to Westervelt's "cold and dead materialism," to Hollingsworth's divisive, self-deceiving philanthropic system, and to Zenobia's display of self. Even more crucially, Coverdale's "accordance," though stimulated by Priscilla's "tender faith," involves an effort to understand (with all the risks involved) which "a character so simply constituted as hers," and which "has room only for a single predominant affection," can never face. Priscilla's love then is, paradoxically, the opposite of the Hawthornian artist's understanding.

Once Hawthorne has established that an effort to bring about a "manifold accordance" sustains both Coverdale's authority—and his own—it is not surprising that the following sequence clarifies both Coverdale's awakening sense of the shape his narrative will take and the kind of response he expects to develop in his reader. Confident now of his fitness for "the office" of "observer" he continues in chapter 19:

> True; I might have condemned them. Had I been judge, as well as witness, my sentence might have been stern as that of Destiny itself. But still, no trait of original nobility of character; no struggle against temptation; no iron necessity of will, on the one hand, nor extenuating circumstance to be derived from passion and despair, on the other; no remorse that might co-exist with error, even if powerless to prevent it; no proud repentance that should claim retribution as a meed—would go unappreciated. True, again, I might give my full assent to the punishment which was sure to follow. But it would be given mournfully, and with undiminished love. And, after all was finished, I would come, as if to gather up the white ashes of those who had perished at the stake, and to tell the world—the wrong being now atoned for—how much had perished there, which it had never yet known how to praise.

Leo B. Levy detects in such passages "the sternness of the Puritan age . . . [persisting] in Coverdale's fantasy of condemning to the stake those who have failed to confide in him." He fails to recognize that at such moments Coverdale is less concerned with judgment than with appreciation and with tragic waste. Coverdale's terms may serve as a summary of the great themes and attitudes of Shakespearean tragedy. Hawthorne's aim, no less, is to write a tragic romance which will mold and measure the human loss, the tragic waste, at the heart of the love quartet and of the Blithedale experiment in "accordance."

We miss both the distinction and the oddity of *The Blithedale Romance* if we do not realize that Hawthorne deliberately trusts such solemn business to a narrator who "exaggerates" his "own defects," who is, as we have seen, both bewildered and clairvoyant, both eagerly curious and painfully shy, both intuitive and distrustful of his intuitions. In the world of Hawthorne's fictions such opposing responses are just. As Coverdale brilliantly realizes, "a man cannot always decide for himself whether his own heart is cold or warm." In Hawthorne the human heart never knows itself well enough to set up the kingdom of heaven on earth (as the Blithedalians wish)—let alone to securely anticipate the kingdom of heaven itself, as his "good . . . just and sage" Puritans do.

That Hawthorne trusts his narrative to a narrator who "exaggerates" his "own defects" as surely as Hawthorne reveals them and that he so remorselessly pressurizes his narrator and ensures he is accused of every failing and every danger the Hawthornian artist is prone to, means inevitably that Coverdale struggles to establish his authority. As readers, we are obliged to share Coverdale's ambivalent responses to "the goblins of flesh and blood" who haunt, oppose, and finally in the figure of Zenobia, solicit him "to turn the affair into a ballad." In the closing chapters it is not Coverdale who is "witless." Rather his and our pain is that we watch his friends, witless of their fate, accuse him of meddling. Thus in chapter 20 Zenobia anticipates Coverdale's desire to rescue Priscilla from Westervelt: "With all your fancied acuteness, you step blindfold into these affairs. For any mischief that may follow your interference, I hold you responsible!" Zenobia's blind outrage at the only person who is aware of the impending "mischief" is outrageous. She knows better at the close.

Priscilla confesses to Coverdale that "I am blown about like a leaf. . . . I never have any free will" and Coverdale, too, discovers—try as he might—that he, too, cannot "resume an exclusive sway over" himself. He confesses: "Hollingsworth, Zenobia, Priscilla! These three had absorbed my life into themselves. Together with an inexpressible longing to know their fortunes, there was likewise a morbid resentment of my own pain, and a stubborn reluctance to come again within their sphere." Coverdale, however, is inextricably bound to them; apart from them his life is "a restless activity to no purpose." Both his sympathy as a medium and his analytic desire to understand their "old problem" ensure that he cannot escape "the goblins of flesh and blood" who want their story told.

"Two nights" after accidentally seeing Hollingsworth rescue Priscilla from Westervelt in "A Village Hall" he returns to Blithedale "with a yearning interest to learn the upshot of all my story." As usual, he fears that his "sickness of spirits" alone, has engendered "the spectral throng so apt to steal out of an unquiet heart," and thus render him vulnerable to "a spiritual lie"; but his intuition that "some evil thing had befallen us or was ready to befall" is confirmed by the "fantastic rabble" of "the Masqueraders." The masqueraders, like Zenobia, confirm "our heroic enterprise" to be "an illusion, a masquerade, a counterfeit Arcadia"—a kind of extended "The Maypole of Merry Mount"—and when they pursue him he is indeed "a mad poet haunted by chimeras." The fate he has tried to avoid suddenly overtakes him. The moment is surreal. Coverdale is here intensely comic; yet the cry of the masquerader dressed like the devil—"he is always ready to dance to the devil's tune"—expresses both his deepest fear and that of his creator, of the artist's potential doom. "Quite lost in reverie" he stumbles on (note he does not seek out) "the goblins of flesh and blood" who have absorbed him into themselves and will not let him rest. Respectful of their passion, awed and fearful, Coverdale says:

> "I will retire."
>
> "This place is free to you," answered Hollingsworth.
>
> "As free as to ourselves," added Zenobia. "This long while past, you have been following up your game, groping for human emotions in the dark corners of the heart. Had you been here a little sooner, you might have seen them dragged into the daylight. I could even wish to have my trial over again with you standing by, to see fair-play! Do you know, Mr. Coverdale, I have been on trial for my life."
>
> She laughed while speaking thus. But, in truth, as my eyes wandered from one of the group to another, I saw in Hollingsworth all that an artist could desire for the grim portrait of a Puritan magistrate, holding inquest of life and death in a case of witchcraft;—in Zenobia, the sorceress herself, not aged, wrinkled, and decrepit, but fair enough to tempt Satan with a force reciprocal to his own;—and in Priscilla, the pale victim, whose soul and body had been wasted by her spells. Had a pile of faggots been heaped against the rock, this hint of impending doom would have completed the suggestive picture.
>
> "It was too hard upon me," continued Zenobia, addressing Hollingsworth, "that judge, jury, and accuser should all be comprehended in one man!"

On trial here is not merely Zenobia before Hollingsworth, or Coverdale before Zenobia, but the Hawthornian artist before his characters; which is to say Hawthorne before his conscience or what James calls his "morality." Hollingsworth "as Puritan magistrate" is a reincarnation of iron Puritans such as Endicott and Governor Bellingham and Hawthorne's own great, great grandfather John Hathorne, who, as Hawthorne wrote in "The Custom House Sketch," "made himself so conspicuous in the martyrdom of the witches that their blood may fairly be said to have left a stain upon him." Hollingsworth is the very representative of "a goblin of flesh and blood" piping the devil's tune, holding like the Puritan magistrates, the power of life and death over helpless so-called sorceresses like Zenobia or innocent victims such as Priscilla. The magistrates in *The Scarlet Letter* are self-righteously certain that they can use the letter A as "a living sermon against sin, until the ignominious letter be engraved upon her tombstone," but the omniscient narrator states "out of the whole human family, it would not have been easy to select the same number of wise and virtuous persons who should be less capable of . . . judgment on an erring woman's heart." In contrast to the certainty of judgment embodied in Hollingsworth and the long line of Puritans behind him, we have the Hawthornian artist desperate once again to emphasize the secretiveness, the mystery and the freedom of his characters: they have not faced "judge, jury and accuser comprehended in the *one man of the artist!*" Rather the countermovement, as we have seen, is that the characters *demand* their story be told.

Zenobia is crucial to this thrust. As early as chapter 5 she teases Coverdale about his fascination for Priscilla: "Since you see the young woman in so poetical a light . . . you'd better turn the affair into a ballad. It is a grand subject and worthy of supernatural machinery." The culminating moment of this theme occurs after the trial scene when Zenobia and Coverdale are left alone in perhaps the most moving and powerful moment in the whole of Hawthorne's fiction:

> Zenobia had entirely forgotten me. She fancied herself alone with her great grief. And had it been only a common pity that I felt for her . . . the sacredness and awfulness of the crisis might have impelled me to steal away silently . . . But . . . I never once dreamed of questioning my right to be there, now, as I had questioned it just before, when I came so suddenly upon Hollingsworth and herself . . . It suits me not to explain what was the analogy that I saw, or imagined, between Zenobia's situation and mine; nor, I believe, will the reader detect this one secret, hidden

> beneath many a revelation which perhaps concerned me less. In simple truth, however, as Zenobia leaned her forehead against the rock . . . it seemed to me that the self-same pang, with hardly mitigated torment, leaped thrilling from her heart-strings to my own. Was it wrong, therefore, if I felt myself consecrated to the priesthood by sympathy like this, and called upon to minister to this woman's affliction, so far as mortal could?
>
> "But, indeed, what could mortal do for her? Nothing! The attempt would be a mockery and an anguish . . ."
>
> "Is it you, Miles Coverdale?" said she, smiling. "Ah, I perceive what you are about! You are turning this whole affair into a ballad. Pray let me hear as many stanzas as you happen to have ready!"
>
> "Oh, hush, Zenobia!" I answered. "Heaven knows what an ache is in my soul!"
>
> "It is genuine tragedy, is it not?" rejoined Zenobia, with a sharp, light laugh. "And you are willing to allow, perhaps that I have had hard measure. But it is a woman's doom . . . But, Mr. Coverdale, by all means write this ballad, and put your soul's ache into it, and turn your sympathy to good account as other poets do, and as poets must, unless they choose to give us glittering icicles instead of lines of fire. As for the moral, it shall be distilled into the final stanza, in a drop of bitter honey."

Coverdale does not question his "right to be there, now," as he shares with Zenobia the finest moment of accordance in the romance. The secret analogy with Zenobia contains a deeply felt paradox: Coverdale with Priscilla, and Zenobia with Hollingsworth, experience the torment of loss of self to the other without hope of togetherness; but because their hearts have been touched they are both at this moment "beings of reality," united in their anguish and grief.

Zenobia the self-appointed "tragedy queen" of the story thinks "It is a genuine tragedy" because it tells of "a woman's doom." But though Coverdale, after her suicide, accepts her judgment ("the world should throw open all its avenues to the passport of a woman's bleeding heart") the tragedy has wider implications. These are embodied in Coverdale's final reflections on Hollingsworth's "perilous," "exclusive" philanthropy: "I see in Hollingsworth an exemplification of the most awful truth in Bunyan's book of such;—from the very gate of Heaven, there is a by-way to the pit!" That "by-way" is a broad path in the actual slough of this world, in which the road to hell is paved with good intentions—the good intentions of the original pilgrims to whom Coverdale compares the Blithedalians; of the latter in their effort "to establish the one true system"; of Hollingsworth for prison reform; of Zenobia for women's rights; of Coverdale for a better world. All prove in Zenobia's words "varieties of mock life."

Hawthorne's vision of mankind anticipates Conrad's and T. S. Eliot's. The Congo to Marlow like the Blithedale world to Hawthorne is "a dream sensation" and "what redeems" both ventures "is the idea only." But in Eliot's words in "The Hollow Men":

> Between the idea
> And the reality
> Between the motion
> And the act
> Falls the Shadow

"The shadow" in Hawthorne, as Zenobia tells Hollingsworth, is "Self, self, self!" which is inexorably embodied in any project, and which threatens to turn all human plans and ambitions into masquerades. Not least the writing of tales. As Coverdale realizes Zenobia's version of her "genuine tragedy" is the *romantic tragedy,* of the ballad of "village maidens . . . wronged in their first love . . . seeking peace in the bosom of the old, familiar stream." The "drop of bitter honey" "distilled into the final stanza" of her version, and of her life, is the old story of the woman who dies for love. It is a grim irony that in completing *that* pattern Zenobia confirms that the shadow of "the self" was with her until the very end, because her postured romantic death embodies, as Coverdale gloomily realizes, "some tint of the Arcadian affectation."

Whereas Zenobia takes her "soul's ache" to a watery grave which hideously rigidifies her, the shy, frail, self-mocking Coverdale puts "his soul's ache" into a *tragic romance* which truly ends with a "moral" and "a drop of bitter honey." Thus Coverdale's final disclosure confirms that the projected "life of love and free-heartedness" which Zenobia has looked to as the goal of Blithedale is an impossibility. "Love and free-heartedness," as the romance demonstrates, are at odds. And that bittersweet recognition has profound implications for Coverdale. Early in the romance the minor poetaster has enthusiastically explained to Zenobia that he means "to produce . . . poetry—true, strong, natural and sweet, as is the life we are going to lead." By the close he knows better: "As for poetry, I have given it up." But, most importantly, Coverdale's last revelation, which in turn reveals that Hawthorne has deliberately thrown a "veil" over his narrative, draws our attention to the novel as "a masquerade," one that has deliberately mystified and deceived us so that we *realize* the consecrating power of the artist, the fakes and ploys of whose masquerade serve to ensure that Coverdale truly fulfils his role:

> It resembled that of the Chorus in a classic play, which seems to be set aloof from the possibility of personal concernment, and bestows the whole measure of its hope or fear, it exultation or sorrow, on the fortunes of others, between whom and itself this sympathy is the only bond. Destiny . . . chooses . . . the presence of at least one calm observer. It is his office . . . to detect the final fitness of incident to character, and distil, in his long-brooding thought, the whole morality of the performance.

One of the great distinctions of *The Blithedale Romance* is that it captures what it costs in human terms for an author to be "a calm observer." It is at once to live off and in "the fortunes of others." As both Coverdale and his creator know, keen perceptive and analytic powers lead to a deficiency in feeling and the risk of the artist's estrangement from his fellows. On the other hand, the romance captures the consecrating powers of the artist. The artist is "sacra-re" that is "made sacred" because he is "set apart" (*O.E.D.*); but he works also for accordance (con = together). The Hawthornian artist strives to give us "the whole morality" and the whole cost.

Thus "the final passage" is indeed "bitter honey." The oxymoron is precise. Coverdale's life has been *bitter* honey. He cannot understand why Zenobia and Priscilla should be under the sway of such a monster of selfishness as Westervelt and such a distinctively egoistic spirit as Hollingsworth. We come to realize, however, that the very ego and purpose of these figures have seemingly conferred meaning upon the lives of the women who surround them. "*Bitter* honey," too, because Coverdale's analytic curiosity ensures his divorce from the woman he loves. The artist as man pays a high price for his skepticism. Like Theodore in Zenobia's legend he is left to pine "for ever and ever for another sight of that dim mournful face—which might have been his life—long, household, fireside joy—to desire, and waste life in a feverish quest, and never meet it more."

Yet, too, both as a man and an artist he has experienced "bitter *honey*"; he has been haunted by three characters in search of him who, though they have sought definition from him, they have provided, too, the only definition and "proper substance" he himself is ever to know in life. Hence his attenuation whenever he is apart from them, and Blithedale is over. But truly "bitter honey" because, as an artist Coverdale gives shape and purpose to their lives in the tragic romance he has written. It is surely satisfying to the reader to know that at least one person has loved that test case of Blithedale's values, Priscilla. Moreover, because Coverdale's heart is and was touched; because he once did have hopes for Blithedale which he still remembers as "our beautiful scheme of a noble and unselfish life"; because he can attest even at the end "I feel we had struck upon what ought to have been a truth" he has *earned* the "consecrated" right to turn "his sympathy to good account" and to write if not Zenobia's romantic tragedy, his own tragic romance. That is *The Blithedale Romance* in which, for once in his artistic career, he is able "to detect the final fitness of incident to character, and distil, in his long-brooding thought, the whole morality of the performance."

MICHAEL J. COLACURCIO

The Matter of America: "My Kinsman, Major Molineux"

"My Kinsman, Major Molineux" is, by almost all accounts, the masterpiece of the "Provincial Tales," however short or long the table of contents of that "projected" collection is imagined to be. And doubtless it presents us with an unavoidable test of the style of interpretation we have been imagining. On the one hand, its historical locus is unarguably more obvious than that of "Roger Malvin's Burial": to recover the tale at all—from among those which Hawthorne did not reprint in his famous collections of 1837, 1842, and 1846, and which the ongoing tradition of moralistic appreciation did not know how to value—was in fact to observe the evidence of its ("proleptic") relation to the American Revolution. And at some level this fact has always seemed fair enough, for that "event" (along with its fifty-year anniversary celebration in 1826) was altogether more famous than the original doings (or memorial sayings) at Lovewell's Rock. On the other hand, however, its distinctively literary merit has continued to seem more obvious and unflawed; so that ever *since* the initial moment of rediscovery and revaluation, the critical history of this tale can fairly be described as the dialogue created by a series of more or less elegant attempts to set it free from its historical moorings. Critics have found themselves repeatedly insisting that the perfection of "Molineux" is (to change the figure) its ability to ride on its own superb melting.

From *The Province of Piety: Moral History in Hawthorne's Early Tales*. © 1984 by The President and Fellows of Harvard College. Harvard University Press, 1984. Originally entitled "The Matter of America: The Provincial Tales."

Evidently it can do so very well. Few sensitive readers have trouble responding, in a vital and elementary way, to the literal details of Robin's anxious progress. And most tend at once to associate the private results of his strange misadventures with their own experience of adolescent disillusion and adult choice, spontaneously and without the mediation of history. One readily sees why. We watch Robin taking, all innocently, a long and crucial first step into psychic independence. We sense, almost immediately, that he is stepping in over his head, involving himself in a process which, having a structure of its own, he cannot entirely control; we worry that he may get somewhat more than he shrewdly bargains for. When he does, we sympathize with his childlike wish to turn around and go home, even as we conclude, in our own adult wisdom, that "you can't." And we sadly imagine that he too will soon internalize this inevitable conclusion of experience. In all of this the "philosophical" perfection of Hawthorne's plot seems too general and complete to admit the slightest adulteration of historical particularity. The sequence of Robin's nighttime confrontations, rendered in a superb modulation of tones—from callow confidence, to violent frustration, to honest uncertainty, and on the verge of some mature toleration of self-contradiction—seems regulated by some absolutely universal law of growing up. It is as if the entire genre of *bildungsroman* could be epitomized in the single evening of ambiguity and weariness of some Provincial Everyman.

Accordingly, we do not much resist the translation of this inevitable human plot into the appropriate clinical terms. In seeking the economic and social assistance of a worldly uncle, Robin is, truly enough, searching out some more tolerant surrogate for the loving but strict, ministerial father he has left behind. He evidently desires an extension of his sphere of personal freedom, without the loss of social identity which complete self-reliance inevitably entails; indeed, since Major Molineux is a famous and successful relative, Robin is evidently seeking the best of both worlds. It is, therefore, no more ironic than it is appropriate that every male figure he meets turns out to represent a more absolute version of paternal inhibition than the one he left behind: evidently it is even harder to hang between than it is to go back. And though some relatively innocent readers may resist the inference that Robin never did "really" want to locate Molineux, few who know about "Oedipal violence" (from Freud or from his mythic sources) will find Robin's hysterical response to their eventual meeting either gratuitously cruel or outrageously unmotivated. Edifying or not, the process of maturation has a logic of its own. The Unconscious has a reason which the political commitments and even the family sentiments do not know. And it has wrecked more than one enlightened critical system.

Thus the problem of "Molineux" is different from that of "Malvin." And more crucial. With "Malvin" the task has been to suggest that *only* some fairly sophisticated form of historicism can fairly comprehend all the tale's arcane references and adequately unify its fictional logic. With "Molineux," however, the problem is evidently to show that *any* form of historicism is supple enough to avoid reduction. The "Hutchinson Mob" episode of [Hawthorne's] *Grandfather's Chair* throws an astonishingly useful light on the moderate politics of "My Kinsman, Major Molineux"; but the static moralism of the one will never replace the dramatic irony of the other. And not even the strongest evidence in favor of the developing historicity of Hawthorne's imagination can justify a criticism which enlists symbolic richness and psychoanalytic acumen in the aid of a high-school history lesson.

Nevertheless, there is ample reason to imagine that the historical setting does very intensely matter. Even the staunchest "myth critic" will have to concede that the "vehicle" of "Molineux" is as pointedly particular as its "tenor" is timelessly general. To be sure, Hawthorne's prosy headnote seems to call us off from too detailed an investigation of the local history of Boston in the earlier eighteenth century, begging to be excused from the obligation to provide "an account of the train of circumstances that had caused [the] temporary inflammation of the popular mind"; but surely the anti-historical signal may be entirely ironic, as are the similar gestures at the beginning of "Malvin." Perhaps the tale itself will stand in for those events, in a general way, and by some acceptable law of literary substitution. Or quite possibly the "historical" interest touched matters far more significant than the precipitating causes of some unpleasant but forgettable rum riot. Or, most wickedly—as Roy Harvey Pearce long ago suggested—possibly Hawthorne means to alert the reader to the sort of language or habits of perception that have erased all real ugliness from the historical memory. Ugliness there certainly is, in the tale's final parade of horribles; it all seems, somehow, *very* historial; and it must mean *something,* even in a story about the absurdities of growing up.

With or without the gloss from *Grandfather's Chair,* the orchestrated cacophony of the Molineux procession evokes a great deal of the nighttime activity of the pre-Revolutionary 1760s and early 1770s. The lord of this misrule recalls the notorious revolutionary mobster Joyce, Jr., as unmistakably as the name "Molineux" reminded Longfellow, however oddly, of that somewhat more polite Bostonian who was known to sponsor and organize such purposive festivities. Even the name "Robin" (as we shall presently observe) is not without an astonishingly apt significance in the lexicon of eighteenth-century politics, the language of which is elsewhere strewn all over the tale. And surely some sense of history pervades the story's primary "literary" realities, lower down the cognitive scale: tone, attitude, and gesture everywhere bespeak a rising and unruly people, if not quite a revolutionary populace.

We can say, of course, that the tale has to be set "somewhere"; and where *better* than in the Age of Revolution? What better backdrop for a rite of personal passage than a nation's own problematic and, yes, ultimately violent transition? Or we can suggest, somewhat more pointedly, that the political ambiguities of eighteenth-century Boston provide, for Hawthorne, precisely the sort of "neutral territory" he needed for such a tale: following Scott (and perhaps Cooper), he learned to let disputed or non-aligned real estate stand for those neutral times when the bewildered psyche does not know if it is "here or there." Or we might propose—in some ultimate gesture of reconciliation, designed to incorporate both the preceding suggestions and to "split the difference" between the political Historicist and the psychoanalytic Myth Critic—that Hawthorne means *both* his matters, public and private; that he means both *equally*; that in this one instance, at least, he has made it possible to tell tenor from vehicle or to decide what reality is being studied in terms of what image. In this view, the process of personal maturation and the dynamics of political independence go round and round in our mind forever, in the aftermath of Hawthorne's tale, like equilibrists; or, not unlike "My love" and "a red, red rose," Robin and Revolution now exist in that sort of indissoluble union which only literature can create. What Art has joined together, let no man deconstruct.

And yet certain nice questions would always remain, evading solution by such a large, easy, genial, and tolerant view. For example, why should Robin's experience be regarded as the personal equivalent of *both* the 1730s and the 1760s or 1770s? It might well be seen as inseparably like one or the other, depending on whether Hawthorne thought the rite of passage occurred most perfectly in the psychic context of benign neglect or of threatened enslavement; but probably not both, without the plot's coming to seem a little too thick. As in fact it does, for surely one major effect of the story is to leave the reader wondering, uncertainly, whether he is "here" in a minor episode of provincial unruliness or "there" in the glory and chaos of full revolt. Taken seriously, the question can become fairly unsettling: what if this cardinal ambiguity of setting, which amounts to something between a redundancy of plot and a contradiction of theme, were somehow the clue to an interpretation altogether less conciliatory than the one we have imagined?

What if Hawthorne's main purpose were to suggest that the fit between the private-personal and the public-political is hardly ever so perfect as literature can make it seem? Arguably, the major result of *any* such too-perfect identification would be to obscure important differences, to blur certain distinguishing features of each. And thinkably, that effect might be, in certain cases, somebody's deliberate and meretricious intention. What if Hawthorne were perceiving that the American Revolution were *not,* or did not *necessarily* enfigure itself as, some inevitable rite of national passage? If so, then the tale of Robin Molineux is more ironic than we have yet supposed, its patriotism more bitter than anything in Robert Lowell.

What we need to imagine, then, in order to test for the ultimate thematic relevance of the history on the face of "My Kinsman, Major Molineux" is the possibility that the literary identity we are invited to experience as the heart of the tale is less the creation of Hawthorne's own esemplastic imagination than it is a cultural *donnée*; not a last philosophical insight but only another popular story, obscuring the problem it pretends to solve and creating others along the way. And if this is so, then the task of criticism is not to admire but to criticize. It is, in fact, to tear asunder a fabric whose one seam calls critical attention to its evident fabrication. But we may well begin, less drastically, by noticing certain surprising colorations in the historical weave.

At something like the climax of "The Boston Massacre" section of *Grandfather's Chair,* the most sensitive of the youthful listeners painfully protests that he is learning more than he had wished to know about the way things really were back in the 1770s: "'The Revolution,' observed Lawrence, who had said but little during the evening, 'was not such a calm, majestic movement as I supposed. I do not love to hear of mobs and broils in the street. These things were unworthy of the people, when they had such a great object to accomplish.'" Grandfather is moved at once to soften the effect of his "true story." Everywhere on his guard against the danger of tainting the pure springs of youthful patriotism with some premature admixture of irony, he hastens to reassure Lawrence that "our Revolution" was indeed a grand movement, full of "great and noble sentiment," whatever fault the historian could find with its mode of expression. Lawrence takes the instruction, and yet we sense that his innocent pain survives the consolations of political philosophy, and that it is supposed to. Somehow his response, and even his language, has seemed truer and more convincing than Grandfather's own. Probably it is the word "majestic" that gives away Hawthorne's deepest and most adult case. We are surprised to find a youthful observer discover so absolutely just a word to characterize the half truth by which the Revolutionary Fathers have sought to socialize their revolt from authority—and their Sons. We may even remember the word as an echo of the conclusion of "Molineux" where, surprisingly, it characterizes the calm of the deposed ruler, in myth-shattering contrast to the "counterfeit pomp," "senseless uproar," and "frenzied merriment" of the deposing mob which broils in the street.

Majestic indeed had the Revolution come to seem by the time Hawthorne began (in the late 1820s) to write "My Kinsman, Major Molineux"; or by that moment, slightly earlier, when he began to borrow such "annals of Massachusetts Bay" as underwrite whatever history the tale contains. Nowhere, in fact, have the convulsive events of the American 1760s and 1770s been made to appear more simply and calmly majestic than in the public oratory which marked the semicentennial celebrations of 1826. Probably these festivities have to be set down as at least the remote rhetorical occasion of "Molineux"; and arguably they were the immediate and impelling psychological cause. For the appropriately placed observer could hardly fail to mark the drastic difference between the way the events had got themselves recorded and interpreted in the sober pages of Thomas Hutchinson's *History of Massachusetts Bay* and the way they reappeared, miraculously transfigured, in the altogether more occasional productions of democratic visionaries who rejected Hutchinson's theory of history as absolutely as their fathers had anathematized his political commitments.

For Hutchinson, a fatal constitutional error had launched a slow but perceptible drift toward criminal violence. The rumor of the royal governor "driven from the province by the whizzing of a musket ball" really does set the stage, though unintentionally, for his own bitter experience with the tender mercies of his fellow Bostonians—in a historical episode which, in Grandfather's retelling, would also teach Lawrence more than he wanted to know. And yet what had interested Hutchinson most was not the threat of violence lurking within the slumbering "Puritanism" of the secularized New England populace but rather the cumulative (and evidently wearing) effect of a determined (and apparently ideological) "Resistance" to the "six governors" who ruled Massachusetts after "the surrender of the old charter, under James II." Little of majesty here, in their "continual bickerings with the House of Representatives." And yet, as more than one historian of historians has ironically noted, Hutchinson's endlessly patient and tediously "legitimist" constitutional *History* quickly came to serve as the standard sourcebook for past greatness and less directly as a ready textbook for "rising glory."

Latter-day Puritan Jeremiahs used it for their fast- and election-day sermons through more than a decade before Lexington and Concord, as naturally as if it had been but an updated version of Mather's ancient "Wonderbook." And incipient American Republicans continued to draw on its riches in a lengthening series of Fourth of July orations designed to inculcate the lessons of Apocalyptic Whiggism, in spite of the fact that Hutchinson himself was regarded as a malicious traitor to the American cause. That Hutchinson's work tended, in itself, strenuously to resist enlistment of *any* version of the dominant American teleology seemed scarcely to matter. Bancroft's hour having not yet come, one had to make do with what there was; or, rather, make what there was to do what one wanted. What one wanted, evidently, was "majesty." *No one* loved to hear of mobs or broils in the street. And nearly everyone wanted to hear that the Revolution had been a major event in Holy History. It would overstate the case only slightly to say that in 1826 (Hutchinson himself to the contrary notwithstanding) all one could discover about the Revolution was that, in the Cosmic Progress toward a Universal Salvation in Holy Liberty, it figured as only slightly less important than the Birth of Christ and the Protestant Reformation, whose libertarian meaning it essentially fulfilled. And this astonishing fact of public attitude and political rhetoric probably explains the basic literary strategy of "Molineux."

Only in this context of outrageous typological inflation does Hawthorne's deliberate running-together of two rather markedly different moments in the political life of the colonial eighteenth century reveal any plausible motivation or express anything like satisfactory sense, historical or literary. Some drastic reduction is being made, clearly enough, but its *raison* is neither factual ignorance nor that imaginative gratuity supposed by suggestions that Hawthorne altered history to suit his literary purposes. Evidently Hawthorne is striking back at the flagrant idolatries of America's pseudo-Puritan civil religion: in the face of a nearly overwhelming national consensus in favor of the holy-historical significance of 1776, Hawthorne is studying the majestic Revolution in terms of a minor outbreak of provincial unruliness, a mob scene.

Such, apparently, is the strategy of irony and insult of the historical headnote: abandon all critical discrimination you who enter here. Do not inquire too exactly into the local details of the "here or there" in your Great Chain of Becoming, and you can easily discover not only pre-figuration but even pre-enactment everywhere; but beware lest the ordinariness of the type destroy the majesty of its fulfillment. Proceed into this fiction as if safe in a world so politically insignificant *in itself* that only an obsessive legitimist like Thomas Hutchinson (or an unreconstructed romancer like Freud) could love it. Then encounter not only certain historic identities (the mobster Joyce, Jr., and, by association, the scoundrel William Molineux) but also a famous metaphorical logic (coming of age) that cannot *but* imply the Revolution. Then wonder: *am* I here or there? Which is to ask: just what sort of "event" was the Revolution, anyhow? The completion of the Divine Plot so long preparing, the final unveiling of God's own historico-literary *majestas*? Or just another local anxiety, one more utterly "temporary inflammation of the popular mind"—predictably violent and relentlessly ordinary?

The epistemology of the tale is still remotely "typological," if one insists, but only in some negative or ironic mode. And the motive is much more obviously "critical" in the eighteenth-century and modern historiographical sense. Nothing that happens in this midsummer nightmare is elevated or transfigured by its reference forward to the Revolution; not the piteous and terrible tarring of Major Molineux, and not the traumatic hazing of his kinsman. The red-and-black-faced Joyce, Jr., evidently means to claim descent from one of the Regicides of Charles I; and his having exchanged his ancestor's patient ass for an apocalyptic horse seems to express somebody's belief that some last revolution of human affairs is at hand. But as a violence of rhetoric gives way to a violence of fact, the reader is more effectively reminded that the Boston Tea Party would, like any other tactic of resistance, have to be *led,* and by someone willing (at least temporarily) to invoke the powers of darkness. Similarly, the implication of the historic Molineux insinuates (among many other things) that even *American* protests need to be sponsored, organized, planned, and managed as well as led; and that often enough they were paid for by the very rum the British have made an issue "here," in 1733. So that the unlovely but subtle idea of conspiracy is added to the ugly but obvious idea of violence: not only do revolutionary passions express themselves in ways that seldom accomplish God's justice, but they proceed far more intelligibly from somebody's ordinary political design than from God's special providence.

As a matter of distressing fact, Hawthorne has come much closer to dignifying the "Tory" cause with religious significance than he has to endorsing the familiar typological argument which explains "How the Puritans won the American Revolution." For as the tale moves toward its violent and hysterical revelation of Robin's Royalist kinsman, Hawthorne suggests that Major Molineux might recall somewhat more than the Scapegoat King who organizes pagan politics and presides, in "pity and terror," over the birth of tragedy. Borne along by a torchlight procession, he reminds us not a little of a Christ betrayed by an apostle from Gethsemane to Calvary. This, surely, is the view being prepared for when Robin is instructed, all Biblically, to "Watch here an hour" and when, earlier, someone in authority is bold to declare, "I know not the man." We need no crowing cock to remind us that, whoever may be the Judas of the piece, it is finally Robin who fills up the role of the faithless Peter by refusing to come forward and own the man he had taken for a political savior.

But all of this, of course, is also in the mode of irony. It is simply the *other* religious view of the American Revolution—the Tory view, barely hinted at in the scrupulously secular pages of Hutchinson's *History,* but rampantly revealed in all the other conservative critics of 1776 (or 1649) that Hawthorne had likely read. According to this very traditional and august view, *any* form of resistance to established authority not only violates the divine command to "honor thy father" but essentially reenacts mankind's Original Rebellion; and violence against the person of *any* of God's vicarious agents of saving order recommits the crucifixion of Christ. Not a Tory but an Ironist, Hawthorne is as far from endorsing this patriarchal and sacramental, essentially Anglican view of history as he is from precipitating an idolatrous extension of Puritan typology. No doubt a fair number of "Lawrences" in Hawthorne's audience could take useful adult instruction from the Tory view: notably deficient on the score of comparative religion, they needed reminding that God's politics are too much disputed to serve as nationalistic creed. And yet the main purpose of Hawthorne's impressively dramatic "Toryism" is simply to strike the uneven balance.

For, finally, it is the idea of ordinary human conspiracy rather than high theologic violence which organizes most of Hawthorne's prediction of the revolution. The Tory view does not at all reduce the cosmic implications of this provincial ouster of authority; it merely turns them inside out. Hawthorne's own strategy is far different: as he relentlessly reduces Apocalypse to rum riot, he keeps rubbing our nose in the painfully plotted quality of the action in which Robin has got himself involved. And it is in reading the tale from this point of view that we grasp the truly revisionary quality of Hawthorne's provincial imagination.

The "Robin Molineux" who enters the "little metropolis of a New England colony" as eagerly "as if he were entering London city" is more aptly named than we have supposed. His problematic surname reminds us, first of all, that he is very nearly related to somebody who will turn out to be on "the other side"—as soon as it shall have become clear that there *are* sides, in a strife which can be made to appear every bit as "civil" as a later one so named. And, somewhat more teasingly, it serves to remind us that neither we nor Robin himself can be entirely certain which side he himself is going to be on. He may back up from the brink to which he is approaching so near. Or, as seems more likely, he may indeed decide to throw in his lot with the faction his friendly observer refers to, conspiratorially, as "us"; if so, he may yet grow up to be the Molineux of history recognized by Longfellow, and by Professor Pearce, as that "organizer and leader of anti-Loyalist mobs," deemed a "martyr" to the cause or a "Pest to Society," depending on one's side.

Beyond this, however, his name surely recalls another Molineux who also figures in the pages of Hutchinson's account of the ordel of legitimacy in Massachusetts. Way back in Volume I (in the 1670s), the men of Massachusetts had protested the difficulty of conforming to Parliament's "acts of trade," which they apprehended as "an invasion of the rights, liberties, and properties of the subjects of his Majesty in the colony, they not being represented in parliament." This, of course, is a classic statement of the classic problem, so that Hutchinson can scarcely let it pass: thus early, he remarks, did the colonists betray "the wrong sense they had of the relation they stood in to England." Furthermore, the colony's error was so serious that it rightly became "one great article of charge against it" in the proceedings against their original charter. And yet, unforgivable as their error must certainly be judged, it is at least understandable: "The people of Ireland, about this same time, were under the same mistake"; and certainly "they had not greater color for an exemption from English acts of parliament, than a colony of natural born subjects, departing the kingdom with the leave of the prince." Still as loyal and loving a Massachusetts man as any, Hutchinson is actually "glad [to] have the instance of Ireland, and that so sensible a gentleman as Mr. Molineux, the friend of Mr. Locke, engaged in the cause; for it may serve as some excuse for our ancestors, that they were not alone in their mistaken apprehensions of the nature of their subjection."

Much is at stake here, obviously. When the theory of Locke is added to the Molinesque premise of a plurality of "parliamentary" bodies, all equal under the headship of the King (not to mention "taxation without representation"), we have a nearly perfect epitome of the legal and constitutional question of the Revolution as we used to understand it. Very likely, "Molineux" does not mean to address itself to the problem at this technical level. But we know where we are: the colonists conspiring to oust Robin's kinsman and, eventually, to enlist Robin himself in their own partisan cause, are still laboring under the same "wrong sense" of their relation to England. The rum tax lies directly between those difficult-to-obey "acts of trade" England began to pass (and to try to enforce) in the years following the Restoration, and the Stamp Act, which would undo the career of Hutchinson himself. And the local response is as clear as ever: no such act can possibly be legal in Massachusetts; so that those who forcefully oppose it are no more outside the law than those who would forcefully execute it. Thus, if our Young Man

Molineux does indeed grow up to be a version of the "well-to-do radical Boston trader" Molineux, he will only be moving into the political space originally occupied by his Irish-patriot namesake, his "Uncle Molineux."

Before we decide this is a little too "much" to be other than gratuitous—some half-conscious echo of the effect of chance reading desultorily done—we should note that "Robin" itself is scarcely an innocent name in the lexicon of eighteenth-century political conspiracy. In the still Biblical New England, it sounds strangely unlike a given or "Christian" name. Almost certainly it means to put us in mind of "Robin" Walpole, so nicknamed, in mock-affection, by the long list of his true-blue political enemies in England's own neo-Puritan Country Party, and of the "Robinocracy" he was accused of creating in order to stabilize the modern nation and/or to subvert the ancient constitution. The "Robinarch," as the "gloomy" Bolingbroke famously explained, "is *nominally* a minister only . . . but in reality he is a sovereign, as despotic, arbitrary a sovereign as this part of the world affords." And more particularly: "The *Robinarch* . . . hath unjustly engrossed the whole power of a nation into his own hands . . . [and] admits no person to any considerable post or trust or power under him who is not either a *relation,* or *creature,* or a *thorough-paced tool* whom he can lead into any dirty work without being able to discover his designs or the consequences of them." Now obviously Robin is not—and may indeed never grow up to be—that sort of wily usurper and pernicious corruptor. And yet he is, from his very outset, on his way to join what somebody's politics might easily identify as a Robinocracy.

Robin may think of himself, all innocently, as merely seeking to "profit by his kinsman's generous intentions," but what his wealthy and politically influential relative has in mind, apparently, is patronage. Unless he has been *utterly* deceived by Uncle Molineux, he is on his way to some "place" or "post" in a local Royalist "establishment" which clearly predicts the network of interrelated appointments by which Thomas Hutchinson himself would seek to manage the political process in Massachusetts, and for which he would be accused of deeper plotting than Walpole himself. No one has mentioned those "*bribes* which are called *pensions* in these countries." And, as things turn out, Robin never will get himself "tied down with *honors, titles,* and *preferments.*" He can scarcely be said to have "sacrificed [his] principles and conscience to a set of *party names,* without any meaning, or the vanity of appearing in favor at *court.*" But none of the nighttime Revolutionaries Robin encounters has any trouble recognizing him as someone "persuaded to prostitute [himself] for the lean reward of *hopes* and *promises.*"

Of course this political "style" is far less proper to provincial Massachusetts than to Hanoverian England. One of the American problems, in fact—as Hutchinson himself would learn, to his dismay—was that there was not nearly *enough* patronage to make the thing work: two posts for yourself and a single place for your brother-in-law, and the local resources were pretty well exhausted; and so the native political process, with its own peculiar "genius," seemed destined to go its own ragged and illegitimate way. But this fact did not prevent the local Jeremiahs, in a marvelously successful imitation of their transatlantic counterparts, from creating the impression that innocent New England was becoming as deeply mired in "corruption" as Old England at its "Egyptian" worst; or (to change the figure) that Boston was a city hellishly like London. From a sheerly rhetorical point of view, Robin might indeed be entering the one as well as the other. And apparently the outline of the problem could be discerned even at the distance of the 1730s, when the secular (and essentially alien) idea of political "parties" was only just beginning to take shape in the land founded on a myth of holy consensus.

For there it all is in the story of Robin's painful initiation into the politics of conspiracy. Before this political innocent has proceeded very far in his insufficiently shrewd attempt to place himself under the patronage of his royal kinsman, he runs directly up against an impressive display of that sort of transplanted "courtliness" which lent social credence to the imported political style. "Promenading on the pavement" are a number of "gay and gallant figures" who seem on transatlantic loan from Vauxhall Gardens: "Embroidered garments of showy colors, enormous periwigs, gold-laced hats, and silver-hilted swords glided past him and dazzled his optics. Travelled youths, imitators of the European fine gentlemen of the period, trod jauntily along, half dancing to the fashionable tunes which they hummed, and making poor Robin ashamed of his quiet and natural gait." It hardly matters whether these "figures" are *really* the local specimens of those "Anglicized" New Englanders already corrupted by "luxury," or whether this is all, also, part of the evening's ritual *en costume*—any more than it matters whether one is "here" in the 1730s (or Boston) or "there" in the 1770s (or London). Social reality or literary satire, the operative point is the same: an Old English Court Party has insinuated itself into the provincial life in countrified New England.

The point is extended and emphasized as Robin makes "many pauses to examine the gorgeous display of goods in the shop windows." Already "ashamed," the American Jonathan is now being tempted by those imported manufactures which are the social (and economic) counterpart of the political establishment he is already on his way, half-wittingly, to join. Of course

Robin cannot afford to *buy* any of these luxuries: after satisfying the ferryman's demand, his "little province bill of five shillings" has returned him only a "sexangular piece of parchment, valued at three pence," scarcely enough to cover the cost of a couple of "great puffy rolls." Clearly the province is suffering a serious "depreciation in [Robin's] sort of currency," and everywhere the balance of more than trade seems to be running against New England. British taxes on rum, an American "Good Creature," handsomely supports a mercantile empire, which sells its gorgeous manufactures back to the provinces at prices which only those who have sold themselves to the system can afford. It may or may not be all part of some deep-dyed conspiracy of economic, then social, and then religious "enslavement," but one would scarcely be surprised to discover the existence of some local counterplot. Or, at very least, to learn that the values of the Puritanic "Country" will be resisting those of the Aristocratic "Court" in some fairly self-conscious way.

Thus the second, and altogether more telling, *political* irony of Robin's reference to the man with "authority"—he of the "two sepulchral hems"—as "some country representative." Robin is himself, quite obviously, the country bumpkin; but almost certainly the authoritative gentleman he encounters is a "Representative" in the intransigent local "Parliament," of the values and interests of the resistance, the "Country Party." Quite probably he is the Speaker of the Massachusetts House of Representatives: some such function is comically suggested by his continual hem-hem clearing of the throat, as if to deliver a speech; and only that position would seem to justify his reappearing, at the climax of Robin's political initiation, on the balcony of the building where that body was accustomed to hold its Molinesque deliberations. The joke is pretty broad, even though everybody seems to have missed it so far: the first man of whom Robin demands the whereabouts of his courtly kinsman turns out to be the leader of the Country Opposition, Molineux's deepest official enemy and (it seems likely) one of the principal organizers of the evening's political festivities.

Everywhere, clearly, Robin locates himself in the most ironic and dangerous relation to a highly contrived and carefully orchestrated political demonstration. Indeed he seems the only person in the story who is *not* in on the plot. The reader has to learn fast or lapse himself into the psychology of adolescence.

In effect the French Protestant innkeeper tests Robin's political sympathies when he inquires, "From the country, I presume, sir?" And he anticipates the conspiratorial conclusion of Robin's guide later, when he also presumes that Robin "intend[s] a long stay with *us*" (my italics). But Robin knows only one magic name, "Molineux"—at the mere mention of which "there was a sudden and general movement in the room," expressing not "the eagerness of each individual to become his guide" but rather the general hostility, based on the common suspicion that the well-known plan is being exposed, or satirized. No more does Robin know the local words and ways when he encounters "little parties of men . . . in outlandish attire": "They paused to address him, [but] such intercourse did not at all enlighten his perplexity. They did but utter a few words in some language of which Robin knew nothing, and perceiving his inability to answer, bestowed a curse on him in plain English and hastened away." In well over his head, Robin simply does not know the password to the evening's plans and arrangements. And so, again and again, his innocent blundering comes dangerously close to provoking violent retaliation.

His situation is especially perilous just when, cudgel visibly in hand, he rudely accosts the figure with the "infernal visage." Absurdly addressing him as the philosopher's "honest man," he blatantly demands the "whereabouts [of] the dwelling of [his] kinsman, Major Molineux." At first the confrontation seems fated: "Keep your tongue between your teeth, fool, and let me pass," says the "deep, gruff voice," confident of its own power to wield the cudgel. "Let me pass, or I'll strike you to the earth." But Robin, issuing his own violent but pre-political "Don't tread on me," boldly repeats his preposterous demand; and for this repeated impertinence he receives, strangely, not a thrashing but rather the instruction to watch for an hour, when "Major Molineux will pass by." What saves Robin is hardly the threat of his own main strength. Possibly it is his very innocence, provoking the mob leader to reveal his political role, though not his personal identity, by unmuffling what the narrator wickedly calls his "unprecedented physiognomy"—so "strange" to youthful travelers but so familiar to students of political typology. Ultimately, however, Robin is spared out of the mobster's own conspiratorial confidence, and out of that political restraint which the perpetrators of "controlled violence" can so generously afford. Apparently the movement is too well disciplined to lose its temper and waste its force on chance objects awkwardly thrown in its way.

And thus the story's structural irony is never more dramatic and telling than when, at the end, the whole horrible procession comes "rolling towards the church" where Robin has stationed himself. The conclusion seems preordained, as Robin uncomfortably concludes that "the double-faced fellow has his eye on me." Literally, of course, Robin's perception is true enough: the mobster will indeed fix "his glance full upon the country youth," enforcing his earlier revelation, as his horse moves slowly by. But the psychoanalytic reader's nearly irresistible feeling that in some symbolic sense Robin's initiation is the goal or informing *telos* toward which the whole elaborate action tends is as critically partial as it would be politically naive. For in a deeper sense Robin has merely bungled his way to the center of an action entirely independent of his personal anxieties, with which he has only accidentally (and perhaps proleptically) to do. The procession of political events simply moves on, as unconcerned about Robin's maturity as it is unthreatened by his politics.

Explaining Robin's instinctive sense of his own centrality and, at the same time, highlighting some more critical grasp of his relation to the events as late-come and epiphenomenal is our gradual discovery that he has in fact blundered his way to a sort of "reviewing station," past which everyone knows the well-made pageant is scheduled to pass, and from which it is being essentially (though "secretly") controlled. The procession is coming straight "at" Robin's dazed and vibrating consciousness only because he just *happens* to be standing in the place where its organizers wait to watch its dramatic progress and judge its political effect. The authoritative man with the sepulchral hem-hem is, as we have suggested, very likely the Speaker of the House of Representatives; and he appears on the balcony of the Town House to observe the public embarrassment and personal pain of his political enemy, the confirmed Royalist and would-be Robinarch Molineux. He laughs cruelly enough, but not primarily at Robin; the fact that this innocent has been making political enemies thick and fast does not excuse his paranoia or justify our psychologism.

Nor are we at all safe in assuming that the apparently friendly man who stands with Robin on the steps of the church, witnessing his meeting with Uncle Molineux, is himself anything but an *arch*-conspirator. Only a species of critical wish-fulfillment will assume that he is meant to function, mythically, as some kindly superintendent of Robin's initiation. And only some extreme of textual (and political) credulity will conclude that he is actually very concerned about Robin's own best interests. True, he first accosts Robin in "a tone of real kindness, which had become strange to Robin's ears"; but in a tale which explicitly "teaches" that a "man [may] have several voices . . . as well as two complexions," we have to be alert to other tones as well. At least as alert as Robin himself, who does, in the end, finally recognize the motives of his interest in watching him watch the rites of Molineux's "passage."

Surely there is something other than simple kindness in this stranger's "singular curiosity to witness [Robin's] meeting" with his much-sought kinsman. And though there is a strong hint of voyeurism, some political motive is even more obvious. Accidentally, but not in the end unusefully, Robin lends himself as an almost perfect "experiment" or test case: a leader of the rebels can observe first-hand the impact of the evening's demonstration on the political sensibilities of the rising generation. He might well wish that Robin were not *quite* so naive about the ways of the political world in the metropolis of Boston, but perhaps someone even this untutored will prove "shrewd" enough to take the point about the real path to power in the provinces. And, whatever may be true of the future, clearly this stranger knows exactly what is going on here and now.

The irony of his answers to Robin's astonishingly innocent questions is broad enough to be called sarcastic. It may even strike us as a little cruel. And certainly it gives away his own conspiratorial identity. He does indeed know the "ill-favored fellow" with the face "of two colors"; not "intimately," to be sure, but well enough to have "chanced to meet him a little time previous" and well enough to "trust his word . . . that Molineux will shortly pass through this street." The principal irony here is obvious: their meeting was not at all by "chance" but by careful, conspiratorial design. Except for Robin, everyone in the story knows everyone else, and all have been conferring about the progress of the plot; everyone knows very well the established route of the procession, and only just a moment ago has the rough and visible leader made it clear to the smooth and secret organizer, by way of some final report, that everything will go off as planned. But a second, somewhat nastier irony is also discernible: *of course* this polite planner does not know his lieutenant very "intimately"; revolutionary politics may indeed make strange streetfellows, but ultimately one knows one's place.

The stranger's ironies continue broad, and only a little less cruel, in answer to Robin's inquiry about "the meaning of this uproar," as the demonstration begins in earnest: "Why, indeed, friend Robin, there do appear to be three or four riotous fellows abroad to-night." Robin is temporarily distracted from the insult-value of this alien sort of rhetoric by the altogether more vital question of whether a woman may have several voices as well as a man. But ultimately he learns to use just such grown-up talk himself. At last beholding his kinsman, in all his "tar-and-feathery dignity," he finally seizes the political outline of what has happened; and when he does his ironic maturity confirms our cynic suspicion.

No, Robin has *not* been "dreaming," as he bitterly realizes. And "Why yes," he is now able to reflect, "rather dryly," he *can* now be said in some manner to have "adopted a new subject of inquiry." And then, with devastating insight and not a little of that wit by which the eighteenth century knew to turn personal bitterness and political gloom into literary satire, this:

"Thanks to you, and to my other friends, I have at last met my kinsman, and he will scarce desire to see my face again. I begin to grow weary of a town life, Sir. Will you show me the way to the ferry?" Denouement indeed: to mark Robin's passage from the singlemindedness of childhood to the fallen wisdom of adult duplicity, nothing could be finer than his pose of urban weariness, worthy of the London coffeehouse wag or the Parisian *roué*; and to prove his newly acquired political intelligence (and to instruct ours), nothing could be clearer than his ironic identification of the friendly stranger as no better and no worse than all the "other friends" he has met this weary evening. He may or may not decide to "prefer to remain with us," but he now knows perfectly well who "us" is.

Evidently, therefore, a man may smile and smile and be, in despite of a narrator, a conspirator still. Even if that man should turn out to be a Congregationalist minister. For surely we must agree at least this far with Robert Lowell's poetically licentious identification [in *The Old Glory*] of the man who watches Robin watch his kinsman fall from royal grace. Robin has come to be on the steps of Boston's own First Church, directly across the street from the home of Massachusetts' own local "parliament," only by the sheerest and most bewildering of pre-historic accidents; but surely this calm, restrained, polite, decorous, knowing, and (yes) even friendly gentleman is exactly where he is expected to be, at his own proper reviewing post, watching a political demonstration in which the "Black Regiment" has had as deeply conspiratorial a hand as the merchant class and its political representatives. There stands (so to speak) the recognized head of the local church, across from—that is to say, separate from but at least equal to—his secular counterpart, the elected head of the local government. Alike they judge the impressive result of their common machinations: not even the arrest of Andros, way back in the "miraculous" Revolution of 1689, had come off more smoothly.

It is, apparently, the "religious" significance of the evening's not entirely Puritanical sort of "merriment" which Hawthorne means to suggest in the scene of Robin's lovely reverie at the deserted church, just before its proper minister arrives to "watch." Robin begins by fondly imagining that the "large square mansion" across the street is actually Molineux's residence (and not that of the rebellious legislature). He ends by supposing, even more vainly, that this deserted church can somehow put him in touch with the values of the pious, ministerial home he has left behind. And in between, his wayward fancy feeds on even less substantial visions, involving "moon beams" as these come "trembling" in the church, falling "down upon the deserted pews," and extending themselves "along the quiet isles." Haunted mind, indeed. Unless we are tone deaf, or unless we have *already* overinvested in the pseudo-Wordsworthian significance of "moonlight on a child's shoe," we will surely conclude that the narrator's sentimental diction gives away the author's ironic game:

> A fainter yet more awful radiance was hovering around the pulpit, and one solitary ray had dared to rest upon the open page of the great Bible. Had Nature, in that deep hour, become a worshiper in the house which man had builded? Or was that heavenly light the visible sanctity of the place,—visible because no earthly and impure feet were within the walls?

The scene makes "Robin's heart shiver with a sensation of loneliness," but it is supposed to make our skin—and our suspicion—itch just a bit: what *are* we to make of an empty church? And why *should* we speculate about the idea of "visible sanctity" (that strict and definitive mark of Puritan ecclesiology) so oddly warped and romanticized? Here's the church. And here, presumably, is the steeple. Climb (absurdly) up "a window-frame"; and *where are all the people!*

In the street, one readily concludes. Marching "towards the church" in apocalyptic procession, led by a "single horseman, clad in military dress and bearing a drawn sword," a man whose "variegated countenance" caused him to appear like "war personified." The majestic calm of "visible sanctity" has given way to the "counterfeited pomp," the "senseless uproar," and the "frenzied merriment" of that ungodly mob which christened itself "the Boston Saints." So that this totally unwonted merriment can, under the aspect of the problem of "Puritanism and Revolution," be referred to quite fairly and technically as "*congregated* mirth" (my italics).

Evidently these riotous saints are not coming to rest at Robin's particular church. Almost certainly the procession turns the corner and continues on, slowly and by design, to the Old South Church, across from the Province House, the official residence of the royal governor. For there, most usually, were revolutionary meetings most notoriously held, in order to obtain maximum visibility and intimidation. It might take these Boston Saints several more decades to get there, in literal political fact. But given the story's own wickedly figural chronology, we know very well where events are tending—as new taxes breed new riots, and deeper fears of enslavement spawn subtler conspiracies of resistance.

Robin, of course, cares very little about where next the Revolutionary Procession may pause. His own story ends on a very distinctive note of ironic insight and political suspense: a light having gone out of his world, he scarcely concerns himself with the Tendency of Great Events. He may yet grow up to help speed the cause of the American Revolution, but he will hardly think to view the whole affair as "majestic." He has watched the beginners of the process end by "trampling all on an old man's heart," and he may have noticed, in the process, that contrivance is not the same thing as Design. He may even be about to suspect that man's providences are but accidental to the Universal Plan. Other Americans might yet learn the lesson.

Perhaps the last word in "My Kinsman, Major Molineux" *will* always concern Robin himself, the meaning of his own youthful disillusion, the nature and extent of his own initiation. Whatever the audience of 1826 needed to learn, few modern readers (I suppose) will be convinced that Robin's presence on the "reviewing stand" of the Molineux procession is in every sense accidental; or that the political enrichment achieved by locating the tale, subtly, amidst "the Ideological Origins of the American Revolution" can quite account for its full fascination. Clearly, by now, Robin's growing pains cannot be taken for the whole of Hawthorne's plot; and yet they are, just as clearly, an integral part. In contrast to certain of Hawthorne's later political stories, the evident fact is that here some anxious adolescent does indeed gets his first hint of the relative unsimplicity of things-in-general upon the occasion of a chance encounter with some ironic and wildly overspecified political prefiguration. Probably we need to conclude by explaining why this should be so.

And yet we must learn to do this very carefully. We need to recognize, first of all, that it is no longer fair to conclude [with Seymour Gross] that within the terms of historical analysis "the great bulk of the tale, Robin's quest, remains sheer Gothic mystification." For at every step the tale deepens its political irony in direct relation to Robin's enduring naiveté. Probably most readers will feel defrauded if, in the end, Robin proves nothing more than a literary device, a figure off of which the tale repeatedly scores its dramatic ironies. But surely this dynamic accounts for very much of the tale's conscious strategy. And we need to imagine that the gap between historical reach and literary grasp might be narrowed still further, by anyone unorthodox enough to pursue the lead of teasing allusion and to resist, temporarily, the nearly irresistible lure of *passage*.

The obvious example would be Robin's encounter with the "pretty mistress" who shows him a "strip of scarlet petticoat." Conceding that sexual experience is, nowadays at least, everywhere a more vital and interesting subject than ecclesiological or even apocalyptic theory, one may still want to insist that this "lady of the scarlet petticoat," who claims to reside in Major Molineux's own house, probably has a figural-political as well as a literal-sexual identity. No ordinary prostitute set out to lure the farm boys, she is easily recognizable as a figure of that Scarlet woman, the "Whore of Babylon," whose Romish outline American Puritans always seemed to discern behind the shape of the Anglican Church, and whose fatal charms seemed to have been spread abroad, from Babylonish England, as part of some total strategy of slavish entrapment. Apparently a *variety* of "hopes and promises" invite Robin to "prostitute" himself.

And, beyond this classic contest of sexual surface with political symbol, it is absolutely essential to notice how the single most improbable and astonishing formal detail in the entire story—the view the "Man in the Moon" takes of the whole riotous affair—actually confirms our critical sense of the large-scale irrelevance of Robin's painful anxieties. Quite obviously and deliberately, Hawthorne's tale does whatever it can to upset our ordinary range of assumption and response. Ultimately, our psychological empathy must stand against some really *cosmic* view or lapse into the somewhat pathetic fallacy of misplaced sentiment.

Just when the "contagion" of cruel and barbarous laughter has engulfed Robin himself, so that now everyone (except of course Major Molineux) seems united in sending a "congregated mirth . . . roaring up to the sky"; just at the moment when Molineux's abasement seems most piteously and terribly complete and when, accordingly, Robin's own anxious passage from innocent separation to guilty participation seems most painfully accomplished; just when, that is, our primary human sympathies seem most powerfully and primally engaged, the scene (or at least the point of view) suddenly shifts. Suddenly, and just before the human pain lapses into some myth in which "fiends . . . throng in mockery around some dead potentate," everything waxes calm, cosmic, and even jolly. Apparently the "Man in the Moon" can be thought to have "heard the far below," and to have a view sufficiently disinterested to be worth considering; and the rare detachment of this ultimate structuralist threatens to embarrass our moral earnestness even more seriously than the ironies of the "friendly" stranger satirize Robin: "'Oho,' quoth he, 'the old earth is frolicsome to-night!'" Frolicsome indeed, under the aspect of eternity: one more night of rowdy misrule, one more "temporary inflammation of the popular mind," one more "revolution" among the numberless and continual turnings of sublunary events. One more anxious adolescent, it may be; it scarcely matters what—those earthly fellows are at it *again*.

Here, then, would be the ultimate insult which the deflationist strategy of "My Kinsman, Major Molineux" offers to the vaunted claims of American typological historiography; so far from being a unique and climactic event in the unfolding of Divine Purpose, the "majestic" Revolution is no more remarkable, "structurally," than any other local resistance to local authority; and no more distinctive, "psychoanalytically," than the anxious overflow of Oedipal emotion. Compared, from the outset, to a rum riot in the 1730s, and discovered, throughout, to be a thoroughly plotted and stage-managed affair, the entire episode is revealed, at the end, to amount to nothing more than one or another form of utterly local unruliness.

The same deliberately "reductionist" insight will, not incidentally, put into immediate and perfect perspective all of Hawthorne's famous anticipations of Sir James Frazer. Here, as in "The Maypole of Merry Mount" later, pagan myth spreads out to surround the swelling pretensions of Puritanic vision until, at the limits of coherence, we are forced to recognize *nothing* new under the moon. For if the long-ranged definition of Major Molineux as "dead potentate" seriously threatens his more parochial identity as conspiratorial Robinocrat, still that relatively timeless definition is itself embarrassed by and then subsumed into the absolutely "secular" view of the Man in the Moon. The ritual of the "Scapegoat King" is far older and more venerable than the nighttime activities of the Boston Saints or the civil-millennial vision of "Apocalyptic Whiggism"; but the lunar theory of "frolic" comprehends them both. They are at it again. Thus does time, in the midst of some midworld evening's trauma, "fold us music-drunken in."

We respond, of course, by reformulating the political significance and reemphasizing the human pain from our own, equally valid, sublunary point of view. Governments are not *entirely* like streetcars, as mortal men structure their common life; and crises of loyalty and relation are the very substance of our identity, as sexual energy erupts into consciousness. And it is in just such a philosophical mood that we think to *answer* the moon (and solve the critical ambiguity) with a "compromise" theory of the relation between politics and analysis in "Molineux." Without denying the lunar view that political revolutions are just as inevitable (and almost as common) as Oedipal strife, we may want to add that they are, as well, equally violent and painful, as even Grandfather's youthful auditors had to learn. And, reversing our sense of sign and signified, we may want to insist that the passage from adolescence to adulthood is just as definitively significant for the life of the human individual as any political revolution ever was (or was claimed to be) for the life of a nation. We confidently imagine that Hawthorne could well have been interested in the significance of *both,* separately and at once. And, with growing literary confidence, we think to propose that perhaps it has been Hawthorne's intention so to join tenor and vehicle that we cannot assign primacy to either the individual or the social passage. Each one illuminates the other.

Perhaps. And yet another, far more ironic interpretation also suggests itself, especially to anyone who has followed the "progress" of American ideology from provincial Jeremiad to national myth. Such a person might want to suggest that, in the name of literary reconciliation, it is all too easy to pass from one "story" to another, without ever facing the issue of reality. For if the dominant view of the American Revolution was, in 1826, still some survival of that pseudo-Puritan "propaganda" of Holy History used by the participants to justify their revolt, nevertheless that view was even then being challenged by a proto-Freudian "literature" of growing up; and if the new explanation were in many ways opposite to the old one, it was nevertheless at least equal in its power to neutralize the guilty memories of violent rebellion. A culture critic of Hawthorne's severity could easily have noticed that the new, more literary "history," obscuring as much as it clarified, was at least as objectionable as the old one.

Of course the older ideology of Protestant Destiny never really died, susceptible as it was of ever more subtle (and idolatrous) translation; and yet it was, in Hawthorne's Jacksonian Age, beginning to fail as a single persuasive account of the events of 1776. But even as it began to lapse, it was all too easily supplanted by an explanation which, equally large, also refused to face head-on the crucial questions of contingent local conspiracy and voluntary local violence. If the Revolution were not, clearly, the crowning denouement of God's Plot, then surely it was, inevitably, an irresistible part of Nature's Plan. Jefferson had declared it in the quaint idiom of the Enlightened *Philosophe*: evidently there comes a time, "in the course of human events," when nations, just like individuals, need to assume that "separate and equal station to which the laws of Nature and Nature's God entitle them." And then a whole chorus of literary nationalists translated the political insight into its inevitable literary form, the Romantic *bildungsroman*: the American Revolution was *just like* growing up.

The problem, of course, was that human time and ordinary sublunary change continued to drag their slow length along, with the same unapocalyptic insignificance in Republican America as they had in plodding and provincial Massachusetts or in merry and monarchical England. And so what could *not* be rationalized in Divine Teleology needed some justification in human process. All things grow and change, even America. The process is continuous, for the most part; and yet there are moments when national identity undergoes the temporary though painful and confusing process of changing relations. The temporary disorientation is regrettable, in a sense; but not ultimately so, for in the long run maturation is inevitable and necessary. In the vast number of cases, the adolescent comes through. And so—as Robin's features begin to lose their troubled distinction—did we.

And yet that famous psychopolitical story will not *quite* tell itself here, in the midst of the weird moment when Robin's divided consciousness vibrates back and forth between the pastoral pursuits of the rural countryside and the political policies of the Country Party, and when our own doubled vision watches the Revolution pre-enact itself as a rum riot. Surely the particular complexities of Hawthorne's historical emplotment embarrass the simplicity of the new myth, at the outset, as clearly as they reduce the majesty of the old one in the moment of its eclipse. For the two stories Hawthorne is telling are in fact quite different. Neither is anything like a perfect recapitulation of the other. That, ultimately, is the point of insisting on the redundant overspecification of the political world into which Robin has wandered: it has a contingent and even, in a sense, a factitious life of its own. Robin's moment of passage may be scientifically predetermined by "the course of human events," but rum riots and tea parties require local plans and private invitations.

None of the conspirators in the story cares at all about Robin's stage along life's way. And surely all of them are absolutely convinced that *they* (and not he) represent "Young America." He may just happen to start to grow up in the midst of their political demonstration; the thing always happens somewhere; and if he does, then he is welcome enough to join in. But *only* the moon could fail to notice all the differences. Only some excessively simplistic will-to-structure will ever confuse the subtle and necessary pain endured in the natural process of growing up to manhood with the gross and (in a sense) gratuitous suffering inflicted by the political actions required to throw off an alien government.

Accordingly, therefore, we are left with two stories, unreconciled—as Hawthorne resists the conflations of America's political psychologism at the outset. Robin Molineux grows up *just when* his Royalist uncle is being tarred and feathered for Robinocracy; he passes beyond his own "Season of Youth" *just when* America is beginning to exercise its conspiratorial imagination. But his experiences are not *just like* anything else, unless they be like *all other* transitions under the moon. But at that level of generality all political discrimination, like all human intelligence, lapses into cosmic indistinction. Such a view might serve well enough as a sort of religion; indeed the utter secularity of its insistence on "vanity" usefully counteracts the cosmic teleology of Puritan politics. Or it might serve as some new "ideology" of the

American Revolution—as anxious to minimize questions of local causation and local guilt, in the name of literary form, as the older theory had been, in the name of God. But it is a poor way to study life in the provinces.

Here, as elsewhere, Hawthorne's revisionist strategy validates all sorts of conflationist tactics. To emphasize the altogether unabstract suffering of the Revolution, he allows the figurative torture of Major Molineux to mingle with our memory of the real-life hazing of Governor Hutchinson. To increase our sense of the undeniable evil being perpetrated (in whatever cause, toward whatever end), he momentarily permits the tragic view of this event to merge with the Tory theology of rebellion. To remind us—at the same time, but on the other hand—of the un-majesty of political resistance, he structures the whole event as a local riot; and he even comes to the verge of conflating the revolutionary beginnings of the American republic with an Oedipal itch. But there his ironies stop and even begin to reverse themselves. He plainly resists the all-too-reassuring view that revolutionary politics recapitulates adolescent psychology: maturation is painful but it knows nothing of conspiracy.

And so we are left, deliberately, with Robin's *difference*. He has finally entered into an adult world, but he remains very little representative of its historic complexity. He has finally learned what the reader has had to know all along—that, politically as otherwise, grown-ups have a story which boys do not know. But his "moral adventure" is quite different from their historical plot. *His* story is not *theirs*. *His* story is, quite simply, the discovery that they do indeed have one. The reader must know *their* story to appreciate Robin's own (for Robin discovers far more than scarlet petticoats and ambiguity); but he may not, without political naiveté, pretend they are the same. He can decide to choose between the two stories, but any such "reading" must always seem selective and willful, the result of his own literary bias or preferred style of interpretation rather than of Hawthorne's controlling intention. For in the ironic structure of Hawthorne's complex and even deconstructive tale, the two stories are as inseparable as they are different: everybody grows up somewhere, but Robin passes out of adolescence in the process of discovering, first-hand, the distressing secrets of a provincial politics already rather shrewdly adult. In this tale, at least, the formal purity of universal *bildungsroman* will not quite subsume the ragged matter of local conspiracy.

Evidently Robin gets a rather heavy dose of reality—heavier, obviously, than that prescribed for Lawrence and his friends by Grandfather, who really *does* exist to supervise their passage from chauvinism to charity, even as he mediates their experience of political history through a form of personal literature. Accordingly, therefore, we are not unduly surprised to learn that Robin would like to "go back." But we must avoid imitating him, even momentarily; for we have, after all, the advantage of *his* mediation. If his first experience of real politics is significantly stark and not a little cruel, still his own drastic experience is designed to ease the reader's political transition from righteousness to irony. The "old-style" (or Puritanic) reader is supposed to be reminded that as the ways of Special Providence are often a little rough, so America's revolutionary origins can seem relentlessly ordinary and noticeably guilty. And the "new style" (or psychologistic) reader is tempted but forbidden to reduce politics to *passage*. If he does so reduce the complexity of one of Hawthorne's most perfectly crafted tales, he will surely involve himself in a moral regression far worse than Robin's own last-stated wish. For after the lapse of innocence, natural or theologic, nothing protects us from the ugly facts of political life quite so well and comfortably as that literary miracle in which brutal psychic law achieves its formal redemption as national myth.

CHAPTER ONE

A Christmas Letter

"I will honor Christmas in my heart, and try to keep it all the year."
—Charles Dickens

"Christmas is usually my favorite time, but I think I just want it to be over with this year," said Meg, sighing a gigantic sigh and adjusting the colorful striped skirt she was holding on her lap. It had never fit the way it should, so she was attempting to turn it into a throw pillow cover. The project wasn't going very well.

"I know. Me too," said Jo, looking up from her book. She'd read it several times before, and didn't mind her sister's interruption. "Christmas won't be Christmas at all without Dad here. What's the point?"

"It's totally unfair, everyone I know is making fun

plans with their families and we don't get to," said Amy, who was drawing in her sketchbook and feeling sorry for herself.

Beth, who was knitting, was the only sister who almost never complained. She even managed to smile a little. "We have Mom, and Hannah, and each other," she reminded her sisters. "And Dad will be home before we know it."

At Beth's words, all four girls managed to look a little bit less glum. Though the mood in the room was subdued, it was impossible to stay crabby for long in such a cozy scene. The March house, which had been in the family for three generations, was large and full of interesting details large and small, with nooks and crannies everywhere you looked. The shelves in each room practically overflowed with books and collectibles. The fire in the fireplace had been burning for two hours, which meant it was now turning to embers that warmed each young sister right down to her belly.

A few gentle snow flurries swirled around in the twilight beyond the thick-curtained windows, and three candles burned on the mantel. They were scented like apple cider, the perfect complement to the refreshing, earthy smell of the real Christmas tree, which had been lovingly decorated in the corner, and the clusters of fragrant boughs adorning the center of the dining room table and the top of every door frame.

Despite the pretty decorations and nice holiday aromas, Jo was still feeling a lot less cheerful than she usually did during the Christmas season. "He won't be home before we know it," Jo said, allowing herself a moody sob. "He won't be home for almost a year!" All four girls thought of their father, trying to picture what he might be experiencing at that very moment. Mr. March was in the U.S. National Guard and was serving a tour of duty overseas. It had been very hard to say good-bye to him, and now it was even worse being apart.

No one said anything for a few minutes.

"I'm not just sad about Dad," Meg said suddenly. "I sound like an awful person, but I'm also kind of sad about Mom's presents policy!"

A few days earlier, Mom had explained to the girls that there would be fewer Christmas gifts than normal this year, as the family needed to "tighten its belt" a little and use what extra money they did have on care packages for Dad.

"I know Mom said we should be grateful for what we have and try to think about the true meaning of Christmas this year," agreed Jo, "but I was hoping for a huge stack of new books!"

Jo was a bookworm, and Mom and Dad were usually very generous with novels for their second-oldest daughter, particularly at Christmas or when she had a birthday.

But this year was different, and Jo was having a hard time getting used to the idea that she may need to wait an extra month or two before getting her hands on the newest books. It made her cranky.

Meg nodded, thinking about the new outfits she'd love to open up on Christmas morning, if only Santa would bring them to her. Meg was a pretty girl of thirteen, with soft, wavy light brown hair that she liked to wear long and loose. She had big brown eyes and a quiet, motherly nature that was only occasionally a little bossy. But who could blame her? As the eldest of four girls, Meg believed it was her job to set a good example and try to keep her sisters in line. She liked fashion and flower gardens and singing in choir at school, where she was in eighth grade.

Jo was twelve and a little clumsy. Tall and skinny and awkward, her arms and legs liked to be in motion—unless she happened to be reading a book, which she often was. Jo had smart gray eyes that drank in the world around her, noticing every detail for recording in one of her precious writing notebooks. She had long, thick dark brown hair that was usually in a ponytail or simple braid, and she often wore jeans with at least one rip in them paired with a trusty red hoodie that made Meg cringe. Jo, who was in seventh grade, liked to be comfortable and had no interest in anything that was, as she put it, "girly."

Beth was in fifth grade, but if she had it her way, she'd

stay home all day to play with her kitten, practice piano, and bake cookies. Most content when she was with her family, Beth was shy and peaceful. Her smooth auburn hair was generally tucked behind her ear with a simple black barrette, and her bright eyes and rosy cheeks looked content and happy without fail. Though she was too timid and quiet to have many friends, everyone who knew Beth loved her and wanted to protect her.

Amy was, in many ways, Beth's opposite. Yellow haired, blue eyed, and naturally effervescent, she was only nine but somehow managed to seem older. Amy was the most important person in the room—according to Amy—and planned to grow up and become a famous artist. She was very popular in her fourth-grade class and smarter than she let on. Fascinated by Paris and New York and other big, exciting cities, Amy was trying to teach herself French because she thought it made her seem more sophisticated. Mom liked to call Amy a handful, but couldn't conceal the twinkle in her eye when she reminded her youngest daughter to be a little humbler once in a while.

"And I wanted a new set of drawing pencils," admitted Amy with a sigh. "But I know they're very expensive, so there's no way that's happening. I wish I were old enough to babysit and earn my own money like Meg."

Beth patted her younger sister's leg in understanding and murmured that she'd like some new sheet music to practice. But then the large grandfather clock in the corner of the living room caught her eye. It was almost six, which meant that Mom would be home any minute. She worked each day as the director of the community center in their small New England town. It was hard work, with long hours and low pay, but Mrs. March was devoted to it with her whole heart. The girls admired their energetic mother for all she did for people in need, even if they didn't always remember to tell her so.

Beth moved Mom's slippers closer to the fire so they'd be warm for her when she arrived home. Jo set down her book and scrambled out of her overstuffed chair to poke at the fire in an effort to coax a little more heat out of it. She looked at the worn slippers and said, "Eesh, Mom could really use a new pair of these. Maybe I'll see if I can find a pair tomorrow." Jo was a little embarrassed she hadn't gotten Mom a Christmas gift yet, even though Aunt Em, who was very rich, had given each sister a little Christmas money to spend as she liked. Jo felt relieved there was still a little time to shop.

"I wanted to get Mom new slippers!" Beth said.

"No, me!" Amy shouted.

"I'm the oldest," Meg asserted. "I'm going to buy them."

All four girls glared at one another, but then started giggling when Jo stuck out her tongue. Encouraged by her audience, she began making sillier and sillier faces. Amy threw a pillow at her and the giggling started anew.

"Hey!" Meg shouted. "No pillow fights in here. You'll burn the house down!" She pointed to the open fireplace and snatched up all the throw pillows and sat on them. Then she fell over.

"Okay, okay," Beth said, weak with laughter. "Here's what we'll do. We'll stop worrying about what we're not going to get for presents and think about what to get for Mom instead. Jo, you can buy the slippers tomorrow since you said it first. I'll get her some fancy bubble bath from the soap store she loves."

Meg nodded approvingly. "I'll get her some new gloves. I know the ones she has now are worse than her slippers."

"I'll go to the mall and pick out some perfume," Amy said, her eyes dancing at the idea of a trip to the mall, even on Christmas Eve. Jo shuddered at the thought.

"It's settled, then," Meg said.

Each sister felt 100 percent better than she had a few minutes ago, when they'd been thinking of Dad and of all the gifts they wouldn't be opening in two days. It didn't hurt that Hannah, a longtime friend of Mrs. March, had moved in several weeks ago to help Mom take care of the girls in Dad's absence. For many years, Hannah had run the kitchen at a large bed-and-breakfast in Maine. The place had recently been purchased by a developer and turned into condos, so Hannah was between jobs. She had offered to stay with the Marches for the duration of

Mr. March's deployment while she contemplated her next move. Mrs. March had almost wept when Hannah had suggested the arrangement, and everyone in the family was thrilled she was around. Since Mrs. March worked a lot, Hannah had taken over the cooking, cleaning, and other household details. She was a no-nonsense person who wasn't impressed by much, but her kind heart and her love for all the March sisters was plain. Hannah was in the kitchen preparing beef stroganoff for dinner; it smelled scrumptious. Christmas was a mere two days away.

Mrs. March swept into the foyer along with a swirl of cold air and snow. She was happy to see her girls all together, enjoying each other's company and the cozy fire.

"Hello, my girls!" she said, her cheeks flushed and her eyes dancing. Mrs. March was tall and noble, dressed simply but elegantly in straight wool slacks and a thick cream-colored sweater. She stepped out of her boots and into her worn slippers, sitting down comfortably in the middle of the enormous living room couch, which everyone had affectionately nicknamed Couchzilla, as it was sage green and more than willing to swallow up whoever approached. "Did I miss dinner? Where's Hannah? How's your cold, Meg? Did anyone stop by with donations?"

Mom's mind was always going a mile a minute as she had an endless list of people depending on her. But somehow she managed to give each of her daughters her full attention in the midst of all the chaos, and they loved her for it.

Meg brought Mom a fresh cup of chamomile tea and each sister chattered away about her day and her plans for Christmas break from school.

"I have a treat for after we eat," Mom said. "A new e-mail from Dad. I printed out copies for everyone!"

"Let's read it now! I can't wait," Jo cried. The family did get to video-chat with Dad occasionally, but new e-mails were still special. Mr. March preferred to write long, thoughtful notes twice per week instead of just a line here or there, so his messages were always interesting. Jo definitely got her writerly talents from Dad.

"Okay, okay." Mom laughed. She dug in her large satchel and pulled out the copies, passing them around and reading aloud to add to the excitement:

"Dearest daughters,

My days are very different now than they were at home, but nevertheless quite interesting and worthwhile. We are doing good work here, and I am proud of our efforts and of our progress. Still, I can't help but think of home every other minute. I wonder if the snow has covered everything and how the light looks when the day draws to a close. I wonder how you are all doing, what you are learning, and what you are thinking about.

I want to give you all my love and my hugs, girls, and tell you that I find so much comfort in your funny letters, messages, and care packages. A year seems like a very long time to wait before we are together again, but the good news is that while we wait we all have important jobs to do. The time will fly by and the days will not be wasted.

I know you ladies will be loving daughters to your mother and good friends to one another. You'll make good choices, greet the days with energy and hope, and have a wonderful New Year. I trust that you will all grow smarter and kinder in my absence, so that when I come back I will be astounded and impressed by the little women you're all becoming.

With all my love, Dad"

There wasn't a dry eye in the room when Mom finished reading. Even Jo wiped a giant tear from her nose and sniffed loudly.

"I promise to try to make Dad proud," she whispered, vowing she'd do a better job controlling her temper, helping Mom, and cleaning up after herself.

Beth didn't say anything, but began knitting faster, determined to finish a scarf for the community center donation box before New Year's Day. Amy and Meg nodded, thinking of their own ways to impress their father.

With a new sense of purpose, all the girls sat down to a delicious dinner. After everyone had finished eating and worked together to clear the table and wash the dishes, the girls wandered over to the piano and asked Beth to play for them. She obligingly filled the room with a beautiful, melancholy rendition of "Have Yourself a Merry Little Christmas." Each sister chimed in singing when she remembered the words, and Mom filled in the gaps with her clear soprano.

Even though they were young and prone to embarrassment, the March sisters knew they would never be too old to listen to their mother sing to them.

Beth's Pot Holder Knitting Pattern

Supplies:

- Size 8 knitting needles
- 34 yards worsted-weight yarn
- 2 stitch markers (optional)
- Scissors
- Ruler

Gauge:

6 stitches to 1 inch; 6 rows to 1 inch

Beth's tips:

Always ask a parent or guardian before starting a new craft project.

There are lots of helpful, free videos and instructions online to learn how to cast on and make knit and purl stitches. If there is a local yarn store near you, the employees are often happy to help beginners.

For your first few projects, choose a light-colored yarn—it will be easier to see the stitches.

Don't be afraid to pull out stitches and start again if you make a mistake. It happens to everyone!

Stitch markers can be helpful to remind you when to switch the type of stitch you are making in a pattern.

Gauge is a measurement of how large the stitches you are making are. It is helpful for things like socks and sweaters, to make sure your piece will turn out the right size. For something like a pot holder, it's not so important. But it's always good to practice measuring it!

Cast on 30 stitches loosely.

Row 1: Purl 30 stitches.

Row 2: Knit 30 stitches.

Row 3: Purl 30 stitches.

Row 4: Knit 30 stitches.

Row 5: Purl 3 stitches (place 1 marker here if you're using them), knit 24 stitches, (place one marker here if you're using them), purl 3 stitches.
Row 6: Knit 3 stitches (slip your marker from one needle to the other if you're using them), purl 24 (slip marker), knit 3.

Alternate rows 5 and 6 until the piece measures 5.5 inches long down from your needles. End by completing a repetition of row 6.

Then repeat rows 1–3. Last, cast off all stitches knitwise.

To make your pot holder lie flat, get it wet (damp is fine; it doesn't need to be sopping) and lay it flat on the floor sandwiched between two kitchen towels. Make sure all of the edges are flat. Layer some heavy books on top of the towel to press the pot holder flat. Leave the books there overnight while the potholder dries. Once dry, it should stop curling up at the edges.

CHAPTER TWO

A Christmas Feast

"Christmas is doing a little something extra for someone."
—Charles M. Schulz

Jo woke first on Christmas Day, in the small bedroom she shared with Meg. Feeling something strange under her head, she reached under her pillow and discovered a little book, wrapped in striped tissue paper and tied with a simple green bow. Unable to wait, she sat up abruptly and tore it open, waking her sister in the commotion.

"Ooh! *A Tree Grows in Brooklyn*!" Jo opened the thick novel and read Mom's inscription: *One of my favorite books of all time to one of my favorite girls of all time*. Jo smiled. Mom always knew just what she would like.

Meg sat up too, much more gingerly, and discovered a gift

under her pillow as well. It was a collection of flower seeds in all the colors of the rainbow, designed to attract honeybees. Meg loved it. In the next room, Beth and Amy woke up to gifts of fancy yarn and a fresh sketch pad. The care Mom had taken in selecting and wrapping the small gifts touched each girl.

The girls tumbled down to the living room still in their pajamas with smiles on their faces, in a rush to present Mom and Hannah with the gifts they had lovingly purchased and wrapped. Though there were no more gifts under the tree, the girls didn't mind. There was a fresh fire in the fireplace, good smells in the kitchen, and a new layer of snow outside that made the bright morning look soft and clean.

They were greeted by Hannah alone, who was stirring a large pot of cider on the stovetop and putting together a special Christmas breakfast of eggs Benedict, complete with Canadian bacon and homemade hollandaise sauce.

"Where's Mom?" Amy demanded. She was often a little grumpy in the morning, and Christmas was no different.

"She had to go in to work," Hannah replied. "The community center had a last-minute emergency food shortage. She'll be back any moment; I know she wanted to enjoy breakfast with you girls."

With that, the side door banged open and in came Mrs. March, her face flushed with the cold. She hugged all of her daughters as they rushed at her with glee. But Hannah could tell, with one glance at her old friend, that something was amiss.

"Everything okay downtown, Margaret?" she asked.

"They're managing, but the need is greater than we anticipated this year," Mom said. "There's already a line, and I think we may run out of food before nine a.m. I made a few calls and did what I could."

Everyone in the room, including little Amy, who was the hungriest and grumpiest of all, turned toward the Christmas feast almost ready for them on the table. They listened to their grumbling stomachs, but then thought of the letter from Dad.

"I'm glad you got back before we started," said Jo.

"Me too," Beth added. "Let's wrap everything up and deliver it, Mom. Can we?"

"Let's take the cookies," Amy said in a small voice. The Christmas cookies she had carefully decorated the previous weekend were her pride and joy—each one a small work of art covered in intricate patterns of sprinkles, piped frosting, and Red Hots. Still, when the youngest March thought of the hungry people in line in the cold, she wanted to give them away.

Meg didn't say anything, but was already digging around in the Tupperware drawer for containers big enough to hold the spread.

"I'm overwhelmed, girls." Mom's eyes shone with tears of pride. "Let's all go together, and when we get back we'll have cereal and smoothies."

It was decided. They finished packing up their fancy

breakfast and Amy's dozens of Christmas cookies, and piled into the minivan. Mrs. March's staff was thrilled to see her again, and happily added the new provisions to the offerings.

"Angels!" cried the volunteers, and all the girls blushed. They had never been called angels before. Each one rather liked it. Even Jo.

Fortunately, several other families in the community center network had responded to the call for more food, and new donations were rapidly appearing. It looked like the center would be able to feed everyone in line.

Mrs. March let out a breath she hadn't realized she'd been holding.

Now Christmas could begin.

Back at home, the girls presented Mom and Hannah with their gifts and Meg took over blender duties, whipping up Christmas smoothies for everyone with bananas, almond milk, nutmeg, and frozen mango.

Meg's Christmas Smoothies

Ingredients:

1/2 cup almond milk (original or unsweetened)
1/4 cup orange juice, pulp free
3 bananas, broken into chunks
2 cups frozen mango pieces

1/2 teaspoon nutmeg
1/2 teaspoon cinnamon
6 cinnamon sticks

Directions:

Always ask a parent or guardian before starting a recipe.

Place all ingredients except cinnamon sticks in large blender and fit the cover on. Start blending the ingredients on a slow speed, and gradually increase it. When the mixture is smooth (after about 30 seconds of blending), portion it out into fancy Christmas glasses and garnish with cinnamon sticks. Makes approximately six small smoothies. Yum!

There was a lot of laughing and explaining and floating festive wrapping paper as each girl clamored to make sure her gifts were fully understood and appreciated.

Then, all fell quiet, enjoying their new things. Beth planned a new scarf to make use of the delicate yarn she had received. Jo began to read her novel. Meg planned out a flower garden for springtime, and Amy opened her fresh sketch pad to capture the scene.

The quiet peace didn't last for long, however, because right at noon there was a knock at the door. Four of Jo and Meg's neighbor friends from school piled into the March house, ready to perform the play they'd been rehearsing together ever since Thanksgiving—a play Jo had written. One girl promised to record it for them on her phone, and Meg's friend Sophia planned to edit it into a short movie. They were all nearly hysterical with excitement for the production.

"Merry Christmas!" Sophia shouted as she stomped the snow off her boots in the foyer. She had a mass of curly black hair that no hat could ever contain.

"It's freezing outside!" said Mia, one of Jo's classmates. Her twin sister, Ella, shivered and quickly scooted over to the fireplace to warm her hands. The fourth girl, Olivia, was an outgoing sixth grader who had candy canes for everyone and handed them around with a big, gap-toothed smile. She was in film club and eager to be in her very first movie production of all time. "I've been practicing my fainting," she told Jo. "I'm really good."

"Excellent!" Jo said approvingly. "Your scene is the most important one of all."

The group was no stranger to the March house and the girls made themselves right at home. Hannah had prepared for their arrival and handed out mugs in all shapes and sizes filled with hot cocoa and tiny marshmallows. The girls, dressed in a colorful assortment of flannel pajama pants and Christmas sweaters, began donning the costumes Jo and Beth had lovingly prepared.

Since the play was about knights and heroes, villains and princesses, cloaks and gowns and painted cardboard scenery soon began flying around the room. Hannah wisely placed a heavy screen in front of the fire. Couchzilla, tipped onto its back, became a fortress.

Jo put on Dad's heavy leather boots, happy to play the male lead, Don Pedro. She carefully shoved all of her hair under a cloak and began speaking in a deep voice. Amy played the princess, Zara, putting on an exquisite blue-and-silver prom dress Jo and Beth had found several weeks ago at a thrift store. Olivia and Meg played elfin queens imbued with special powers. When Sophia said, "Action!" the performance began with this chant over a cauldron, which was really Mom's largest outdoor planter, rescued from storage in the garage:

"Don Pedro loves beautiful Zara
But only from afar-a.
To see her from his steed he calls
But on her way she trips and falls.

But worry not, oh sweet knight.
These queens do plan to help your plight.
We'll see your passion through,
Now, which charms and potions will we brew?"

The dramatic story played out beautifully, with only a few scenes dissolving into giggles that Sophia promised Jo she could edit out.

With no warning, Couchzilla tipped over forward with a deafening *BANG!* and every last actress, even the dedicated Olivia, began to shriek, thinking poor Beth was pinned underneath. Nothing could save the scene. When it was determined Beth was completely fine and, in fact, nowhere near the vanquished fortress, each girl stopped shrieking and started giggling.

Much to Jo's frustration, the last scene didn't get performed at all thanks to a quiet interruption from a very bemused Hannah:

"Mom invites all of you girls to come in for dinner," she said, gesturing for all to follow her into the dining room.

This was a surprise. No dinner was planned that Jo or Meg or anyone else knew of. In fact, the girls all thought Mom had to work that night, with the idea that her staff and most of the volunteers at the center would want at least part of Christmas Day off with their families.

When everyone walked into the dining room, they gasped in amazement.

The enormous table was absolutely covered in treats out of their wildest imaginations: a towering cupcake stand holding three different flavors, an assortment of mini French pastries that Amy immediately identified as being from the fanciest bakery in town, several dishes of ice cream with bowls and bowls of toppings, and even a platter filled with cocktail shrimp and sauce, a particular favorite of Jo's.

Their eyes struggled to take it all in: a beautiful glazed ham, tea sandwiches with the crusts cut off, the shrimp, chocolate truffles in every shape and size, and even four immense bouquets of tropical flowers that made the entire room smell like a Hawaiian island instead of a New England winter.

Each girl stared as Mom smiled at them happily. "Dig in!" she admonished them all, handing out plates. "There's more than enough to feed an army, so I'm sending everyone home with extras for your parents, too," she added, nodding at the neighbor girls.

"Is it fairies?" whispered Beth.

"It's Santa Claus," Amy said with certainty. "He knows I love chocolate truffles and almost never get them."

"It must've been Aunt Em. Maybe she just read *A Christmas Carol*," Jo said, her voice filled with wonder.

Aunt Em, who was very rich, was not generally known for her generosity, though she did have her moments.

"Jo!" Mom said. "It wasn't Aunt Em. We'll visit her later this evening. Mr. Lawrence, our next-door neighbor, sent it all."

"What?" Meg said, truly surprised. "But we don't even know him!" Meg and Jo had noticed a boy their age around the house recently, but had never met him. Jo suspected he went to private school, which is why their paths had never crossed despite the fact that their town was on the small side.

"Hannah ran into Mr. Lawrence this morning while she was salting the sidewalk," Mom explained. "She mentioned you girls had donated your breakfast and it impressed him. He knew your grandfather a long time ago, and gave me a call while you all were performing. He said he hoped I would allow him to send over a few treats for Christmas dinner. Of course, I was happy to say yes. I had no idea he'd be so extravagant. Eat up!"

With that, all eight girls loaded their plates and the entire party moved back into the living room, where they all had an impromptu picnic among the detritus of their moviemaking adventures. Jo sighed contently after eating at least twelve shrimp, six tea sandwiches, three pastries, and one red velvet cupcake. "I gotta meet Mr. Lawrence's son. Just because we go to different schools doesn't mean we can't be friends," she said.

"Is he cute?" asked Mia.

"Yeah, is he?" asked Ella. "My mom says his parents died and he doesn't get to play sports at St. Jude because Mr. Lawrence is overprotective. I feel bad for him," she added, considering the thought for the first time. St. Jude was the private school in their small town.

"I don't know," Jo said, dismissing the idea. "But it doesn't matter. He sounds lonely. I'm going to be his friend."

"Good. We need a boy in our next production," said Sophia.

It was decided.

CHAPTER THREE

A New BFF for Jo

"Friendship is born at that moment when one person says to another: What! You too? I thought I was the only one."
—C. S. Lewis

A week later, Jo was in the attic reading her well-worn copy of *The Princess Bride*, which, she liked to loudly tell anyone who would listen, was superior to the movie, but not by much. The attic was by far Jo's favorite spot in the house, even though it did not have a fireplace like the living room, or any fresh potted herbs like the kitchen. Instead, it had something far more valuable to Jo: her book collection. Hastily constructed and ever-sagging shelves of paperbacks and hardcovers filled the space, collected almost since the moment she'd been born and reached for her father's beloved tomes.

The attic was organized exactly to Jo's liking. No one else in the family had much use for the tiny garret, with its low ceilings and crisscrossed beams. Dad, the fellow March bookworm, had a study filled to bursting with books of his own.

On one side of the room, there was a window seat nearly swallowed up by pillows in every color. On the other, a small writing desk was covered in teetering stacks of notebooks in which Jo recorded the stories and plays she was always writing. A valuable first edition of her favorite book, *Treasure Island*, enjoyed a special perch on a shelf with a glass door to protect it from dust. It had been given to Jo by her father when she was only five.

Jo knew she only had a few more minutes to read because she had promised Meg she'd attend the much-anticipated winter dance in their middle school gym.

It was pretty much the last thing on earth she wanted to do, but a promise was a promise. Meg had made her two new throw pillows for the attic when she could've been reading magazines, and now it was payback time.

"Jo! Jo? Where are you? Are you ready?" Jo cringed as she heard Meg's voice call up to her from the bottom of the attic opening. She reluctantly closed her book, hopped down from the window seat, and lowered herself down the ladder and into the second-floor hallway outside the bedrooms.

"Yup," Jo replied, flinging herself onto her bed. Meg was sitting at her little vanity, carefully applying lip gloss. "Totally."

"You're wearing your hoodie. You are not ready," Meg said. "You can borrow one of my dresses."

"No way," said Jo. "It's way too cold to wear a dress. And I hate dresses and I don't care what people think."

"It's not too cold. You just have to wear leggings or tights with it. Like mine." Meg gestured to her own legs and frowned. She was wearing her very favorite pair of leggings, but they were easily a year old and starting to look faded. Meg knew Mom didn't have enough room in the budget to buy new clothes right now, so she never asked. But it was hard, knowing her best friends at school would have lots of new outfits to show off, extravagant Christmas gifts from all the most popular stores in the new mall the next town over.

"Okay, okay," Meg relented. She didn't have the energy to argue with her boyish sister. "At least comb your hair and put on your nicer jeans, okay?"

"Deal." Jo released her long brown hair from its ponytail holder, brushed it, and put it right back in its ponytail. Meg sighed and Jo grinned. She did put on nice jeans, though. They were even a very dark color, which helped to hide the stains.

• • •

Mrs. March dropped the two girls off at seven p.m., even though their school was only six blocks away from the house. Meg didn't want to walk through the cold because she had painstakingly curled her hair and wearing a hat would mess it up. She was also wearing pretty ankle boots with low heels that wouldn't work in the snow at all.

The gym looked quite festive. Someone had decorated it with huge crepe-paper snowflakes and even hung a big disco ball on one side. Nervous kids grouped together in clusters in the darker parts of the space, and a few confident eighth graders were dancing already. Meg's science teacher, Mr. Calhoun, was DJing, which meant they'd be hearing a LOT of music from the eighties.

Jo immediately felt completely out of place, especially when Meg disappeared into the girls' bathroom with Annie Moffat to exchange lip glosses. Jo felt irritated she'd let her older sister talk her into going. *Why do I always get myself into these situations?* she wondered. *There's no law that says just because you're in middle school you have to go to dances. Ugh. Ugh. Ugh.*

Jo was just about ready to bolt for the door and demand that Mom come back to rescue her when a familiar boy standing awkwardly near the folded-up bleachers caught her eye. It was the Lawrence kid! He looked almost as miserable as she felt, so she went over to him.

"Hey," Jo said.

"Hey," he said.

"You're my next-door neighbor." Jo stood next to him. They watched the other kids in the gym dance and stand in clusters.

"I know," he said.

"I'm Jo."

"Laurie." They shook hands. Jo noticed he had a nice handshake and that his hands were not sweaty. She approved.

"Weird name for a boy," Jo said.

"Tell me how you really feel," he replied.

"Always," she promised.

He smiled.

"Most people agree with you," Laurie said. "About my name. I get bothered a lot about it. But lucky for me there's another new kid in my class whose name is Peaches, so everyone is getting used to me."

Jo smiled, very familiar with the short attention spans of her own classmates. "So, if you go to St. Jude, how come you're here?"

"Our class is so small—only twelve kids—that we're invited to go to your school's events. I'm supposed to try to have fun, I guess." He blushed. Jo could tell, even though it was kind of dark in the corner where they stood. She liked Laurie. He got to the point and had a thoughtful way of talking. She took a moment to look him over, noticing his dark hair that curled a little around the edges; tan, olive-toned skin; and kind brown eyes. He was also taller than Jo, which was saying something.

"Well, I'd ask you to dance, but I don't dance." Jo crossed her arms with finality. She wanted to make Laurie feel welcome in her school, but there were limits to her generosity. Firm limits.

"Me neither," Laurie said, sounding relieved. The pair watched a knot of eighth graders all jumping up and down under the disco ball.

"So, what kind of stuff do you like to do?" Jo asked.

"Stuff?"

"Like, for fun? Do you have fun? Or do you just stand in dark corners at dances and look miserable?"

"Well, standing in dark corners and looking miserable is one of my top five interests." Laurie grinned. "But when I'm not doing that I like to read. Play video games. Play hockey."

"Cool." Jo nodded approvingly. "Those are actually three of my top five interests. Do you have skates?"

"Yeah." Laurie looked much less miserable than he had a few moments ago. He looked almost happy.

"Me too! They're too small, but it doesn't matter. We should play. The pond is definitely frozen over; we just have to clear the snow."

"Okay."

"So, what's your favorite book?" Jo asked. "If you weren't talking to me, I'd already be home reading."

"Mmm, probably *Ender's Game*." Laurie loved classic sci-fi.

"Ooh, I love *Ender's Game*," Jo said, clapping her hands. She went through the occasional sci-fi streak herself. "I also love *A Wrinkle in Time* and *Ready Player One*. My favorite book is old-school, though: *Treasure Island*."

"I haven't read it," Laurie admitted. "But I'd like to," he added. "I'm also a Tolkien nerd."

"All the best people are," Jo said. They smiled at each other.

Laurie looked at the crowd of kids in front of them and noticed some kind of commotion. His eyes narrowed. "Hey! Isn't that your sister?"

Jo gasped and ran into the middle of the group gathered around Meg, who was sitting on the gym floor with one foot out of its ankle boot and in her hands. "Meg! What happened?"

"It's nothing," Meg said, sounding slightly mortified. "I just twisted my ankle is all. It was these stupid boots. I should've worn my flats."

"Let me help you," Laurie said, breaking through the group holding two folding chairs. He carefully guided Meg onto one of the chairs and helped her elevate her ankle onto the other. The chaperones came over and examined the situation, noticing there wasn't any swelling. Jo ran off to get Meg some fruit punch, but spilled most of it on herself in her rush to get back to her sister's side.

Jo knew Meg felt uncomfortable being the center of attention. Indeed, Meg's face was bright red. "I just want to go home," she said. "It's really nothing."

"I already called Grandpa to come get us," Laurie announced. "He'll send the Lincoln so you can stretch out your foot."

Jo looked at him gratefully, happy for his quick thinking. Mr. Lawrence's huge black town car would be perfect to get them home and save Mom a trip in the van. "But it's so early! Are you sure you're ready to leave?" she asked Laurie.

"Completely," he said. The chaperones helped Meg to the school's front entrance, where she wouldn't have much distance to cover when their ride arrived.

The two sisters were whisked home before they even knew what happened, each rushing to thank Mr. Lawrence's driver. Jo promised Laurie she'd bring him a stack of books in the morning, and everyone said their good nights.

At home, Mom wrapped up Meg's ankle with an ACE bandage, and the two younger sisters begged to hear every detail of the dance, imagining it to be a grand ball. Meg and Jo indulged them, embellishing every detail of their evenings.

"Even with your ankle, and my spilled punch," Jo

admitted, "we had fun. Middle school dances aren't so bad. I mean, on a scale of one to ten, they're like a four."

It was high praise.

When everyone had gone to bed and Jo and Meg went to their room to get into pajamas, Meg finally asked Jo the questions she'd been saving for an hour, not wanting to embarrass her sensitive younger sister in front of Mom.

"So, you and the boy next door were adorable together. Do you think he's *cute*? Do you *like* him?"

"What? What are you talking about?" Jo said, sounding crabby. "Can't a person talk to another person without everyone thinking about romantical nonsense?"

Jo's voice was sharper than she intended it to be. Her relaxed face immediately turned sour and she set down the hairbrush she'd been using with a clatter. It made Jo angry that her normally sensible big sister was acting exactly like one of the silly gossips in her class, who seemed to talk about nothing so much these days as which boy they thought was cute or which celebrity they wished they could meet. It was so annoying.

"Whoa. I'm sorry. I just . . . You guys seemed into each other is all." Meg felt bad for ruffling her sister, especially when she'd taken such good care of Meg and her lousy ankle.

"Well, we're just friends. He's nice," Jo said in a huff, flopping onto her bed and curling up toward the wall.

"Hey. Hey," Meg said in a soft, apologetic tone. "I'm sorry. I really am. I get it; you're just friends. I promise not to ever tease you again about boys, okay?"

"Deal," Jo said, muffled by her pillow.

Meg's Pretty Pillow Pattern

Materials:

- Piece of fabric, at least 34 by 17 inches (Old curtains, sheets, or clothing can be fun materials, but make sure to ask an adult before you cut anything!)
- Ruler
- Scissors
- Piece of chalk
- 20 straight pins
- Spool of thread in a color that matches your fabric
- Sewing needle (a slightly thicker one will be easier to work with)
- Needle threader (optional)
- About 13 ounces of pillow stuffing
- Iron

Directions:

1. Carefully measure out two 17-by-17-inch

squares onto your piece of fabric and mark them on the "wrong side" (the side of the fabric that looks like the back, without any pattern on it) with the chalk. Cut out the two squares.

2. Lay the squares down flat with their "wrong sides" up. On each side of each square, measure half an inch from the edge and put a chalk dot to mark the spot. Make several of these dots along the edge of the fabric on each side. Connect the dots with the ruler and trace the line with the chalk so there is an outline all the way around each square half an inch from the edge. This is where you'll sew.
3. Put the "right sides" of the fabric together, so the "wrong sides" of the fabric are facing out. Put a pin at each corner of the squares, holding them together. Then, place four more pins on each side of the squares, evenly spaced, perpendicular to the edge so the pin and the edge form a T shape.
4. Thread your needle (a needle threader can make this easier) and pull the thread through about 30 inches. Then cut the thread off so that there are 30 inches of thread on each side of the needle hole. Bring the strands together and tie a knot at the end.

5. Starting at a corner, make small stitches straight along your chalk line. 1/4-inch stitches are a good size. If you run out of thread, just tie a knot, cut the thread, rethread your needle, and start again where you left off.
6. Stop sewing about 2 inches from where you started. Tie a knot and cut your thread.
7. Turn the pillowcase right-side out using the 2-inch opening you left. Make sure to poke out the corners so you can see the points.
8. Lay the pillowcase down and ask an adult to help you iron it so that the seams are flat.
9. Stuff the pillowcase with cotton batting through the opening. You can make it as firm or squishy as you like.
10. Fold the edges of the fabric at the opening over 1/2 inch on each side and use 2 pins to hold them together. Use small stitches to sew across the opening. Make a knot and cut your thread.

CHAPTER FOUR

Back to Reality

"I hate being good." —P. L. Travers

Jo felt wretched. The sky was gray, the air was cold and damp, and the snow that had looked so perfectly picturesque at Christmas time had morphed unattractively into dirty slop coating every outdoor surface. As she trudged from school to Aunt Em's house, Jo noticed that each car driving by was covered in the salt and sand that the city had placed on the roads to make things less slick.

Usually Jo loved winter. It meant ice-skating and hockey, and snowball fights and delightfully huge mugs of hot chocolate in front of the fire. But today, the dark season weighed on her. The merriment of Christmas had passed, she missed Dad horribly, and life felt like one long chore list with no end in sight.

Today, her main duty was visiting Aunt Em. In theory, all four March sisters were supposed to take turns keeping her company in the afternoons, but the chore mainly fell to Jo as Meg had a steady babysitting gig, Beth wanted to stay home to bake and practice piano, and Amy was too young to read as smoothly aloud as Aunt Em liked. Jo dreaded having to read magazines to her aunt. For one, her favorite was *Ladies' Home Journal*, which Jo had zero interest in whatsoever. And for two, all the issues in the house were at least seven or eight years old. It was like a time capsule inside Aunt Em's house, but not in a good way.

Jo reached the cobblestone walk that led up to the mansion's grand front porch, complete with pillars. She sighed deeply. If the March house had been built mainly with usefulness and comfort in mind, Aunt Em's home had been built to impress people. Which made it cold and foreboding.

She knocked, and the door immediately swung open. Em had obviously been waiting for her.

"You're late!" she exclaimed.

"I am?" Jo was genuinely surprised. "But I came right from school."

"You must've walked pretty slowly," Em said, her eyes narrowed.

"Can I make you some tea? It's so damp today," Jo said, wisely changing the subject. She found that afternoons went much more smoothly when she remembered to take deep breaths and do nice things for her charge. Arguing never, ever worked.

"I suppose."

Aunt Em liked to hold court in the formal living room at the front of the house, though she received few visitors. Jo felt the room was the least comfortable of all, with its rock-hard wingback chairs and not even one ottoman or footstool. The sofa was pristine, almost as if it had been covered in plastic for the last thirty years and only recently unwrapped. Mom said Aunt Em had it replaced every two years, the exact same model, in the exact same upholstery. Jo thought the very notion was the silliest thing she'd ever heard, but Mom said to try to be nice and that Aunt Em was "eccentric."

It took no time at all to make the tea and get settled. Jo reluctantly opened an article about how to properly pluck one's eyebrows and started to read. She tried to infuse the dull instructions with some verve, pretending it was a tale of danger and suspense: "Plucking perfect eyebrows to possess a flawless, face-framing shape can hurt a lot," Jo read, her voice trembling as if she were describing a pirate mutiny. "But since full and thick brows can look out of control, you should spend a little quality time with your tweezers each and every week. Get perfect eyebrow arches every single time, and remember—you can always fill in mistakes with your trusty pencil!"

Aunt Em studied Jo's eyebrows carefully. She didn't say a word, but Jo knew what she was thinking.

Jo wrinkled her nose. It was true that her eyebrows were thick and a bit unruly—just like Dad's—but Jo liked them that way. There was no chance she'd let anyone near her with tweezers, least of all her elderly relative. But, since she didn't want to ruffle her aunt's feathers, she carefully tore the instructions out of the magazine and placed them gently on her backpack. (She'd throw them out later.)

"How is your tea, Auntie?" Jo asked.

"It's good. Thank you." Aunt Em yawned.

Jo smiled a big smile but covered it up with a cough. She knew that if her charge fell asleep, she'd be free to read what she wanted, as long as she sat perfectly still and didn't make too much noise turning the pages. With that, Jo changed her reading strategy. Instead of trying to make the home decorating tips sound exciting, she subtly started using a more monotonous tone. This, combined with the soothing chamomile tea she'd prepared, did the trick. Aunt Em was out like a light and Jo was free!

Inch by careful inch, she reached for her backpack and her copy of *The Book Thief* by Markus Zusak, which she was reading for the first time and loving.

This way, the two passed the next two hours peacefully. At five thirty, it was time for Jo to return home for dinner and homework, which she did gleefully.

The mood at the March house was dim as the unfortunate facts of winter settled in. It was cold, it was gray, it was drafty, Dad was still gone, and there was no extra money for dinners out or special treats. The girls, who were eating leftovers in the kitchen with Hannah while Mom worked late, were gloomy.

"The twins were extraterrible today." Meg sighed, hoping for sympathy from her sisters and from Hannah. Meg babysat the King twins, who were three, most days after school to give their mother time to run errands and see friends. Though the Kings lived in a big, beautiful house, Meg didn't particularly like spending time there. The twins were spoiled and allowed to do almost anything they wanted. It was pretty chaotic. "Today, Chloe spilled an entire bowl of cereal, with extra milk, on the carpet. When I was trying to clean *that* up, Jacob knocked over a houseplant. The dirt went *everywhere*. I almost cried."

Beth patted her older sister's shoulder consolingly. "Maybe next time you *should* just cry," she said. "Three-year-olds understand tears. They'd probably put *themselves* in time-out."

"Not these three-year-olds," Meg said, shaking her

head. “Besides, the Kings say they don’t believe in punishment. What a nightmare.”

“I’m sorry, Meg,” Jo said sincerely. “Your job is definitely harder than keeping Aunt Em company. But not by much,” she added, explaining to everyone how Em had looked critically at her eyebrows.

“Your eyebrows are beautiful!” Beth exclaimed.

“No, they’re not,” said Amy in a quieter voice. “They look like caterpillars.” Jo heard her youngest sister, but fortunately the comparison struck her as funny, and she started giggling and wiggling her caterpillars menacingly.

Jo’s laughter made all the sisters smile, but most of all Beth, who wanted everyone to get along. Beth had actually stayed home from school that day complaining of a stomachache. She didn’t like school very much and preferred to stay home whenever Mom would let her. School was loud and complicated; home was quiet and peaceful. Beth liked to pass the time playing with her kitten, Snowball, or making new pieces for her elaborate dollhouse. She also loved to bake. Hannah was teaching her how to create the perfect apple pockets, and Beth relished the project.

Beth and Jo were a pair. Jo took special care to look out for her sensitive younger sister, and felt that Beth understood her better than anyone else, maybe even better than Mom sometimes.

Meg, on the other hand, felt that Amy was her

counterpart. The oldest March and the youngest March could spend hours at the mall together if Mom would ever let them, or in the bathroom playing with the curling iron, a magazine open between them.

"Well, I had a miserable day too," Amy announced. "I think my nose is getting worse. If that's even possible." She started rummaging in the kitchen drawers and produced a small chip clip, which she ceremoniously placed on her nose, hoping to coax it into a more pleasant shape.

Jo, with a twinkle in her eye, said, "I don't think noses are like teeth, Amy. You can't, like, put braces on them to straighten them out."

"Who says? You're not a doctor," Amy replied petulantly.

"If Amy wants to wear a chip clip all night, she can wear a chip clip," Hannah said, settling the matter and winking in Amy's direction. Amy's willfulness sometimes gave Hannah a headache, but she found the youngest March amusing in the extreme.

"I'm sure it'll help," Beth said kindly. Amy smiled at her and stuck her tongue out at Jo.

"Let's go sit by the fire," Hannah said. "I have a treat for you. But first, put your dishes *in* the dishwasher. There are no elves here cleaning up after us."

The girls cleaned up the kitchen and eagerly moved into the living room, where Hannah had placed Beth's perfect, delectable apple pockets on a large platter for dessert. She also had a big bag of marshmallows for them to roast on sticks over the fire. “Yay!” Amy shouted, her nose completely forgotten at the prospect of sweets. “Thank you, Hannah!”

As everyone got settled in the glow of the fireplace, Mom arrived home. She changed from her coat into her robe and got comfortable in her chair. Meg brought her the first melty marshmallow, which Mom ate with a smile.

“How was your day, girls?” she asked. “Mine was bonkers.”

“Terrible!” Meg said. But she didn’t sound upset as she put a fresh marshmallow onto her stick.

“Wretched!” added Amy, as she bit into an enormous piece of apple pocket.

“Pretty good,” Beth said, picking up her knitting project. She wasn’t eating dessert because she’d had so many samples after baking earlier and her stomach really was quite sensitive.

“I’d give it a three,” Jo concluded. “Is there a new e-mail from Dad?”

“Not today, sweetheart. I’m sorry. Sounds like January around here,” Mrs. March said, nodding. “It can be hard work getting back into the swing of things after such a nice Christmas. But we do all right, don’t we, girls?”

Everyone grumbled in reluctant agreement. No one

wanted to tell Mom they felt grumpy, even if they all did a little bit, even Beth.

"The winter doldrums can be difficult and regular life isn't always fun, but we have everything we need to be happy—most of all each other," Mom reminded them.

"That's true," Meg said. "We'll try to be grateful."

"Can we get cable?" Amy asked. "Everyone on earth has five hundred channels except for me. How can I live?"

Jo gave her chip clip a squeeze. Amy squealed.

Beth's Apple Pocket Recipe

Ingredients:

1 pound frozen bread dough, thawed
6 cups peeled and sliced apples
1 teaspoon lemon juice
1 tablespoon cinnamon
1/4 cup sugar
1/2 cup butter

Directions:

Thaw frozen bread dough ahead of time in the refrigerator (at least 8–12 hours before you plan to bake). Preheat oven to 350 degrees. With the help of an adult, roll out the dough on a floured bread board to 1/3-inch thick. Cut into squares (4 inches by 4 inches).

Mix sliced apples with cinnamon, lemon juice, and sugar in a large bowl. Place three tablespoons of the apple mixture on each square. Fold corners together, pinching tightly. Place on greased cookie sheet, pinched side down. Let rise 20–30 minutes. Place in oven and bake for 25–30 minutes. Serve warm with butter.

CHAPTER FIVE

Good Neighbors

"Always be on the lookout for the presence of wonder."
—E. B. White

Even winter couldn't stop the weekend from arriving. The March girls eagerly welcomed a day to do as they pleased—at least after the family chore list was completed. Beth had to clean up Snowball's litter box, Amy had to pull the sheets off of all the beds and carry them down to the basement to be washed, and Jo and Meg worked together to clean the bathroom.

"There is enough hair around this house to make six wigs," Jo said, wrinkling her nose as she cleared the tub drain and emptied the garbage can. "It's gross."

"That's true. I nominate you to chop *yours* off," Meg

said, admiring her own long, pretty locks in the mirror as she wiped away the toothpaste spray in front of her with a paper towel and some glass cleaner.

"Maybe I will," Jo said, liking the idea.

"No!" Meg protested. "Your hair is nice."

"Whatever. I just don't like cleaning."

"Who does?" Meg said sensibly.

Soon it was time to relax. Normally, Jo would head straight for her attic to do some writing and reading, but today she felt restless. She decided to go outside to shovel snow off the walk; about three inches had fallen overnight, and both Mom and Hannah hated shoveling. Jo didn't mind it.

"Are you serious?" Meg asked Jo, watching her younger sister put on snow boots and a scarf. She was curled up by the fire watching a romantic comedy on TV with Beth and Amy. The three were sitting close together for warmth. "It's freezing out there!"

"It's not that bad," Jo said. "I'll be fine. Adventure awaits!"

Meg laughed and shook her head.

To Jo, it felt good to breathe in the cold air and get her muscles moving. After clearing the sidewalk in front of the house and a path around the garden, she got busy on the driveway. This was a lot harder to shovel, because underneath the snow was a layer of loose gravel. Even though it was all frozen together, the driveway was very bumpy, and extremely long. The garage was not attached to the house. Rather, it sat far behind it at the back of the March property, which meant the driveway had a lot of ground to cover. It would be so much easier to do the job, Jo thought, if she only had access to a backhoe. Just a small one, really. How awesome would that be?

Fortunately for everyone, Jo had no means of procuring construction equipment, not even a small model.

Feeling worn out after clearing less than half of the drive, Jo took a break and let her shovel fall into the snowbank. She looked around. The sky was white, with a thick layer of very high clouds blocking the sun. There wasn't much traffic because it was still pretty early in the day. Jo noticed a bird's nest in one of the eaves of the March house, and saw a lot of peeling paint all around it. The place had needed a fresh coat of paint for at least two years now; maybe when Dad got back they'd finally tackle the job. The Lawrence house next door had no peeling paint. It was perfectly maintained and very distinguished-looking, with already-cleared walks (Mr. Lawrence hired a service), precisely trimmed trees, and squared-off evergreen shrubs.

Jo stomped her feet to warm up and something caught her eye in one of the Lawrence's windows. Laurie! She saw him wave and made a motion for him to open the window, which he did. Jo crossed the large lawn between their houses and shouted up to him.

"Hey! I have books for you!"

"Good!" he shouted down. "I have a cold and I'm bored out of my mind. Come over?"

"Okay. Give me five minutes." Jo grinned and ran back to her own house to put the snow shovel away.

Inside, she gathered up the titles she'd been meaning to deliver to her new friend, along with a selection of treats from her secret food stash, and Snowball in his small kitty carrier. She knew Beth would be okay with her borrowing the pet, since it was for a good cause. No one could stay bored when there was a kitten in the room. "Mom! I'm going to Laurie's," Jo shouted.

"Okay," came Mom's muffled reply from the basement. "Remember to take off your boots before going inside!"

She ran over to Laurie's front porch and rang the bell. He answered two seconds later.

"*Hola*," she said solemnly, attempting to remove her boots without using her hands. "I come in peace. Thanks for saving me from shoveling the rest of our driveway."

"You're welcome." Laurie smiled, opening the front door wide. "I'll try not to sneeze in your direction. Grandpa is at breakfast with some of his friends from the country club. Want to play video games?"

"Definitely. I brought snacks and Beth's cat to keep us company. Whenever I'm sick, all I want to do is read and stuff my face."

"Me too," Laurie said. His nose was a little red, but other than that he seemed healthy enough.

Laurie led Jo upstairs, past several interesting paintings, to a comfortable loft space overlooking the living room below. It had clearly been set up just for gaming. There was a big flat-screen TV and several low chairs and bean bags scattered around. Jo let Snowball out of his carrier, and the kitten proceeded to sniff everything in sight. Then she unpacked her backpack, producing a chocolate bar, tinfoil-wrapped apple pockets, and homemade fruit leather. She pulled out books and stacked them on a table for Laurie to look at later: *The Giver*, *The Hitchhiker's Guide to the Galaxy*, *The Martian Chronicles*, and *The Graveyard Book*.

"You've probably read all of these, but I thought I'd make sure," Jo said.

"I've only read two. Thank you," Laurie replied. They both watched Snowball for a few minutes and laughed when the kitten found a small piece of paper and batted it around in an adorable frenzy. "So, is the kitten yours or your sister's?"

"Snowball is Beth's," Jo said. "But we all love him to pieces."

"Is she the youngest?" Laurie asked. Jo could see he was curious to know more about her family, so she filled him in on everyone's ages and particularities and promised to bring them over to meet him soon. She also invited him over to the March home to hang out anytime he wanted.

"Although I have to warn you Meg usually has some sappy movie on, and Beth will hide because she's so shy, and Amy will probably make you sit as still as a statue so she can draw you." Jo smiled. "I just want you to know what you're getting into when you knock on our door. Oh, and you'll definitely have to be in our next movie. I'm writing the script now. It's about a radioactive dragon."

"That sounds fun. More fun than here, for sure," Laurie said, sounding sad. Jo wanted to ask about his parents and what had happened and where he had lived before here, but she wisely decided their friendship was too new to get into that sort of thing just now.

"Well, don't be shy. Come over anytime. Your grandfather would be cool with it, wouldn't he?"

Laurie didn't mind being accused of shyness, because Jo was so friendly and her smile was so big.

"I will," he promised. "Grandpa pretty much lets me do what I want. He looks scary, but he's not bad."

"That's good." Jo nodded. She adjusted her beanbag chair so she was looking at the ceiling. "What's St. Jude like? I've never even been inside."

"It's okay. I'd rather go to your school, but I guess my family has belonged to St. Jude since, like, the beginning of time, so there's no chance. One good thing about it is the high school is in the same building, so I might get to play JV soccer as an eighth grader next year."

"That's awesome!" Jo liked soccer almost as much as ice hockey. She was on her own school's team, playing midfielder. They had finished their season six weeks ago with a trip to state, but hadn't advanced, much to her dismay. Unfortunately, Mom said Jo couldn't go out again next year unless her grades improved. "I play soccer too, but I'm majorly benched unless I start getting more As in my classes."

"Yeah." Laurie nodded in commiseration. "I'm getting a C in math, so Grandpa got me a tutor, this freshman named Brooks. He's all right. I wish I could just do band all day. I'm learning jazz guitar."

"Cool. Let's play," Jo said, lunging for a controller. "I'm superexcellent at this one."

They played. It was a racing game with lots of twists, hills, and flying debris. Even though Jo had only played a half dozen times at friends' houses, she was definitely doing better than poor Laurie, who seemed more interested in watching his new friend than in winning. He didn't mind her racing superiority, which Jo found impressive. Compared to the troglodyte boys in Jo's class, Laurie definitely stood out for being so normal.

An hour later, they heard the back door of the house open and Mr. Lawrence's voice, calling up to his grandson. "I brought you soup, Laurie! Come down and have some; it'll do your throat good."

"I better go down there," Laurie said to Jo. "But it's

okay if you stay up here a little longer and finish your race."

"Okay. I'll be right down." Jo nodded, her eyes a little glazed by the game. After a moment, she realized she was probably being rude and should find Laurie. She stood up, shook out her legs, and took a moment to look at the shelves surrounding the television. There were a few books there and lots of framed photos, mostly of Laurie with his parents and a few of him with his grandfather.

"He doesn't look that scary to me," Jo murmured aloud.

"Well, thank you," a deep voice said, from not twelve feet behind her. Mr. Lawrence stood at the top of the stairs, smiling bemusedly. He wore a golf sweater and khakis. "I do my best."

Jo blushed deeply. "I only meant . . . ," she began, with no idea how to end the sentence. "Um, thank you so much for all that food at Christmas. It was really something."

Mr. Lawrence laughed. "I'm glad you liked it. Er, 'really something' is good, right?"

"It's totally good."

"You remind me of your grandfather," Mr. Lawrence said. "He liked to tell it like it is too. A fine man."

"Thank you, sir. I wish I could remember him." Jo relaxed. Mr. Lawrence seemed quite friendly.

"I could tell you some stories," he said, grinning. "But I'll wait till you're older. What are you and Laurie up to?"

"Video games. He was lonely and I was tired of

shoveling snow, so we've been hanging out. I hope that's okay," Jo added. She realized Mom probably didn't know Mr. Lawrence wasn't home when she gave Jo permission to visit Laurie. *Oops*.

"I'm glad he's made a new friend." Mr. Lawrence nodded. "Join us for tea?"

"Sure!" Jo liked every kind of tea she'd ever met. "I love tea!"

"You're very wise," Mr. Lawrence replied.

The trio sat down at the kitchen table, and Mr. Lawrence poured Laurie a lemon blend with honey. Jo chose vanilla rooibos, and Mr. Lawrence had Irish Breakfast.

"Cream and sugar, Miss March?" Mr. Lawrence asked.

"I'll take one cube of sugar and lots of cream, please, Mr. L."

Jo could tell Laurie wanted to hang out in the loft more than he wanted to have tea with his grandfather, so she was extracheerful and talkative to balance things out and to let him know she didn't mind the change in their activities, especially since Mr. Lawrence had served delicious glazed orange scones alongside the tea. After a few minutes, seeing how well his friend was getting along with his grandpa, Laurie relaxed and his regular grin returned.

As Jo explained—in great detail, and with lots of excited gestures—how she was trying to get the empty lot in their neighborhood turned into either a soccer field or hockey rink, or both, Mr. Lawrence watched his grandson and saw the good effect Jo had on him. Laurie's eyes danced, and his laugh was genuine.

When it was time to go, Mr. Lawrence invited Jo to bring back her whole family over for brunch. Jo left with a smile on her face, happy to have such wonderful neighbors and new friends.

On her short walk home, she didn't even feel the winter cold.

Jo March's Care Box Instructions

When one of your sisters, or your new best friend, is sick or suffering from the winter blues, it can help to make a care box. Everyone loves getting a care box. The best ones have books, food, and other cheerful items. Here are my ingredients for a good one.

Ingredients:

4 books (one classic, one new, two favorites)

1 sugary treat (I suggest chocolate-based choices, including but not limited to brownies or candy bars)

1 healthy snack (good options include veggie chips, fruit leather, roasted nuts, or string cheese)

Something unexpected (a kitten, a magic trick you just learned, fireworks . . . just kidding)
1 box of tea

Directions:

Assemble all the items in a pretty gift bag or decorated shoe box and deliver. You can't just drop it off and leave, though. The most important part about putting together a care box is hanging out with the recipient. Because really, YOU are the care box. ☺

CHAPTER SIX

Beth Comes Out of Her Shell

"I can't go back to yesterday—because I was a different person then."
—Lewis Carroll

Several weeks later, Jo assembled her entire family for a visit to Laurie's house.

"You'll love it, Amy," she promised her youngest sister. "There is totally weird art all over the place. Like, a whole canvas painted with just one big blotch of color. It looks very nice, though," Jo added quickly, remembering her manners.

Amy grinned. She was on a modern art kick, having dragged Dad's biggest coffee-table books out of storage recently. They had been carefully collected over decades of Mr. March's occasional visits to the Met in New York

City and the Institute of Contemporary Art in Boston. Amy was the only March sister who seemed to understand, in her soul, what made a particular work of art special.

"I think I'll stay here," Beth announced. Everything that interested Beth was pretty much within the walls of their home.

"Just come for a minute," Jo said gently, tucking the tag sticking out of the collar of Beth's shirt back in. "You can peek at Mr. Lawrence's spectacular baby grand piano and then come right back home." Jo always knew how to prod her most sensitive sibling without upsetting her. Beth nodded, her eyes gleaming. A baby grand piano? Right next door? It boggled the mind.

"What are we waiting for?" Meg asked impatiently, bouncing from foot to foot. She was very interested to see for herself what sorts of luxurious delights were contained inside Laurie's house.

"Nothing, nothing," Mom said, rushing out of the kitchen with a covered plate of muffins. She couldn't resist bringing something delicious to their neighbor. "Let's go."

After a lively and pleasant brunch prepared by the Lawrences' housekeeper, Riva, and shared around the large dining room table, each girl found something to love in the Lawrence house. Meg was completely enchanted by an incredible greenhouse tucked in the back of the estate. Mr. Lawrence liked tropical flowers, so he kept the space heated to a balmy eighty degrees, and ran humidifiers constantly to accommodate an amazing array of orchids and fruit trees. He had both mangoes and oranges growing inside, so the room had a beautiful aroma. Meg said several times, only half joking, that she planned to visit the greenhouse daily. "Humid air is good for my complexion," she solemnly explained to Mr. Lawrence, who agreed that it was good for his as well, and that she was welcome anytime.

Jo loved the well-appointed library on the first floor and marveled at all the books. Her only criticism was the room was quite stuffed with business theory and had very little fiction.

"You can borrow anything you like, Miss March," Mr. Lawrence said, amused to watch Jo survey each shelf with intensity. It looked as if she was searching for the meaning of life in there.

"Thank you, Mr. L.," Jo said. But then, unable to help herself, she made a face as if tasting something too tart.

"Miss March, do you find my taste in books poor?" Mr. Lawrence asked. Laurie, who was also in the room, looked embarrassed. But Jo didn't hesitate.

"I do. Where's the adventure? The romance? All I see are books about how to make money."

"I see what you mean." Mr. Lawrence laughed. "Perhaps you could accompany Laurie and me to a bookstore one of these days and help us round out my collection."

"I'd be happy to!" Jo cried, clapping her hands. Laurie grinned at her and at his grandfather, for being so kind to his friend. "It's good to start with the classics, you know."

"Oh, really? Why is that?" Mr. Lawrence asked.

"It makes all the other books feel more important," Jo said. "Like, if you go to a party, and the most respected and most intelligent people in the world are there, wouldn't you feel extra good about being there yourself?"

"I suppose that I would." Mr. Lawrence smiled. "Indeed. Which classics do you enjoy the most?"

"Well, my very favorite is *Treasure Island* by Robert Louis Stevenson. I actually have a first-edition copy; it's my most prized possession."

"Impressive." Mr. Lawrence nodded. "I adored that book as a boy. What an incredible thing to own. You have exquisite taste, young lady."

"Thank you." Jo smiled.

Amy was indeed impressed with the mansion's art. One piece in particular caught her attention. It was hanging in the dining room; the only painting in the room. Thick daubs of overlapping oil swirls in greens and blues covered the canvas, which was easily ten feet long. She stared at it in a trance.

Beth looked at the grand piano from around the corner where it stood, as if it might make some kind of sudden movement. She yearned with her whole heart to play it, for it was a fine instrument, but she couldn't get up the courage to ask Mr. Lawrence if it was okay. So she merely stared.

Laurie knew, from Jo's stories about her family, that Beth was exceptionally bashful. Watching her timidly look at the piano with longing in her eyes, he decided to see if Grandpa could do anything about it. Mr. Lawrence was always bugging Laurie to take piano lessons, but Laurie was much more interested in the guitar.

"Grandpa, I think little Beth wants to play your piano, but she's too shy to ask you," he said. Mr. Lawrence nodded. He casually opened several drawers in a hutch next to the piano, and pulled out a collection of music to show to Mrs. March.

"Your father loved to play," he explained to her, just loud enough for Beth to hear as well. "In fact, some of this is his music." He cleverly launched into several stories about how the two friends had once played piano together at parties. He also mentioned some performances he'd seen and described them in such beautiful detail that Beth was drawn from her hiding spot around the corner, fully into the room, and eventually onto the ottoman in front of Mr. Lawrence's chair. He pretended not to notice her, still talking about music and how much he loved it.

"It's too bad," he concluded with a sigh, "that this piano never gets played. I'm so busy with work, and Laurie is so busy with guitar and sports and video games. So here it sits, day after day, lonely for someone to play it."

"Maybe I could help," Beth said, almost in a whisper. One thing that could stir Beth out of her shell was the thought that she could help.

"Oh? Do you play?" Mr. Lawrence said gently, careful not to startle her.

"I do. A little. Not very well," Beth said. Mom elbowed Jo, who was about to loudly contradict her.

"Well, even a little bit of playing now and then would be wonderful. I tell you what, I'm usually gone in the afternoons or working quietly in my study. I'll give you the code to the front door keypad. You can come in whenever you like and play a few songs. I'd be most grateful."

"I'd like that, sir. Thank you." Beth's face flushed in excitement. "I'll come tomorrow after school if it's okay," she added.

"Perfect," Mr. Lawrence nodded, writing the code on his business card and handing it to her.

The next day, true to her word, Beth silently entered the Lawrence mansion at three fifteen on the dot. She quickly scurried to the exquisite piano, opened it up with reverence, and proceeded to play Beethoven with great feeling.

Mr. Lawrence, who was working quietly in his study nearby, made not a peep as he listened to her play. Her talent was so overwhelming that it brought tears to his eyes, for it reminded him of his son, who had once played with a similar depth of emotion. Careful not to alert Beth to his presence, he said not a word and moved not a muscle, only hoping that the girl would return.

And she did. Every day the next week, at precisely three fifteen, Beth visited the Lawrence home to play for exactly one hour. Over time, Mr. Lawrence risked making more and more noise, gradually alerting her to his presence in the study and even occasionally clapping for her. Laurie also greeted Beth several times as he rushed through the house on a search for snacks before a tutoring session or before his Tae Kwon Do class. She got used to it and didn't even jump anymore.

Beth felt so grateful to Mr. Lawrence for letting her enjoy his piano, she decided to knit him a special scarf as a gift. She explained her plan to Mom and Meg, who both agreed it was a great idea and helped her purchase some fine merino yarn. Beth worked on the project every evening for three weeks until the scarf was complete. She'd had to go back and undo stitches several times to fix mistakes, but she was pleased with the result. The scarf was a deep burgundy color with one debonair gray stripe. Beth wrapped it in tissue paper and placed it in a gift box. She tied the package with a bow and attached a gift tag written in Mom's pretty script:

To Mr. Lawrence,
from Beth March

Handmade with care

Thank you for sharing your
beautiful piano with me.

The next day, she placed the box just outside of Mr. Lawrence's study and backed slowly away, wanting him to discover her gift only once she was safely home. He waited a few minutes after hearing his front door click closed, and scooped up the box. When he saw what she had made, he smiled and his eyes teared up. Not only was the gift beautiful, it was well made and perfectly to his taste. The thought of his young neighbor working on it for weeks touched his heart.

Beth waited patiently for a response from her elder neighbor, fearing he didn't like her gift when a whole day passed without a word. But then, the following morning, as she sleepily made her way to the kitchen to find some cereal, she noticed all her sisters already at the table, clearly excited about something. A box sat among them with a letter attached.

"Beth, you're such a sleepyhead! We've been waiting for you for ages! Laurie brought this over this morning. It's from Mr. Lawrence!" Jo was using all her willpower not to open the present herself.

"A present? But . . ." Beth felt embarrassed. The whole reason she'd made Mr. Lawrence the scarf was that he'd already given her more than she'd ever imagined receiving.

"Open it!" Amy yelled. "You're killing me!"

At this, Beth smiled. She dutifully opened the package. It contained an intricate-looking music box that played "Clair de Lune," one of Beth's favorite pieces.

"Wow," Meg said, stunned. "That's gorgeous. And it sounds amazing."

"I love it," Beth whispered. She reluctantly tore her eyes from the gift to read Mr. Lawrence's note:

Dear Miss March,

I have had many scarves in my life, but none have suited me so well as yours. Burgundy is my favorite color, and I plan to wear it every day as a pleasant reminder of its gentle and talented maker. This old gentleman likes to pay my debts, so I hope you will accept and enjoy this music box, which once belonged to someone dear to me.

With many thanks, I remain your friend,

James Lawrence

"You'll have to go thank him," Jo said, though not really expecting her timid sister to actually do it. The whole family was astonished at what happened next.

Beth nodded and said, "Yes. I'll go now, before I get too scared." And with that, she put on her coat and boots and went right out the front door, still in her flannel pajama pants.

With only a slight hesitation at Mr. Lawrence's study door, Beth walked in and went right up to "the old gentleman."

"Thank you, sir. . . ." She trailed off, feeling suddenly self-conscious. But Mr. Lawrence looked so friendly and happy to see her that she simply gave him a hug.

If the roof of the house had flown off, the man wouldn't have been more shocked than he was. He felt many years and many sorrows fall away in that moment.

As if a spell had been broken, Beth stopped being scared of the old man right then. She realized there was much she wanted to tell him, and the two talked cheerfully until it really was time for Beth to go to school.

When Beth returned home, looking happy and chattering excitedly about all she and Mr. Lawrence had discussed, Amy fell right off her chair and Meg said simply, "You know, if Aunt Em came over right now and did a headstand, I wouldn't even be surprised. That's how odd this day is."

Mr. Lawrence's Scarf Pattern

Supplies:

- About 253 yards of super-bulky-weight yarn (Wool is very warm!)
- Size 11 knitting needles
- Crochet hook, any size
- Scissors

Gauge:

4 stitches to an inch, 5 rows to an inch

Scarf:

Cast on 22 stitches.

Row 1: Knit 1, purl 1, alternately across the row.

Row 2: Purl 1, knit 1, alternately across the row.

Repeat rows 1 and 2 until your scarf is about 54 inches long. Feel free to make it longer or shorter as you wish.

Fringe (optional):

Cut two 6-inch strands of yarn. Fold these strands in half to form a loop. With a crochet hook, draw the loop through a stitch at one end of your scarf, then pull the 4 ends through the loop and pull tight. Do this in every other stitch along both short ends of the scarf. Trim fringe so it is all the same length.

Tips:

This pattern will make your scarf about 7.5 inches wide. If you would like a wider or skinnier scarf, cast on more or fewer stitches at the beginning. Make sure you cast on an even number of stitches.

If you lose track of which row you are on, do the opposite of whatever stitches you see in the row below your needle. If the first stitch in the previous row is a knit stitch (the one that looks like a loop), you should start the new row with a purl stitch. If the first stitch in the last row was a purl (the one that looks like a round bump), start the new row with a knit.

CHAPTER SEVEN

Amy Gets in Big Trouble

"I'm not young enough to know everything."
—J. M. Barrie

Every member of the March family was tired of winter as February dragged on, but Amy imagined that she felt even worse than any of them. The problem was her classmates. Every girl in her group suddenly seemed to have something special to show off at lunch, and Amy had nothing. On Monday, Jamie brought in her playbill from the musical everyone wanted to see but no one could actually get tickets for. She'd seen it over the weekend—her father had gone to college with one of the understudies in the cast—and couldn't stop talking about how amazing it was. On Tuesday, Sonja brought to school her collection of shark's teeth, which she had recently acquired during an amazing Florida beach vacation. On Wednesday, Jenny showed up to school with her nails expertly painted in a polka-dot pattern; she'd gotten a mother-daughter manicure with her mom the night before.

Amy could tell that everyone noticed she never had anything new or interesting to wear or talk about. She feared that her friends even pitied her and couldn't stand it. Something had to be done.

"Mom, I can't go to school today," she announced one morning at breakfast, hopeful that a midweek break from school would be just the thing to raise her dragging spirits.

"Why? You're not sick," Mom said in a tone that suggested pretending to be so wouldn't get her very far.

"I don't have any clean underwear," Amy tried.

Jo started giggling and couldn't stop.

Mom sighed. "We do laundry every weekend, Amy. How is that possible?"

"I don't know. It just is."

"Well, borrow a pair of Beth's. You're going to school."

"No! I can't! That's gross!" Amy squealed. But Mom gave her the Look and she gave up.

Amy got a new idea the next day, while flipping through one of Meg's glossy celebrity magazines. Several of the actresses and singers carried their pets with them when they went on coffee runs or even on vacation. Amy loved the shots of tiny dogs peeking out of purses, especially when the pups had bows in their fur.

So on Friday morning, while everyone was distracted, Amy carefully placed Snowball in her backpack with several kitty treats, making sure to put his head by the open mesh part, and walked to school with Beth, who conveniently trailed far behind her younger sister. She was distracted by the sight of several cardinals in the trees and didn't hear her kitten's occasional meows at all.

Amy went straight to her classroom and took her normal seat by her friends. It took about three seconds for all the attention in the room to swing to her as Snowball's meows became more insistent. Fortunately, Mr. Davis was looking at his phone and didn't seem to realize that everyone was crowded around Amy's desk, eager to pet the kitten, who seemed happy with the attention.

That's when Amy first realized that maybe her plan was slightly . . . flawed. What was she going to do with the kitten all day? Where would he go to the bathroom?

It didn't end up being a problem.

"Is that a . . . cat?" Mr. Davis asked incredulously.

"Yup!" Jenny said, not-so-secretly thrilled that Amy was about to get in trouble. "Amy brought him to school in her backpack!"

"I thought we needed a class pet," Amy said weakly.

"Really," Mr. Davis replied. It wasn't a question. He looked pretty mad.

"He's so cute!" Sonja said, trying to be helpful.

At that moment, Snowball decided to seal Amy's fate. He peed, right on top of Amy's desk. The room went wild. "He's peeing! He's peeing," several boys shouted. "EWWWW!" several girls yelled in unison. "SOME GOT ON MY SWEATER!"

Amy blushed a deep shade of red. She loved attention, but this wasn't exactly what she'd had in mind. Mr. Davis was furious.

To make matters worse, Snowball was an excellent climber. Right after he finished going to the bathroom on Amy's desk, he leapt gracefully to the bookshelves nearby and used his sharp little claws to climb right up the bulletin board. In two seconds flat, he was perched above the classroom on the little ledge that usually just displayed maps and the periodic table. The classroom turned into a pandemonium; not one student was sitting at their desk anymore.

"Amy March, what were you thinking? Clean up this mess, and figure out a way to get that poor, frightened animal to the principal's office, where you can call your parents to come pick it up. I'm giving you two detentions."

Amy was mortified. She'd never gotten a detention in her life, and now she had *two*. It was so unfair! Didn't most classrooms have a class pet? Just because Mr. Davis had no imagination at all shouldn't mean the entire fourth-grade class should have to suffer! She was doing everyone a favor, breaking up the dull winter week with some entertainment and excitement. Her young heart burned with indignation.

Fortunately, Snowball did not seem frightened at all. He calmly licked his paws from his high perch and surveyed the scene of yelling and pointing children below him with satisfaction. Luckily for Amy, he decided to jump down, first onto Mr. Davis's desk, and then back onto hers. From there, he pranced over to a pillow in the classroom's reading nook to look for a nice comfortable spot to snooze.

Feeling deeply humiliated, Amy cleaned up the kitty pee using paper towels from the science station in the corner and trudged to the office after she'd successfully placed poor Snowball in her backpack with zero help from her "friends." He seemed pretty calm about the whole ordeal.

Hannah ended up being the one who came to Amy's school to retrieve the pet, since Mom was at work. She wasn't the sort of person who gave lectures to the girls, and today was no different. But what Amy really wanted was understanding and comfort, and she didn't get that either. Hannah was efficient when things needed to be done; she wasn't warm and cuddly.

Amy was miserable when she returned to class a bit later, miserable when she served the first of her two detentions after school, and miserable when she finally returned home at the end of the day. She was in no mood to apologize to Beth or anyone else for her behavior.

Mom sized up her gloomy youngest daughter at the dinner table and decided to be gentle with her. She knew what had happened.

"Amy, we need to talk about what happened today," she began.

"Haven't I suffered enough?" Amy asked cheekily. Her face flushed and her voice wobbled.

"I'd like you to apologize to Beth. I got a call from your principal when I was at work today. It sounds like you made an unwise decision this morning," Mom said.

"I just wanted to do something fun for a change! Every day is the same! Nothing good ever happens!" Amy wailed. "And then I got *two* detentions! Cody didn't even get one detention last week for *pinching* me on the playground and pulling my hair! It's *so unfair.*"

Mom, and everyone else at the table, stayed silent while Amy dissolved into tears.

"Mr. Davis is pretty harsh," Meg said in a voice just above a whisper. She couldn't help defending Amy, at least a little.

Mom nodded. "I agree the punishment was a lot, Amy. But I hope it gives you a little bit of time to think. School is for learning, not for showing off."

"Tell that to my friends," Amy muttered.

"I suppose you are right," Mom said kindly, "that every day can feel a little repetitive in the middle of the winter, but it's up to us to find little things to make us happy and to appreciate what we *do* have."

Amy thought about this for a moment and sighed a big sigh. "I'm sorry, Beth," she said finally. "I didn't mean to cause problems. I hope Snowball isn't upset."

"It's okay," Beth said gravely. "He's fine."

"Can we go to Florida on school break like Sonja's family?" Amy asked hopefully.

Now it was Mom's turn to sigh deeply. "Definitely not."

Amy and Beth's Kitty Grass Planter

Materials:

- Grass seed (choose a shade variety)
- Container (a wooden box looks nice as long as it's lined)
- Misting spray bottle
- Soil (topsoil or potting soil will do the trick)
- Pebbles

Directions:

1. Find a sturdy container with sides. We used a wood box 2 feet long and 10 inches wide that

Jo had made for Beth, lined with thick plastic on the bottom to prevent leaks.

2. Place a 1-inch layer of small pebbles in the bottom of the box for water drainage. You can also use marbles from a crafting store.

3. Cover the pebbles with a couple of inches of potting soil and sprinkle the soil with grass seeds.

4. Press the seeds into the soil. Be gentle!

5. Mist with water until the whole surface is slightly wet and put your box in a spot where it will get at least a little sunlight each day.

7. Mist the seeds 3 or 4 times per week. You'll see baby grass in a few days; when it gets longer you can keep it neat and trim with scissors! Let your kitty chew on the grass; it's good for her.

CHAPTER EIGHT

A Scary Day

"We should regret our mistakes and learn from them, but never carry them forward into the future with us."
—Lucy Maud Montgomery

One Friday night, when the first signs of spring were just starting to appear in the air, Meg and Jo got a special invitation from Laurie and Mr. Lawrence to attend a play with them in a small, recently restored opera house downtown. Mr. Lawrence was a show sponsor, and he thought the two eldest March sisters might enjoy it. They were both very excited, especially Jo, who didn't even mind the thought of wearing a dress.

As she and Meg got ready, hogging the bathroom for a full hour as Meg curled her hair and Jo put on a headband and fought with her tights, Amy refused to leave them alone.

"But I want to go! Why can't I go?" she cried, over and over, bouncing up and down and begging Jo to call Laurie and wrangle an extra ticket.

"Amy! Calm down!" Jo shouted, getting exasperated. She almost tugged a hole in her tights. "I already told you that Laurie only invited us for opening night. Mr. Lawrence gave Mom a pack of extra matinee tickets, so you and Beth and Hannah are going with her on Sunday."

"I want to go nooooow," Amy whined. "I want to get all dressed up and ride in the town car and be fancy."

"We aren't that dressed up," Meg tried reasonably. "I got this outfit on a clearance rack. Besides, you can wear a dress on Sunday."

"It's not the *same*," Amy wailed. "My life sucks!"

"Your life is just fine. Stop being such a huge pain," Jo said, starting to get seriously annoyed with her ungrateful sister. "Now leave us alone! I'm serious." Jo pushed past Amy on her way out of the bathroom.

"Fine," Amy said, and stomped away with tears streaking her face, furious with Jo for not feeling the least bit bad about excluding her. It seemed like Jo was *happy* Amy couldn't go. "You'll be sorry for being so mean to me, Jo March!"

Jo and Meg walked to Laurie's house and indeed got to ride downtown in the fancy town car. They had an amazing evening, but Jo did feel the tiniest bit guilty about

Amy when she noticed that one of the actresses on stage had golden curls. She realized she would have enjoyed the show even more if her youngest sister had been by her side. Amy loved every kind of art, including the theater, and Jo vowed to make her part bigger in the next movie they all made together.

Amy, for her part, was truly angry when Meg and Jo left the house. Her anger was white hot—it demanded action. She felt like destroying something.

So that's exactly what she did. In a flash, Amy went up to Jo's garret and grabbed the top notebook in her sister's precious stack. Then she ran all the way back down to the living room and tossed it right into the fire before anyone could stop her. Finally feeling a little bit better, she crawled into her bed and fell into a fitful sleep.

When Jo and Meg returned home that night, they saw nothing had been disturbed in the bedroom they shared, and that the household was peaceful. Perhaps Mom had talked to Amy and calmed her down. It wouldn't have been the first time.

But the next morning, Jo made a discovery that created a hurricane of drama.

Her newest notebook, the one that contained 90 percent of her latest movie script, was missing.

Jo crawled down from the attic and found her sisters in

the living room enjoying breakfast: mini breakfast pizzas with three different cheeses that Beth had helped make.

"Has anyone seen my notebook with the green cover?" Jo asked hopefully. "It has my draft of *The Glowing Dragon*. We're supposed to start filming at Easter break, and that's only two weeks away."

Meg and Beth said, "No," right away, looking surprised. Jo's notebooks were always in the attic or in her hands.

Amy looked guilty. She took a big bite of her food to try to hide it.

"Amy! You know where it is. Hand it over!" Jo demanded.

"I don't have it and I don't care where it is!" Amy yelled, spewing bits of egg in every direction.

"Amy, calm down," Meg admonished. She saw the fury in Jo's eyes and felt nervous about what might happen next.

"You know where it is. Tell me before I wrestle you to the floor," Jo said, moving toward Amy menacingly.

"I threw it into the fire. You deserved it," Amy said with a sniff, and retreated into the couch cushions, as if they could protect her.

"You what?!" Jo screamed. "My script!" She ran over to the fireplace, which was cold and empty of everything save for a few blackened logs. The notebook had been completely consumed. "How dare you?" Jo yelled, turning back to Amy, her temper raising the volume of each word. "I can never rewrite what was lost, and I'll *never* forgive you." She lunged for Amy, but Meg got between them before Jo could hurt her. With rage flashing in her eyes, Jo ran from the room and up the stairs.

When Mom came in a few seconds later with groceries, she could tell right away that something was wrong. Amy was crying silently into the couch. Beth and Meg looked upset, but were making no effort to comfort her. There were several plates of half-eaten breakfast pizza strewn about.

"What's going on?" Mom asked.

"Amy threw Jo's notebook into the fire last night," Meg said. Amy glared at her oldest sister. Beth said nothing. She felt terrible that her sisters were fighting. Quietly, she slipped away from the living room and went upstairs to comfort Jo.

"Oh, dear," Mom said, seeing the seriousness of the situation. "Is that true, Amy?"

"Yes," Amy sniffled. "But she deserved it. And she tried to tackle me too, but Meg stopped her."

"Well, that's good. Meg, can we have a minute to talk?" Mom asked.

"Sure. I need to take a shower anyway," Meg said, a little put out that she hadn't been thanked for keeping her sisters from killing each other. It wasn't easy being the oldest, but Meg always did the job well. In her opinion.

Mom regarded her youngest daughter gravely. "Amy,

you know how much Jo's notebooks mean to her. She puts her whole heart into them. How would you feel if she destroyed one of your sketchbooks?"

Amy started to feel bad about what she'd done. A little bit. "I'd be mad," she admitted. "But she and Meg went to the play without me and didn't even feel a little bit sorry for me. It was mean."

"I know you were upset last night. But sometimes it's not possible for all of you girls to do everything together. Meg and Jo also went to the winter dance at their school without you. And sometimes you'll do things without them. It's natural . . . You're all different ages and you'll all start to get different kinds of invitations from your friends."

"I guess so," Amy admitted. But it felt like the only invitations *she* ever got were to sleepovers, not to fancy plays downtown. Being nine was the worst.

"The next time you feel angry," Mom said, "you have to find a way to manage your feelings without destroying things. I think you should apologize to Jo."

Amy gulped, and saw that Mom was right. Not even Meg, who usually made an effort to see Amy's side, had defended the way she'd behaved.

"I'll say I'm sorry," Amy said. And she meant it.

But when Jo came downstairs later that day for lunch, her face was a thundercloud. She wouldn't even look at her youngest sister. Even when Amy said, "I'm really sorry, Jo," all she got in reply was a snort.

Everyone left Jo alone, even Mom, who understood her bookish daughter needed some time. The whole house relaxed a little when she decided to put on her hockey gear and go find Laurie.

He was already outside, lazily guiding a puck around, in the part of the river behind their two houses that widened enough to make a nice little rink. Occasionally, he shot into the net he'd placed near one bank.

"Hey!" Laurie said, pleased to see Jo. He'd been hoping she'd pop up and was just getting ready to call her house.

"Let's play," Jo said, skipping hellos altogether. Her angry face looked a little less menacing than it had an hour ago since it was now half-covered by her scarf, but Laurie could still tell something was bugging her.

They swatted the puck around the rink and Jo started to relax. One of her favorite things about Laurie was that they could hang out and have a great time without having to talk. It was a big relief. Laurie and Jo were evenly matched as players and took turns playing offense and defense. The sky was blue instead of white and a few clouds hung above them, spectating their game. Trees that had been coated in ice for a week's time were starting to drip, drip, drip as the sun warmed their small corner of the world.

Back at home, Amy decided she had to try harder to

get Jo to forgive her. She knew that Laurie always put her sister in a better mood, so she decided to meet them on the river and make things better.

"Let's race," Jo suggested to Laurie, still feeling she had energy to burn. "First one to hit the dock in front of McLaren's with their puck wins."

"Cool," Laurie said, familiar with the spot Jo mentioned, a half mile downstream. "Let me just check the ice a sec," he warned. "It's getting kinda warm out here."

"Yeah, good idea," Jo agreed. "We probably shouldn't skate in the middle of the river."

A flash of movement caught Jo's eye as Laurie poked at the ice fifty yards away from her. It was Amy, rushing to put on her skates on the bank. Jo rolled her eyes and skated away, determined to keep some distance between herself and her ex-sister.

She was still angry enough at Amy that she forgot to warn her about the cracking ice.

Still, something made Jo turn around to check back before she went around the bend to catch up with Laurie and begin their race.

In that split second, she saw and heard something awful: Amy slipped down and crashed below the weakened ice with an earsplitting scream.

Terror leapt through Jo's heart. "No!" she bellowed, scrambling back to the place where Amy had disappeared.

Jo tried to call to Laurie, but she was frozen in terror. Amy's head and arms were above the water, but she had nothing to grab on to. The hole she'd fallen into was big and getting bigger. Amy was struggling to breathe as her heavy winter clothing dragged her down.

Fortunately, Laurie heard both Amy's scream and Jo's. He was there in a flash. He lay down flat on the ice, on his belly, as he'd once been taught to do. Though he was still several feet away from where Amy struggled in the frigid water, he was much closer than Jo. He had his hockey stick and planned to use it. "Grab my legs," he yelled at Jo. "I'll get her by the arms and you'll have to help pull us both back.

"Amy! You're going to be fine! Grab my hockey stick!" he yelled at the flailing girl. "Just hold on to it and I'll pull you closer."

For the next minute, Jo operated as if possessed by someone with double strength. Laurie clutched Amy and Jo pulled them both back from the cracking, unstable ice to the shore, clutching some branches. Amy wasn't hurt, but her lips were bluish and her eyes were terrified. Every single part of her was soaked.

"We have to get her inside right away," Laurie said, who was pretty wet and cold himself. "She'll freeze to death out here."

Jo ripped off her skates and Amy's, and put her own coat on her sister. Laurie added his to the pile as well. They got her home, and in front of the fire, shivering, frightened, and crying. Jo's hands were cut and her eyes were wild, even after Amy had fallen into a peaceful sleep and was clearly fine.

Laurie quietly returned home, but only after Beth had plied him with hot chocolate and a fresh batch of gingersnap cookies to share with his grandpa. Jo was so distraught she forgot to thank him for helping to save her sister.

"Is she going to be okay?" Jo whispered to Mom, who handed her some Band-Aids and antiseptic wipes so she could clean up her hands.

"Oh, yes," Mom said calmly. "You were smart to get her home so fast."

"That was all Laurie. I didn't do anything. What if . . . what if she'd drowned? It would be all my fault!" Jo began crying passionately, sobbing in remorse and fear. "I just got so angry and I couldn't control it."

"Well, you come by your temper honestly, my dear," Mom said. "As does Amy."

"What does that mean?" Jo said, still crying, but less energetically now. She settled into pitiful hiccups.

"It means I have a temper, too," Mom admitted.

"You?" Jo said this in disbelief. Her mother was the calmest, nicest person on the face of the planet. "You don't know how it feels, Mom. I felt like I could hurt Amy and enjoy it. I'm horrible, horrible."

"I know exactly how it feels. You're not horrible. Your job, like mine, is to remember how this day feels and use it to control your anger when it shows up again. Look at it, recognize it, and refuse to give in to it. I find taking deep breaths helps a lot."

"It's so hard," Jo said. "*So* hard. But I'll try. I feel awful and I don't want to feel like this again."

"It *is* hard." Mom nodded. "You know, a lot of people struggle with anger when bad things happen. But we have to put some distance between ourselves and our feelings sometimes. Do you understand what I'm saying?"

"Kind of—" Jo hiccupped again and had to readjust one of her bandages, which had gone on crooked.

"We also have to try to see things from the point of view of others when we can. It will help you handle your temper."

Jo sighed. "I guess I could've been a little nicer to Amy when she was so upset about the play on Friday." She felt so guilty about Amy falling through the ice that she was ready to feel guilty about everything.

Mom smiled. "It's very intelligent of you to see that, Jo. I'm proud of you. I'm not saying you had to bring her with you that night just because that's what she wanted. But if you had taken a moment, looked her in the eye, and *understood* why she was so upset, she wouldn't have lashed out quite so badly. Listen. I'm going to have this talk with her, too. She shouldn't have done what she did. If sisters are also to be best friends for their whole lives, everyone has to work at it. A lot."

Jo nodded thoughtfully. "Having sisters is tough."

"Sure it is. But also great," Mom said, laughing. "Of course, if I'd had three of your aunt Tabitha instead of just one, I'd probably have lost my mind by now."

Jo giggled at that, happy she had such an understanding mother. She thought about all the good memories she had with Amy, and about how, even though Amy was only nine, she often impressed Jo with her sense of humor or smart observations. Jo reluctantly remembered how many times she used something Amy had said in her writing, and how those lines were oftentimes the best ones.

Amy stirred then, and Jo went to her, gently brushing the yellow curls back from her flushed and tearstained face. Amy opened her eyes and smiled a small smile that made Jo feel better. The two hugged each other close and everything was forgiven between them.

Beth's Mini Breakfast Pizza Recipe

Ingredients:

8 frozen multigrain dinner rolls

1/4 cup olive oil
1 tablespoon minced garlic
1 small can of diced tomatoes
1 tablespoon Italian seasoning
4 eggs, scrambled
1/4 cup diced white onion
1/4 cup chopped fresh basil
1/2 cup grated Parmesan cheese
1/2 cup crumbled Feta cheese
1/2 cup grated cheddar cheese
1 cup sliced fresh mushrooms

Directions:

Let the multigrain dinner rolls rise. Preheat the oven to 350 degrees. Spread out the dough into 6-inch pizza crusts. Put each pizza on a cookie sheet (you'll need two cookie sheets to bake all eight). Brush or spoon on the olive oil, and smear minced garlic over the top of that. Next, spoon on diced tomatoes from a can. Then, sprinkle on Italian seasoning, scrambled eggs, fresh onions, fresh basil leaves, all three cheeses, and fresh sliced mushrooms. Bake for 15–20 minutes, or until everything looks a little golden and delicious.

These little pies are going to be part of your regular breakfast rotation from now on. The best part is you can buy the multigrain dinner rolls in bags of 24, and just pull out a few as you need them.

CHAPTER NINE

Meg's Makeover

"Before you can be anything, you have to be yourself. That's the hardest thing to find."
—E. L. Konigsburg

Spring arrived quietly and lightened everyone's mood. The trees in the Marches' quiet neighborhood grew buds and looked as if they could burst out in a celebration of green at any moment. The river was completely clear of ice now, and the smell of life and of dirt filled the air.

Each girl noticed the season change in her own way: Meg saw the tulip shoots coming out of the ground and smiled each time she saw them grow bigger. Jo got her bike out of the garage and checked the air pressure in the tires. Beth opened the window in the bedroom so Snowball could sniff at that newly verdant air and hear the excited baby birds twittering in the trees. Amy's sketchbook exploded with new life: huge, unfurling green leaves and vibrant flowers as she chose to work with her brightest paints and most vivid pastels.

One Friday after school, Meg rushed around the bedroom throwing clothing into piles Jo didn't understand at all. She was packing for a weekend at Annie Moffat's house, and Jo was making a sincere effort not to tease her sister for being so hyper about it.

"What difference does it make what you wear?" Jo asked. She was lying on her bed with her chin propped up on her hands, watching her older sister pick up and discard shirts and leggings and dresses one by one.

"It makes a huge difference!" Meg said, flustered. "I wish I had something new. Tonight we're meeting up with a bunch of boys in my class for a movie, and tomorrow there's a huge birthday party for Annie. I want to look nice!"

"But you always look nice," Jo said. "You can borrow my hoodie," she added playfully. "I think it'll really set off your eyes."

Meg stuck out her tongue at her sister. "You are zero help, Joey. Zero."

"Sorry. I'll leave you alone."

Jo wandered downstairs to find some food, and Meg finished her preparations. She decided to wear a striped

T-shirt that looked interesting because she'd sewn lace to its hem after being inspired by a picture she'd seen in a magazine, paired with cropped skinny jeans and purple flats. Since it was still cool outside, she actually did borrow something from Jo's side of a closet: a white jean jacket from Aunt Em that her younger sister almost never wore. The outfit was pretty. Meg just hoped she'd done a good enough job on the lace. If it ripped, she'd be mortified.

In her overnight bag, Meg placed her nicest pajama pants and flannel pajama shirt, and packed two different dresses for the party because she couldn't decide which one was better. She also added a random selection of scarves, underwear, and other clothing items since she wasn't sure what the girls would be doing in the morning. A few minutes later, Meg heard a car horn honk lightly in her driveway and flew out the door with a sleeping bag, a birthday gift for her friend, and a loud shout. "Bye, Mom! I'll call you on Sunday for a ride!"

"Bye, honey, have fun!" Mom called after Meg. "Be good and say hi to Mrs. Moffat for me!" Mrs. March had been a little hesitant to let Meg go away all weekend. But she did know Mrs. Moffat personally as they both served on the board of the local United Way, so she wasn't too concerned. The Moffats were very wealthy, but also known in the community for their generosity and style.

Meg piled into the car with Annie and two of her other

friends, Bella and Claire. It was being driven by Annie's older sister, Courtney.

"Ooh, I like your shirt," Annie said approvingly to Meg. "Where did you get it?"

"Um, I can't remember," Meg answered. She blushed a little bit at her fib and hoped her friends wouldn't notice.

When they arrived at Annie's house and jumped out of the car, Meg remembered to thank Courtney for picking her up and had to stifle a gasp as they all entered the Moffats' home. It was one of the grandest in town, significantly bigger and fancier than even Laurie's place. Though Meg had been there many times before, each time she walked through the door its splendor and elegance shocked her. The living room looked more like a hotel lobby than a place where you'd watch movies or hang out.

"Picture time," Bella announced when they reached Annie's room. All the girls crowded together and held out their phones, making their faces look as cute as possible. Meg knew the drill and participated enthusiastically, hoping no one would notice she didn't have a phone of her own.

"Where's yours, Meg?" Claire asked.

"I don't have one," Meg admitted. "My mom says I can't until I'm in high school."

Mrs. March hadn't actually said this. The truth was the family couldn't afford fancy phones for all the girls. But Meg didn't want to explain all that.

"Ugh, that's the worst," Bella said sympathetically. "My parents were totally saying that too, but they finally gave in when I turned thirteen. I think I wore them down by asking for one every single day. You should try that."

"Yeah, definitely," Meg said, feeling a little uncomfortable, but glad that Bella was being so understanding. "I'm sure I'll get one soon." She decided to change the subject. "Does anyone want a manicure before the movie?"

"Me, me!" Annie shouted. "Meg does the best flowers."

"It's true," Meg said, showing the other girls her fingernails, which had ten perfect daisies on them.

Each girl got at least one fingernail flower before it was time to go to the movies. They arrived early; the theater had a café where you could get soda floats and fries. Meg didn't know everyone Annie had invited. Some of them were her friend's older cousins who were already in high school, and a few of the boys went to Laurie's school. Even though she felt a bit shy, Meg had a nice time until she overheard two older girls talking in the bathroom after the movie was over.

"I think her family lives next door to the Lawrences," the first girl said. Meg's ears perked up. They were talking about *her.*

"Lucky them. I heard Mr. Lawrence is very generous, and that they could use the help. Did you see the T-shirt she's wearing?"

In her bathroom stall, Meg blushed a deep shade of crimson and stayed completely silent. She stared down at her shirt, which was still perfectly intact and looked fine.

"Yeah. But she seems sweet. If she's smart, she'll date that boy. What's his name? I can't remember."

"I can't remember either. Whatever." The two girls left the bathroom with a bang of the door and Meg was left in there alone, feeling awful.

Not only did those mean girls think she was poor, they thought she should go out with Laurie! Which was ridiculous! He was an *entire grade* younger than Meg, and besides, he was Jo's friend. She didn't know if she felt more embarrassed about that or about her shirt.

The worst part was now she had to rejoin the party, which was full of kids who were all totally at ease and happy. Meg would have to do something very difficult: pretend nothing was wrong when everything was.

She did it. Why, Meg wondered, were there no Academy Awards given out to eighth-grade girls in acute emotional distress who managed to smile anyway?

That night, as the other girls gossiped and giggled and eventually fell asleep strewn about Annie's room, Meg wrestled with her hurt feelings and worried that the two dresses she'd brought with her for the party were woefully wrong and even more proof that her family didn't measure up.

The next morning, Meg wanted to go home, but noticed

her friends were being perfectly nice to her. The mean girls from the bathroom weren't at Annie's house, and Meg didn't even know if they'd be at the party later. She started to relax.

Annie's mom set up an amazing waffle bar for the girls. It had sixteen different kinds of toppings, including maple butter, sprinkles, sliced strawberries, and chocolate sauce.

"Here's your waffle, hon," Annie's mom said. "The rule is you have to add at least three toppings!" She winked.

"Mom! She does not!" Annie giggled. "But I'm adding seven to mine."

The girls tried one another's concoctions, all of which were delicious. Meg's favorite was Bella's, which had apple pieces, toffee, caramel sauce, and real whipped cream.

That afternoon, everyone swam in Annie's indoor pool, and then it was time to get ready for the party. Meg still felt unsure about what to wear, so she decided to let her friends help her.

"What are you guys wearing tonight? I brought two dresses, but I'm not sure if they're cute." She opened up her overnight bag and carefully spread them on Annie's bed.

"I think they're both pretty," Claire said sincerely.

"Me too," said Annie. "But you can totally borrow one of mine if you want. Bella is."

"I am," Bella said. "My mom never lets me buy

anything I like. Anyway, I can also do your hair if you want. I brought this!"

Bella pulled a bottle of pink temporary hair dye out of her bag. Meg gasped. Mom would absolutely have a coronary if Meg returned home with dyed hair. But it did say *temporary*. . . .

"Ooh, sweet," Meg agreed.

"And I can do your makeup," Claire cried. "Makeover!"

"Um . . . ," Meg said.

But any hesitation she felt at the idea of being made over by her friends was soon overcome by their enthusiasm. Meg had never really worn much makeup, and she'd definitely never dyed her hair.

Annie, Bella, and Claire were so excited to work their magic on a blank canvas that they didn't give Meg much of a chance to object. The next thing Meg knew, she was in one of Annie's bright green party dresses with flat-ironed hair, complete with dozens of pink streaks, wearing eyeliner, mascara, blush, and lip gloss. She wore a pair of Bella's low-heeled shoes and Claire's dangly earrings.

Meg looked older. And, she could see in the mirror, beautiful.

"OMG, you look amazing," Claire said. "I'm so jealous," she added, but not in a mean way. "My turn!"

Meg helped the other girls get ready, but none of them were quite so transformed as she was. They'd all worn makeup and used flat irons on their hair before, so they looked more like themselves than Meg did. Meg felt good, and special, but also a little uncomfortable. She was very glad none of her sisters could see her. Jo, in particular, would freak out about Meg's new look.

The party, which was in the Moffats' basement, got rolling when Annie lowered the lights and turned up the music. There was a small dance floor, a foosball table the boys immediately commandeered, and a fridge stocked with soda and snacks. Streamers and balloons bounced around the room. Mr. and Mrs. Moffat kept an eye on things and repeatedly teased their daughter by threatening to play their music instead of hers.

Determined to have a good time, Meg acted more like Annie and Bella, who were naturally outgoing, than herself. She giggled loudly whenever anyone said anything remotely funny and even danced a few times.

When Mr. and Mrs. Moffat suggested everyone sing Annie "Happy Birthday," Meg rolled her eyes along with all the other kids, even though she knew Mom wouldn't approve when her hosts had been so incredibly generous.

Meg had fun. Until something unexpected happened: Laurie arrived.

She didn't even notice him at first, since it was kind of dark and he was standing with some boys from her class.

"I definitely love Baby Vampire," Meg said, leaning

toward Ned Moffat, who was extending his earbud in her direction and asking her if she'd heard the DJ he liked.

"Hey, Meg," Laurie said when she and Ned ended up next to him at the chip bowl. "Baby *who*?"

"Laurie! What are you doing here?" Meg was immediately flustered, and touched her hair, which was still very, very pink.

"Annie and I know each other from Tae Kwon Do, and Jo said I had to come. To check on you." He laughed. "You look alive to me. The snacks are excellent, right?"

"Um, right," Meg said, unsure of what to say. She usually liked seeing Laurie, but she felt totally weird about her worlds colliding. The last time Laurie had come over to play video games with Jo, she'd been knitting on the couch with Beth, watching *You've Got Mail* in her pajamas. She'd insisted he wait to plug in his Xbox until the movie finished and she and Beth had had a chance to watch *all* the credits.

"You look different," Laurie said.

"I, uh, had a makeover. It's not a big deal." *Don't tell Jo*, she added silently, hoping he'd get it. "Do you like my hair?"

"Not really," Laurie said.

"What? Why not?"

"I don't know. You just don't look like yourself, and I liked you the way you were."

Meg frowned. Laurie clearly did not understand anything. What could you expect from a seventh grader? "You are totally rude," she said, and stomped away from him in a huff.

Meg decided to go upstairs to get some fresh air. Before she reached the door to the huge back porch, however, she got lost. Somewhere between the powder room and a laundry room that was bigger than her kitchen, she heard Annie's parents talking about all the kids at the party.

"Did you see little Meg March? She's all grown up. Her mother is going to kill me for letting the girls put that pink stuff in her hair," Mrs. Moffat was saying to her husband.

"Eh, tell her to relax. She looks like Annie's twin." He laughed. "Adorable."

Meg turned around and headed back to the party, feeling almost the same way she had the night before: weird.

She was seized by an urge to put her own clothes back on and wash the dye out of her hair so she could go back to feeling like herself instead of like Annie's clone.

But that would have to wait. First she needed to apologize to Laurie. She found him playing foosball and caught his eye. Warily, he walked over to her when he finished his game (he lost).

"You okay?" he asked, noticing her eyes, which were a little bright.

"Yeah, I'm fine. Listen, I'm sorry for calling you rude.

You're right that this is all . . . a little much," Meg said, gesturing to her outfit, and her hair, and her face. "I just wanted to try it."

"Sure. I'm sorry too. I was just surprised," Laurie said. "Let's have some ice cream. There's an ice cream bar with all these toppings. . . ."

"Yeah. The Moffats are, like, really into the whole toppings-bar concept." Meg laughed, feeling better.

"I'm into it too," Laurie said.

Instead of sleeping over again, Meg decided to let Laurie and his grandfather take her home later that night when the party ended and the birthday presents had been opened and the thank-yous properly distributed.

Back at home, Meg hoped Jo would be asleep when she gently opened the door to their bedroom. Her sister's light was on, but it looked like she had fallen asleep reading her book. It was spread open askew, half on her face. Meg moved around the room silently, changing into her pajamas and carefully placing Annie's dress on the chair, so she'd remember to wash it in the morning. She used a couple of disposable wipes to try to clean off her face and accidentally knocked the hairbrush onto the floor. Jo stirred and sat up.

"Meg! Hey! I thought you were coming back tomorrow morning," she said, immediately alert. "Your hair is flat."

"Hey, yeah, I decided to come back a little early. Laurie dropped me off," Meg explained.

"Did you have fun?" Jo asked, rubbing her eyes.

"I did, actually," Meg said, nodding. "A lot of fun. But I'm glad to be home."

Jo became more alert. "What is with your face? It's . . . I don't . . . What did you do?"

"Um, nothing," Meg said, thinking the light was too low for Jo to really notice the makeup she'd only half removed.

"Something," Jo insisted, moving closer and peering at Meg's eyes like she was some sort of detective.

"Okay, okay. Stop looking at me like that. I let Annie and Bella give me a makeover."

Maybe it was because the two were only fourteen months apart, or maybe it was because Jo was just so *Jo*, but Meg did care what her younger sister thought of her. It felt nice to tell her about the weekend, even though Meg was still trying to work out how she felt about it.

"A makeover?" Jo wrinkled her nose. "Why?"

"I don't know," Meg said. "For fun, I guess. Annie and Bella and Claire have so many dresses and accessories and new kinds of makeup and I just wanted to see what it would feel like to look . . . you know, older."

"So what *did* it feel like?" Jo asked, genuinely curious. Meg liked this about Jo. Her sister could occasionally be easy to talk to if you caught her in the right mood, open to whatever thoughts happened to come her way.

"Pretty cool. But also weird. I didn't feel like myself. And when Laurie arrived, I felt extra awkward, especially because he caught me, like, flirting with Annie's brother."

"With *Ned*?" Jo said. "Ew!"

Meg laughed. "He's kind of cute, Jo."

"No, he is not," Jo said definitively. "Laurie is a *million* times better-looking than *Ned*."

Meg raised one eyebrow at that, and then let it drop. "Anyway, I had fun getting the makeover, but I think I'd rather just look like my regular self most of the time."

"Good," Jo said. She was open-minded in a lot of ways, but Jo also strongly disliked change of most sorts and did not want Meg to look like Annie Moffat, of all people. Jeez.

"Hannah is going to kill me if this stuff stains the pillowcases," Meg said, tugging at her highlighted hair and looking around for a towel to put down on her bed.

"She won't kill you. She told me she had an eyebrow ring in college and that she has a tattoo on her hip."

"Really?" Meg gasped. "How come no one ever tells *me* anything interesting?"

"You gotta ask," Jo said. "Like, seventeen times. Anyway, I think it's fun to try different things. Even eyeliner . . . I *guess* . . . ughh. But the stuff you try should be what *you* want, not just what Annie Moffat says is cool. Maybe you should wear all black, Meg," Jo added solemnly, her eyes dancing.

"I'm not wearing all black; that's depressing. And all of that's easy for you to say, Joey, because everyone thinks you're awesome," Meg said, sighing.

"In what universe?" Jo said, flabbergasted.

"In this universe! You're so popular at school and you don't even have to try! Maybe it's because you're good at sports," Meg added thoughtfully. "It's so unfair. I do not have one ounce of athletic talent at all."

"Sure you do," Jo said consolingly. "You're very good at badminton."

"Shut up," Meg said affectionately, sitting on Jo's bed and wrapping her arms around her knees.

"Hey." Jo squeezed her sister. "Everyone thinks you're awesome too. And if I'm popular at school it's only because I seriously do not care about that kind of thing at all. I'd rather be on the hockey rink or writing in my notebook."

"Thanks."

"And you know why *I* love you?" Jo asked. "You're nice and you care about other people and always notice when one of your little sisters needs a smile or a wink."

"Okay, stop." Meg went to her own bed and crawled in.

"Are you going to make out with Ned?"

"Ew! No!"

"See! I knew you didn't really think he's cute."

"Jo, go to sleep."

"Okay, okay. G'night."

Jo rolled over and started fake snoring. Then *real* snoring. Meg smiled and turned out the light.

Ice Cream Toppings Bar Ideas

By Laurie Lawrence

You can never have too many toppings when it's time to make an ice cream sundae. Here are my favorites:

Crumbled chocolate cookies
Crumbled bacon
Sliced strawberries
Chocolate chips
Chopped pretzels
Sprinkles
Crumbled toffee
Crumbled peanut butter cups
Chopped peanuts
Crushed graham crackers
Pop Rocks
Marshmallows
Salted caramels

CHAPTER TEN

JAMB 'Zine Club

"A story was something you made up out of something that might have happened. Only you didn't tell it like it was, you told it like you thought it should have been."
—Betty Smith

Once per month, all four March sisters gathered in Jo's attic space for a very important meeting of their JAMB 'Zine Club. It had been Jo's idea: She'd wanted real experience editing, as she called it, a premier literary publication, so they'd formed the JAMB 'Zine two years ago to report the monthly goings-on of the household and neighborhood.

"The 'B' is silent, just like me!" Beth had explained to Laurie, giggling.

"You're not silent! You're perfect," Jo had protested.

Jo decided what would go in the 'zine, Amy did the illustrations and decided on the color scheme each month, and

Meg arranged it all to fit on three pages and printed the copies. Beth was everyone's assistant. They all contributed poems, stories, recipes, updates, and classified ads. It was a lot of fun and kept them completely occupied for an entire day when it was time to put out an issue, so Mom loved it.

On this particular day, the sun was shining and spring was in full flourish, almost tilting right over into summertime. Everyone—even Snowball, who was licking his paws serenely in between wrestling matches with scattered kitty toys—knew it would be a short meeting. In fact, Jo had thrown open both dormer windows in the attic to let in the floral breeze from outside, and the space felt fresher than it had in months. The sunlight streaming in seemed to cleanse the air even as the beams highlighted all the dust swirling about. The trees outside, which were now green and lush, begged to be climbed. It was finally time for shorts and sundresses and sandals again!

Jo, who was often content to spend all day in the attic, had big plans to head outside and not return home until dusk. But not until her beloved 'zine went to press.

JAMB 'ZINE // MAY EDITION

Editor in Chief . . . J. March
Design . . . A. March

Publisher . . . M. March
Editorial Assistant . . . B. March

May Poem • by Jo March

Again we meet to celebrate
With smiles of delight,
Our second anniversary,
At headquarters, tonight.

We all are here in decent health,
None gone from our small team:
Again we see each well-known face,
And laugh at well-worn meme.

Our editor, at her great post,
Distinguished leader of word nerds,
As carefully she reads our work
And smiles on all the words.

Although she suffers from a cold,
We love to hear her speak,
For words of passion from her come
Along with croak and squeak.

The determined chief looms on high,
With punctuated grace,
And beams upon the company,
With tan and cheery face.

Poetic fire lights up her eye,
While germs turn her nose red.
See ambition on her face,
When she should be in bed.

Next our peaceful assistant comes,
So rosy, fun, and sweet,
Who chokes with laughter at the puns,
And tumbles off her seat.

Senior designer is here too,
With every hair in place,
A model of great style and grace,
Though hates to wash her face.

Our publisher sits on a rug
And keeps our work so keen
With fearless talents she gets it done
Our baby, our love, our ’zine.

The year is gone, we still unite
To joke and laugh and read,
And walk the path of creativity
That right to fortunes lead.

The Treasure Hunt • by Meg March

When the school week began one bright Monday morning during Spirit Week, the friendly principal announced that a treasure had been hidden somewhere on school grounds. Each day before and after school, and during the lunch hour, students could look for it by decoding clues scattered in each classroom.

Everyone began the treasure hunt with a lot of enthusiasm, finding clues, figuring them out, and getting closer and closer to the prize. But by Thursday, not one student had actually found anything. The big eighth graders were very upset, because they felt, after so many years in the building, that they owned the place and knew each one of its hiding places. But they were wrong.

A small sixth grader watched the older and more well-known students on the treasure hunt all week. She wasn't sure she could compete with them on such an exciting task, but she collected each clue once it had been pored over and discarded.

She began to notice that the clues were too confusing to figure out on her own. One had to do with sports equipment in the gym. One concerned the library. Another, the band room. The fourth? The backstage area of the school's small theater. This small sixth grader didn't know many students yet, for she was a bit shy, but she was also persistent, friendly, and very curious.

One by one, she found and talked to the people who could help her decipher each clue. She talked to seventh graders. She talked to sixth graders. She talked to eighth graders. She talked to teachers. She talked to the cafeteria volunteers, the janitors and basketball coaches. She met the whole alto section in choir and the cheerleaders and the chess team.

Finally, by lunch on Friday, she thought she knew where the treasure might be. All the clues pointed to the same place in the school: the underside of one of the tables in the cafeteria. She didn't want to crawl under each one herself because that would be totally embarrassing, so she spread the word at lunch that everyone should check the place they sat. Sure enough, a pack of eighth graders found a small, flat box taped to their table. The treasure box was filled with candy, gift cards, a school T-shirt, and other silly spirit items.

The small sixth grader grinned. She'd done it!

Her best friend frowned. "Hey! That's so unfair. You should have the prize! You're the one who talked to everyone and figured it out!"

The small sixth grader nodded but didn't say anything. She felt happy, even if she didn't actually have the treasure. The eighth graders who located the box looked like they planned to keep the prize.

But then something happened. Everyone started

talking at once, and pointing to the small sixth grader. Because she'd had everyone's help decoding all the clues, everyone knew she'd been the one who had figured it out. Within moments, the eighth graders handed over the treasure and said congratulations. The small sixth grader took it and smiled a big smile.

She was happy to have the treasure but even happier about something else: She knew *everyone* now.

MONTHLY RECIPE

by Beth March

Quinoa Fruit Salad

Mix together in a big bowl:
2 cups cooked quinoa
1 cup halved red grapes
1 cup cubed green apple
1 cup cubed mango

1/2 cup chopped fresh mint
2 tablespoons extra virgin olive oil
2 teaspoons lemon juice
1 tablespoon sugar

Serve in small bowls. Makes 5-6 servings.

MONTHLY UPDATE

Miss J. March has been promoted on the set of *The Glowing Dragon* from writer and director to executive producer. She would like to thank her supportive family and draw attention to the classified ads section of this publication, as extras are still sought for this groundbreaking film production.

We are pleased to report that friend of the magazine Mr. L. Lawrence has succeeded in joining the summer soccer league of his choice and will no doubt lead it to many victories throughout the northeast region.

Miss B. March will graduate fifth grade next month, completing an elementary school journey marked by optimism, friendship, and particularly strong grades in music and science classes. The entire March family is devastatingly proud of B. and wishes her a wonderful transition to middle school. The editor in chief of this publication would like to emphasize, for the millionth time, there is absolutely no reason to be scared of middle school. It is a perfectly lovely place filled with decent kids and funny teachers. Furthermore, the editor in chief confidently resolves to watch out for dear B. at all times and make sure everyone treats her with the utmost respect and kindness. Or else.

CLASSIFIED ADS

FOR SALE

Very gently used collection of hair bows in near-perfect condition. $5. Current wearer has outgrown the collection, which is exceptional in taste and quality. Call 555-5050 and ask for A. March.

BABYSITTER AVAILABLE

Experienced babysitter with three younger siblings is taking on new charges for occasional weekend care. References available. Reasonable rates; loving and responsible care given. Call 555-5050 and ask for M. March.

WANTED

Movie extras. Extreme preference given to anyone in possession of a large dinosaur or dragon costume. Also seeking movie set painters and production assistants. No experience necessary. Call 555-5050 and ask for J. March.

A weekly meeting will be held in the kitchen to teach young ladies and young gentlemen how to conduct a proper tea service. Contact B. March for details.

FOR SALE

Hand-knitted pot holders and mittens. Place orders now for winter. Talk to B. March at the weekly farmers' market for details.

After a long break for dinner, the issue was almost "put to bed," as Jo said, and Meg was just about ready to push print on the ancient Epson printer hooked up to the family's equally ancient computer. Calling their last meeting of the day to order, the editor in chief had something important she wanted to discuss with her staff.

"I want to invite Laurie to join JAMB 'Zine Club," she announced with a big grin. Everyone loved Laurie, so she expected a quick vote.

"Okay," Beth said, nodding immediately. "What would his title be?"

"Maybe staff photographer or something," Jo said. "I hadn't thought ahead that far."

"Wait a minute," Meg said, looking uncertain. "Are you

sure he even wants to join? Our 'zine is mostly about what happens here in our house."

"No, it isn't!" Jo objected. "Besides, I've been thinking we need to widen our journalistic focus."

"By reporting on what goes on in the Lawrence house too?" Amy asked, grinning.

"Exactly," Jo said. "And a whole 'nother school. And stuff." Jo loved grandiose projects, but she wasn't a big planner. She liked to make things up as she went along . . . it was more fun that way. This trait was one reason the casts of her movies generally had only partial costumes when they began filming and needed lots of cue cards.

"Well, I guess it's okay with me. I like Laurie. Just as long as his photos don't take space away from my drawings. I think the 'zine would really suffer without them," Amy said imperiously.

"So we're nearly unanimous, then!" Jo shouted. "Meg?"

"Okay, fine. He can join. But if he starts teasing us for having a 'zine instead of a blog, he's out."

"Yay!" Jo started jumping up and down and clapping her hands. "Laurie! You can come out!"

Laurie burst out of the old wardrobe in the corner of the attic just then. "I'm in?"

"You're in," Jo said, and the two giggled to see Meg's horrified face. Amy and Beth just looked confused.

"How long has he been in there?" Amy asked.

"I climbed in before the meeting started," Laurie said. "So, ten minutes?"

"We were so sure you guys would love to have a new member," Jo explained. "And I wanted Laurie to join right away, not have to wait a whole month."

Meg composed her face. "Well, welcome, Laurie. I'm sorry I was the only one who hesitated. I just thought you'd think our 'zine was old-fashioned."

"I think it's awesome," Laurie assured her. "And I'm honored to join your club."

"Okay. Cool. Well, let's brainstorm some articles for next month, then!"

Meg hit print on the current issue and the staff whooped. JAMB 'Zine Club had another successful issue on the books and a brand-new staff photographer.

Or something.

CHAPTER ELEVEN

A Summertime Experiment

"Tomorrow is always fresh, with no mistakes in it."
—Lucy Maud Montgomery

June ninth was a very happy day in the March household. It was the first official day of summer vacation, and each girl was ecstatic. The gardens outside were blooming in a cascade of garrulous roses, bright sunflowers, and fragrant lavender, and the whole house was opened up to let in fresh, sun-warmed air.

Jo planned to do nothing but read each day. Aunt Em had booked herself a river cruise tour up in Canada with other ladies from her weekly canasta game, so Jo no longer had to visit her most days. Meg was also free, as the Kings were headed to the shore for vacation and didn't need her babysitting services for two whole months. Hannah was visiting her mother in Boston and wouldn't be back until July.

"What will you do all day?" Mom asked her daughters at the breakfast table. She was nearly ready for work; the girls were all still in their pajamas.

"Sleep," Meg said with great satisfaction. "Nothing but sleep."

"Me too!" Amy piped up. They all looked at Beth's cat, who was sprawled out in a puddle of sunlight on the hardwood floor in the living room. "Just like Snowball. Maybe I'll work on my tan."

"Tanning is bad for you!" Beth cried. "But he does look pretty happy. . . ."

Mom usually didn't approve of her girls lying around doing nothing, but she decided to let them have an experiment.

"You can do absolutely nothing this week if you like, ladies," she said, with a twinkle in her eye. "No chores, no eating your vegetables, no laundry, no set bedtimes. You don't even have to organize your school papers yet. I just ask that you stay close to home, since Hannah isn't here to keep track of your activities. Let's see how you all really feel about all play and no work. Meg is in charge when I'm gone during the day."

"Yay! I'm going to love it," Jo said. "Fun forever!"

"Vacation!" Amy smiled. She was particularly pleased at the thought of not dealing with nine months' worth of school stuff, which was scattered in a pile in her room that seemed to be growing by the hour. There were gym socks in that pile that should've been washed months ago.

"I'm going back to bed," Meg announced, placing her cereal bowl in the dishwasher. "Don't burn the house down," she added, looking at Jo, who crossed her eyes.

"Me too," said Beth with a yawn. "Vacation makes me sleepy."

The day passed slowly. When Meg reappeared downstairs at eleven, no one was around and the living room was a mess: Amy had left all her pencils and pastels scattered everywhere when she was looking for one in particular. Meg felt a little bored, so she put on the television and watched reruns for a while, trying to think of something fun to do by herself.

Amy spent her time outside trying to draw a pretty river landscape, but kept getting bitten by mosquitos. Jo read and napped outside until she gave herself a headache, and Beth played every song she knew on Mr. Lawrence's piano, twice.

"How was your day, girls?" Mom asked that evening when she returned home, noticing everyone looked a little lethargic.

"Amazing," Meg said, not willing to admit to her boredom. "So relaxing."

All the girls nodded their heads vigorously. "What's that smell?" Jo asked, wrinkling her nose.

"Ick, that's the litter box," Amy said, looking fearfully at Mom. It had been her turn to clean it that day, but she hadn't done it. "Sorry, I didn't clean it today."

"It's okay, I'll do it," Mom said. All four girls stared at her, shocked, as she disappeared into the back hallway to clean up after Snowball. Each one felt uncomfortable; Mom had just worked for almost ten hours straight and now she was taking care of their pet. Beth in particular felt so guilty that she ran off to help.

Monday turned into Tuesday turned into Wednesday. Jo got a sunburn and found she couldn't write anything good at all without any natural boundaries on her time. Her blank notebook pages stared at her menacingly until she put them away and the old computer seemed to be mocking her, even though she never even turned it on. She was starting to have thoughts she couldn't believe, like wondering how Aunt Em was doing on her cruise.

Meg began wishing she had asked to go to the shore with the Kings for a change of scenery, and Amy was the crabbiest of them all, as she was the most social March girl and really missed her friends from school, none of whom were bothering to make an effort to hang out with her.

Beth was mostly fine. She was content just sitting around knitting or baking. But she did feel a bit unsettled by the unhappiness and restlessness of her sisters.

By Thursday, the bathroom the girls shared was beginning to get extra-gross. It was usually Jo's job to tidy the sink, toilet, and mirror, Beth's job to wipe up the floor, Meg's job to clean the shower and tub, and Amy's job to make sure the towels were all washed and the garbage emptied. Since none of that had been done in almost a week, the room had turned into a humid petri dish.

The girls were also getting peevish with one another.

"Take that chip clip off your nose. You look ridiculous," Meg said to Amy one day when they finally got up. It was eleven.

"*You* look ridiculous," Amy spat back at her oldest sister, glaring. She usually admired Meg and wanted to be like her, but today was different. Today Meg's very presence made her feel furious.

"I'm going outside. You're both annoying," Jo said, slamming the door on her way out.

By the weekend, it was fair to say the whole house was out of sorts. Junk mail was sliding everywhere in the hallway after a haphazard pile of it tipped over, with no one taking it to the recycling bin. The laundry piles in the girls' rooms covered their beds—now Amy *really* didn't have any clean underwear, and it was starting to smell all the way into the hall. The weeds, which all the girls usually worked together to pull out a little every day, choked the garden.

The girls stayed up later each night of the week and slept in later and later as well; soon it was noon before they stirred. When they finally did get up, they all felt wretched. Jo noticed she had a persistent headache from reading so much and not exercising. She vowed to find Laurie and play some soccer as soon as possible.

The worst thing that happened that week happened on Saturday.

"Have you seen Snowball?" Beth asked Amy.

"No. He's probably hiding in the basement," Amy said. "It's cool down there."

Beth asked Jo and Meg as well, and no one had seen him. The kitten, who was now pretty much a full-grown cat, was officially missing.

"But he's never run away before!" Beth cried, wringing her hands with worry. "I just don't get it! He's not an outdoor cat!"

Secretly relieved to have something to do, all the sisters fanned out across the March property to look for the animal, peeking under the creaky front porch and under the rosebushes. Hours went by with no sight of him.

Beth was nearly inconsolable. "It's all my fault," she wailed, tears streaming down her face. "I forgot to feed him this morning!"

"It's not your fault," Jo said, nearly in tears herself. "I saw that his food dish was empty and I didn't do anything about it either. He's everyone's responsibility, not just yours."

"I'm sorry, Beth," Meg said, feeling extremely guilty. She was the oldest and Mom had put her in charge. "We'll find him. Let's eat something and then go out again. And I'll check the basement again too." Amy nodded solemnly at Meg, determined to do whatever it took to find the cat. Everyone loved Snowball, and now he was gone.

After looking for several hours with no luck, the sisters, with Jo in charge, decided to make a special summer dinner themselves to try to cheer up Beth. Unfortunately, there were no groceries in the house or fresh veggies from the garden because no one had picked them.

"It's okay! There are berries in the garden. I'll get them!" Jo shouted.

"No, me!" Amy said. Jo let her take over that chore so she could whip up some cream as a topping. Next, she attempted to make a simple pasta salad with garlic, olive oil, and canned tomatoes. But Jo ended up overcooking the noodles and using a little too much garlic.

"Making dinner is harder than it looks," she said when she taste-tested her creation. "Oh well, it's better than nothing."

When all the girls and Mom sat down to eat, they gamely managed to choke down the pasta but couldn't stomach the berries and cream.

"Yuck!" Amy cried, never one for subtlety. "What is *with* this cream?"

"I'm not sure," Mom said, trying not to laugh. "Let's just have the berries without it, shall we?"

"The cream wasn't spoiled; I double-checked . . . ," Jo said, trailing off. Then she glanced back at the counter where she had added the sugar before using the handheld blender to whip it up. "Uh-oh. I know what happened. I added salt instead of sugar. Oops."

That did it. Everyone giggled and Jo's face turned bright red before she saw how funny it was and smiled weakly.

"It's okay, Joey," Meg said kindly. "Cooking takes practice."

"I think everything is delicious," Beth added, hugging Jo. "But I'm still so worried about Snowball. Where *is* he?"

Quiet settled over the table as each sister tried to think of a place they hadn't yet checked for their beloved cat. Fortunately, this was the exact moment Snowball decided to come out of hiding. Everyone heard a small meow from above, and looked out the open window. He was perched high up in one of the trees, stretching deeply as if emerging from a long, deep nap.

"Snowball!" Beth yelled. "There you are!"

The cat meowed at them, louder. He appeared to be quite stuck.

"We have to call nine-one-one!" Amy shouted, eager

for the excitement of a visit from the fire department. She stood up so fast her chair tipped back as she lunged for the phone on the counter.

"Definitely not," Mom said, blocking her. "No one is calling anyone. Jo, help me get the ladder from the shed."

Jo leapt up from the table, extremely happy to do something that required strength, not cooking skills. In minutes, she had the ladder positioned right under the tree and Snowball in her arms.

"My hero!" Beth said. Jo grinned and handed Beth the well-rested animal.

When everyone had settled down and eaten sandwiches made by Mom to supplement Jo's culinary adventure, they talked honestly about their week.

"So, how was your forever-fun experience?" Mom asked the girls.

"Pretty good," Jo began, feeling only a little sheepish.

"Not bad," Amy added, not making eye contact with anyone. She hadn't finished even one decent drawing all week. It didn't make any sense to her. She'd had hours and hours and hours to make something great, and it just hadn't happened.

"Oh, stop it," Meg said. "I was bored, the garden looks horrible, and our bathroom is giving me nightmares. All play and no work is just as bad as all work and no play."

"She's right," Beth said. "I don't miss school, but I do kind of miss our regular life."

Mom smiled. "I'm proud of you. Meg is right. Life only feels right when you have a good balance of work and play. And our household only runs well when everyone does a little bit each day to keep it going. I'm not saying this to lecture you or to make you feel bad. That's why I wanted everyone to have a chance to truly relax and just see."

The girls nodded.

"One thing I've noticed," Mom continued, "is that when my days have a little structure to them, I'm happier and I get more accomplished. I sleep better too. So how about this: Each day of summer vacation, everyone starts the day at a reasonable hour. Do your chores, get some exercise, and THEN relax and work on your projects. Sound good?"

"What's a reasonable hour?" Amy asked, sounding concerned.

"I think nine at the latest," Mom replied. "But eight would be better. There's no reason for you all to be up half the night. It's not healthy for growing girls."

Amy sighed but didn't say anything. She was a night owl and believed two a.m. was a very artistic time of day.

"Okay, Mom. I think we can handle that," Meg said. "Can we start by cleaning the bathroom? Or maybe we could just leave it and move into a different house?"

"I'll start packing my stuff right now," Amy said solemnly.

Everyone laughed.

"Let's start the washing machine instead and get caught up," Mom said. "We'll begin with Amy's gym socks."

And with that, the experiment was over.

Everyone was glad.

Natural Air Freshener

1 cup of water
3 orange peels
3 lemon peels
2 drops of essential oil

Place the water in a pot and bring to a boil. Add the other ingredients and turn down to a low simmer until the house fills with a nice fragrance. Don't leave the stove on longer than 1 hour! Thirty minutes should do the trick.

CHAPTER TWELVE

Jo Masters Her Temper; Meg Meets a Boy

"Always be a little kinder than necessary."
—J. M. Barrie

The Lawrences decided to throw a barbecue party for the Fourth of July. Jo was excited about it because Laurie promised some of his cousins from London were going to visit, and they were rumored to love Ultimate Frisbee, Jo's latest obsession. She and Laurie helped Mr. Lawrence set up a big tent canopy in the yard and select fireworks for the nighttime portion of the party. Mr. Lawrence promised there'd be a bonfire as well. When the caterers began arriving with a giant smoker and all the fixings, Jo returned home to change her clothes and gather her sisters.

"Amy! You're still in pajamas! It's nearly four," Jo said, exasperated. "Let's go!"

"It's too *hot* for barbecue," whined the youngest March. "Besides, all of Laurie's friends ignore me. And I don't like Frisbee."

"But you do like cake, and there's going to be some. And *fire*works! What's wrong with you? Find Beth and let's go!" Jo was losing patience. "Oh, and I know that Laurie's family from London have a sister, Grace, who is exactly your age."

"O-*kay*," Amy said, and went to go get dressed. Meg, Beth, Mom, and Hannah were ready. Within minutes, the whole family was out the door. Jo wore jean shorts and a plain blue T-shirt with her Nikes. Meg was her opposite in a pretty orange sundress, big sunglasses, and white sandals.

The party was already in full swing when the Marches arrived. The Moffats were there, as was Meg's friend Sallie and Laurie's math tutor, Brooks, who immediately noticed Meg. Laurie introduced everyone to his British cousins. Fred and Frank were his age, Kate was fifteen and looked bored, and Grace was ten. Frank had a cast on one of his wrists; he'd broken it several weeks earlier.

"I heard you like Ultimate Frisbee," Fred said to Jo. The sentence sounded extracharming in his British lilt, but Jo detected a challenge in his words.

"Love it," Jo said, sounding confident.

"What are we waiting for?" Fred returned. "I'll take Brooks, Meg, and Kate. You can have Laurie, Ned, and Sallie. We're going to crush you."

"Let's go," Jo agreed with a grin.

The teams lined up. They were evenly matched and everyone had fun, pulling the disc so fast that Beth, Amy, and Grace, the cheerleaders, sometimes lost track of it. Jo and Fred were clearly the most competitive players on the field, and both nearly forgot their sportsmanship several times. When Jo fumbled a pass from Ned, she was particularly ruffled. Then she spied Fred running with the disc before his team scored, which was strictly forbidden by the rules.

"Foul!" Jo cried, pointing in Fred's direction. Unfortunately, it seemed no one else on her team had seen it.

"It was not!" Fred protested. "The point stands."

The blood in Jo's veins pulsed with indignation. She could live with losing a game, but it made her furious to think her team might lose to a cheater. Jo took a deep breath and mumbled that they didn't cheat in America. "Nature calls," she announced to the field. "Take five."

Jo jogged to the house and returned in a much cooler mood than she'd started with. Though the game stayed tied in the second half, Sallie made a brilliant underhanded pass to Jo and her team won. Laurie leapt up and down, cheering, before remembering he shouldn't gloat in front of his guests. He calmed down and threw his arms around Jo, saying, "Fred is for sure a cheater; I'm glad we got 'em."

Meg shook her sister's hand with a congratulatory grin. A few minutes later, as they both filled their plates with brisket and slaw, she said, "I can't believe you didn't blow a gasket at Fred, Joey. I thought there was going to be trouble for a second there because I could see the smoke coming out of your ears. Way to keep it together."

"Ugh, I know. He would've deserved it too," Jo said grimly. She thought of everything she'd talked about with Mom the day Amy had fallen into the ice and felt glad she hadn't let her temper get the better of her in front of Laurie's guests. "That's why I took the bathroom break."

"Yeah. Smart." Meg felt proud of her sister, but couldn't figure out how to tell her so without sounding condescending. She forgot about it a second later, though, when Brooks caught her eye and gestured to a chair next to him that he appeared to be saving for her.

"What do you think of Brooks?" Meg asked Jo.

"Laurie's tutor? I dunno. He seems pretty nice," Jo said. It was clear she'd never given him a single thought. She was still triumphant about the game and replaying its best moments in her mind.

"I think he's kind of cute," Meg said, noticing his longish blond hair and nice tan.

"You think everyone is kind of cute," Jo said dismissively.

"I do not! Anyway, I'm going to go sit by him."

Jo rolled her eyes and found a place on a large picnic blanket by Beth and Laurie. Everyone ate the delicious food greedily, starving from running around. The scene was perfect: The sun was bright and the clouds were few. The Lawrence house looked cheerful, decorated as it was with patriotic bunting. The deck was strewn with tiki torches, and all the adults were in good moods.

"What should we do now?" Laurie asked his friends and cousins, when everyone set down their empty plates and looked in danger of napping.

"Let's play Truth!" Sallie squealed. "It's so fun."

Kate, Meg, Ned, and Brooks decided to take the canoe out on the pond; Amy and Beth had disappeared with Grace to explore Mr. Lawrence's garden. Fred, Sallie, Jo, and Laurie stayed behind to play Sallie's game. Each got to take turns asking the others a question; the only rules were the questions couldn't be boring and you had to answer truthfully. Laurie had to be the first answerer.

"Who are your heroes?" Jo asked first.

"Boring question!" Sallie said, but gave up when Jo glared at her.

"Grandpa and Cristiano Ronaldo," he said, thinking of his favorite famous soccer player.

"Which girl here do you think is the prettiest?" Sallie asked.

"Meg," Laurie said.

"Which girl do you like the best?" Fred asked.

"Jo, obviously," Laurie said, without hesitation.

"What a stupid question!" Jo said, feeling herself beginning to blush. "Of course he likes me; we're best friends," she added, trying to dispel the flutter of anxiety in her stomach at the idea that Laurie might *like* her. She didn't feel any better when Sallie announced it was Jo's turn to answer questions next.

"Let Fred go. I have a question for him," Jo insisted. Laurie shot a worried look in her direction, and she crossed her eyes back at him.

"Okay, fine," Sallie said.

"Did you run with the disc on purpose?" she asked.

"Maybe a little," Fred admitted.

"I knew it!" Jo yelled, satisfied.

"What do you want from me?" he protested, laughing. "You won! Americans are so competitive."

Laurie snorted. "Yeah right, Freddie. Jo's just very into honesty. And you're even more competitive than she is. Which is saying something."

Jo smiled at Laurie, pleased he understood her so well.

The day was turning into evening and the setting sun made everything and everyone glow. Summer nights in New England contained magic, and Jo wished she could bottle it.

Sallie, the flirt, next asked Fred which girl he liked and he answered, truthfully, that he had a girlfriend at home. Jo was starting to get bored, so she decided to ditch the game and go find Meg, who was sitting on the Lawrences' dock on their little river, talking to Brooks.

Jo swerved away from the pair when she saw the love-sick look on Brooks's face and heard Meg's sweet giggle as she soaked up his attention.

"Everyone is *so* annoying," she said to herself, and decided to get more cake and ice cream.

Healthy Peanut Butter Ice Cream

Ingredients:

4 frozen bananas

4 tablespoons peanut butter

Directions:

Peel ripe bananas and put them in a Ziploc bag to freeze.

Freeze for 2–3 hours (if you leave them longer, let them defrost a little bit before starting)

Break bananas into large pieces and place them in a food processor or blender.

Turn on the blender on a slow speed and gradually increase. If your blender has an "ice pulse" function, use it.

Turn food processor/blender off to push bananas down with a wooden spoon as needed. Blend bananas until smooth and texture resembles ice cream (this can take a few minutes and a few pushes down, but it will eventually become the right texture).

Add peanut butter and blend slightly until combined. Makes 6 small servings.
Enjoy. You will not believe how delicious this is! ☺

CHAPTER THIRTEEN

Summer Dreams

"If you look the right way, you can see that the whole world is a garden."
—Frances Hodgson Burnett

August drew to a close, and each of the March sisters was determined to squeeze as much fun and enjoyment out of the rest of summer vacation as possible. Laurie felt the same. He set himself a strict schedule of hammock swinging, swimming, and gaming with Jo. One afternoon he began kicking the soccer ball around his yard and saw all four sisters headed for the hilly woods behind their houses, carrying a backpack, a huge blanket, and a picnic basket.

"Hey!" he yelled to them. "What're you doing?"

"Picnic," Jo shouted back. "Come with us!"

"Cool," Laurie said, happy to tag along. He caught up

with them and, after walking for about fifteen minutes deep into the woods, they found a beautiful spot to spread out their blanket. It was a shady nook tucked on one side of a hill overlooking the valley below with a wide river at its base, and the outskirts of their town beyond.

The sun flickered through the leaves, and a light breeze ensured no one felt too hot. In addition to a nice spread of snacks, the girls had brought lots of activities. Jo had her newest writing notebook, Amy her sketch pad and pastels, Beth her latest knitting project, and Meg a sudoku puzzle. "Are you sure I'm not bothering you?" Laurie asked. It seemed the girls had plenty to keep them busy.

"Of course not, weirdo," Jo said affectionately. "We decided to do a picnic since it's so nice. We totally plan to stay out here until dark because Mom and Hannah are on a decluttering kick." She wrinkled her nose. "The only thing to do when they get like that is to escape."

"I should've stayed to help," Beth said, biting her lip. "You don't think they'd get rid of any of my dollhouse accessories, would they?"

"Are you crazy?" Amy said. "Of course not. Besides, this is much nicer. And wouldn't you rather finish those socks for Dad?" Amy gestured to the misshapen sock Beth was attempting to complete for the latest care package they'd be sending in a few days.

"I guess so," Beth said, smiling a little. "They're not

coming out very well, but I'm sure Dad will like them anyway."

"He'll adore them, just like he adores you," Meg assured her. "Amy, are my sunglasses in the picnic basket? I can't find them anywhere."

"No," Amy said, taking the chip clip off of her big bag of SunChips and placing it directly onto her nose. "You'll have to squint."

"I haven't seen them either, Meg. Sorry. Here, have some potato salad," Jo said, handing the container to Laurie. "I hate potato salad."

"Gee, thanks," he said, laughing. "This is a pretty spot; I can't believe I haven't found it before."

"Yes, we like it," Amy agreed, looking around to appreciate the view. "I'm trying to draw it, but I can never really capture the sky properly."

"We've been coming up here every summer for a long time," Beth confided to Laurie. "We like to dream when we're here," she whispered, feeling a little embarrassed even though it was only Laurie she was talking to, and he was the nicest boy any of them had ever met.

"Dream about what?" Laurie said, lying back to check out the shapes in the clouds.

"Fame and fortune," Amy explained confidently.

Jo giggled and threw a blueberry at her. "The future," she said. "I'm going to write eleven bestsellers and get my pilot's license and fly all over the world and then buy a big farmhouse out in the country with bookshelves from floor to ceiling in every room, including the kitchen and bathroom."

"So modest," Meg said, teasing her. "What about you, Laurie? What do you want to do when you grow up?"

"I want to move to New York and be a musician, but Grandpa will never allow it," Laurie said, sighing deeply. "Instead he says I have to get better grades in math so I can study business in college. What about you, Meg?"

"I want to stay here in town after college. I mean, in my own house, not Mom and Dad's. I think I'd like to be a teacher, but for older kids, not preschoolers or anything." She shuddered, thinking of the misbehaving King twins, whom she was again babysitting most days now that they were back from the shore. Their latest prank had involved pressing as much Play-Doh as they possibly could into the rug. Meg hadn't discovered the extent of their shenanigans until nearly an hour after they'd finished, when it was mostly dry and nearly impossible to clean up.

"I want to go to Italy and be a world-famous artist," Amy piped up, though no one had asked her. "I'll live in one of those grand salons like you see in pictures in the travel magazines, with gold leaf on the walls and a huge canopy bed with ruffles falling all over the place like a waterfall. And I'll have gelato for dessert three times a day, and every evening, I'll eat in a different restaurant in Rome."

"You'll have to learn Italian," Meg said sensibly.

"No problem," Amy answered. *"Prego!"*

Laurie smiled, sure that if anyone could figure out a way to live such a life someday it was pretty, clever Amy. "What about you, Beth?"

Beth blushed. "I never really think about it very much, but I guess I'm like Meg. I want to stay here in our town forever. Maybe I could do the same kind of job Mom does when I finish school. I think I'd like that."

"You'd be wonderful at it, Bethy," Jo agreed, smiling at her sister. And she would. They all imagined that Beth would never leave home, and all inwardly agreed that was perfectly fine. "I just know that all of these dreams will come true. We should all meet here in exactly twenty years to see if we got our wishes!"

"I hope I've done something impressive by then," Laurie said, "but I'm afraid I won't."

"Sure you will! Why are you worried about it?" Jo asked, puzzled.

"Because Grandpa is so determined for me to get good grades and become a businessman like him. But I'm not interested in any of that. I only want to play guitar and soccer and be happy."

Laurie spoke quickly and with great agitation, as if

these thoughts had been bothering him for a long time. Jo felt badly for her friend. She never got perfect grades either, and neither Mom nor Dad bothered her about it. They saw how truly devoted Jo was to her writing. They didn't worry about her being lazy or unmotivated if she forgot she had a geography quiz; they understood she was forging her own path, and it didn't always include straight As. She felt glad her parents didn't care what she decided to be when she grew up, as long as she was happy.

"Well, when you finish high school, you should just skip town and do whatever you want," Jo advised. "What can your grandfather say about it? You can come back here when you're a rock star and see what he says *then*. I'll be your roadie in between my book tours! We'll see the whole world!"

"Jo! That's a terrible idea," Meg said, horrified. "Don't listen to her, Laurie. College is important, and I'm *sure* your grandpa wants you to be happy. I bet he'll let you choose your major. He's just trying to make sure you have a good life, and so he's showing you the way he understands. He'd be *so* upset if you ran away."

Meg was being sensible, but Laurie wasn't ready to take her advice. He much preferred Jo's adventurous plan. "I doubt it," he scoffed. "You sound just like Brooks," he added.

Meg blushed. "I don't mean to lecture," she said quietly. "I just think running away would be scary, and that your grandfather needs you."

Laurie looked at her shy face and felt his cheeks redden. "Hey, I'm sorry, Meg. I'm just stressed out because Grandpa's been saying I have to take algebra this year and I barely understand fractions."

"I know what you mean," Meg said kindly, accepting his apology with a nod. "School would be a lot more fun if we didn't have to have grades. Or tests."

Everyone agreed with this except for Amy, who got nearly perfect grades without trying.

Laurie still felt bad, but tried to just think about the warm summer day and not his entire future. Sometimes it was fun to dream about the days and years ahead, and sometimes it was better to leave them alone to take care of themselves. Jo caught his eye and winked conspiratorially. She wanted Laurie to know that no matter what happened, she'd be around to make sure he wasn't sad or bored. He winked back at her and felt a lot better.

The mood lightened and Jo and Laurie got up to throw a Frisbee for a while. Meg completed her puzzle, Beth almost finished one sock, and Amy made good progress on her sketch.

As the sun set, they all felt it had been an afternoon

perfectly spent and promised each other they'd have at least one more picnic together before the weather turned cold and the leaves fell from the trees.

Potato Salad Even Jo Could Love

1 pound red potatoes
1/4 cup olive oil
1 tablespoon balsamic vinegar
2 teaspoons salt
1 teaspoon pepper
1 teaspoon tarragon
1/4 cup finely chopped chives
1/4 cup finely chopped fresh parsley
1/2 cup cooked and chopped bacon
1/2 cup grated sharp cheddar cheese

In a large pot, boil the red potatoes. This should take about 20–25 minutes. Remove from heat and cut them into cubes with the peels still on. Place potatoes in a large bowl and add all of the other ingredients. Mix up using a wooden spoon or flexible spatula and serve. Makes approximately 6 servings.

CHAPTER FOURTEEN

Growing Up Is Hard to Do

"Perhaps if I make myself write I shall find out what is wrong with me."
—Dodie Smith

The week before school resumed in the fall, Jo spent every spare moment in the attic, writing her latest poem in a frenzy. When a fit of writing came on, Jo gave herself up to it completely, abandoned to the words swirling around in her brain until they landed on the paper in front of her in the correct order. Jo was a superstitious writer that summer, always trying to wear the same baseball cap each time she sat down at her desk, and the same T-shirt. She was determined to submit something for publication before the summer ended, and she succeeded.

Her latest work felt like her best yet, so Jo submitted it

to the local alt weekly's young writers contest. Though she sent it in online, she wanted to make sure the newspaper received her work. One day, she resolved to bike all the way downtown just to double-check at their offices.

She set off, determined, and reached the address in record time even though it was a very windy day. It was only late August, but some of the leaves were already falling off the trees and swirling around the streets in minicyclones. When Jo reached the offices, she felt confused because there was no door on the street. Instead, she had to enter a boring-looking building and find the name *Worchester Weekly* on a list by the joyless elevator. She saw that the paper was on the fourth floor and almost lost her nerve.

Jo went up to the correct floor and spoke to a very nice receptionist, who was able to check their recent writing content submissions list and assure Jo that her work had indeed been received. Jo felt relieved and glad she'd made the journey. When she went back outside to retrieve her bike, she was so full of distracted energy that she ran directly into another young passerby, who was coming out of his Tae Kwan Do studio.

"Laurie!"

"Jo! What are you doing down here?"

"I came on my bike to visit the newspaper," Jo explained to her friend. She unlocked her bike and walked it, keeping step with Laurie. "I've entered their contest for young writers and I wanted to make sure they got my poem. I really want to win," she added, feeling thrilled.

"Nice!" Laurie said enthusiastically. "Jo March, Great American Writer. I'm sure you *will* win. Will they print your writing in the newspaper?"

"Yup! How was your class?" Jo asked, looking back to the studio.

"It was really good today," Laurie said. "I'm pretty close to getting my blue belt."

"That's awesome. You have to show me some stuff so we can add stunts to our next film production."

"Sure. Hey, you want to hear something funny?" Laurie said suddenly.

"Always." Jo grinned.

"You know how Meg couldn't find her sunglasses last week?"

"Yeah . . . ," Jo said, not really remembering. Someone in her house was missing something pretty much every single hour of the day. Mom was always saying they needed "a system" for managing belongings more efficiently, but thankfully so far no such system had been implemented.

"I know where they are!" Laurie smiled. "Brooks had them!"

"What? Why?" Jo was truly baffled. What use would a boy have for Meg's sunglasses? It's not like he was going to go around wearing them or anything. If Jo remembered correctly, they had either white or pink frames. Or white and pink striped.

"She left them behind at our party and he's been meaning to return them to her like a knight in shining armor, I guess." Laurie laughed. "But he forgot all about it until I saw them in his bag yesterday. Now he's embarrassed that he's had them so long and doesn't know what to do. So he gave them to me to give to you. Here." He pulled them out of his backpack and gave them to Jo. "You're supposed to put them in the house somewhere and, like, pretend they've been there all along, I guess. Isn't that hilarious?"

Jo hooked the glasses onto the collar of her T-shirt and looked dismayed. She didn't say anything.

"What?" Laurie said, seeing her odd expression. "I thought you'd think it was funny. I had a good time teasing him. It was a completely excellent way to avoid doing math."

"Yeah, yeah, it's kind of funny," Jo said. "It's just that Meg is *waaaaay* too young to have a boyfriend or nonsense like that."

"She is? I thought she turned fourteen last spring. Is that too young?"

"Absolutely," Jo said firmly. "Brooks should really find someone else to like. I mean, Sallie Gardiner is okay. I guess. He could kidnap *her* stuff."

Laurie laughed at this but stopped when he saw Jo's furrowed brow. He let out a low whistle then, and looked at his friend from the corner of his eye.

They walked in silence for a few blocks. Laurie felt Jo was being extremely weird for no reason at all, but he couldn't figure out how to snap her out of it, so he let her be.

Girls were so confusing sometimes, he decided.

Jo was glad Laurie was being quiet and letting her think. All she kept coming back to was that she missed Dad, who by now had been gone for what felt like an eternity. His e-mails and letters were still regular and celebrated, but the more time that went by, the more important stuff he was missing. The stuff it was hard to explain in an e-mail. The stuff you told the people you loved with a flick of your eyebrow or the tilt of your head. The stuff you saw in each other's eyes. How could Jo ever catch him up?

As she walked with Laurie, Jo forgot all about the excitement she'd felt about the writing contest and felt worse and worse.

Why did everything have to change?

"Let's race," she mumbled to Laurie, out of the blue. The only thing between them and their houses was a big hill.

"What?" he asked, startled. They were almost home.

"Let's race!" Jo repeated. "I'll come back for my bike later. Now!"

"Okay," he said, and was off, a full two paces ahead of her.

Jo caught up and passed Laurie, happy to let some of

the bad feelings escape as she ran her heart out and filled her lungs with the crisp air. They were breathless when they reached the top of the hill and tagged Laurie's front porch at exactly the same time.

"See, that's why I like you," Jo said to Laurie after waiting a moment to catch her breath. "You don't let me win, even when I'm being crabby."

"I never will," Laurie said solemnly, and opened his front door.

"Later." Jo nodded, and walked the quarter mile back to the place where her bike lay by the sidewalk. She rode it home and put it away in the garage, thinking as she went about the poem she'd written and how much she hoped it was good enough to be published.

The Space Between
by Jo March

The space between myself and the world
Is really wide indeed.
The world is stress and calls and jobs to do
While I am life and need.

The world can be a little rough
And must keep moving on.
While I can be a little soft
And want to watch the dawn.

I miss someone so dear to me
But the world doesn't care a lot.
It offers me some empty words
But doesn't stop the plot.

I wonder about the world
About how it's always been.
The loving and the fighting
I capture with my pen.

The grown-up world? No friend of mine
I'll find a different way.
All that stuff will hurt you
I'd rather stop and play.

The inside to the outside
Is a schism that can't be crossed.
I wish I had more sense in me.
I wish I wasn't lost.

When Jo entered the house for dinner, she was unusually quiet. Amy and Meg were arguing about what to watch on TV and Beth was busy in the kitchen, slicing some zucchini bread she'd baked that day, so no one noticed Jo's moodiness except for Mom, who'd had a quiet day at work for a change and asked Jo if she wanted to help her set the table. Jo nodded silently and set out place mats, plates, silverware, and glasses for everyone.

"How was your day, sweetheart?" Mom asked her second-oldest daughter.

"It was okay," Jo said.

"What did you do?"

"I biked downtown to make sure the newspaper got my young writers contest submission. Then I ran into Laurie and we raced home."

"That sounds fun. Did Laurie do something that upset you?" Mom pressed. "You seem a little quiet."

Jo sighed massively and shot a look at Meg, who was still wrestling for the remote with Amy in the living room.

"Not exactly. He just mentioned something that reminded me Meg is starting high school in a few days and it made me grumpy thinking about it again," Jo confessed in a voice low enough that her sisters wouldn't hear.

"I get it," Mom said sympathetically. "I know it will be strange not to be at the same school with your sister. I'm sorry you're feeling sad."

Mom hugged Jo, letting her know that she understood her daughter's mixed-up feelings and fears about the future.

"I just want things to stay the way they are," Jo whispered, feeling comforted by Mom's embrace, but still unsettled. "I don't want Meg to make a bunch of new friends and abandon me. Abandon us."

Mom nodded. "Meg isn't going anywhere, sweetheart. Not really. And besides, what if growing up makes life better?"

"There's no way," Jo said, frowning deeply.

"Sure there is," Mom said. "Think about your writing contest. Could you have entered it when you were only, say, five? Of course not. Getting older *does* mean that things change, but it also creates more exciting adventures and big opportunities . . . especially for the brave and the bold. I promise, growing up is not all bad."

"Mmm," Jo said, doubtful. "I don't think Meg is ready for high school."

"It is sweet of you to be concerned about her, dear," Mom said, not contradicting Jo, but not agreeing with her either.

"And I don't know if I like Brooks. As a person," Jo added.

"Have you gotten to know him? Has Laurie said something negative about him?" Mom was curious, but very calm.

"I guess I don't really know him, no. And Laurie seems to think he's okay. But still," Jo said, pursing her lips and looking unhappy.

"I see." Mom nodded. "Everyone always says you're so tough, don't they, honey? I bet it feels strange to be told that all the time and then not *feel* it all the time."

"Yeah," Jo said, sniffing.

"That happens to me sometimes, because I'm in charge of the Center," Mom said. "I'll be feeling overwhelmed or even a little scared or unsure what to do next, but everyone else who works there acts like I'll automatically have all the answers. It's scary."

"It is. I liked being at the same school as Meg," Jo grabbed a Kleenex from a box on the shelf and dabbed her eyes. "I don't want her to get a boyfriend and stop doing our 'zine and our film productions and picnics and stuff. I think all the regular high school stuff might be a form of brainwashing."

"High school stuff?" Mom said, working hard to conceal the smile pulling up the edges of her mouth.

"You know. Homecoming dances and football games and geometry. I'm deeply suspicious. Meg's going to grow up and the fun will be over. We have to do something."

Mom smiled and gave Jo another hug. "Meg will make new friends. But so will you. Think about it as a 'the more the merrier' deal."

"I guess so," Jo said darkly. "But before you know it, Meg'll be talking about gas prices and visiting colleges far away, never to be seen or heard from again."

"Talking about gas prices?" Mom repeated, confused.

"Yeah. You know. Like all grown-ups."

"We do talk about gas prices a lot, I suppose. But I think Meg's a few years away from that. And even when she does become an adult, you can just tell her you'd rather discuss other things, honey. And let's worry about college visits another day, okay?"

"Can you tell Meg she's not allowed to be friends with Brooks?" Jo sniffed.

"Um . . . no," Mom said, trying again not to smile. Her eyes looked at Jo kindly. "Meg is too young to have a serious boyfriend, but she's not too young to spend time with a boy she likes who likes her. Wouldn't you be mad if I said you weren't allowed to hang out with Laurie?"

"That's completely different!" Jo said.

"Mmm," Mom replied. "Maybe so."

"Mom. It is. Anyway, getting older is bogus."

"Elegantly said, my dear. There are many people who would agree with you. But I'm proud of you," Mom said, changing the subject.

"For what?" Jo asked.

"For finishing your poem and entering it into the contest. That takes discipline. A lot of people say they want to do something creative in their lives, but you're actually doing it. I hope you never stop."

"Oh, I won't," Jo said. The idea of stopping her writing for any reason sounded completely impossible. "Thanks, Mom."

They hugged again, and Jo did feel a little better. Over the next three weeks, everyone in the March family couldn't help but notice that Jo checked the mail the second she returned home from school.

Finally, one day, she received the letter from the *Worchester Weekly* that she'd been waiting for. She screamed.

Everyone rushed toward her, wondering what was the matter.

"Jo! Are you okay?" Meg asked, worried.

"Are you hurt?" Beth asked, ready to run for the first aid kit.

"Dude, you made me drop my pencil," Amy said, scowling. She was doing homework; it turned out that fifth grade was a lot harder than fourth had been.

"I placed! I placed! They're going to publish my poem!" Jo yelled. She quickly explained to her sisters about the writing contest, and told them she'd received third place and that her work would be published in the next edition of the paper. They all jumped around in celebration, whooping for joy.

"You did it!" Beth said, bursting with pride. "This is just the beginning!"

"Nice job, Joey," Meg said, smiling her biggest smile.

"I'm so happy for you!" Amy cried, giving Jo a big hug. "Dance party!"

All the sisters crowded around Jo, dancing and laughing. Jo did something very out of character then. She started to cry.

"I'm just so, so happy." She gulped, surprised at herself.

Meg, Beth, and Amy gave Jo a big hug and spent the rest of the day celebrating.

CHAPTER FIFTEEN

Bad News

"Maybe you have to know the darkness before you can appreciate the light."
—Madeleine L'Engle

"November is my least-favorite month," Meg announced one morning, drinking a hot mug of cinnamon tea at the breakfast table. The sun was nowhere to be seen; the gloom was thick and the wind was cutting. Despite the awful weather and bleak mood, all the girls still had to get themselves to school.

"Not mine," Jo said, although not very convincingly. "I like it because I was born in it. Besides, being contrary is kind of my thing, so I'm glad I came into the world during a grumpy month."

"Since it's yours, can you tell November to hurry up

and get over with?" Amy asked. Her eyes were barely open as she ate a bowl of Raisin Bran. Her normally curly hair frizzed around her head in a giant snarl, because the air in the house was so dry and brittle.

"If something good happened, we'd think it was a perfectly great month," Beth said. She always tried to look on the bright side of things. If she were anyone else, this trait would have annoyed her sisters, but since they all loved sweet Beth so much, it didn't.

"But nothing good ever does happen," Meg said hopelessly. "It's just school, work, chores, and no fun. Ever."

"If I were writing your story, Meg, I'd send you on a grand adventure to a tropical island," Jo offered.

"Thank you," Meg said, a little bit comforted. A tropical island was exactly what she needed, she decided. She thought of how Annie's family got to travel frequently and how even when they stayed home, they were cheered by fancy foods and new outfits and premium cable channels. It felt deeply unfair to Meg that the Marches couldn't live like that.

"Oh, man! It's sleeting!" Jo said, peeking out the window. The already-drafty house felt even draftier.

"Don't worry, girls," Mom said, entering the kitchen already dressed for work in her thickest sweater. She started making coffee. "I'll ask Hannah to get a fire going this afternoon so it's warmer in here when you get home from school."

"And Hannah and I are going to make a cheese dip

later," Beth said. "With marinara sauce. It'll make the whole house smell yummy."

A knock sounded at the door. It was Laurie, who took the same school bus as Jo and Beth, even though they had different stops. Jo let him in since he was a few minutes early. Normally, he met them at the corner, but it was too cold and miserable outside to stand there any longer than necessary.

"Hey, neighbor," Jo said. "We're almost ready; we just need coats."

"Hey. Nice day out there," Laurie returned, attempting to grin. He sneezed.

The phone rang.

"That's weird," Mom said. "The Center usually calls my cell phone if they need anything this early."

A pit formed in the center of Jo's stomach. When you had a family member in the military, a call at a weird time was the last thing in the world you wanted to hear.

"Hello?" Mom answered. "I see. I see. Thank you for calling. Yes, I'll arrange to arrive as soon as possible. Please . . . okay. Yes. Good-bye."

She hung up and everyone stared at her in silence, praying the news wasn't bad.

"Girls, that was a military official," Mom said, sounding unnaturally calm. "Your father has been hurt, but not too badly, so we can be very grateful for that. He is being treated for a concussion. They're bringing him back to the States, to the army hospital in D.C."

Beth burst into tears.

Jo bit her lip hard, terrified and relieved. Terrified at the thought of Daddy hurt; relieved at the news he was alive and headed to a safer place.

Meg and Amy looked stunned. All the girls rushed around Mom. They hugged and offered reassurances.

Hannah, who'd gotten up a little earlier than usual due to the ringing phone, wiped her eyes and turned to business. "I'll start packing your things, Margaret. The girls and I will be fine."

"Yes," Mom said. "I'll need to go to his hospital. I'll need to find a flight. . . ." She trailed off. It had been many years since she'd flown anywhere, and couldn't remember, at the moment, the most efficient way to buy a ticket.

"Please let me help, Mrs. March," Laurie said quietly. He'd been trying to stay mostly out of the way as the family processed the scary news. But now he knew that he—or, more accurately, his grandfather—could help. "Grandpa goes to the city frequently, and I know he'd want to help you with your travel arrangements."

Mom nodded gratefully, and Laurie took out his phone and fired off a text to his grandfather. "Actually, I'm just going to run back home. He'll understand my being a little late to school on a day like this."

Laurie gave Jo a quick hug and was gone.

"We'll need to let Aunt Em know what's going on," Mom said distractedly. "Jo, can you go visit her? I'll call the school to let them know you'll be tardy."

Jo nodded. The other girls had the misfortune of having to go to school as if it were a normal day, though it was anything but. Mom asked them to be brave and assured them she wouldn't leave the house until the next day at the earliest.

Jo knew that her mother didn't have the extra funds needed for an unexpected trip. She didn't want her to worry, not when Dad needed her at his bedside to get better.

So Jo made a decision. Before leaving the house, she quietly went up to her little attic sitting room and retrieved something dear to her heart. Then she went about her day, resolving to help her family as best she could.

That evening, Mom was ready to go. Mr. Lawrence had booked her a flight in the morning using his vast collection of frequent-flier miles. There would be a car to take her to the hospital when she landed, and a place for her to stay in Washington.

Each girl had made Dad a card and assembled other small gifts and treats for Mom to deliver as well. They wished they could all go, but it wasn't practical. Mom had been able to get a little more information from the doctors and nurses in her husband's ward, and Mr. March needed to rest, so he was sleeping most of the time.

"Mom, I have something for you," Jo whispered late that evening, once Amy and Beth had fallen asleep on Couchzilla. Mom had been reluctant to send the two younger girls to bed, knowing that the family needed to be together. She wasn't sure exactly how long she'd be gone. Jo handed her mother an envelope.

"What's this?" Mom said, surprised. She peeked inside and saw a healthy stack of bills. "Jo, this is a lot of money."

"What did you *do*?" Meg said, catching a glance at the cash. She looked at Jo, worried.

"I didn't do anything wrong." Jo sniffed, offended at the suggestion. "I just didn't want you to worry about money when you're gone, Mom. And I want you to be able to buy Daddy anything he needs to feel better. So I sold my first-edition *Treasure Island* to Mr. Lawrence. I'll earn enough with my writing to buy it back from him someday. And don't worry, he loves it as much as I ever did," she added bravely, her lip quivering.

"Oh Jo, you didn't have to do this," Mom said. But she was proud of her daughter for making such a sacrifice.

"Wow," Meg said, impressed at Jo. She knew exactly how much her sister treasured her book and what it had taken for her to part with it. "What made you do it?"

"Well, I just wanted to help Dad. And having that old

thing locked up behind glass wasn't helping him. So it was an easy decision."

After more hugs all around, Mom got all of her girls off to bed, even the exceptionally sleepy Beth and Amy.

When the house had fallen silent, neither Meg nor Jo could sleep. Meg had heavy thoughts in her mind and knew she'd feel better once she heard Jo's regular snoring. But it never came. Instead, she heard a quiet sob from Jo's side of the room.

"Joey!" she whispered. "Are you okay? Are you worried about Daddy?"

"No," Jo said. "I feel bad about selling my book. But it's okay, I did the right thing. I'm just a little sad is all."

"I'm sad too. Let's try to think of some happier things. Like Christmastime. Or movies. It's been too long since we've made one with everyone, don't you think?"

Jo smiled. She'd always figured that Meg was only humoring her when she agreed to be in Jo's movies. But maybe that wasn't the case.

"You're right. I'll get busy on a script again first thing in the morning. I find social studies to be the perfect time to really get some work done," Jo said with a giggle.

"Jo! You'll flunk out of school!"

"I will not. Let's go to sleep."

And so they did. As the house quieted down for real this time, Mom went to each of her daughter's beds in turn, tucking their blankets cozily around them like she'd done when they were sweet little toddlers. She kissed all of their cheeks and smoothed the hair back from their faces, her heart filled with love for her girls.

The whole house held its breath then, waiting for the news of the world to get better.

Hannah's Baked Cheese Dip

In difficult times, girls need comfort food. This will do the trick! Love, Hannah

Ingredients:

1 11-ounce log of plain chevre cheese
1 16-ounce can marinara sauce, any brand
1/4 cup chopped fresh basil leaves (for garnish)
1 package of crackers or mini crostinis

Directions:

Preheat the oven to 375 degrees. Place the cheese in the middle of a medium-sized casserole dish. Open the jar of marinara and pour it all around the cheese log into the dish so it surrounds the log. Place in the oven and bake for approximately 25 minutes until the sauce near the edges of the dish starts to caramelize and the cheese begins to turn slightly golden in spots. Remove from oven, let cool for five minutes, and sprinkle fresh basil leaves all over the top. Then dunk your crostinis into the cheese and sauce and enjoy! Makes 8–10 servings.

CHAPTER SIXTEEN

Things Fall Apart

"Don't judge each day by the harvest you reap but by the seeds that you plant."
—Robert Louis Stevenson

With Mom gone to Washington, the dreariness of the March house grew even worse. Hannah did her best to keep things cheerful, stoking the fire and cooking delicious meals with Beth's help. But the girls' spirits sagged. Despite hearing from Mom as soon as she reached the hospital that Dad would eventually make a full recovery, the sisters felt like normal life and regular happiness were far away.

"Amy, what is that smell?" Meg asked suspiciously, putting her nose into her younger sisters' bedroom one day before dinner.

"Don't boss me. Nothing," came the retort. Amy was

eating something on her bed while halfheartedly doing homework.

"Is that chili-cheese sauce? You're stinking up the whole house! Can't you eat in the kitchen like a civilized human being? Besides, we're having dinner in fifteen minutes."

"No, I cannot. Mind your own business," Amy said. But she did get up and brush past Meg, chili cheese and all.

Meg sighed and decided to let it go. She cracked a window for a few minutes to clear out the smell and wiped up a spot on the carpet where Amy's snack had spilled.

The wind whipped, the snow began to pile up, and the days shortened.

Each girl continued to trudge to school every day, and Jo continued her afternoon routine of visiting Aunt Em while Meg babysat the King twins. Amy started hanging out at friends' houses when she could, and Beth asked for Hannah's permission to visit the Community Center after school each day to help with its day-care program. It made her feel closer to Mom to help out at her work, and the little kids adored her. Beth had a natural talent when it came to quieting fussy babies, so she was a very welcome presence when she arrived each day.

One afternoon, when Mom had been gone about a week, Beth arrived at the Center to find that her favorite little one wasn't feeling well. The baby, who was only six months old, had a low-grade fever and was clearly uncomfortable.

The mother had been called and was working on finding someone else to cover her shift so she could pick up her daughter. Though the regular caregivers were reluctant to let Beth hold the feverish babe, it was only when Beth insisted that the tiny infant finally relaxed and went to sleep in her young arms.

Beth rocked the baby in a quiet corner of the room for a full forty minutes, right up until her mama was able to pick her up. The pair made a peaceful picture: Beth, only eleven years old yet seemingly much older, holding and rocking the baby girl; the twosome's breathing perfectly in sync and Beth's voice barely audible as she sang her charge sweet lullabies.

Two days later, when Beth returned to the Center, she learned the baby was home sick with influenza. Her mother had taken her to the pediatrician and she wouldn't be coming to day care again until she got better, which could take as long as a week. Beth began to play with the other kids, yet felt more tired than usual. All she wanted to do was lie down on the play mat and take a nap. Her eyelids felt weighted down and her skin felt hot.

"Beth? You look a little flushed. Are you feeling okay?" Cynthia, the head day-care teacher, looked at Beth with concern and immediately placed her hand on Beth's forehead.

"Actually, I'm a bit tired," Beth admitted. "I guess I must not have slept enough last night. I've been waking up at the slightest sounds lately." It was true: Each March sister was restless at night with Mom gone.

"I hope you're not getting sick, sweetheart," Cynthia said. "You feel a little bit warm to me. Why don't you go home early today and get some rest, okay? Do you need a ride?"

"Okay," Beth said. "Yes, I do. I'll see you on Friday."

Beth got a ride home with one of the Center's volunteers, and crawled right into her bed and pulled the covers up to her chin when she got there even though it was only five p.m. Hannah took her temperature and saw that it was 100, a little high but not dangerous. She made Beth some soup and tea, then they both agreed she should try to sleep and see how she felt when she woke up.

Beth had a fitful night and sat up at dawn feeling a lot worse than she had the day before. Hannah brought her some water, toast, and orange juice on a tray.

"How are you feeling, dear?" she asked as quietly as possible, as Amy was still asleep in the same room. "Did you get some rest?"

"Beth! What's wrong? Hannah, what are you doing?" Amy sat up in bed, alarmed. Hannah wasn't in the habit of bringing anyone breakfast in bed, so Amy knew right away something was up.

"I don't know," Beth said in a voice just above a whisper. Hannah took her temperature and saw that it was a lot higher than it had been the night before.

"Yikes. I think we better get you to Urgent Care. Amy, can you grab some comfy clothes for Beth to put on? She's sick."

Amy and Hannah whisked around the room then, getting poor Beth bundled up as quickly as possible to visit the doctor, even though it was so early. Hannah jotted a quick note to Jo and Meg and left it on the kitchen table.

Fortunately, there was almost no one in the waiting room at six a.m. Beth was seen quickly and received antibiotics. The doctor listened to Beth's chest and said she was a bit concerned about some rattling she heard there. There was no way Beth would be going to school.

Back at home, Hannah got Beth tucked into bed again, made her as comfortable as possible, and Snowball curled up next to her in bed, keeping her company. Then Hannah called a family meeting in the kitchen. As she waited for the girls to gather around the breakfast table, she started cleaning every surface in sight with antibacterial wipes, hoping to prevent the whole household from getting sick.

Jo and Meg were bleary-eyed, having just gotten up for school. Amy was wide-awake and uncharacteristically silent. The cereal bowl in front of her was mostly forgotten.

"Girls, Beth is sick. The doctor thinks it's probably the flu. I'm going to keep her home from school," Hannah explained. "When you get back home today, let's keep things as quiet as possible so she can rest."

"Oh, no!" Jo said, instantly 100 percent awake. "I have to stay with her."

"Me too," Meg added, stifling a yawn. She was not a morning person, but totally forgot about that fact in her worry over poor Beth.

"Let me," Amy whispered, thinking of how pale Beth had looked when she had gotten dressed.

"I know you girls all want to help, but she's very contagious. In fact, I think it would be best if you, Amy, slept in a different room for now. Can you bunk on Couchzilla? Or maybe stay at your aunt's? We don't need the whole house sick."

"I guess," Amy said miserably.

"And I think you all need to go to school as usual," Hannah added. "I'll call your mother as soon as it's a reasonable hour to let her know what's going on."

Tears filled Jo's eyes. With Mom gone, Dad hurt, and Beth sick, it felt like her whole world was collapsing. "I have to check on her," she sobbed, and was off like a flash up the stairs. Jo didn't care if she got sick; she had to take care of her sister if she could.

Beth's fever was breaking, so she was very sweaty when Jo sat on her bed and smoothed back her hair. Jo helped her drink some cold water and change into fresh pajamas.

"Thanks, Jo," Beth whispered, managing a small smile. "I feel a lot better than I did last night. The doctor gave me medicine; it's no big deal."

"I should've been in here with you," Jo said, her lip quivering. "I didn't know you were sick last night. I had to stay at Aunt Em's later than normal to help her reorganize the china cabinet."

"I went to bed early. The doctor said I probably have the flu."

"I'll stay here with you all day and read to you," Jo announced. "And fluff your pillow and make sure you're okay."

"Mom will be mad if you don't go to school," Beth said. "And I'm just going to sleep."

Jo bit her lip, knowing it was true. She also had a huge test that day. "I'll run home the second the last bell rings," she conceded. "Get better, Bethy!"

"I will," Beth said, and closed her eyes.

Jo heard a knock at the front door—Laurie—and sat at Beth's side for one more minute, to make sure her breathing sounded normal. Reassured, she backed slowly out of the bedroom, resolving to get back there the second she could.

Barely even noticing which coat she grabbed, Jo flew out the front door with her backpack, as if getting to school faster than normal would make it possible to get home earlier as well. Her long hair swirled around her head in the wind and she fought to try to get it contained in a ponytail holder.

"Hey," Laurie said, immediately noticing the odd look on Jo's face. "Everything okay?"

"No," Jo said, walking very fast past the place where they normally caught their bus. "Beth has the flu. Hannah already took her to the doctor and she just needs to rest, but I wish I could stay home with her. Can we walk today? I can't deal with the bus. . . . I need some fresh air."

Laurie looked relieved and hurried to make her pace. The flu wasn't the worst thing in the world, and he'd had a lot on his mind lately, so a walk sounded good.

There was a fall dance at Laurie's small school in a week, and even though he knew Jo disapproved of middle school dances—or at the very least, found them ridiculous—he wanted to ask her to go with him. Practically every boy in his class already had a date, and he didn't want to be the only one to show up alone. There was no one Laurie could have more fun with than Jo, and he wanted her to meet his friends at school.

"I hope she feels better soon," Laurie said in a rush. "I had the flu last fall and it was miserable, but after I went to the doctor I was totally better in a week."

"Thanks." Jo was so distracted by worry for Beth, she didn't notice when Laurie kept clearing his throat.

"Listen, there's something I have to ask you," he finally choked out after they had walked about two blocks in hurried silence.

Jo noticed Laurie slowed down a lot just then, and a pit of dread formed in her stomach. She'd known for a long time, practically since they first met, that her insistence she and Laurie were just friends was pretty one-sided. But she'd desperately hoped he would quietly come around to her way of seeing things and not bother her about anything more. Today it seemed she would not get her wish.

"Laurie . . . ," she said, trying to figure out a way to make him stop before he started. But he was determined to say what he needed to say. He stopped walking completely and faced her.

"There's a dance at my school next week and I know you hate dances but I want you to go with me. It's on Friday. As my date." Laurie's speech was jumbled and rushed, but he was proud of himself for getting it out. He looked at Jo expectantly, his heart filled with hope and his face flushed with fear.

Jo let a few moments go by. Now that she'd heard what he'd had to say, she felt a little shocked, even though she'd seen it coming. Jo didn't mean to leave her friend hanging, but she had no idea what to say.

"It's true I hate dances," she began, giving Laurie a halfhearted grin.

"I know," he said, giving her a small grin back. They both knew that what Laurie had said wasn't really about the dance, though.

"I'll go with you because you're my friend and I like hanging out with you," Jo said, trying to be nice.

"Thank you," Laurie said. He still felt unhappy. "But . . ."

"I can't go with you as your date, Laurie," Jo said firmly. "I can only go as your friend."

"But *why*?" Laurie said miserably. "And don't say we're too young. It's not like I'm asking you to marry me. I just . . . I like you."

"I know you do, Laurie," Jo said. All she wanted to do was drop her backpack and run as fast as she could, away from him and away from the awkward conversation. But she knew she had to stay. Why did this have to be so hard? "And I don't deserve it at all."

"Yes, you do. I have more fun with you than I have with anyone. And I think you're pretty," he added, his nose bright red.

"You are killing me," Jo said, and made a face, trying to get him to stop acting romantical by being silly. It wasn't working.

"I am not," he said, starting to get upset. Why did Jo have to make everything serious a joke?

"Laurie. I'm sorry. I'm not making fun of you. I just don't . . . I don't want a boyfriend or anything like that. I don't know if it's because I'm not ready or if it's because I see you almost like a brother or what. But all I can be is your friend. I'm sorry. I really am."

Laurie felt terrible. He started walking again and looked at Jo with a pained expression. "Okay. Okay, then I take it back. Let's not go to the dance. Forget I asked. This is my turn; I'll see you around."

It wasn't his turn. Jo watched his slumped-over form walk away from her and sighed.

It didn't seem possible, but Jo felt even worse than Laurie did at that moment. Why, *why* did he have to choose today of all days to talk about this stuff?

Jo kept walking and cataloged her problems one by one: Dad was injured. Mom wasn't home. Beth was sick. Laurie had gone bananas. It was impossible. She started to feel angry. Seriously, why did Laurie have to choose today to ask her to a dance? He *knew* she was upset about everything going on in her family, and he *still* asked. She kicked some rocks and decided she didn't need that kind of stress in her life.

But then she thought about not playing video games with him or kicking the soccer ball around. She thought about how she'd feel when the river froze over and her skates and hockey stick waited by the door.

When she finally reached school and slid into her desk a half second before the first bell, Jo wanted to cry. Instead, she took out her notebook.

No words came to her.

Somehow, Jo made it through the school day. She'd spent equal amounts of time worrying about Dad, Beth, and Laurie. The funny thing was, she really wanted to see Laurie and make things normal somehow, but she knew it was impossible. The only kind thing to do was to leave him alone. So, that evening she turned her attention completely to getting Beth well, as if she could make it happen through sheer force of her will.

"I'm going to sleep in Beth's room tonight and watch over her," Jo announced to Hannah. Jo had just about every single item in the refrigerator out on the countertop. She was trying to put together a tray of food that Beth would actually eat, and she couldn't figure out what she might like.

Hannah opened her mouth to object, but then saw the set of Jo's jaw and decided to leave her alone. Jo was famously stubborn and sometimes it was just easier to let a girl learn her lesson by catching the flu than it was to insist she be sensible. "All right. Amy's already gone to Em's for the night, so you can have her bed."

"I'm staying with my sisters too," Meg said. She was trying to help Jo with the tray of food, remembering to add things like utensils. She was also busily making hot cocoa for herself and for Jo and Hannah. "I'll put my sleeping bag on the floor if I have to."

Hannah looked up to the ceiling as if asking her higher power to make the girls change their minds, but again she declined to argue with them. "When all three of you end up sick, your mother is going to kill me," she said, resigned. "You're more stubborn than the horses I used to raise, and that's saying something."

"No, she won't," Jo said, one notch more cheerfully than before. "She knows we're impossible. And thanks, I'm taking that as a compliment. Dad says stubbornness is a fine quality in a girl."

"Yup," Meg added solemnly. "He does."

Hannah smiled in spite of herself and gathered Jo and Meg in a quick hug.

Everyone went up to Beth's room and made sure she drank some juice and ate a few bites of toast. Her fever had been intermittent all day, and at the moment, it was in full force. Her rattling cough had also deepened and she was whimpering a bit because her whole body ached, from the ends of her limp hair to the tips of her toes. To make matters worse, a blizzard was gathering steam outside, the snow piling up on all the roads with impressive speed.

"Can't we give her more Tylenol?" Meg asked. Beth was buried under her comforter and looked miserable. "Extra-extra-strength?"

"I'm afraid not." To Beth, Hannah said, "Shhh, shhh, sweetheart. It's going to be okay. Try to close your eyes and just breathe, honey." To Jo and Meg, she explained. "She's just had a dose. It hasn't kicked in yet, which is why she's so miserable, but it will. Here's a washcloth; you can use it to cool her forehead."

Hannah let Jo and Meg tend to their sister, keeping watch over them all. "I heard from your mother today, and she's getting a flight in the morning. She'll be back by tomorrow afternoon."

The news cheered Meg and Jo, but then Jo remembered the snowstorm and glanced out the window. "Planes won't be able to land in that. But it *could* stop snowing any minute now."

"Let's just get through the night and let the weather worry about itself," Hannah said. But her face betrayed her concern. Jo was right. Planes would definitely not be able to land in that. Nor would any vehicle be able to drive through it, save a large pickup truck with a plow attached to the front.

All three nurses kept watch over Beth for the next hour. Jo and Meg took turns cooling her head with the cloth, and Hannah reassured them. Then Jo read Beth the best parts of her favorite book, *Anne of Green Gables*.

Finally, it was time for everyone to try to get some sleep. Hannah went to her room next door and collapsed in exhaustion, but not before issuing the instruction to wake her at any time if Beth needed anything or if her fever rose even one tiny notch.

Jo told Meg to take Amy's bed and she spread out the sleeping bag directly next to Beth's bed. She didn't fall asleep. Instead, she kept vigil, patting Beth's back and watching her breathing. When Beth coughed in her restless sleep, Jo was right there to give her water to drink out of a bendy straw.

Meg couldn't sleep either. The hours ticked by and the house was so still, but not in a comforting way. It felt like everything and everyone was trapped in a tumbling, unhappy snow globe. It seemed impossible that the sun would eventually rise. Over at Aunt Em's, Amy also had a restless night, tossing and turning and wishing she were in her own bed. In Dad's hospital room many hundreds of miles away, Mom sat up on her cot and barely even tried to sleep.

"Is this the worst night of our lives?" Meg whispered to Jo. She had no idea what time it was, but it felt like it had been dark forever and would stay that way. There was no hint of the dawn. She crawled out of bed and sat next to Jo on the floor, as close to her as she could possibly be. Together, they kept watch over their sick sister, and waited.

"Yes," Jo said with no trace of doubt in her voice. "Poor Beth. If she gets better, I'll never complain about anything ever again. I swear it. I'll be a better person every single day. I'll clean our room. I'll find Laurie a girlfriend, even."

"Um, what?" Meg had been nodding along to everything Jo was saying, making her own silent pledges to do a better job with her homework and be a more playful babysitter to the twins and help Hannah more with meal preparations. But when Jo got to the part about Laurie, she was puzzled.

"Ugh, never mind," Jo whispered. "I don't want to talk about it."

"Okay," Meg said. She knew Jo would talk about it. Jo wasn't the secretive type, even when the secrets were her own.

"He asked me to go to a dance with him at his school,"

Jo whispered, and put her head onto her bent knees. Then she wrapped her arms around her head as if she could make herself disappear.

"Oh," Meg said. "What did you say?"

"I said I'd go as his friend," came Jo's muffled reply. Meg couldn't understand her.

"Jo! What?" Meg's whisper was insistent.

Jo raised up her head. "I said I'd go as his friend. But that's not what he wants. He wanted me to go as his regular date. He said he thinks I'm pretty."

Meg smiled. Jo was pretty. But then she saw how unhappy her younger sister looked, and understood. "I'm sorry, Jo. I know you just want to be friends with Laurie."

"Exactly. And the stupid thing is, since he asked me, he's all I can think about. But not like *that*," she added hurriedly. "I just want things to be normal, like they were last week."

"I get it. Sometimes I wish I were still in eighth grade. It's weird being a freshman. The high school is so huge, and it seems like everyone knows exactly what they're doing except for me."

Jo smiled. Meg understood. "What should I do?"

"I don't know. I really don't."

Beth stirred then, and struggled to sit up. She was sweaty again, a good sign. Her pale face was less pained than before, and she looked peaceful in the small bit of light coming in to the room. Meg and Jo got up in a flash and got closer to her to see what she might need.

"Meg? Jo?" Beth whispered, confused. "What are you guys doing here?"

"Beth! How do you feel? We're here to take care of you," Jo said. "We've been right next to you all night."

"I'm okay. Better. Thirsty," Beth whispered. Meg handed her a water bottle and she drank eagerly. She coughed and settled back into bed. Jo took her temperature.

"Ninety-nine-point-one!" she cried, triumphant. "That's almost normal! She's getting better."

"Shhh!" Meg said with a relieved smile. "You'll wake Hannah. I think 'almost normal' is perfect."

Hearing Beth's peaceful snores, Jo and Meg relaxed. They both fell asleep right on Beth's small twin-size bed with her, and woke up several hours later to a beautiful sunrise streaming into the bedroom through the tiny, frost-coated window.

The golden light shone down on a pillowy, glistening world covered in drifts of snow and jeweled ice crystals. It was dazzling.

"It looks like a fairy wonderland," Meg whispered, the first one to peer out the window.

Jo joined her. "Wow," she whispered. "You're right. It's so amazing."

Meg and Jo smiled at Beth, who was still sleeping soundly. The next sound they heard filled their hearts with joy: It was the door downstairs opening and the familiar sound of their mother's heavy boots stomping the snow off onto the rug.

They rushed downstairs and into her arms before she had a chance to take her coat off.

Fudge Nut Bars

When the going gets tough, the tough make fudge nut bars. Here's my favorite family recipe!

—Meg

Ingredients:

Cookie mixture:

1 cup butter, softened

2 cups brown sugar

2 large eggs

2 teaspoons vanilla

2 1/2 cups flour

1 teaspoon baking soda

1 teaspoon salt

3 cups quick rolled oats, uncooked

Fudge filling mixture:

12-ounce package of dark chocolate chips (or semisweet)

2 tablespoons butter
1 teaspoon salt
1 cup sweetened condensed milk
1 cup chopped pecans
2 teaspoons vanilla

Directions:

Preheat oven to 350 degrees. Begin by making the cookie mixture. Cream butter and sugar together. Mix in eggs and vanilla. Mix in flour, baking soda, salt, and rolled oats. Set aside and make the fudge-nut filling. Melt the chocolate chips, butter, salt, and sweetened condensed milk over low heat in a saucepan. Stir until smooth, then add nuts and vanilla.

Spread about 2/3 of the oatmeal cookie mixture in the bottom of a greased large jelly roll pan. Cover with the fudge-nut filling and smooth it out for even coverage. Dot with remaining oatmeal mixture. Bake for 25–30 minutes and let cool. Cut into squares. Makes 30 bars.

CHAPTER SEVENTEEN

Single Digits

"True happiness comes from the joy of deeds well done, the zest of creating things new."
—Antoine de Saint-Exupéry

"I'm very proud of you, Amy," Mom said later that morning. It was a Saturday, and the entire family was having a celebratory brunch of waffles and scrambled eggs around the dining room table. Beth was at the table, looking peaked but healthier. Her fever was gone and she was left feeling weak, but still much better than before.

"Of me? What did I do?" Amy was wolfing down her food. There was never anything good at Aunt Em's, so she'd arrived home an hour before, completely ravenous.

"Hannah asked you to sleep at Aunt Em's so you wouldn't catch Beth's flu, and you did it with no complaint.

Thank you," Mom said. She was pleased to hear that her youngest daughter had thought not of her own wishes, but simply complied with instructions without fuss.

"That's right, she did," Hannah confirmed, smiling. She was eating almost as fast as Amy, having mostly forgotten to do so yesterday while she was taking care of Beth.

Amy smiled. It felt good to be appreciated; she was worried that in all the drama she'd be completely forgotten at Em's. Instead, Mom herself had arrived on foot that very morning to collect her. Amy felt she'd never been happier or more relieved in her entire life. All Aunt Em had for breakfast was high-fiber cereal that reminded her of little sticks and tasted like something you'd feed to your misbehaving pet rabbit. It was good to be home. "You're welcome, Mom. I'm so glad you're back. And I'm so glad you're feeling better, Beth. Never get sick again."

"I'll try not to," Beth said in a quiet voice.

"She can't control that!" Jo shouted. But she was in a good mood. Beth was going to be fine, Mom was back, and she had good news about Dad.

"When will Dad be out of the hospital, again?" Meg asked. Mom had told them everything she knew right when she arrived home that morning, but Meg wanted to hear it all again.

"Pretty soon, maybe even by Christmas," Mrs. March said, smiling. "He's still got a lot of resting and healing to do, and then some rehab. But they have an excellent facility and incredible doctors and nurses. He's in good hands and he sends his love. We'll try to talk with him a little later today if he's feeling up to it."

"Wooo!" Jo whooped. Her heart felt like it might explode from relief. She looked outside, eager to get out there, do a little shoveling, and maybe take the sled out. Then she thought of Laurie and her enthusiasm dampened. It wouldn't be any fun to play in the snow without him, but maybe he wouldn't want to see her at all this weekend. The thought made her very sad.

Everyone at the table had been quite hungry, so brunch disappeared quickly. Mom asked each of her girls to do a few extra chores to get the house back in shipshape order, and they all got to work. To help them along, she tuned the old stereo system in the living room to an oldies radio station and started to sing along.

An hour later, the house was clean and the girls were free to do as they liked. Beth chose to take a nap. Amy took over the dining room table—she was currently into watercolors and needed a lot of space. Meg retreated to her room to read; she was deep into a juicy dystopian novel and wanted to finish it. Jo started following Mom around the house, first down to the basement, where she helped her sort the giant pile of laundry into lights and darks, and then up to Mom's room, where she helped her unpack.

"I'm surprised you're not outside, dear," Mom said casually.

"Yeah, I really need to shovel the sidewalk," Jo said. Shoveling had always been her job.

Mom didn't say anything more and waited.

"But I think Laurie is mad at me, and I'm worried I'll go out there and I'll see him in his window and he won't come out."

Mom nodded. "Sometimes being good friends with your neighbors can be challenging," she said.

"Yup."

"So do you think you'll be inside all day? I could use some help writing thank-you notes to all the people who sent your father flowers. I think I need to write almost forty of them," Mom added. She knew that writing thank-you notes was one of Jo's least-favorite tasks. She liked it even less than going to the mall to buy new school clothes.

"Oh," Jo said, looking stricken. "No, I'm sure Meg could help you with those. I think I'll go shovel after all."

"Okay. Thanks, dear. And if Laurie doesn't come out today, don't worry too much. He can't stay inside forever, and I'm sure you two will make up before too long. Friendship like yours is special, and I think he knows that."

Jo sighed and went into her room to change into warmer clothes. Then she put on snow pants, her coat and other gear, and went outside, determined to shovel the sidewalk as quickly as possible and avoid thinking about the sledding hill.

She worked ferociously, feeling like she'd been cooped up and was now freed. The fluffy snow didn't stand a chance against her efforts. Within thirty minutes, the sidewalk was cleared. Jo carefully spread a thin layer of rock salt over the whole length as well, thinking about the few elderly neighbors nearby who liked to walk their Goldendoodles every day and wouldn't be able to manage if things melted and got slippery.

"Hey, March!" Jo's head snapped up. Laurie! As he got closer, dressed head to foot in a fancy snowsuit, Jo saw that he was towing his sled. She thought about the fact that Laurie had never called her by her last name before. It sounded strange, as if he was trying to put distance between them, but she was just glad he'd come outside and sounded not-unfriendly.

"Laurie! Hi!" She quickly returned the bucket of rock salt to its place on the front porch and ran over to greet him.

"Can you believe that blizzard?" He gestured all around them to the huge piles of snow. It was nearly impossible to see out into the street as the banks were that high.

"I know. It was crazy. We were up half the night with Beth, but she's feeling better this morning. And my mom is home!"

"Oh, good," Laurie said. Jo searched his face for a sign of where she stood, but it seemed like he was determined to pretend nothing out of the ordinary had happened between them. It made her feel both relieved and uneasy. She wanted to be sure things were okay.

"Laurie . . ."

"Jo, it's fine. I shouldn't have asked you to the dumb dance. It was too soon; you still think boys have cooties, even me."

Jo laughed. But she saw a hint of something in Laurie's little speech that bothered her: He thought the problem was just timing, and she knew it wasn't. "I'm sure you're *coated* in cooties" was all she could say. It felt good to stand on solid ground, but Jo knew Laurie's declaration was still there, just waiting to appear again.

"Let's sled!" he cried. "Race you!"

Jo hesitated for one second, then ran to the garage to grab her own saucer before running—or rather, wading—through the deep snow after him. It was true that Jo had decided, then, to let Laurie have hope about the two of them and whatever silly future he imagined. It might have been a mistake not to set him completely straight, but it felt too messy, and Jo didn't know how to fix it. She just wanted to sled.

So that's what they did.

Mrs. March's Thank-You Note Tips

When to write them:

- you've received a gift from someone
- you've enjoyed someone's hospitality or visit
- you've had a job interview
- someone helped you

How to write them:

- be specific: explain why the gift or gesture made you happy
- be brief: a few sentences are just fine
- be personal: handwritten is best!

CHAPTER EIGHTEEN

Chilly Mischief

"A little nonsense now and then, is cherished by the wisest men."
—Roald Dahl

Beth continued to feel better and better until her cough disappeared altogether. The March girls were so grateful to receive news of their father's improving health that they all acted like angels right through Thanksgiving and into December, doing the household chores, turning in their homework on time, and helping Mom at the Community Center on the weekends. The holidays were a busy time for her, with more donations than usual, but also more people in need as the weather continued to plunge below zero.

As the days grew shorter and shorter, the girls began

to feel a little restless. They were waiting for Dad to get home, and it was difficult to stay patient because the doctors wouldn't say when he'd be released. Everyone was dreading the beginning of the week. There were lots of tests coming up, and the weather was forecast to be extra miserable.

"Can't we just *go* to him?" Amy asked Mom nearly every day. "I'm sure the minivan could make it. It's not that far."

"It *is* that far," Mom said. "And besides, I can't take more time away from the Center, and you all have school. He'll be home before we know it. Until then, it's our job to be patient and keep sending him our notes and gifts and love."

"What's this?" Jo said, picking up a dog-eared envelope lying half under the front hall rug one Sunday afternoon. The girls were scattered around the living room, and Mom was out in the garage, unsuccessfully trying to start an ancient snow-blower that had been given to her by one of her coworkers who'd recently moved into a condo.

The envelope looked like it had been there a while, dusty and rippled from being wet and drying again. "Did this fall out of the mail? There's no stamp or address."

"Weird," Meg said, snatching it away from her and opening it. "Huh, it's for me."

Dear Meg,

Would you like to see a movie with me sometime? We could split some nachos. I think you are the prettiest girl I ever saw in my life.

[ ] YES [ ] NO

-Brooks

Meg blushed a deep shade of red and showed the note to Jo, who immediately started laughing. Amy and Beth rushed over and began giggling, too. They all tried to stop when they noticed Meg's horrified face, but only Beth was successful.

"Oh Meg, I think it's sweet," she said. "He's finally asking you out. Hasn't he liked you since summer?"

"Meg and Bro-ooks sitting in a tree," Amy sang. *"K-I-S-S-I-N-G!"*

"I don't think he's the one who wrote this," Meg said, ignoring Amy, who was prancing around her like a demented fairy, continuing to sing her taunt in an off-key warble. "Someone's making fun of me. Was it you, Joey?"

"Me! No!" Jo vehemently denied the charge. She almost wished she *had* written the silly note, because she had a feeling she knew who had.

"I don't believe you," Meg said, glaring at her younger sister.

"I swear! I didn't write it!" Jo shook her head. "I bet it was Laurie. He's mad at me for saying I wouldn't go to his school dance with him, but pretending he's not. He's getting back at me. I'll punch his lights out!"

"Whoa, slow down there, champ." Mom entered the hallway then, drawn by the commotion. "What's going on?"

Meg showed Mom the note and Jo explained it was a prank. Just then, the doorbell sounded, making them all jump.

Mom opened the door to see Laurie himself, holding a can of oil.

"Grandpa heard someone struggling with a snow-blower and said to bring this over," he explained, handing Mrs. March the oil. "He said it works miracles."

"Thank you, Laurie," Mrs. March said kindly. "That's very nice of you." She barely got the words out before Jo got right in their visitor's face with Meg's note.

"Did you write this?" she demanded, waving it at him. He immediately looked guilty. "AHA!" she cried. "Caught you!"

Mom ushered Amy and Beth into the kitchen so Meg and Laurie could talk. She shot Jo a look as she retreated as well. A look that said: *Go easy on him.*

Laurie felt badly when he saw how deeply Meg was blushing. She was such a nice girl, and much more delicate than Jo. "Look, Meg. I'm sorry. I didn't mean to make fun of you or anything. It's just that Brooks goes on and on and *on* about you when he's supposed to be tutoring me. He gets up from the table every half second to try to catch a glimpse of you. I just thought I'd put him out of his misery by trying to get you guys to actually admit you like each other. Is that so bad?"

"Since when are you a matchmaker?" Jo said, annoyed. "Meg's love life isn't your business! Have you been watching reality TV or something? Why are you being so weird lately?"

"I know, I know," Laurie said. "I'm really sorry."

Jo was impressed with Laurie for not getting defensive. She immediately forgave him, seeing how sorry he really did look. Meg did too.

"It's okay. I guess if Brooks weren't so shy, he would've asked me himself," Meg said. "But his shyness is something I like about him. Don't tell him this happened, okay? It's embarrassing."

"I promise I won't," Laurie said solemnly. "But you should come over sometime when he's at my house, okay? You two can be shy and mushy together, and I'll be free to play video games. Every Tuesday and Thursday afternoon."

"Maybe I will," Meg said, unable to conceal the thrill in her voice. She'd been wanting an excuse to see Brooks, but couldn't figure out how to pull it off without being awkward since they went to different schools. She almost felt like hugging Laurie. Instead, she happily bounced up the stairs to her room, where she planned to try a new kind of braid in her hair.

"Well, Meg has forgiven you, but that doesn't mean I have," Jo said with finality. "Go away."

Laurie nodded, looking hurt, and trudged back to his house, leaving the oil can behind for Mrs. March.

Jo immediately felt she'd been too harsh and thought back to the day all those many months ago, when her temper had flared at Amy and she'd been so very, very sorry about it. After pacing around in her attic for only twenty minutes, she grabbed a book she'd borrowed from Mr. Lawrence and decided to go make up with her best friend.

After Jo rang the Lawrence doorbell twice, the large front door was opened by Mr. Lawrence's housekeeper, Riva, which was unusual.

"Uh, is Laurie around?" Jo asked, uncertain.

"He is, but he's sulking in his room," Riva answered. "I think he had an argument with his grandfather. But you can go up and check on him if you like."

Jo nodded and bounded up the stairs. She knocked on Laurie's door and only got a gruff "Go away!" in reply.

"Laurie, it's me!" she said through the door. "Let me in!"

"No way," came the reply.

Jo sighed and walked back down the stairs, trying to figure out how to cheer up Laurie if he wouldn't even see her. When she passed Mr. Lawrence's office, she heard her old friend's voice.

"Miss March? Is that you?"

Jo poked just her head into the room, unsure whether to enter. "Yes. But I was just going. I guess Laurie and I are in a fight," she added, frowning.

"Well, that makes two of us. Come in and have some tea with me." Mr. Lawrence rose from his large, intimidating desk and walked to his sideboard, where an elaborate tea service was set up, complete with a newly brewed pot of something that smelled like nutmeg, and an extra cup. There were also pretty little tea sandwiches arranged in a circle on a platter next to the pot. He poured Jo a cup and, remembering how she liked her tea, added a cube of sugar and a generous pour of cream. He also placed two tasty tea sandwiches on her saucer.

"Thank you, Mr. L.," Jo said, taking a big sip. "This is really good."

"You're welcome, Miss March. Now, tell me what's going on with our boy. He came home a half hour ago in a foul mood and refused to explain himself. When I tried to make him talk, he disappeared into his room, and there he stays. I have half a mind to turn off the Wi-Fi in this house once and for all!"

Jo smiled at this. Her house didn't even have Wi-Fi, ever, because Dad said he didn't believe in it. "He's mad at me because . . . well, I'm not really sure why. I guess I was a little mean to him when he came over to our house before with the oil can. Boys are very sensitive, you know."

Mr. Lawrence smiled. "You always charm me, Miss March. Boys are very sensitive indeed. I just wish he'd talk to me when something's bothering him."

"I tell my sister Meg everything," Jo offered. "But I never would if she tried to *make* me do it. She's very good at waiting until I'm ready to 'fess up about what's on my mind."

"Meg is a wise sister. I suppose I'm so used to ordering people at my company to do what I want that I forget sometimes adolescent boys are not employees." Mr. Lawrence looked sad then, and older than he usually did.

"It's obvious you love Laurie very much, Mr. L. I'm sure he knows that," Jo said, trying to make her neighbor feel better.

"He's lucky to have a friend like you, Jo," Mr. Lawrence said. "You're a fine young woman."

"Thanks, Mr. L. I try to be, but it's really hard. Sometimes it feels like all I ever do is hurt someone's feelings and then try to apologize, only to hurt them worse somehow. And all I really want to do is play hockey and write stories."

"I know exactly what you mean," Mr. Lawrence said. He turned to the door and noticed Laurie lurking there. "Ah, look who's decided he's thirsty. Come in, dear boy, and have some tea with us."

Laurie came into the room, grabbed two tea sandwiches and stuffed them into his mouth at one time. He still looked unhappy.

"Laurie! Good. Listen, I'm sorry I was such a grump before," Jo said. "You've got to stop taking me so seriously all the time," she added, crossing her eyes. "Have some tea, and let's go build some grotesque snowmen to scare all the neighbors."

Laurie smiled and swallowed. "Okay. That sounds fun."

"Friends?" Jo asked.

"Friends," Laurie answered.

Mr. Lawrence's Chicken Salad Tea Sandwiches

Ingredients:

2 cups chopped cooked white meat chicken

1/4 cup celery, finely chopped

1/2 cup chopped pecans
3/4 cup seedless grapes, cut in half lengthwise
1 tablespoon poppy seeds
1/3 cup mayonnaise
1 teaspoon chicken bouillon
1 teaspoon sugar
dash of salt
dash of white pepper
8 slices of white bread, with crusts removed

Directions:

In medium-size bowl, combine chicken, celery, pecans, grapes, and poppy seeds. In small bowl, blend mayonnaise, boullion, sugar, salt, and pepper. Fold dressing lightly into chicken mixture to coat. Chill for at least two hours. Spread the chicken salad onto four slices of crustless bread, top with the other four, and slice into triangles with the help of an adult. Makes 16 minisandwiches.

CHAPTER NINETEEN

Jingle Bell March

"Home is the nicest word there is."
—Laura Ingalls Wilder

Jo was determined to make this Christmas merrier than the last one at the March house. She drove Mom nearly crazy asking if they could have a neighborhood bonfire or at least a few fireworks.

"Jo! Stop! There will be no holiday explosives. We can be perfectly merry with our usual traditions," Mom said one evening as everyone decorated cookies, including Beth, who was now fully healthy. "There are Christmas cards to make and send, and caroling to do, and gifts to wrap, and church. . . . We don't need to blow anything up."

"Okay, okay." Jo sighed. "I'll cancel my order from RomanCandles.com."

"You better be joking."

Christmas morning dawned unusually warm, and Jo woke before everyone else. Determined to do something extra special, she put on her boots and snow pants and went outside. With the help of the heavy snow leftover from days before, she started building an enormous snowman meant to look like Santa. Her plan was to display the gifts she'd made for all of her family members on his shoulders.

Jo worked efficiently in the bluish light of the dawn, and Santa came together spectacularly, especially when Laurie came out of his house to help, bringing with him a large bottle of red food coloring to complete the effect.

"Merry Christmas, Laurie!" Jo was full of the joy of the day and gave her friend a huge hug.

"Merry Christmas, Jo!" Laurie hugged her right back and began building out Santa's curled beard by adding snowball after snowball to the behemoth's chin and chest. They worked silently but happily until the sun came up fully and showcased their efforts beneath the glistening trees.

"He's perfect, Laurie. Thank you. The food coloring looks amazing," Jo breathed, feeling Christmas butterflies in her stomach. She quietly gathered the gifts she'd placed on the front porch and perched them all on top of Santa, a pretty Christmas display for her family.

"He's going to melt by noon. Let's take some pictures," Laurie said, and captured a few of Jo standing by her creation, her cheeks rosy. "I've got to go back home and open presents with Grandpa, but I'll come to your house again in an hour or two. We've got a surprise for you!"

"A surprise?!" Jo clapped her hands and thought of last year's feast. "What kind of surprise? I demand you tell me! Is it edible? I bet it's edible. Is it chocolate?"

Laurie laughed and backed away from her, shaking his head. "Nope! You have to wait."

Jo ran after him, pelting him with half-formed snowballs as he retreated. "Tell me! Tell me!"

"Later! Go inside and tell your sisters to get excited!"

Jo nearly tackled Laurie, but he was too fast for her this time. She sighed and returned home. When she opened the back door, she was immediately greeted by the amazing smells of burning candles, simmering apple cider, and the sound of Beth playing the piano: "Old King Wenceslas," one of Jo's favorite carols. The whole household was fully awake and wrapping paper was already starting to fly.

The Christmas tree, which was always big enough to swallow up the entire living room, was extra-enormous this year and filled with ornaments, glittering lights, and tinsel. Jo loved it and routinely stuck her face directly into it to enjoy its real pine scent.

"Joey! Where did you go?" Meg cried, flinging red and green and white confetti in her direction. "Sing with us!"

"I was outside making something special," Jo said, grinning and pulling back the huge dining room curtains to reveal her creation. "Santa's here!"

Amy laughed and clapped her hands. "Thank you, sis. But where are everyone else's presents?"

Jo put Amy into a loving headlock and ruffled her curls. "Go be a good little elf and bring all the packages in, okay?"

Amy looked at Jo like she was crazy, but then the spirit of the day came over her and she said, "Oh, all right." She put on her present from Mom, a brand-new pink snowsuit and matching pink boots, and went to get Santa's bounty and bring it all inside. Jo smiled. Amy had grown up a lot in a year.

Mrs. March was happily sitting in her comfy chair, sipping on hot cider and watching her girls swirl around her, filled with good cheer. They all competed to bring her the best cookies and biggest gifts in the room. "The only thing that could make the day more perfect would be if Dad could be here today. But he'll be home soon," she said.

"I can't wait," Jo said.

"Me neither," Beth agreed, taking a break from her piano playing to eat a cookie.

Amy came back inside and everyone opened presents in one big, happy, chaotic tumble. They were supposed to take turns, and Mom kept saying, "Slow down!" but no one could. Instead, Jo stoked the fire, Meg turned up the radio station that played only Christmas carols, and everyone amused the cat by balling up little pieces of wrapping paper and tossing them in Snowball's direction. He hopped around maniacally and made everyone smile. Hannah and Mom started making breakfast: eggs Benedict, just like last year.

A knock sounded at the door just then and Jo raced to open it. "It's Laurie!" she cried, flinging open the door. "I'd invite you in for breakfast," she said to him, wagging her finger, "but you're on my bad side for not telling me what the surprise is!" It was obvious she didn't mean a word she said, as the smile on her face was wide. Beth immediately brought Laurie a plate of cookies and a fresh mug of steaming cider.

"You only have to wait one more minute. Look!" Laurie pointed past the front porch and to the street directly in front of the March house. Mr. Lawrence was parking his large black town car himself. "We've just been to the airport," Laurie said mischievously, building the suspense. "To bring you a very special delivery."

"The airport?" Mrs. March said suspiciously. "On Christmas morning? But . . ."

"AUGHHHHHH! DAD!" Jo shouted and flew right out the front door without a coat in her socks, into her father's outstretched arms. He'd just emerged from the car and beamed up at his whole family, now crowded onto the porch and shivering in disbelief. He looked strong and healthy in his National Guard dress uniform, even with Jo clinging to him as if for dear life. Everyone burst into cheers and tears.

Mrs. March put her hand to her heart and looked truly shocked. "But the doctors said you needed another week. . . . I can't believe . . ."

"It's a Christmas miracle, honey," Mr. March explained, his voice barely audible above his daughters' shouts and laughter. "I told them I intended to get home for Christmas whatever it took, and they relented yesterday and officially released me. Mr. Lawrence here was kind enough to arrange my transportation. I hope you're not upset I didn't call ahead."

"I—I can't believe it!" she said again, and joined in on the group hug, tears streaming down her face to match her daughters'.

The next several minutes were pure chaos as everyone crowded into Dad's arms and thanked Mr. Lawrence and Laurie and God and whomever else they could think of. All four girls cried from sheer happiness, relief, and shock. Meg nearly fainted, and Amy tumbled over the last porch stair and ended up hugging Dad around the knees. Beth managed to get closer to Dad than anyone else, wiggling her way past Jo and Meg. It was a touching scene with no dry eyes by the end of it. Laurie was particularly touched and felt like part of the family, hugging everyone.

"It's good to be home," Dad said finally, as everyone began to calm down and move back inside. "There's no better place in the entire world."

The entire party sat down to eat, with Hannah, Mom, and Mr. Lawrence all working together in the kitchen to make sure there was more than enough for everyone. There never was a merrier Christmas feast than the one that transpired that morning in the March home. The sisters' words jumbled over one another's as they filled Dad in on all that he had missed. Each was eager to share with him her latest project, passion, and 'zine issue. He eagerly soaked it all up, expertly giving his full attention to each girl as if she were the only person in the world that morning.

It was possible to see each of the four March sisters in their father's face. Jo had his big gray eyes; Amy his dimples. Meg had the tilt of his chin and Beth his warm smile. For the first time in a whole year, the family was together, and each member felt their heart filled to the brim with happiness and contentment.

"Just a year ago we were complaining about our bleak

Christmas, and this year, everything's different!" Jo remembered.

"That's true," Meg said. "Even though we were so sad you were gone, Daddy, it ended up being a pretty good year, all in all."

"I thought it was a hard year," Amy said truthfully. "I'm glad it's over."

"It was hard at times because we missed you so much," Beth explained. "But we found good things to do and we made the best of it."

"That you did," Dad said approvingly, looking around him at how much his daughters had grown. "I'm so proud of all of you for working together, making good decisions, and learning so much. I hear that little Beth has become bolder and made a new friend," he said, nodding at Mr. Lawrence. "I know that Jo has had a poem published and Meg has begun high school, already getting excellent grades. And I think perhaps Amy has grown up the most, thinking of others and being a helper. But more than anything else, I'm proud of each of you for being good and kind sisters to one another. That's a gift not to me but to one another and one I hope you treasure forever."

"We will, Dad," Meg assured him. The other girls nodded as well, thinking about how much they really did love one another when you got to the bottom of it.

"A toast!" Mr. Lawrence said then. "To good health,

to family, to country, and to Christmas! May it live in our hearts all year to guide us and keep us happy, grateful, safe, and strong!"

"Here, here!" Jo shouted. Everyone clinked their glasses together and drank to the new year, new possibilities, and new adventures.

And so we leave the Marches as we found them, at Christmastime, but another year older and another year wiser, with more friends, greater hopes, and big plans. It was a new year, and each sister knew that it would be a great one.

EPILOGUE

JAMB 'ZINE // JANUARY EDITION

UPDATES

In celebration of the New Year, each of our four original staff members has chosen to reflect on the ways in which they have grown. Sources tell us Editor in Chief J. March has not let her temper rule her in months, and is making good progress with her writing. The word on the street is she is creating longer and more detailed screenplays as well as more ambitious poems, several of which will debut in this very publication, so be sure to renew your subscription today.

According to another reliable source, our publisher has declined an invitation to sleep over at A. Moffat's again, deciding instead to get more involved with her mother's Community Center on the weekend and spend time with local sophomore B., who is now her official boyfriend despite many objections from our wise editor in chief.

A very important commission has been awarded to our art director, A. March. According to several well-placed sources, she will design and paint a new mural at the downtown Community Center, donating all of her time and expertise to bring joy to the community. Materials to be donated by Mr. March, father of the artist.

Perhaps the biggest news of all is the bulletin that Miss B. March, assistant extraordinaire, has agreed to play piano in a local youth choir recital, which makes both her mother and Mr. Lawrence, her friend, very proud. This is B. March's first public recital, and will no doubt be a smashing success that leads her directly to an engagement at Carnegie Hall one day.

New Year's Ginger Cream Cookies

Cookie ingredients:
1/4 cup soft shortening
1/2 cup sugar
1 small egg
1 teaspoon baking soda
1/2 cup hot water
1/2 cup molasses
2 1/2 cups sifted flour
1/2 teaspoon salt
1 teaspoon ground ginger
1 teaspoon nutmeg
1 teaspoon cloves
1/2 teaspoon cinnamon

Frosting ingredients:
2 1/2 tablespoons flour
1/2 cup milk
1/2 teaspoon vanilla
1/4 cup shortening
1/4 cup butter
1/2 cup sugar
Pinch of salt

Preheat oven to 375 degrees. Mix shortening, sugar, and egg thoroughly. In a separate large bowl, dissolve baking soda in hot water. Add the rest of the ingredients and add shortening/sugar/egg mixture. Drop spoonfuls of dough on cookie sheet, two inches apart, and place in oven. Bake for 8-10 minutes.

While the cookies bake, make the frosting. Put the flour and milk in a saucepan and cook over low heat, stirring, until the mixture achieves a pudding-like consistency. Cool. In a bowl, place vanilla, shortening, butter, sugar, and salt. Add the cooked flour mixture and beat together at high speed until it looks like whipped cream. Spread the frosting on the slightly warm cookies and serve. Makes 18 cookies.

JO'S BOOK LIST

A Wrinkle in Time by Madeleine L'Engle
The Princess Bride by William Goldman
A Tree Grows in Brooklyn by Betty Smith
Ender's Game by Orson Scott Card
The Fellowship of the Ring by J. R. R. Tolkien
Anne of Green Gables by L. M. Montgomery
Treasure Island by Robert Louis Stevenson
Ready Player One by Ernest Cline
The Giver by Lois Lowry
The Hitchhiker's Guide to the Galaxy by Douglas Adams
From the Mixed-Up Files of Mrs. Basil E. Frankweiler by E. L. Konigsburg
The Book Thief by Markus Zusak
The Martian Chronicles by Ray Bradbury
I Capture the Castle by Dodie Smith
The Graveyard Book by Neil Gaiman

LETTER FROM THE AUTHOR

Dear Reader,

I first read *Little Women* as a sixth or seventh grader at St. Peter's School in Oshkosh, Wisconsin. I was eager to read such a big book and get lots and lots of points on my Accelerated Reader test, truth be told. But I was also touched by all of the March sisters, especially Jo.

Jo stood out to me because she wasn't afraid to be herself, even if that self was a little different from what people may have expected of her. I admired that trait then, and I admire it even more now.

When I reread *Little Women* before beginning this project, I was newly blown away by its warmth, insightfulness, and strong, wonderful characters. These are people—Meg, Jo, Beth, Amy, Hannah, Mrs. March, Laurie, Mr. Lawrence—who are simply wonderful to spend time with. They are thoughtful. They are genuine. They make mistakes and figure out ways to fix them and do better. They *try*. They don't take shortcuts as they attempt to find happiness and be good people in the midst of everyday responsibilities, and they value the things that really matter, like family, friendship, creativity, charity, and kindness. Perhaps most important, they're funny!

I love the Marches, and it was an absolute pleasure and dream come true to bring them to life again with this version of the story. My hope for this book is that it attracts you to the original version of the tale. There is something very special about these little women, and I think they exist outside of time simply because they are so human, so fully drawn, and so interesting, no matter the era they happen to find themselves in.

These girls are each one of us, trying to figure out who we are as we grow up, how to get along with everyone in our families and in our lives, how to help one another, and how to use our talents in a meaningful way. Little women—even littl*er* women—do big things.

I hope you enjoyed the story. It was an honor to write it.

With love,
Laura Schaefer